T0374734

A Cultural History of the Medieval Sword

Armour and Weapons

ISSN 1746-9449

Series Editors

Kelly DeVries
Robert W. Jones
Robert C. Woosnam-Savage

Throughout history armour and weapons have been not merely the preserve of the warrior in battles and warfare, but potent symbols in their own right (the sword of chivalry, the heraldic shield) representing the hunt and hall as well as the battlefield. This series aims to provide a forum for critical studies of all aspects of arms and armour and their technologies, from the end of the Roman Empire to the dawn of the modern world; both new research and works of synthesis are encouraged.

New proposals for the series are welcomed; they should be sent to the publisher at the address below.

Boydell & Brewer Limited
PO Box 9
Woodbridge, Suffolk, IP12 3DF

Previously published titles in the series
are listed at the back of this volume

A Cultural History of the Medieval Sword

Power, Piety, and Play

Robert W. Jones

THE BOYDELL PRESS

First published 2023
The Boydell Press, Woodbridge

ISBN 978 1 83765 036 1

The Boydell Press is an imprint of Boydell & Brewer Ltd
PO Box 9, Woodbridge, Suffolk IP12 3DF, UK
and of Boydell & Brewer Inc.
668 Mt Hope Avenue, Rochester, NY 14620–2731, USA
website: www.boydellandbrewer.com

A CIP catalogue record for this book is available
from the British Library

The publisher has no responsibility for the continued existence or accuracy of URLs for
external or third-party internet websites referred to in this book, and does not guarantee
that any content on such websites is, or will remain, accurate or appropriate

This publication is printed on acid-free paper

Printed and bound in Great Britain by TJ Books Limited, Padstow, Cornwall

Contents

Illustrations

The author and publisher are grateful to all the institutions and individuals listed for permission to reproduce the materials in which they hold copyright. Every effort has been made to trace the copyright holders; apologies are offered for any omission, and the publisher will be pleased to add any necessary acknowledgement in subsequent editions.

Acknowledgements

As with all books, this one could not have appeared without the support and enthusiasm of a great many people.

Everyone at Boydell and Brewer is to be congratulated for their work in turning my manuscript into the excellent volume you have before you. I am grateful to the history faculty at Franklin and Marshall College in Pennsylvania for making me a Visiting Scholar in History there, a position which has been of enormous assistance for accessing research materials, as well as connecting me with an excellent community of scholars. Ted Pearson, Maria Mitchell and Richard Reitan have been particularly welcoming, and supportive of my studies, as have my colleagues, students, and friends at Advanced Studies in England.

Thanks are due to Peter Coss and Andrew Ayton, who have been long-standing supporters of my academic work. So have been two former denizens of the Royal Armouries: Karen Watts and Bob Woosnam-Savage. Both have been enthusiastic about my work, have shared their time and expertise over the years, as well as helping me with access to one of the finest collections of medieval weaponry in the world. As a historian who firmly believes that one must do in order to understand, being able to handle original swords was both essential and a great privilege.

I am grateful to Mike Loades – another man who does in order to understand – not only for talking with me about his understanding and experience of swordsmanship on stage and screen, but also for a day's workshop on rapier and dagger fighting in Scotland nearly twenty years ago, which gave me my first taste of what real swordplay was all about. That understanding of the use of the sword has developed through my contacts within the HEMA community, and I would like to thank Alan Knowles, my first instructor, and all those I have crossed swords with over the years, whether it be in Swindon, Newnham-on-Severn, or beyond.

The amount of research being produced by the Historical European Martial Arts (HEMA) community is bewildering, and it is impossible to thank everyone whose material has shaped my thinking on the subject (most of them, but I fear not all, appear in the footnotes and bibliography). The community of HEMA scholars with whom I have shared the podium at numerous conferences (Erik Burkart, Fabrice Cognot, Jacob Deacon, Daniel Jaquet, and Iason-Eleftherios Tzouriadis in particular) have been a constant source of inspiration. Eric Burkhart is to be thanked for instigating my initial foray into the possible parallel evolution of the herald and fencing masters; I do hope we can explore this avenue together in the near future. Kelly DeVries and Sixt Wetzler's close reading of an earlier draft of this work has made it a far better book (and its German far more grammatically accurate). As always, any remaining errors remain wholly my own.

Peter Johnsson and Roland Warzecha, both excellent scholars as well as hugely talented craftsmen, were kind enough to allow me to use their artwork in this volume, illustrating far better than I important aspects of the structure of the sword, and of its scabbard.

Finally, I must thank my family and friends. The course of this book has not run smooth, and their support and understanding have been essential in seeing it to its conclusion. Once again, it has been my wife Liz who has borne the brunt of its trials and tribulations. Without her this book could most certainly never have been completed, and so it is to her that it is dedicated.

Introduction

> I am the sword, deadly against all weapons. Neither spear, nor poleaxe,
> nor dagger can prevail against me. I can be used at long range or close
> range, or I can be held in the half sword grip and move to the Narrow
> Game. I can be used to take away the opponent's sword, or move to
> grapple. My skill lies in breaking and binding. I am also skilled in
> covering and striking, with which I seek always to finish the fight. I will
> crush anyone who opposes me. I am of royal blood. I dispense justice,
> advance the cause of good and destroy evil. To those who learn my
> crossings I will grant great fame and renown in the art of armed fighting.
>
> Fiore de'i Liberi, *Flos Duellatorum* (c. 1404)[1]

WE HAVE A CONTRADICTORY attitude towards the medieval sword. We expect
it to be an object of nobility and status, the weapon and emblem of the
knight and king. In our popular view of the medieval world, it is a magical object,
imbued with power and symbolism. It is Roland's *Durendal*, Aragorn's *Andúril*,
Arthur's *Excalibur*, Elric of Melniboné's *Stormbringer* – whether the sword is part of
a historical myth or a modern one matters little, the imagined mythic properties are
the same. Our modern myths are of magical swords, and so we assume the medieval
ones must have been magical too. They are things of beauty. Their blades flash in
the sun and their hilts gleam with opulent decoration. Yet they are also objects of
violence and brutality. On television and the movies, they are often depicted as
cumbersome weapons, requiring great strength to wield, cleaving armour, flesh, and
bone in graceless and vicious fights.

These contradictions have fed into the traditional study of medieval swords. This
field has been dominated by the work of Ewart Oakeshott, the leading authority
on high medieval swords throughout the twentieth century.[2] He had an interest in

---

[1] 'Spada son contro ogni arma mortale, ne Lanza ne Azza ni daga contra mi vale. Longa e curta me
posso fare. e me strengho e vegno alo zogho stretto, e'vegno allo tor de spada e allo abrazare mia
arte si'e roture e ligadure so ben fare de coverte e ferire sempre in quelle voglio finire, chi contra me
fara, ben lo faro langure. E son Reale e'mantengo la Justicia, la bonta acresco e destruzo la malicia.
Chi me guardera fazendo in me crose, de fatto de armizare gli faro fama e vose'. Fiore De'i Libere,
Fior Battaglia, Getty MS Ludwig XV 13, fol. 25r, trans. Michael Chidester (https://www.wiktenauer.
com/wiki/Fiore_de'i_Liberi/Sword_in_Two_Hands/Wide_Play (accessed 1 August 2021).

[2] Historical convention divides the Middle Ages into three phases. The 'early medieval' begins in the
late fifth century and ends at the start of the eleventh century (it is often referred to as the 'dark
ages' but this is a term that is now avoided where possible). The 'high Middle Ages' spans the period
1000 to 1300, and then the 'late Middle Ages' follows, from 1300 to 1500. This is followed in turn
by the 'early modern period', which ends around 1800. Histories of swordsmanship will often divide

swords from boyhood and started his own personal collection at a young age.[3] He supported this with extensive personal research, which was accompanied by his own drawings (his job, up until he became a full-time researcher, was as an illustrator). Building on the work of Jan Peterson and R.E.M. Wheeler on so-called Viking-era swords, Oakeshott developed a typology of medieval swords of the high Middle Ages.[4] Whilst Peterson had focused on the pommel and the cross of the swords as being the diagnostic element, Oakeshott followed Wheeler in adding the shape and profile of the blade into his typology. Oakeshott's typology and chronology continue to be the go-to resource for most who are interested in the sword.

Oakeshott focused very much on the taxonomy of swords. The core of his two major works – *The Sword in the Age of Chivalry* and *Records of the Medieval Sword* – is the provision of examples that support his typology and locate them chronologically. However, this was not his sole concern. As a collector he had a genuine passion for his subject. Challenging the commonly held belief that swords were clumsy, heavy lumps of metal, he spoke eloquently about them. The blackened and corroded survivals dug out of the ground, he explained, bore no relation to the 'living examples' of the sword-smith's art, which held 'an austere perfection of line and proportion … comparable with splendid and majestic pottery' of China. Far from heavy, the average weight of these swords was 'between 2lbs and 3lbs, and they were balanced (according to their purpose) with the same care and skill in the making as a tennis racket or fishing rod'.[5]

The analogies are telling. Whilst Oakeshott was a passionate collector of swords, he was not a swordsman and, whilst he had an affinity for the subject of his collection, and for the chivalric milieu in which they had been used, he still understood them first and foremost as artefacts. His primary approach was to treat swords as *objets d'art*: to be categorised and appreciated as an object, a thing of beauty.

This is not to say that he did not understand its practical use. He could see the development of the sword through the centuries: blades became longer so that they were more effective from horseback, and then stiffer and narrower the better to thrust into the vulnerable areas between the steel plates with which combatants were increasingly protected. Yet, there was rarely any description of their actual use in his

---

this last into the 'Renaissance', (1500 up to the mid-seventeenth century) when the rapier was the dominant form of sword, and the 'early modern' when the smallsword took its place (approximately mid-seventeenth to early nineteenth centuries). It almost goes without saying that boundaries between each of these periods are arbitrary, and therefore mutable.

3   'Ewart Oakeshott' (Obituary), *Daily Telegraph* (12 October 2002).
4   This typology is most clearly expressed in Oakeshott's book *Records of the Medieval Sword* (Woodbridge, 1991). For Peterson's typology, see *De Norske Vikingesverd* (Kristiania, 1919). For R.E.M. Wheeler, see *London and the Vikings* (London, 1927). James Elmslie has produced a similar typology for the falchion (published in *Das Schwert: Gestalt und Gedanke*, eds. Grotkamp-Schepers, Immel, Johnson, Wetzler (Solingen, 2015)), and A.V.B. Norman has used the same approach for the Renaissance/ early modern rapier and smallsword (*The Rapier and the Smallsword, 1460–1820* (London, 1979)). For a critique of such typologies, see Iason-Eleftherios Tzouriades, "What is the Riddle of Steel?": Problems of Classification and Terminology in the Study of Late Medieval Swords', *Sword: Form and Thought*, ed. Lisa Deutscher, Mirjam Kaiser and Sixt Wetzler (Woodbridge, 2019), pp. 3–11.
5   Ewart Oakeshott, *The Sword in the Age of Chivalry* (Woodbridge, 1994), pp. 11–12.

writings, beyond references to the point of balance. When he talked about his Type XIIIa swords, which he connected with the 'great' or 'war' sword of thirteenth- and fourteenth-century written sources, he noted that they were 'admirably adapted for the work they had to do – to deal slow, ponderous slashing blows from the back of a horse at a well-protected adversary some distance away'.[6] They were, he suggests, a response to the early developments in plate armour, 'an extension of the age-old idea of smiting an adversary with mighty, shearing blows by providing an even stouter and heavier cutting blade'.[7] It would seem that Oakeshott could not escape the fallacy of crude medieval swordsmanship, even when he recognised the 'austere perfection of line and proportion' that made the sword 'the very essence of beauty', as he put it.[8]

A contemporary of Oakeshott's took a rather different approach to the study of the sword. Hilda Ellis Davidson, a historian specialising in Norse religion and mythology, studied the sword in Anglo-Saxon and Scandinavian cultures in a holistic manner.[9] She sought to combine the archaeological evidence with the literary to understand what swords meant to men in the culture of pre-Conquest England and Scandinavia. She talked about the sword's significance for the warrior elite, recognising that the aesthetic qualities of the sword were intrinsic to its rarity and function in marking the owner as a man of status and power. She saw the magic and mythic properties a sword might have, and examined the practicalities of the sword's manufacture and carriage as a means of better understanding from where these properties came. She also considered their use, both in terms of the physical wielding of the sword and the contexts in which they were used in combat. Here again, though, the swordsmanship is characterised as powerful but crude. Taking the literary evidence at face value, she says that fights were 'largely a matter of blow and counter-blow, the helmet and shield acting as a defence against the cutting strokes of the sword, brought down upon the head of the adversary', with devastating effect, striking off limbs and splitting skulls.[10]

Only some aspects of Davidson's approach to the sword have been taken up in more recent times.[11] Most recently, Sue Brunning has looked again at the swords of early medieval northern Europe.[12] Like Davidson, she seeks to understand the

---

[6]   *Ibid*, pp. 42–7. Oakeshott, *Records*, pp. 95–114.
[7]   Oakeshott, *The Sword in the Age of Chivalry*, p. 51.
[8]   Oakeshott, *Records*, p. 1.
[9]   H.R. Ellis Davidson, *The Sword in Anglo-Saxon England: Its Archaeology and Literature* (Woodbridge, 1994).
[10] Davidson, *The Sword in Anglo-Saxon England*, pp. 196–98.
[11] On the scholarship surrounding the early medieval sword, see Sue Brunning, *The Sword in Early Medieval Northern Europe: Experience, Identity, Representation* (Woodbridge, 2019), pp. 1–15 and 158. Another key work, alongside that of Davidson and Brunning, is Friedrich Grünzweig's *Das Schwert bei den "Germanen" Kulturgeschichtliche Studien zu seinem "Wesen" vom Altertum bis ins Hochmittelalte* (Vienna, 2009).
[12] The term 'early medieval northern Europe' is carefully selected, over the more succinct, but loaded, 'Viking age' or 'pagan'. We should be aware (and Brunning most certainly is) that many of our sources for the 'pre-Christian' attitudes towards the sword in northern Europe are written much later and in a firmly Christian context. However, whilst the Icelandic sagas (some of our most extensive sources for the understanding of swords in the early medieval period) are not themselves products of the 'Viking age', but thirteenth-century compositions, it seems to me highly likely that the way in which they depict the sword is an artefact of that earlier cultural understanding (see below, pp. 15ff).

significance that the sword had for that culture through the archaeology, artwork, and literature connected with it. She too identifies the sword as a symbol of power, status, and authority, recognising sword ownership as being the basis of a hierarchy within the warrior elite, with sword-owning warriors ranking more highly than those without, both socially and martially.[13] She argues that the cultures of early medieval northern Europe saw the sword as a 'living' thing, serving as the warrior's companion. They could be thought of as 'person-like', the blade acting like a warrior's body, the hilt as recognisable as an individual face, the scabbard serving as clothing, 'dressing' and protecting the 'body' of the weapon.[14] Some of the weapons in art and literature seem to have had a physicality, acting independently of their wielders.[15] She suggests that with the advance of Christianity (but not necessarily because of it) the sword lost much of this anthropomorphised character, but remained, nonetheless, an object of great significance and power.[16]

Such work on the symbolism, status, and significance of the early medieval sword is hugely important to the study of weapons in society. It emphasises that it is not our appreciation of the sword, but that of the medieval owner and wielder that counts. It is how *they*, not we, respond to its aesthetic qualities, and to its function as a weapon, that is important. The sword was a tool for war, not just an object to be admired (although it could be that too). Yet the complexity of its manufacture, the expense of the materials of which it was made, and its use in homicide, all raised it up to be far more than just an implement of the warrior, or a thing of beauty. In early medieval society the sword was fetishicised, imbued with a power and agency by its wielder and those who viewed it.

The approach of the scholars of the swords of early medieval England and Scandinavia has not, on the whole, been used for the swords of the high and late Middle Ages. There has been little attempt to apply the same cultural historical and anthropological approaches to the swords of the twelfth century onwards.[17] In part, I think that there has been an assumption that the early medievalists have already done the job. This, of course, presumes that swords throughout the Middle Ages shared the same symbolic significance and were used in the same way. A sword, after all, is still a sword: 'pointy' at one end and 'pretty' at the other. They were very much symbols of power and authority and can be presumed to be every bit as magical and spiritual as their 'early medieval' counterparts. Others might argue that the converse is true, and that the sword in the high and late Middle Ages had become so common as to have

---

[13] Brunning, *The Sword*, p. 146.
[14] *Ibid*, p. 143.
[15] *Ibid*, p. 124.
[16] *Ibid*, pp. 132–3.
[17] The two volumes edited by Lisa Deutscher, Mirjam Kaiser and Sixt Wetzler – *Das Schwert. Symbol und Waffe* (Leidorf, 2014) and *Sword: Form and Thought* (Woodbridge, 2019) – each contain submissions that are notable exceptions. Kristen B. Neuschel's *Living by the Sword: Weapons and Material Culture in France and Britain, 600–1600* (Ithaca, NY, 2020) and Martin Aurell's *Excalibur, Durendal, Joyeuse: La Force de l'épée* (Paris, 2021) also take an approach which views the sword as more than just an object – I am sorry that both these works appeared too late to incorporate more of their analysis into the appropriate chapters of this work.

lost all significance, or that Christianity had destroyed the notion of a sword having agency and intrinsic power. As a result, there is less cultural significance to analyse, and that which remains, the sword as a symbol of knighthood, of royal authority and power, is all too obvious to provide much to discuss or debate.

The situation is similar in the matter of the sword and women. Indeed, some readers may be surprised that there is not a separate chapter discussing the sword in relation to gender roles within the high Middle Ages. The subject is very much alive in the study of the early Middle Ages, particularly following the genetic identification of the remains in a grave at Birka in Sweden – buried with two horses, axe, knife, spears, arrows, sword, and shield – as female, and not male as had been assumed when the grave was excavated in the late nineteenth century.[18] At around the same time work was done to reconstruct the face of another Scandinavian woman buried with a sword, whose face showed evidence of trauma suggestive of an active military life, from the tenth-century cemetery at Asnes in Norway.[19] These reassessments were quickly picked up by the media, and reinforced in the public consciousness by the depiction of powerful female warrior characters on TV shows such as *Vikings*, *Game of Thrones*, or the film *The Northman*, and by the growing popularity of HEMA amongst all genders, with its widespread culture of inclusivity.[20] The discussion around the issue has been a polarising one, entwined with modern debates on gender identity and societal roles.[21]

The debate has not been as fierce for the high Middle Ages. It is far harder to connect a sword directly to a woman. Burials with swords are less common, and are invariably male. There has been no equivalent to the popular image of sword-wielding women to match the character of Lagertha from *The Vikings*, and no high medieval cultural tradition of women warriors or equivalent to the (oft-misunderstood) Valkyries.

That is not, of course to say that women could not use a sword. Medieval women were as capable as any man of wielding a sword, given the opportunity and training.

18 Neil Price, Charlotte Hedenstierna-Jonson, Torun Zachrisson, Anna Kjellström, Jan Storå, Maja Krzewińska, Torsten Günther, Verónica Sobrado, Mattias Jakobsson, and Anders Götherström, 'A Female Viking Warrior Confirmed by Genomics', *American Journal of Physical Anthropology* (2017), pp. 1–8, and 'Viking Warrior Women? Reassessing Birka Chamber Grave Bj.581', *Antiquity*, 93.367 (February 2019), pp. 181–98.
19 Ursula Dronke, *The Poetic Edda I: Heroic Poems* (London, 1969), p. 58. The reconstruction was done for the television program *Viking Warrior Women*, dir. Stuart Strickson (National Geographic, 2019). It revealed a wound on the forehead that could have been caused by a sharp edge. On the difficulties of interpreting trauma evidence, see below, pp. 147–52.
20 *Vikings*, created by Michael Hirst (MGM Television, 2013–2020). *Game of Thrones*, created by David Benioff and D.B. Weiss (HBO, 2011–2019). *The Northman*, dir. Robert Eggers (Regency Enterprises, 2022).
21 Challenges to the assumptions made by the team working on the Birka burial included those of Judith Jesch ('Let's debate female viking warriors yet again', *Norse and Viking Ramblings* (9 September 2017) http://norseandviking.blogspot.com/2017/09/lets-debate-female-viking-warriors-yet/ accessed 1 August 2021) and Howard Williams ('Viking Warrior Women: An Archeodeath Response – Part 1', *Archeodeath*, https://www.howardwilliamsblog.wordpress.com/2017/09/14/viking-warrior-women-an-archeodeath-response-part-1/ accessed 1 August 2021). See also Brunning, *The Sword*, pp. 8–9, 50–3 and 108–9, M. Fabian-Wittenborn, 'Schwertfrauen' und Schwertadel' in der Urnenfelder- und Hallstattzeit', *Das Schwert. Symbol und Waffe*, pp. 51–64, and Leszek Gardela, *Women and Weapons in the Viking World: Amazons of the North* (Philadelphia, PA, 2021).

Noblewomen were active participants in chivalric culture.[22] They read or listened to the same stories of heroic combat, and they stood in the grandstands watching the tourneys and jousts, wholly involved in the combat, encouraging and urging the knights on. They were active participants in the hunt, whether with hawk or hounds. If Richard Kaeuper is right in that a major element of chivalric culture was to extol violence and physical prowess as a virtue, then one might argue that the female participants were imbued with that same sense and so we should not be surprised if they made the decision to take up swords and fight.[23] Certainly, noblewomen appear in our sources leading men in battle.[24] The twelfth-century chronicler Orderic Vitalis tells of the Countess Isabel of Conches riding out in armour amongst her knights, likening her to a number of 'warlike, Amazon queens'.[25] Jeanne de Montfort, Duchess of Brittany, who led the Montfortian faction during the Breton civil war of the fourteenth century, did likewise at the siege of Hennebont, riding out to burn the enemy camp. On another occasion Froissart describes her wielding a rusty sword in her defence during a naval engagement in the Channel.[26] Most famous of all, of course, is Jeanne d'Arc, Jeanne *la Pucelle*, who led French troops against the Anglo-Burgundian forces in northern France in the early fifteenth century. Her sword is discussed in this work, but because it informs our understanding of the mysticism (and the lack thereof) attached to swords in the high Middle Ages, not because it was being wielded by a woman.[27] Indeed, Joan was at pains to assert, during her trial, that she did not wield her sword in combat, instead placing faith in leading men with her banner. Now this may have been special pleading on her part, as she was trying to refute claims that she had transgressed the limitations of her sex, but the situation does highlight that whilst a woman might well have had the strength and competence to wield a sword it was far from the norm for them to do so.

The other example given by those seeking to assert sword use by women in the high Middle Ages is the appearance of a female figure, identified in the text as 'Walpurgis' or 'Walpurga', in the fourteenth-century fencing manual I.33 but, as we shall see, this figure's appearance within the text is not straightforward nor as literal as she might seem.[28]

---

[22] See Louise J. Wilkinson, 'Gendered Chivalry', *A Companion to Chivalry*, ed. Robert W. Jones and Peter Coss (Woodbridge, 2019), pp. 219–40.

[23] Richard Kaeuper, *Chivalry and Violence in Medieval Europe* (Oxford, 1999).

[24] For an overview of women as military commanders, see Katrin Sjursen, *Peaceweavers' Sisters: Medieval Noblewomen as Military Leaders in Northern France* (Ann Arbor, MI, 2011) and Megan McLaughlin, 'The Woman Warrior: Gender, Warfare and Society in Medieval Europe.' *Women's Studies*, 17 (1990), pp. 193–209.

[25] *The Ecclesiastical History of Orderic Vitalis*, ed. and trans. M. Chibnall. vol. 4 (Oxford, 1973), pp. 212–14, quoted in Susan Johns, *Noblewomen, Aristocracy and Power in the Twelfth-Century Anglo-Norman Realm* (Manchester, 2013), p. 14.

[26] Jean Froissart, *Chroniques*, ed. Siméon Luce et al, vol. 2 (Paris, 1869), pp. 142–46, and vol. 3, pp. 8–10, quoted in Katrin J. Sjursen, 'The War of the Two Jeannes: Rulership in the Fourteenth Century', *Medieval Feminist Forum*, 51.1 (2015), pp. 4–40.

[27] See below, p. 24.

[28] On Walpurgis and I.33, see below, pp. 127ff.

The aspect of swords that has seen the least active consideration by academics since Davidson's work, until very recently, is the *use* of the sword.[29] The understanding of the sword as a tool for killing, and an appreciation of the practice of swordsmanship, has been largely ignored until quite recently. However, studies in these areas have developed dramatically since the 1990s. With the growth in 'Historical European Martial Arts' (or HEMA, pronounced *He-Ma*), whose practitioners seek to recreate the swordsmanship of the past by the study of so-called *fechtbücher* – 'fight books' – and apply the techniques they describe in training and sparring using modern weapons analogous to medieval forms, there is an increasing appreciation of how we think medieval swords handled and what they were capable of. Whilst for Oakeshott the medieval sword was every bit as finely balanced as a tennis racket or fishing rod, for the HEMA practitioner the medieval sword is every bit as finely balanced as... well, as a sword.

Whilst the HEMA community is a broad one, the approach of the majority of HEMAists to swords is pragmatic. Oakeshott's work is reviewed almost purely for its typology, to identify the weapons around which the *fechtbücher* were developed, but often this is as far as the interest in the historical swords goes. It is the martial art that is important; the wider cultural and social context of the sword and its use has little of interest because it is not obvious how it serves to inform the recreation of the art. HEMA is a hobby with few roots in academic study. As a result, the publication and dissemination of research tends to be through social media, blogs and internet videos, and although the insights they provide can be sound and should be of wider interest, they have often been overlooked by academics because of the disconnect with formal academic scholarly works, and a sense that HEMA is just 'playing with swords'. There is, however, an increasingly important and well-published community of scholars who combine the practice of HEMA with historical study.[30] They look at the wider context of the *fechtbücher*, the masters who produced them, and the schools and the context in which they were understood. For these scholars, the focus is less often on the sword itself as on the society and culture of those teaching swordsmanship, and on gaining an understanding of the pedagogical and codicological issues of the manuscripts produced to 'teach' its use, both for the original medieval audience and the modern HEMA practitioner.

Each of these different approaches helps in the wider understanding of the sword, and its significance for medieval society. Ideally, what is needed is an inclusive approach, one that combines the taxonomic approach of Oakeshott, with the experiential knowledge of the HEMA community, and the cultural and anthropological understanding of the early medieval sword specialists. This would help to reinforce

---

[29]   Brunning's approach is typical, in that her section on 'the sword in action' passes very quickly over the use of the sword in combat, to return to its active participation in 'realms beyond the martial', and emotional and personal connection with the warrior. (*Ibid*, pp.143–5). For a study of weapons' injuries, see S.J. Wenham, 'Anatomical interpretations of Anglo-Saxon weapon injuries', *Weapons and Warfare in Anglo-Saxon England*, ed. S.C. Hawkes (Oxford, 1989), pp. 123–39.

[30]   We shall consider some of their writings in the last chapter, but key figures include Matthias Bauer, Eric Burkhart, Michael Chidester, Olivier Dupuis, Jeffrey Forgeng, Daniel Jaquet, Jeff Lord, Roger Norling, and Tilman Wanke.

the connection between the form of the object, its function, and its social and cultural significance, and better illuminate how each aspect informed the others.

In writing this book, it has been my intention to create not a history of the medieval sword, but something that begins to consider the sword in this holistic way. In doing so I wanted also to challenge some of the general preconceptions that modern society has about the medieval sword. Thus, in the following chapters we will consider what really was magical and mystical about the sword, and the way in which it served as a symbol for the powerful. We will look at some of the practicalities of the sword, considering the evidence for when it was worn, how it was used, and how men learnt to use it. We will discover that the sword of the high and late Middle Ages was not solely the preserve of the martial elite, but that others used the medieval sword, especially amongst the burgeoning middle class. Their culture of swordsmanship was distinct, and significant, not only because it is one that is rarely considered, but also because it is *this* culture that is the birthplace of the fencing schools and *fechtbücher* on which the modern sword culture of HEMA is built. The final chapter looks at the modern culture of the medieval sword, at the different ways in which people have sought to interpret and recreate its use, on stage and screen as well as in the form of a martial art, and so have shaped our modern (often imperfect) understanding.

This work is very much focused on the periods known as the high and late Middle Ages; that is to say the period from around 1100 until 1500. I have not wanted to retread the path blazed by Davidson and Brunning, except to compare and contrast their findings with my own. The culture of the sword they analyse is not the same as the one I am looking at, in spite of the inevitable similarities. For much the same reason I have tried not to stray too far beyond the end of the Middle Ages. The development of the rapier, a sword specifically designed to be worn as an accoutrement to everyday wear, heralds a dramatic shift in the culture of the sword. *That* culture of the sword, built around a different paradigm of chivalric behaviour, masculine identity, and personal honour, requires a book in and of itself.

This study also has a definite northern and central European focus in its primary and secondary source material. This is largely because – particularly with regards the fencing schools, fencing masters, and *fechtbücher* – Germany predominates, both in terms of the source material, and (by extension) scholarship. This having been said, and recognising that there will inevitably be regional nuance, the combination of chivalric culture, the Latin Church and universities, and a common framework for the investiture and practice of kingship all help provide a commonality to the culture of the high medieval sword that transcends regional identities.

Within these self-imposed boundaries, I have aimed to range widely in a social and cultural context. This book looks more broadly at the sword of the high and late Middle Ages than previous studies, to show that it was far more than the emblem of the knight or the symbol of royal or imperial power and authority. In later chapters we will see a very different, far less elite culture of swordsmanship, and one which is not, perhaps, truly 'martial'. However, because it is the most familiar to a modern audience, and links to some of the most iconic and famous of swords, it is the sword as a high-status and totemic artefact where we will begin our exploration.

I

The Mystical Blade

WE ARE CULTURALLY ATTUNED to swords being objects of mysticism and magic. The cruciform shape of the medieval weapon connects it with the cross of Christianity and makes it a spiritual emblem, reinforced by its metaphorical use in religious literature: the Bible itself and later doctrinal works, most notably Bernard of Clairvaux's *De consideratione* and Pope Boniface VIII's Bull *Unam Sanctum*, both of which espoused papal power through the metaphor of there being two swords.[1] The magical sword is a strong image in the popular imagination, thanks in no small part to the *Lord of the Rings*, in which named swords, of power and pedigree almost as strong as the magical rings, are wielded by hero and villain alike.[2] Whether it be *Narsil*, the sword used by Isildur to cut the ring from the finger of Sauron, and whose fragments were re-forged into *Andúril* to be the sword of Aragorn as Isildur's heir, or *Sting*, the weapon found by Bilbo Baggins, whose blade glows blue in the presence of orcs and goblins, Tolkien's weapons are invariably ancient, forged by elves or dwarves in earlier ages, and imbued with the magical cunning of those eldar people.

Other fantasy writers have followed suit, equipping their characters with swords of power and potency. Tolkien's contemporary, C.S. Lewis, gives a named sword – *Rhindon* – to Peter Pevensie in his *Chronicles of Narnia*.[3] In more modern literature their powers can be complex. The sword of Michael Moorcock's anti-hero Elric of Melniboné – *Stormbringer* – is one of a number of demons in sword form, having the ability to drink the soul of any it strikes, feeding the vitality and energy to Elric and imparting a bloodlust that leads the tragic figure to attack friends and lovers against his will.[4] Terry Brooks' *Sword of Shannara* forces its wielder to face the full truth about

---

[1]   On the Church's use of swords as a metaphor for spiritual power, see below, p. 32.

[2]   *The Lord of the Rings*, dir. Peter Jackson (New Line Cinemas, 2001–2003). Whilst the swords are a feature of Tolkien's trilogy of novels, it is Peter Jackson's realisation of them for cinema that has fired the imagination of the modern audience. The Royal Armouries Museum in Leeds even has a display of weapons used in the movies, with description of their 'history' as well as comments on their relationship to the forms of medieval weapons.

[3]   The sword is given to Peter by Father Christmas at the end of the Long Winter (C.S. Lewis, *The Lion, the Witch and the Wardrobe*, *The Chronicles of Narnia* (London, 2001), pp. 159–60). The series of movies directed by Andrew Adamson make more of this sword than Lewis did in his novels, and invented the Seven Swords for the Seven Lost Lords in *The Chronicles of Narnia: The Voyage of the Dawn Treader*, dir. Michael Apted (Twentieth Century Fox, 2010).

[4]   The weapon first appears in Michael Moorcock's *The Dreaming City* (New York, 1972), and then recurs in another twelve novels featuring Elric.

themselves.[5] If they can accept their failings, flaws, and shortcomings they are able to wield the weapon. That ability to force people to acknowledge the truth can be used to destroy anyone 'evil' enough. Even the Harry Potter series has its magical sword – the Sword of Gryffindor – which is Goblin-made and able to absorb any substance that will make it stronger, such as Basilisk venom.[6]

Of course, all these magical swords draw on ancient myth and legend for their inspiration, on the tales of such magical swords as Arthur's *Excalibur*, Roland's *Durendal*, or *Dáinsleif* from the Prose Edda.[7] These mythical medieval weapons share many of the same traits as those created by the fantasy authors.

Or at least that is our perception. In fact, the swords of medieval stories are rarely as magical as is commonly believed. The swords in the tales of the early Middle Ages can have complex magical or ritualistic elements connected with them, but the swords of the romances of the high Middle Ages, including perhaps the most famous of all – *Excalibur* – are almost commonplace.

Excalibur is an important example because it looms so large in the modern consciousness. If there is one 'medieval' sword that everyone knows it is *Excalibur*. It is perhaps the most iconic weapon, at least in the English-speaking world. Ask most people and they can tell you that it was the sword of King Arthur, that he was given it by the mysterious Lady of the Lake, or that he drew it from a stone, thereby indicating his right to become the king of the Britons. Some might know that it was forged on the mystical Isle of Avalon. They will remember that, on Arthur's death, the sword was flung into the lake and reclaimed by the Lady, possibly remembering that Sir Bedivere, who Arthur had entrusted with this task, failed to follow Arthur's command the first time. Most will agree that *Excalibur* is magical, and a very few might know that the scabbard was equally magical, ensuring that its wearer should never suffer loss of blood. If pressed, however, very few if any will be able to suggest the specific power with which the sword itself was imbued.

In actuality, none of the different medieval versions of Arthur's story assign any great magical powers to *Excalibur*. In the earliest version, Geoffrey of Monmouth's *Historia Regum Britanniae* – cribbed from older Welsh traditions such as those encoded within the *Mabinogion*, the sword – *Caliburnus* (derived from the Welsh *Caledfwlch*) – is merely one of the named pieces of war-gear belonging to Arthur, appearing alongside his shield *Pridwen* and his spear *Ron* (again Latinisations of Welsh names from the *Mabinogion*'s telling of the Arthur myth).[8] The twelfth-century Romance writer Chrétien de Troyes, so important for adding a number of new elements to the tales which would become central to the later versions, puts the sword in the possession of

[5] Terry Brooks, *The Sword of Shannara Trilogy* (London, 2002).
[6] The sword appears in several of the novels, and is described in Rowling's official website, *Pottermore*. J.K. Rowling, 'The Sword of Gryffindor.' *Pottermore*, 10 August 2015, https://www.pottermore.com/writing-by-jk-rowling/the-sword-of-gryffindor (accessed 1 August 2021).
[7] *Dáinsleif* was the sword of Hǫgni in the Prose Edda of Snorri Sturluson. It caused wounds that could never be healed and, when drawn, always killed a man. Snorri Sturluson, *The Prose Edda*, ed. and trans. J.L. Byock (London, 2005), p. 115.
[8] Geoffrey of Monmouth, *The History of the Kings of Britain*, trans. Lewis Thorpe (London, 1966), p. 217.

Arthur's nephew, the peerless knight Gawain.[9] In the reworking of that tale, known as the first continuation, written in the late twelfth century, Arthur gives *Excalibur* (*Escalibor*) to Gawain, who uses it to defeat the knight known as 'le Riche Soldoier'.[10] The Vulgate cycle of the first half of the thirteenth century gives *Excalibur* something more of a role; originating the idea of *Excalibur* as the mystical sword in the stone, this branch of the tradition also sees Arthur give Gawain, his nephew, *Excalibur* when the young knight represents him in tournament and adventure. In the romance of *Guiron le Courtois* it is Meliadus, the father of Tristan, who benefits from Arthur's largesse by receiving *Excalibur*.[11]

In the majority of tales *Excalibur* is not Arthur's only sword, nor indeed his favourite. In the *Vulgate Merlin*, part of the Vulgate cycle, *Excalibur* is literally outshone by the sword of a rival king, Ryons, named *Marmiadoise*.[12] In this iteration Arthur becomes obsessed with this other sword, which he sees glows brighter than his own *Excalibur*, and he is so envious that he attacks its owner in order to possess it. Having won it Arthur is said to prize *Marmiadoise* above *Excalibur* and indeed any other sword.

Although Malory's fifteenth-century reworking has *Excalibur* as the sword which Arthur draws from the stone, in most versions this is not the case, and it is the Lady of the Lake, who gives *Excalibur* to the king.[13] Again, she may be mysterious, even other-worldly, but, like the sword in the stone, she is a way for Arthur to obtain the sword. Its origins and its making seem not to be mysterious. There is nothing to suggest that the Isle of Avalon, from where the sword is said to have come is a magical place. Geoffrey of Monmouth does not consider it so, merely as remote.[14] This makes it exotic, perhaps, but little more. References to the forging of *Excalibur* in the medieval traditions are rare. Unlike *Marmiadoise*, which the *Vulgate Merlin* tells us was forged by Vulcan in the time of Hercules, there is no mythic property to *Excalibur*'s creation. Indeed, it is modern writers who give the sword its most enchanted origins. Mary Stewart's 1970s *Merlin Trilogy* puts *Excalibur*'s creation in the hands of Weyland, whilst Marion Zimmer Bradley's *Mists of Avalon*, published in 1983, is the first retelling of the myth to describe it as being hammered and quenched

[9]   Chrétien de Troyes, 'The Story of the Grail (Perceval)', *Arthurian Romances*, trans. W.W. Kibler (London, 1991), p. 453.

[10] Kathy Toohey, 'The Swords of King Arthur', *The Grail Quest Papers* (Sydney, 2000), p. 6. *The Continuations of the Old French "Perceval" of Chretien de Troyes, Volume 1: The First Continuation*, ed. William Roach (Philadelphia, PA, 1949), p. 328.

[11] Michelle R. Warren, *History on the Edge* (Minneapolis, MN, 2000), p. 202. Toohey, 'The Swords of King Arthur', p. 8.

[12] On *Marmiadoise,* see Warren, *History on the Edge*, pp. 202–11.

[13] In his retelling of the story, Malory is trying to rationalise the different traditions that have gone before. When it comes to *Excalibur*, he seeks to fit both the swords Arthur is given as a symbol of his right and power – the sword in the stone and the sword given by the Lady of the Lake – into the narrative, by having the former break in a fight against King Pellinore, leaving Arthur in need of a sword, which is duly delivered by the Lady of the Lake. That both swords bear the name *Excalibur* is not easy to explain, unless it is an error on Malory's part.

[14] Geoffrey of Monmouth, *History*, p. 217.

by dwarves and fairies.[15] All in all, the most that can really be said of *Excalibur* as it appears in any of the medieval tales and retellings of Arthur's story is that it was a very fine sword of high quality, that shines incredibly brightly when drawn.

It probably goes without saying that if *Excalibur* has no real magical properties, then nor do those of any of the swords wielded by Arthur's knights or his foes. None of the other named swords within the medieval traditions of the tales – not *Marmiadoise*, not *Seure* (a sword that appears as the sword of Arthur in the *Prose Lancelot*), not *Courte* (the sword belonging first to Tristan then to Ogier the Dane), nor the sword given to Perceval by the Fisher King – are anything other than very fine weapons: beautiful, and strong, even shining, but not at all magical in the way in which we expect swords to be.

The Arthurian romances are, of course, not the only tales of heroic warriors to be current in the culture of the medieval west in the Middle Ages. Yet named swords are less frequent in these, and swords with magical properties even more rare. The swords of Charlemagne and Roland in *The Song of Roland* – *Joyeuse* and *Durendal* – are probably the next most famous swords after *Excalibur*, and neither of them have magical properties. It is true that they have a spiritual element to them; they were supposedly gifts from the Almighty, and the hilt of *Durendal* is encrusted with holy relics – a tooth of St Peter, some blood of St Basil, a hair of St Denis and a fragment of the dress of the Virgin Mary.[16] Just as with *Excalibur*, however, there is no indication in the tales that the swords have any special powers other than to be very finely worked weapons, easy to wield, and that they do not fail their owners.[17]

In the epic *Doon de Mayence*, another of the cycle of chansons de geste connected with Charlemagne, we get a hint of magic. Doon's sword *Merveilleuse* is described as having been forged by 'Galan' (a rendering of the name of the mythical smith Wayland), who is described as the son of a fairy mother. After Galan forged it his mother 'uttered her prayers and spells and made her signs, like the woman skilled in magic that she was'.[18] As a result the sword can cut through iron. This is the extent of its power, however, and later in the work its provenance becomes less impressive, as it is described as having been made not by Galan, but by one taught by him, and that it cut in such a way 'it seemed under a spell'.[19] Within the space of the tale, it has become the sword of an apprentice not a master, and its magical power has become a metaphorical one.

Another historical figure of heroic proportions, the great Spanish hero Rodrigo Díaz de Vivar, *el Cid*, has two named swords connected with him in his myth: *Tizón* (later *Tizona*) and *Colada*. There are no mystical origins to either of these weapons – the former the Cid wins from Yusuf ibn Tashfin in Valencia, whilst the latter he takes from

---

[15] Mary Stewart, *The Hollow Hills* (London, 1973). Marion Zimmer Bradley, *Mists of Avalon* (New York, 1983).

[16] *The Song of Roland*, trans. G. Burgess (London, 1990), p. 103.

[17] Indeed, this is one of the issues in *The Song* as *Durendal* fails to break even when Roland tries, in order to prevent it falling into the hands of the Moors. *Ibid*, pp. 102–3.

[18] 'Et dit ses oreisons, seignie et conjure, Com chele qui estoit de faement senée', quoted in Richard Barber, 'Arthurian Swords I: Gawain's Sword and the Legend of Weland the Smith', *Arthurian Literature*, XXXV (2020), pp. 11–12.

[19] 'qu'ele fet enchantement sembla'. Barber, 'Arthurian Swords I', p. 12.

the Count of Barcelona – and their only attributes, like *Excalibur* or *Marmiadoise*, are that they shine brightly and inspire fear in their wielders' foes.[20]

So, if the swords of the great heroes of medieval literature are not magical, soul-drinkers, or bound with dark destinies, why are they named at all? And where do the cursed and magical blades of modern fantasy come from? The answer to both these questions is that such attitudes treatment of swords stems from a different tradition common to English, Icelandic, and Norse literature, that appears to be based on a pre-Christian understanding of the significance and power of the sword.[21] In these early medieval cultures, swords are not only named; they have peculiar properties that enable their wielders to be victorious in combat, and also, very often, are cursed with misfortune. This combination of *siegschwert* and *álög* – the victory-granting sword and the cursed sword – are common throughout these cultures' heroic stories.[22]

Perhaps the best example of this combination of victory-giving properties and threat to or flaw for the wielder is *Sköfnung*, a blade appearing in *Kormák's* and *Laxdœla sagas*.[23] *Sköfnung* was the sword of the Danish King Hrólf Kraki, a mythical monarch of the sixth century. On his death, the sword and king were buried together in a burial mound.[24] Centuries later Skeggi of Midfirth broke into Hrólf's mound to plunder it, and took the sword. This part of the sword's story is not uncommon; 'Mound swords', taken from the graves of great warriors, are frequently seen in the sagas.[25] In the *Laxdœla saga* the sword appears again, in the hands of Eid, Skeggi's son. Eid loans the sword to Thorkel Eyjólfsson, his kinsman, for the latter's fight against the outlaw Grim. Thorkel keeps the sword and, on his death, is buried with it.

As well as having a long pedigree, and passing hand-to-hand between the heroes of sagas, the weapon also has several mystical traits. Eid explains them as he loans the sword to Thorkel:

> *Sköfnung* has very special properties because of which the sun may never shine on the hilt, and it must never be drawn when there are women present. Also, if someone is wounded by the sword, the wound won't heal unless it is rubbed by the healing stone that is mounted on the sword.[26]

---

[20] *The Song of the Cid*, trans. Burton Raffel (London, 2009), pp. 59 and 119.

[21] As Brunning notes, it is incredibly difficult to 'excavate' pagan attitudes towards swords from the written sources, all of which are from a date where Christianity is well established. (Brunning, *The Sword*, pp. 111 *ff*). The depiction of swords in the sagas is certainly different from that of central, and especially francophone Europe, but the tradition of earlier Eddic poetry on which they draw, and similarities with the way in which they are depicted in earlier English poetry and skaldic verse, make me feel reasonably secure in using them in the way that I have here. (My thanks to Sixt Wetzler for his insight on this point).

[22] Friedrich E. Grünzweig, 'Siegschwert und *álög*: literarisches Motiv oder Reflex eines kulturellen Phänomens?', *Das Schwert: Symbol und Waffe*, pp. 187–96.

[23] Both sagas are first written down in the thirteenth century, but deal with people from the tenth to twelfth centuries.

[24] *The Saga of King Hrolf Kraki*, ed. Byock (London, 1998).

[25] See, for example, Olaf's *Hneitir*, taken from his body on the battlefield, or *Tyrfingr*, which is drawn from a stone by Boðvar Bjarki in the 'Saga of Hrolf Kraki', Skeggi not only takes Hrolf's sword *Skofnung*, but also tries to take Boðvar's sword *Laufi* (*The Saga of King Hrolf Kraki*).

[26] *Laxdœla Saga*, trans. Magnus Magnusson (London, 1975).

Similar injunctions in its use appear in *Kormák's Saga*. Skeggi tells Kormák that:

> the management of it may seem difficult to thee … a covering goes with it and thou shall leave it quiet; the sun must not shine on the upper guard, nor shall thou draw it except thou preparest to fight; but, if thou comest to the fighting place, sit alone, and there draw it. Hold up the blade and blow on it; then a small snake will creep from under the guard; incline the blade and make it easy for it to creep back under the guard.[27]

When Kormák ignores these instructions, attempting to draw the blade in the presence of his mother, and allowing sunlight to strike the hilt, the sword refuses to come out of the scabbard. Instead, it creaks and groans. When he fails to make it easy for the serpent to creep back under the guard, we are told that 'the good luck of it was gone' and, in the ensuing fight, a shard is broken out of *Sköfnung*'s blade that cuts Kormák, causing his blood to be spilt onto the duelling ground, thus losing him the combat.[28]

Tyrfingr, a sword said to have been made by dwarven smiths for King Svafrlami (according to the thirteenth-century *Hervarar Saga*), shares similar traits to *Skofnung*. It might not be hidden under the warrior's head, nor stood on its pommel. Every time it was drawn it would cause the death of a man, but it could only be urged into action three times, after which it would not be drawn again. Ultimately it would be the death of its owner.[29] In the *Gísla Saga*, another thirteenth-century work detailing events of the ninth and tenth centuries, the sword Grásíða shatters when it is used to kill its owner Kolr.[30] In the Anglo-Saxon tale of *Beowulf* (the sole surviving manuscript of which has been dated to the eleventh century) two swords fail Beowulf at key points: *Hrunting*, the sword lent to him by Unferth, which proves unable to harm Grendel's mother, and *Nægling*, the sword with which he tries to defeat the dragon, but which snaps because of the hero's own strength.[31]

By contrast, there is only one tradition in the high medieval heroic stories of a sword which has a similar impact on the warrior's destiny, that of Sir Balin, the so-called 'knight with two swords', whose story is told in the Post-Vulgate Merlin Continuation, a further reworking of Robert de Boron's version of the Arthurian tales, written in the first half of the thirteenth century.[32] A lady arrives at court, girded with a sword, which she is unable to draw or remove herself. Indeed, it can only be taken by the best, most loyal knight of the country. Sir Balin, a poor knight and of low rank, proves able to untie the thongs of the belt and take the sword from the lady. However, when the lady asks him to return the sword, stating that it was not part of their bargain that he should keep it, Balin refuses. The lady warns him that the sword will bring him evil. The first man he kills with the blade will be the man he loves

---

[27] *The Life and Death of Cormac the Skald*, trans. W.G. Collingwood (London, 1903), p. 64.
[28] *Ibid*, pp. 64–7.
[29] Grünzweig, 'Siegschwert und álög', p. 187.
[30] *Ibid*, p. 190.
[31] *Beowulf*, trans. Howell D. Chickering, Jr (New York, 2006), pp. 136–7 and 202–5.
[32] 'The Post-Vulgate Merlin Continuation', trans. Martha Asher, *Lancelot-Grail: The Old French Arthurian Vulgate and Post-Vulgate in Translation*, gen ed. Norris J. Lacy, vol. VIII (Cambridge, 2010), pp. 40*ff*.

most in the world, and Balin will be killed by the same man.[33] Inevitably, in a typical Arthurian episode of borrowed armour and disguised arms, he and his brother Balan end up fighting to their mutual destruction. In Malory's retelling of the story, Merlin fixes the sword within a stone, from which it is drawn by Galahad, being passed to Lancelot, who uses it to strike down Gawain. Here we have a rare example of a high medieval sword with *álög*. But this sword is not the weapon of a particular hero. It has no name and is not intrinsically tied to their owner's character, in the way that Brunning sees the blades of the early medieval literature being.[34]

The swords of the Arthurian and Carolingian heroes are pale reflections of these earlier, more magical weapons. Why did they change? Why did the great swords of the sagas and Germanic tales, central to the narratives, become bit players and plot devices, with little more than a name to distinguish them from the ordinary swords wielded by the non-heroes?

Things become clearer if we look at another aspect of the mystical sword – the inscribing of blades.

'The Word in the Sword': Inscriptions on medieval sword blades

In August 2015 the British Library made a public plea for help, as part of the publicity for its 'Magna Carta: Law, Liberty, Legacy' exhibition.[35] Part of the exhibition included a sword of thirteenth-century date, on the blade of which was an inscription inlaid in gold:

+NDXOXCHWDRGHDXORVI+

The blog entry was picked up by the international press and caused a sensational public response, with a number of potential interpretations being sent in, some more plausible than others. Some argued that it was Welsh, meaning "No covering shall be over me". Others claimed that it was Gallic, Gaelic, Sicilian, or even Hindi. The more scientifically-minded suggested that it was written in some form of ROT-13, a letter substitution code. Some saw encoded within it an attribution of the sword to St George, the inscription referring to his dragon-slaying exploits. There was a claim that the four-letter combination DRGHD formed the consonants of 'DroGHeDa', an ancient Irish place name, or that hidden within it was the name of Cadwgan, son of the King of Gwynedd and one of the leaders of the Welsh contingent at the Battle of Lincoln in 1141.[36]

[33] *Ibid*, p. 42.
[34] Brunning, *The Sword*, pp. 157–58.
[35] Fig. 1. 'Help Us Decipher This Inscription - Medieval manuscripts blog', blogs.bl.uk, 3 August 2015, British Library. https://blogs.bl.uk/digitisedmanuscripts/2015/08/help-us-decipher-this-inscription.html (accessed 1 August 2021). The sword is known as the 'Witham Sword', and dates to between 1250–1330. (Donated by the Royal Archaeological institute, accession no. 1858, 1116.5).
[36] This last concept comes from the fullest and most scholarly of the response; Carla Rossi, 'A proposal for the interpretation of the inscription on the British Museum sword', *academia.edu*, n.d.https://www.academia.edu/14828685/A_proposal_for_the_interpretation_of_the_inscription_

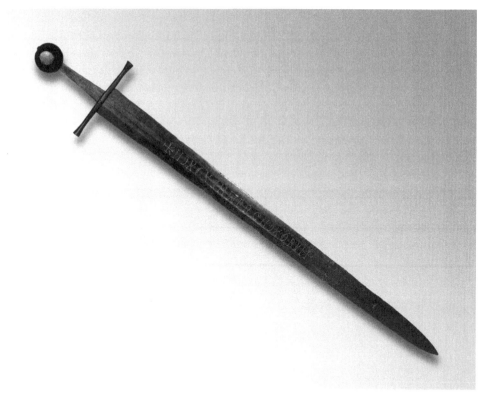

Figure 1. The Witham Sword (c.1250–1330). (Donated by the Royal Archaeological institute, accession no. 1858, 1116.5. Image courtesy of The Trustees of the British Museum).

What the public response showed, apart from the ongoing fascination with mystical swords and with quasi-medieval myths, was that without the proper context inscriptions such as these can be interpreted as meaning almost anything. Ewart Oakeshott wrote of inscriptions in sword blades that

> We have to remember that these swords were decorated not for twentieth-century academic scholars to pore over, but for silly, sentimental, unsophisticated, deeply religious, superstitious and illiterate people who had to rely upon them in heat of battle. We do not know what the inscriptions mean, but we do know that to the men who used the swords there was deep significance, mystery and power in them as well as meaning.[37]

His backhanded compliment is only partly right. It is indeed very difficult to decipher the exact meaning of such enigmatic inscriptions; their codicology is complex, nuanced, and full of unknowns and variables. However, by putting the

---

on_the_British_Museum_sword (accessed 1 August 2021). Whilst Professor Rossi's valuation of the inscription is the most thorough and draws on existing scholarship concerning sword blade inscriptions and religious invocation, the connection with the battle of Lincoln and the Cadwgan of Gwynedd remains highly speculative.

[37] Oakeshott, *Records*, p. 260.

swords and their inscriptions into broader historical and cultural context, it is possible to understand something of their meaning, both literally and in terms of symbolism.

Swords have been decorated and marked since earliest times, but in medieval western Europe the inscribing of sword blades with texts is first seen in the ninth century. The shift away from pattern-welded blades, where rods of different qualities of iron were twisted together so as to form the blade, to blades where an edge was forge-welded onto a core, allowed iron strips to be hammered into the blades surface during construction in order to create letters and patterns.

These words are comparatively easy to decipher. Almost all of them are personal names. A large number bear the Latin suffix ME FECIT (made me), indicating that these are all some form of maker's mark. There are eight or so makers' names, including 'Gicelin', 'Ingelrii' and the most famous, 'Ulfberht'.[38] These marks, inlaid into the blade with small bars of iron, occur from the ninth through to the early thirteenth century: 'Ulfberht' occurring between the ninth and eleventh centuries, 'Ingelrii' between the tenth and the twelfth, and 'Gicelin' between the eleventh and thirteenth. The 'Ulfberht' blades are the found most often, with around 170 extant examples to date, ten time the number of 'Ingelrii' swords, and far more than the six known survivals of swords inscribed with the name 'Gicelin'.[39]

The identity of the individuals recorded on the sword blades has been the subject of much debate.[40] That of Ulfberht has been particularly hotly contested. Alan Williams has argued that the quality of Ulfberht blades was peculiar and special, made with a form of crucible steel called 'wootz', a technology imported from the Indian subcontinent via the middle east, and supposedly not known in Europe before the nineteenth century.[41] Although his hypothesis has been strongly challenged, this has afforded swords bearing the Ulfberht mark a reputation as high-quality blades, a reputation reinforced by the existence of what are clearly contemporary fakes or 'knock offs', where the inscription has been mis-spelt or completely garbled. These have been interpreted as the work of ill-educated smiths attempting to copy the Ulfberht brand, as it were, in the same way as one finds 'Nkie' or 'Knie' trainers, 'sdidsa'-branded clothing, or fake Rolex watches.[42] If so, it would suggest that the

---

[38] Ewart Oakeshott, 'Introduction to the Viking Sword', in I. Peirce, *Swords of the Viking Age* (Woodbridge, 2002), p. 710. Anne Stalsberg, 'Herstellung und Verbreitung der Vlfberht-Schwertklingen. Eine Neubewertung', *Zeitschrift für Archäologie des Mittelalters* 36 (2008), pp. 89–118.

[39] Oakeshott, *The Sword*, p. 34.

[40] See Alfred Geibig, *Beiträge zur morphologischen Entwicklung des Schwertes im Mittelalter: Eine Analyse des Fundmaterials vom ausgehenden 8. bis zum 12. Jahrhundert aus Sammlungen der Bundesrepublik Deutschland*. Offa-Bücher, New Series, 71 (Neumünster, 1991).

[41] Alan Williams, 'A metallurgical study of some Viking swords', *Gladius*, XXIX (December 2009), pp. 121–84, and 'Crucible steel in medieval swords', *Metals and Mines. Studies in Archaeometallurgy*, ed. S. La Niece, D. Hook, and P. Craddock (London, 2007), pp. 233–42. His findings found a wide public audience but have been strongly contested; see as an example E.E. Astrup and I. Martens, 'Studies of Viking Age Swords: Archaeology and Metallurgy', *Gladius*, XXXI (2011), pp. 203–06, and Ingo Petri, 'Material and properties of VLFBERHT swords', in *Sword: Form and Thought* (Woodbridge, 2019), pp. 61–88.

[42] The garbled inscription on the blade of the supposed Ulfberht sword held in the Roman Baths

name is that of an individual smith or workshop. The former is highly unlikely; the swords found have been dated to a period that lasts longer than a single lifespan. The latter is more likely; we could be looking at the mark of 'Ulfberht and Sons, sword-smiths since 907'.

Anne Stalsberg has argued that Ulfberht was an overseer or line of overseers: a churchman or churchmen appointed by the Carolingian royal government to monitor the quality of swords produced within Imperial lands, in much the same way that moneyers worked in overseeing the production and guaranteeing the quality of coinage.[43] Again this seems an improbable scenario. Firstly, there is the long duration of the use of the mark. The swords are being made over a period far longer than one individual's lifespan, so one would have to accept that there were a series of men placed in charge of sword production, all of whom shared the same name. Secondly, and more crucially, there is no evidence for the Carolingian Crown, let alone the Church, having any kind of monopoly over or oversight of sword production, in the way that they did coinage. The references to the Carolingians forbidding the export of swords beyond their borders does not prove centralised production, but is a practice reflected by a number of monarchies across Europe throughout the Middle Ages, making a vain attempt to control the export of arms. The bans are not specific to swords. That of 781, in the *Capitulary of Mantua*, prohibits the sale of all weapons, and both Christian and pagan slaves, outside of the realm.[44] Similarly, the only evidence for Church control or oversight of weapons manufacturing is that they were expected to provide the weapons for the troops they were to supply to the imperial armies, and had smiths on their property too.[45] This is no indication of the centralised control of manufacturing. The abbeys and churches held lands by grant or by purchase and acted as landlord over the people who worked on it. As such the overseeing of production was inevitable, but only to ensure that the abbey was receiving its dues, just as any secular lord would. The most likely explanation for the inscribed names remains that we are looking at the moniker of a workshop which was known for producing especially fine blades.

The decoration on the reverse of these inscribed swords is even less easy to explain. Rather than words, there are geometric patterns, again made by embedding iron bars into the blade.[46] Invariably they comprise a number of vertical strokes (when

---

Museum in Bath may be such a 'fake'. (See Fig. 2).

43 Anne Stalsberg, 'Herstellung und Verbreitung'. This argument has also been taken up by Peter Johnsson, see below.

44 'ut nullus mancipia Christiana vel Pagana nec qualibet arm avel amissario foris regno nostro vendat…' 'Capitulare Mantuanum', *Monumenta Germaniae Historica: Capitularia Regum Francorum, Nova Series I*, ed. Gerhard Schmidt (Hanover, 1996), p. 190. There are further bans on the sale of weapons outside the realm in the capitularies collated in 827 ('Collectio Capitularium Ansegisi', *Monumenta Germaniae Historica: Capitularia Regum Francorum, Nova Series I*, ed. Gerhard Schmidt, pp. 572–3 and 607–8).

45 Stalsberg, 'Herstellung und Verbreitung'.

46 *Ibid*. See also Mikko Moilanen, *Marks of Fire, Value and Faith. Swords with Ferrous Inlays in Finland during the Late Iron Age (ca. 700–1200 AD)* (Turku, 2015): My thanks to Bob Woosnam-Savage for bringing this work to my attention.

Figure 2. An 'Ulfberht' sword (probably a 'faux-Ulfberht') circa 1000, found in Bath, Somerset in 1980. (accession no. BATRM 1980.707. Image by kind permission of Bath and North-East Somerset DC).

the blade is viewed horizontally) followed by a interweaving fretwork pattern and then a similar number of vertical strokes.[47] There has been little interpretation of the meaning, if any, of these decorative forms, the only serious suggestion being that they could be a crude attempt to mimic the flowing patterns seen in earlier pattern-welded weapons.[48] The rationale for this is that the Anglo-Scandinavian literature makes much of these patterns within the blade; they are the basis for a number of the kennings and may be an explanation for the little snake present under *Skofnung*'s hilt. The tenth-century blades, no longer being forged from twisted rods of differing quality irons, would not share this dramatic and magical patterning, and so the design might be seen as trying to recapture something of the pattern-welded blade's magic. The crudity of the imitation is problematic. Surely if the 'watermarks' in the blade were of such significance then the smiths would have continued to use the pattern-welding technique of manufacture. Even though to do so would be more time consuming and less necessary with better quality ores, the magical power of such a blade should surely have trumped such practical considerations. Even a hybrid production technique, with an element of pattern welding being worked alongside the brazing on of an edge, could have been a consideration. The designs seen in 'Ulfberht' and other blades appear to be a poor reflection of the ability of the smith, especially given the supposed high quality indicated by the 'Ulfberht' mark.

The accomplishment of the design matches that of the lettering, and this should perhaps warn us against making too many assumptions about the apparent crudity of the design. A design that appears roughly worked to us, may answer a different aesthetic in its own culture, an argument increasingly made by students of insular art in Roman Britain.[49]

By the twelfth century the inscriptions on sword blades had changed dramatically. Gone were the clear and obvious 'maker's' names. Instead, we see religious phrases and invocations. Some are very clear and easily read, whilst others are of the type found in the British Library's sword blade, increasingly obscure and seemingly meaningless strings of letters and symbols, now more often inlaid in brass or gold wire rather than as slivers of iron or steel.

The change seems to be an abrupt one. One 'Ulfberht' blade, from Eastern Germany, has been found with the invocatory phrase IN NOMINE DOMINI on the reverse.[50] The half dozen blades bearing the maker's mark GICELIN ME FECIT inscription also have those words rendered on the blade in various forms.[51] Other than these, the maker's name disappears from all blades, leaving only the religious inscriptions.

---

[47]   See Figs. 2a and 2b.

[48]   F. Cognot, 'L'armement Médiéval: Les Armes Blanches dans les Collections Bourguignonnes. Xe – XVe Siècles', Unpublished PhD thesis (Paris, 2013), p. 330.

[49]   *Roman Imperialism and Provincial Art*, ed. Sarah Scott and Jane Webster (Cambridge, 2003).

[50]   Stalsberg, 'Herstellung und Verbreitung', quoting J. Herrman and P. Donat (Hrsg.), *Corpus archäologischer Quellen zur Frühgeschichte auf dem Gebiet der Deutschen Demokratischen Republik (7.-12. Jahrhundert)* (Berlin, 1985), p. 376.

[51]   Ewart Oakeshott, 'Introduction to the Viking Sword', p. 9. See, for example, the late eleventh- or early twelfth-century example in the Suomen kansallimuse, Helsinki (NM 3631:1), published in Peirce, *Swords of the Viking Age*, pp. 134–5.

Why this should be is far from clear. If we follow the line argued by Stalsberg that the names are those of churchmen set by the Carolingian royal government to oversee sword production then the obvious conclusion would be that, with the decline of Frankish royal government, the centralisation of sword production also ceased, the overseers disappeared, and their marks with them.[52] Similarly, if the *Me Fecit* inscriptions are a quality assurance stamp placed on a blade from any particular centre of production, then it may well be that the manufacturers had ceased to produce swords. Other centres may have taken their place, but they were using smaller, far less obvious makers' marks (the most famous of which is the 'running wolf' mark of the swordsmiths of Passau).[53]

Another possibility, especially given the nature of the inscriptions, is that the change in message reflects the increasingly sacralised nature of the medieval warrior. By the end of the twelfth century, the knightly class was increasingly seeing itself within a religious context rather than in opposition to it, and the Church was becoming better at incorporating the *miles* into a Christian context. These inscriptions may be seen as reflective of that change. There can be little doubt that these new inscription forms are religious in nature. The use of the phrase IN NOMINE DOMINE, the word BENEDICAT, the names of Christ, Mary, and several of the saints are common, as are longer and more complex passages. Oakeshott describes a sword dating between 1040 and 1060, then housed in the Kunstgewerbemuseum in Düsseldorf, on which were inscribed two Latin phrases: +QUI FALSITATE VIVIT, ANIMAM OCCIDIT. FALSUS IN ORE, CARET HONORE+ 'Who lives in falsehood slays his soul, whose speech is false, his honour' and +QUI EST HILARIS DATOR, HUNC AMAT SALVATOR. OMNIS AVARUS, NULLI EST CARUS+ 'The Saviour loves a cheerful giver, a miser's dear to no-one'.[54] Oakeshott notes these to be the words of Bishop Wipo of Burgundy, for a set of moral precepts he wrote in the years 1027–8.[55] A sword of the first half of the fourteenth century, in the Metropolitan Museum of Art in New York, has the phrase 'SUNT HIC ETIAM SUA PRAEMIA LAUDI' (Here too Virtue has its due reward), drawn from Virgil's *Aeneid*, inscribed around the pommel.[56] Such full inscriptions, with their religious and moralistic text may provide us with a key and context for understanding those blades whose inscriptions are far less clear.

[52] Stalsberg, 'Herstellung und Verbreitung'.
[53] W.M. Schmid, 'Passauer Waffenwesen', *Zeitschrift für Historische Waffenkunde*, 8 (1918–20), pp. 317–42, and Heinz Huther, *Die Passauer Wolfsklingen: Legende und Wirklichkeit* (Passau, 2007).
[54] The Kunstgewerbemuseum was demolished in 1979, and I have been unable to trace the sword.
[55] E. Oakeshott, *The Archaeology of Weapons* (London, 1960), p. 218.
[56] Metropolitan Museum of Art, 32.75.225. Helmut Nickel, 'A Knightly Sword with Presentation Inscription', *Metropolitan Museum Journal*, 2 (1969), pp. 209–10. Oakeshott, (*Records*, p. 116) has the alternate transcription and reading, 'SUNT HIC ETIAM SUA PRECUNE LAUDI, 'Here also are the heralds of his praise'). His suggestion that the phrase on the blade might be a record of the presentation of the sword, including the word 'DONUM' is almost certainly wrong, the far more likely reading being 'DOMINI [illegible] TEMPORE SANCTI [almost illegible but most likely MARIA]'.

There is no distinction in date between those swords with full phrases and those with the strings of seemingly meaningless letters, so we cannot argue for a progression from one form to another. Stylistically the inscriptions are also very similar. It is logical and sensible, therefore, that there should be a link in the subject matter of the two different approaches to the inscriptions. Making the connection is not going to be easy, however. A direct correlation between a 'complete' inscription and a 'redacted' one has never been found. The 'redacted' letter-strings are not a simple case of providing the initial letters of words in a coherent phrase. Rather there are very definite similarities with the sorts of scribal suspensions and contractions that we might find in a manuscript, albeit to an extreme degree.

We cannot even be certain of the language of the letter-string inscriptions. Whilst the majority of the full inscriptions are in Latin, as we might expect it being the language of the Church, study of some of the individual swords seem to show that they display a mixture of Latin and the local vernacular languages.[57] If we add in the possibility of the inclusion of proper names (for example an owner or commissioner's name, or that of a saint), it can be seen that the process of deciphering these redacted inscriptions becomes immensely more complex.

We can make the task of decryption even more difficult by questioning whether the inscribed letters were correctly inserted into the blade. Scribal errors occur frequently enough in manuscript copying, where the scribe was a lettered man who knew what it was he wrote and where any mistake might be corrected (if not deleted) if spotted. It is generally assumed that the bladesmiths were illiterate. Not understanding the context of the inscription, they were likely following a template or design drawn up or described to them by a third party, so an error was more likely. Clearly a mistake made in the decoration of a blade is almost impossible to correct. We then must ask whether the smith was likely to abandon a perfectly good blade, the product of intensive labour and substantial investment in raw materials, because of a minor error in the inscription, or would such a high-status piece have to be perfect? Of course, the imperfectly worked blade might become a stock item, a sort of factory second as it were, whilst a new sword was prepared for the original commissioner. Thus, the weapon, with its erroneous and indecipherable inscription, could still enter the archaeological record.

On balance, and possibly for the sanity of the investigator, we must assume that the inscriptions that we are reading on these blades are accurate, and as intended by the smith and commissioner of the work. This means that, no matter how obscure, we should also presume the inscriptions have a decipherable meaning, and that, given the right context, we should be able to make some determination as to what they mean.

[57] T. Wagner, J. Worley, A. Holst Blennow, and G. Beckholmen, 'Medieval Christian invocation inscriptions on sword blades', *Waffen- und Kostümkunde*, 51.1 (2009), pp. 11–52. T. Wagner and J. Worley, 'How to make swords talk: an interdisciplinary approach to understanding medieval swords and their inscriptions', *Waffen-und Kostümkunde*, 55.2 (2013), pp. 117–18. For a detailed study of a specific example in this context, see M. Lewis, '"Names of great virtue and power": the sword Szczerbiec and the Christian magical tradition', *Waffen- und Kostümkunde*, Heft 2 (2021), pp. 1–28.

By comparing the 'complete' inscriptions with the 'redacted' examples we can sometimes ascribe a probable meaning to parts (if not the whole) of the latter. For example, we have swords with the invocation *SANCTUS*. This can be seen in abbreviated format and repeated as *SCS*, or (with the added exclamation 'O') *OSOSOS*.[58] The invocation of Christ's name can also be rendered as a repetitive pattern using the Greek Chi or *X*, with repeated *OXOXO* patterns. Other repetitions have been assigned a similar meaning, such as *NININ* for 'Nomen Iesu'. Several inscriptions have repetition of the letters *NED*, and it has been suggested that these are the initials of the phrase 'Nomen Eternum Dei' but might equally be a contracted form of 'benedicat', a phrase used in full on other blades

Even with these cues, large parts of the 'redacted' sword inscriptions remain indecipherable. Going back to the British Library's sword, we can now suggest that the first four characters should be interpreted as the invocations 'In Nomine Domini' and 'Christus O Christus', and that the sixth and fifth letters from the end represent 'Domini Christi' or similar. This still leaves seven characters in the centre of the inscription and three at the end whose meaning is undetermined.

When the comparison of 'complete' and 'redacted' inscriptions no longer provides answers, then we should refer to other aspects of high medieval culture. The knight, and his arms and armour, did not exist in a vacuum, after all. He was a participant in a wider culture which impacted on every aspect of his martial ethos, his behaviour, and his equipage. Decades of studies on knighthood and chivalry have sought to show this to be the case.[59] It seems obvious, therefore, that the inscriptions on swords must also fit within the oeuvre of this chivalric culture and, given the clear evidence for an element of religious invocation, within medieval religious practice as well.

A team of scholars in Uppsala, working on the 'Fyris Sword Project', have catalogued a series of inscribed swords found in the River Fyris and have made a link with the magical and mystical invocations common to the high and late Middle Ages.[60] They note that the use of a combination of sacred and arcane magical phrases was commonly used by all elements of society for protection and healing, citing in particular the St Benedict medal, with its abbreviated inscription that draws on a combination of scriptural quotes and invocatory phrases connected with the saint.[61]

Whilst there are similarities here, a closer analogue to our high medieval sword inscriptions would appear to be so-called 'textual amulets' – strips or rolls of parchment on which were written charms, that, when worn or carried close to the body, were thought to protect the wearer from danger.[62] Unlike the Benedict medal, which has a fixed inscription, these amulets varied considerably in their content

---

[58] *Ibid*, p. 14.
[59] See for example Maurice Keen's *Chivalry* (New Haven, 1984), Richard Barber, *The Reign of Chivalry* (Woodbridge, 2005), Nigel Saul, *For Honour and Fame: Chivalry in England, 1066–1500* (New York, 2011), and *A Companion to Chivalry*, ed. Robert W. Jones and Peter Coss (Woodbridge, 2019).
[60] Wagner et al., 'Medieval Christian invocations', and Wagner and Worley, 'How to make swords talk', pp. 113–32.
[61] Wagner and Worley, 'How to make swords talk', pp. 119–22.
[62] D.C. Skemer, *Binding Words: Textual Amulets in the Middle Ages* (Philadelphia, PA, 2006).

and, although local priests appear to have been the primary authors, the amulets themselves are an example of personal piety and lay mysticism. As such, they accord well with our understanding of blade inscriptions as reflections of personal spiritualism on the part of the commissioner and wielder.[63]

The Church's attitude towards these amulets was ambivalent and cautious; the Church authorities saw them as a holdover from pagan superstitions and felt that their content, unless carefully scrutinised, could lead individuals into heterodoxy or heresy, and might even conjure demons rather than act as prayers for the intercession of God, the Trinity, or saints.[64] The trial of Jeanne d'Arc offers us a very clear, sword-related example of this caution or concern. Jeanne's sword had somewhat mystical origins. She had been told by her voices that the sword could be found behind the altar in the church of Ste. Catherine de Fierbois. Although it was rusted over, the rust miraculously fell away leaving a perfect sword. During her captivity, her Inquisitors asked a series of questions about the sword that are quite telling, as are her reported answers. What blessing had she said over the sword? Had she ever put her sword on the altar, to bring it better fortune? Had she ever prayed for the same?[65] Jeanne's replies are all in the negative. No, she had not said a blessing over her sword, and would not have known how to do so. No, as far as she knew the sword had not been placed on an altar in order that it should be more fortunate. It was well known that she wished that her armour might be very fortunate.[66] These answers, especially the last which makes no mention of a prayer or of the sword, suggests that she was aware that her questioners were looking for an indication of unorthodoxy in her attitude towards the weapon, and to the practice of blessing the same.

In spite of the Church's fear that 'textual amulets' might lead the ill-educated into heterodox practices, the range of 'acceptable' invocatory phrases in the amulets remained very broad. They might include words written in Latin or the vernacular, as well as particularly powerful words drawn from Greek or Hebrew. The phrases themselves could be elements from liturgy, biblical passages, the names of God, Christ, or figures from both the Old and New testaments, the Jewish Kabbalah, even nonsensical 'magic' words (such as the very ancient and long-standing ABRACADABRA).[67] Just as with the sword blade inscriptions, the passages did not need be written out in full. They might serve as *historiolae* – a story in which the power of the full passage was held.[68] A common one was that of Luke 4:30 'Ihesus autem transiens per medium illorum ibat' – 'Christ, passing through them, went on his way'. The passage in itself had very little meaning, but it would serve as a reminder of the fuller story of Christ

---

[63] On texts and blessings specifically designed to prevent harm in battle, see C. Benati, 'À la guerre comme à guerre but with caution: Protection charms and blessings in the Germanic tradition', *Brathair*, 17.1 (2017), pp. 155–91, and Lewis, '"Names of great virtue and power"', *passim*.
[64] Skemer, *Binding Words*, pp. 22, 65–73.
[65] *The Trial of Jeanne d'Arc*, trans. W.P. Barrett (New York, 1932), pp. 61–2.
[66] *Ibid*, pp. 61–2.
[67] Skemer, *Binding Words*, pp. 75ff. In this context it is interesting that Vulgate Merlin tradition should suggest a Hebrew etymology for the name *Excalibur* (Warren, *Images on the Edge*, pp. 192–5). Lewis, '"Names of great virtue and power"', *passim*.
[68] *Ibid*, pp.105–7.

passing through an angry mob unharmed. Unsurprisingly its main apotropaic use was the protection of travellers. It was also the inscription on both faces of gold Nobles, the coin of Edward III minted between 1344 and 1351 in commemoration of his victory over the French at the battle of Sluys in 1340.[69] Whilst thus far not found on a sword blade, the phrase does occur in a martial context, decorating the brass borders of the breastplate of a fourteenth-century harness in the armoury of Schloss Churburg, Austria ('Churburg 13').[70]

As well as the similarity in the texts used, there is a more direct martial correlation between the textual amulet and the inscription on swords. Textual amulets might be carried by warriors, in order to give them an edge in combat. One of the most notorious is that of Richard Shawell. He was the professional champion representing Robert Wyville Bishop of Salisbury in his claim on Sherborne Castle against the Earl of Salisbury, and was accused of illegally filling his armour with charms, which resulted in the trial being called off.[71] In a number of the published rules for jousts, *pas d'armes*, and duels, there are ordinances against all sorts of '*malengin*', or evil devices, including hidden spikes, barbs, and hooks on their harness, but also spells, herbs, and charms.[72] In light of this it is, perhaps, unsurprising that we should find the inscription of what appear to be magical symbols on the unsharpened section midway down the blade of a sword of around 1500, designed to accommodate the wielder's hand for use in 'half-swording'.[73] We might well imagine a belief that the wielder's hand coming into contact with the symbols triggered their protective function somehow.

Of course, if there is a similarity between the textual amulet tradition and the inscription on sword blades, then this means that those inscriptions are likely to be even more complicated than we have hitherto believed. In addition to the suggestions of elision and contraction, the inclusion of personal names, the chance of error, and the use of the vernacular as well as Latin, we now have to add in the possibility that the inscriptions might include Hebrew and Greek words, and that the subject matter need not be a single, coherent phrase but could be a list of names, mystical words, or even a random phrase which brought to mind another biblical passage.[74] If anything,

---

[69] The iconography on the face of the coin reinforces the message, as it shows the king on a ship, crowned and with bare sword, his shield bearing his arms of England and France quartered.

[70] See Oswald Graf Trapp, *The Armoury of the Castle of Churburg* (London, 1929), p. 19 and Mario Scalini, *The Armoury of the Castle of Churburg* (Udine, 1996), pp. 44–5.

[71] John Goodall, *The English Castle* (London, 2011), pp. 2–3. *Chief Justice's Roll*, 29 Edw III, Hilary term, NA CP40/380.

[72] Ralph Moffat, 'The Medieval Tournament: Chivalry, Heraldry and Reality. An Edition and Analysis of Three Fifteenth-Century Tournament Manuscripts', Unpublished PhD thesis (Leeds, 2010), pp. 45–6.

[73] Kunsthistorisches Museum Wien, Hofjagd- und Rüstkammer, A 168 (https://www.khm.at/de/object/f2b005ea6d/ (accessed 1 August 2021). My thanks to Fabrice Cognot for bringing this weapon to my attention).

[74] We see this on the Polish coronation sword *Szczerbiec*, whose pommel is decorated with a combination of Latin and Hebrew or cod-Hebrew text. See Marcin Biborski and Janusz Stępínski, 'Szczerbiec (the Jagged Sword) – The Coronation Sword of the Kings of Poland.' *Gladius*, XXXI (2011), pp. 116–20, and Lewis, '"Names of great virtue and power"', pp. 1–3.

a comparison with textual amulets makes it less rather than more likely that we will be able to discern the meaning of sword blade inscriptions.

The example of the textual amulet does more than further obfuscate the inscriptions, however. It also poses questions about their authorship and readership. A large part of the textual amulet's effectiveness came from their composition by clergy.[75] The actions of a priest had power, and his writing of the words on the parchment imbued them with extra spiritual force.

As we have said, the evidence for the direct involvement of the Church in the manufacture of weapons is rare, and it is even less likely that clergymen were inscribing sword blades themselves. It is tempting to suggest that perhaps there was a similar power in the hands of the smith himself. Smiths in pagan mythology had always held special powers, as witnessed by the tales of Wayland the Smith, or reflected in the dwarven smiths of the sagas, all of whom were able to work magic into the objects they made.[76] Could it be that this belief continued down into the Christian era, so that an inscription by a smith held a similar power as the words written by a priest? Whilst such a possibility is enticing, there is little evidence to support it. Just as with the swords themselves, the romance and epic literature, in which we might expect to perceive such a belief, mention Wayland only to suggest high-quality workmanship, creating the hardest and sharpest swords, and to give the sword a sense of age and *gravitas*.[77] As we noted in the discussion of Doon de Mayence's sword above, like the magic of the blade, the smith's magic has also waned. The focus has shifted to those with a religious vocation, and swords were no longer forged for the heroes, but appeared ready-made in the hands of hermits and priests.

The assumption that the smith was also responsible for the decoration of the blade is a sensible one for the early medieval ME FECIT inscriptions, where the bars had to be added during the forging of the blade and before the quenching of it. However, by the high Middle Ages inscriptions were most often created by hammering gold or lateen wire inlaid into channels chiselled into the blade, and this can only have been done after the blade was completed. This new process suggests the possibility of a specialist decorator undertaking the work. Indeed, the finesse of these inscriptions compared to the crude lettering of the early blades would reinforce this impression. Again, however, whilst the knowledge of scripture and liturgical texts, as well as the clerical abbreviations makes it likely that that the choice of words was by someone with clerical training (although we should not dismiss too quickly secular knowledge of religious or mystical texts), that knowledge need not have been held by the decorator, who most likely was provided with a template to work from.

[75] Skemer, *Binding Words*, p. 130.
[76] Wayland the Smith is a figure of a number of Germanic myths, first attested in the sixth century, he appears as a craftsman of prodigious, if not magical skill, and the maker of weapons and armour. See G.B. Depping, *Wayland Smith: A Dissertation on a Tradition of the Middle Ages* (London, 1847), Barber, 'Arthurian Swords I', and Isobel Rennie Robertson, 'Wayland Smith: A Cultural Historical Biography', Unpublished PhD thesis (Leeds, 2020).
[77] Barber notes twenty-two swords in the chansons that relate to Wayland ('Arthurian Swords I', p. 14).

As has been noted, the Church was cautious in its acceptance of amulets. Not only was it uncomfortable about the mixture of spiritual, mystical, and magical language used, but it was at pains to point out that it was not the amulet and its words that provided protection, but rather that it was the indirect intercession of the Divine resulting from the wearer's contemplation of the amulet and the meaning of its inscription.[78] Some textual amulets were not intended to be read at all; once written the invocations retained their efficacy by being sealed up and remaining secret. Others, however, were meant to be recited aloud, or were an aide-memoire for contemplation and prayer.[79]

Sword inscriptions may well have been intended to be used in a similar fashion. When seeking an audience or reader for an inscribed blade, we can quickly disregard anyone on the battlefield. They were not for the enemy to read as the blade flashed towards them. Whilst a warrior might be tempted to show off his inscribed blade to comrades as they prepared to take the field, these were inscriptions that were not intended to be read quickly or idly. The complexity of the inscription means that it might be appreciated casually in terms of the overall quality and beauty of the sword, but the detail and significance of the inscription would have required time and concentration (and in the case of the letter-string inscription, some sort of key or understanding of what had been inscribed).

That the lettering on almost all blades is best read with the blade horizontal and the pommel to the reader's left, starting at the hilt and running towards the tip, reinforces the sense that they were for contemplation.[80] It suggests that the swords were decorated in order to be laid out, and their inscriptions read. This is not unheard of within the context of arms and armour. According to both William of Malmesbury and Wace, Arthur's shield bore an image of the Virgin Mary on the inner face which he was able to view and contemplate, whilst in the arming sequence of 'Gawain and the Green Knight' we are told that Gawain lifted his helm and kissed it before placing it on his head, which reflects the classic knighting ritual, the prospective knight's sword and harness is laid out before the altar as part of the vigil.[81] The idea of the knight praying over his sword because of its cruciform shape is a common one, (although perhaps less obvious in medieval sources than it is in Victorian imagery), whilst the active use of the sword within the dubbing ceremony itself (on which more in the next chapter) almost goes without saying. We see the sword playing a more active role in the statutes of the fourteenth-century *Ordre de Saint-Esprit au Droit Desir*. When a member of the Order was in peril of death his sword was to be sent to the head of the Order, who would arrange for it to be placed on the altar of

---

[78] Skemer, *Binding Words*, pp. 64–5.
[79] *Ibid*, pp. 144–56.
[80] There are a few rare occasions, including the Dusseldorf sword described above, where the inscription runs from point to hilt, but in these cases the blade could be placed horizontal with the hilt to the reader's right and the tip to the left.
[81] William of Malmesbury, *Gesta Regum Anglorum*, ed. and trans. R.A.V. Mynors, vol. 1 (Oxford, 1998), p. 27. Wace, *Roman de Rou*, trans. Glynn S. Burgess (St Helier, 2002), p. 235. *Sir Gawain and the Green Knight*, ed. and trans. W.R.J. Barron (Manchester, 1998), pp. 62–3.

the grandest local chapel. The prince and any other members of the Order within a day's journey would pray for the stricken knight's soul, one of their number taking the sword by the point and proffering it to the altar.[82] The sword served as a surrogate for the knight, and its presentation on the altar a plea for God to work through it in saving the Order's brother.

The idea that an inscribed sword might be used actively in the vigil and inauguration of a new knight is reinforced by the connection that has been made between some sword inscriptions and the rituals ordained for the blessing of such weapons. Marek argues that the inscription of elements of Psalm 143 (144) – in particular the first verse: 'Blessed be the LORD my strength, which teacheth my hands to war, and my fingers to fight' – is inspired by the texts used in a number of benedictions, of knights, kings, and swords.[83]

We can see, then that the inscribed sword blades of the high Middle Ages might well have served a number of different functions. They may have been an active element within the rituals around the making of knights. They may have served to memorialise that event.[84] However, they also turned the sword into a vehicle for the warrior to express his spirituality, and to seek divine aid in the fulfilment of his martial calling.

By the fifteenth century, these inscriptions had almost completely disappeared.[85] Why should this be the case? There is no diminution in the use of amulets (indeed, they continue to be significant into the Renaissance and early modern periods), so it is not that the use of apotropaic phrases goes out of fashion. There is no dramatic change in the number and availability of swords over this period either, so it is not that we get a glut of cheap, mass-produced swords that were not worthy of inscription (and certainly not in the survivals, which are inevitably weighted towards high-status, ornate, and expensive pieces).

The reason would appear to be very prosaic. Fabrice Cognot argues, convincingly, that it is the change in blade form after the middle of the fourteenth century that sees the end of the inscription in blades.[86] Increasingly the sword is designed for the thrust; and the blades take on a diamond cross-section. As a result, the fuller disappears, removing the field into which the inscription could be easily inlaid. In this context it is worth noting that the inscription on the sword made for *harnischfechten* and half-swording described above is not only on the position where the wielder

---

[82] *Statuts de l'Ordre du Saint-Esprit au droit désir ou du Noeud, étably par Louis d'Anjou, roy de Naples et de Sicile, en 1352, 1353 et 1354*, BnF MS 4274, fols. 8v and 9r.

[83] L. Marek, 'The Blessing of Swords. A new look into inscriptions of the *Benedictus* – type', *Acta Militaria Mediaevalia*, X (2014) pp. 9–20. On the use and significance of the sword in the inauguration of king's, see below, pp. 46ff.

[84] The use of objects as tokens and remembrances of particular occasions is discussed by Michael Clanchy in *From Memory to Written Record* (Oxford, 1993). We will discuss the use of a sword in this way below (see pp. 75ff).

[85] Although it is fair to say this, they still appear: c.f. the two 15th-century 'Castillon' swords in the Royal Armouries which both bear gilded, but sadly now illegible, inscriptions on their blades (IX. 5409 and IX.2226). Again, my thanks to Bob Woosnam-Savage for bringing these examples to my attention.

[86] F. Cognot, 'L'armement Médiéval', pp. 331–2.

would place their hand, but also on the only section of the blade to provide a flat space for inscription. The next time we routinely see extended inscriptions on blades is on sixteenth-century civic or bearing swords, or German executioner's weapons, whose blades have a very lenticular cross-section, providing a good flat surface on which to add the words.[87] Once again the inspiration for the inscription tends to be sacred, sometimes biblical, but rarely as obscure as those we have been discussing heretofore. Rather than needing contemplation or deciphering, these are clear statements with moralistic tones, very much in keeping with the weapons' civic function.[88]

A Sacred Geometry?

Another way in which swords of the high Middle Ages might embody a sacred significance is suggested by the intriguing work of the Swedish scholar and swordsmith Peter Johnsson. Echoing Oakeshott's comment about the aesthetic of the sword, he argues that the weapon's beauty stems from its form; the simplicity of its line, and its proportions.[89] This comes about, he argues, because swords were being designed according to 'clear and coherent geometric principles'.[90] In detailed study of hundreds of swords Johnsson has applied the geometric analytical techniques used by architectural historians, and discovered that a large number of weapons from the eleventh to fifteenth centuries appear to conform to the principals that underpinned gothic architecture.[91] Like the architecture of the cathedral, the elements of the swords are in proportion to each other and to key geometric forms, in particular the circle, the square, and the octagon. Thus, the pommel can be seen to be in harmony with the cross, and the whole hilt furniture. In turn, the hilt and its component parts are in harmony with the blade's width and length. The use of the term 'harmony' is a deliberate one. Johnsson explains that the medieval aesthetic principle was based upon Pythagorean ideas of musical interval and proportion, and that these same proportions are to be found in all aspects of medieval art and craft, including swords.

Johnsson describes three different geometric types. In Type I the cross sits in the centre of a circle, the radius of which defines the length of the blade. In Type II the hilt sits in the centre of a *Vesica Pisces* (an almond shape formed by two intersecting circles), created by the first two of a series of interlocking circles, again these interlocking circles determine the length of the blade, with a ratio of hilt to blade of three

---

[87] On these objects, see below, pp. 71ff.

[88] On executioner's swords, see below, pp. 71ff.

[89] I am grateful to Peter for talking to me about his hypothesis. Peter Johnsson, 'Geometry and the Medieval Sword', *Das Schwert: Gestalt und Gedanke*, eds. B. Grotkamp-Scepers, I. Immell, P. Johnsson, and S. Wetzler (Solingen, 2015), pp. 16–27 and endpapers, and 'Higher Understanding and Deeper Reckoning', *Peter Johnsson – Sword Smith*, n.d. https: http://www.peterjohnsson.com/higher-understanding-and-deeper-reckoning/ (accessed 1 August 2021).

[90] 'The Søborg Sword: A Study of a 12th Century Weapon', *Peter Johnsson – Sword Smith*, n.d. http://www.peterjohnsson.com/the-soborg-sword/ (accessed 1 August 2021).

[91] A key text Johnsson uses for these principles is Robert Bork's *The Geometry of Creation: Architectural Drawing and the Dynamics of Gothic Design* (London, 2016). Examples of swords adhering to these principles are illustrated in the exhibition catalogue *Das Schwert: Gestalt und Gedanke*.

to an odd number. In Type III the hilt of the sword is defined by a full circle, and the blade is defined by a series of interlocking circles whose diameter is equal to the radius of the first.[92]

Johnsson would be the first to note that not every sword conforms to these harmonious principles. Nor would he argue that swords made according to them are intrinsically better or more beautiful weapons. He also recognises that there is no evidence for the use of these principles in setting out the sword except for the fact that so many fit within their parameters.[93] There are no images of smiths using compasses, for example, nor do we have surviving medieval drawings showing the application of the principles to the design of a sword. But then, we have very little surviving evidence relating to sword manufacture at all, and even that which we have for the application of such techniques to architecture is scarce in comparison to the vast number of buildings and building elements that must have been laid out. In England, for example, there are only two surviving examples of a 'tracing floor' – a plaster floor into which masons scribed the designs for various pieces of stonework – at Wells Cathedral and York Minster.[94] If we rarely find such laying out drawings in buildings which have survived for a thousand years, it is hardly surprising if we do not find similar drawings which would have been created in smithies and workshops that have long since vanished.

Johnsson suggests that there would have been a practical advantage to the using of a geometric layout for the sword, in that the various craftsmen who contributed to its manufacture – the maker of the blade, the grinder who worked its edge, and the smiths who produced the hilt furniture – would have been better able to ensure the fit and quality of the various components by using a shared understanding of geometry.[95] However, he also argues for there being another, less prosaic reason for the adoption of the principles. Noting that swords that are dated to before the end of the eleventh century rarely conform to harmonious proportions, he argues that the change comes about because the Church took control of the supply and manufacture of weapons within the Carolingian Empire, with several abbeys specialising in weapon production at this time.[96] This involvement in weapon manufacture, Johnsson argues, may have led to the incorporation of the same sacred geometric forms that were being used within religious architecture and art. 'In a time when the mystical understanding of objects was commonplace, the use of geometry in the design of the sword trans-formed it into a divine instrument, possessed of a perfect wholeness derived from the unity and harmony of its parts'.[97]

---

[92] For an example of Johnsson's illustrated principles, see Fig. 3. For more examples, see Johnsson, 'Geometry and the Medieval Sword', pp. 22–3.
[93] Peter Johnsson, pers. comm. 5 August 2021.
[94] J.H. Harvey, 'The Tracing Floor of York Minster', *The Engineering of Medieval Cathedrals*, ed. Lynn T. Courtenay (London, 1997), pp. 81–7.
[95] Johnsson, 'Geometry and the Medieval Sword', p. 20.
[96] *Ibid*, p. 17.
[97] *Ibid*, p. 18.

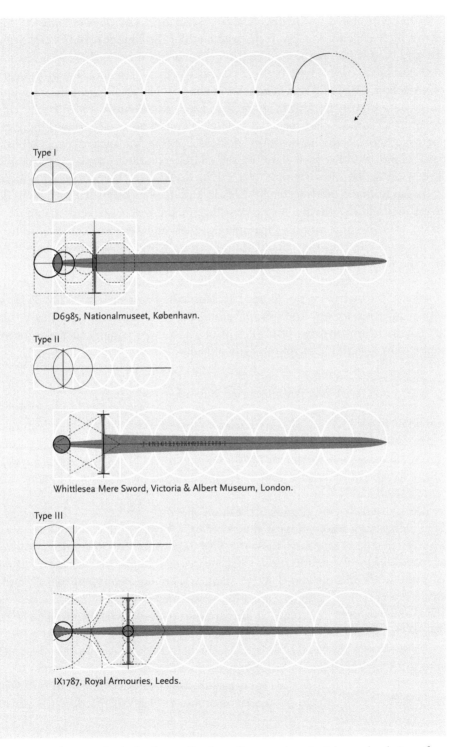

Type I

D6985, Nationalmuseet, København.

Type II

Whittlesea Mere Sword, Victoria & Albert Museum, London.

Type III

IX1787, Royal Armouries, Leeds.

Figure 3. Three methods for the application of geometric principles to the design of medieval swords. (Illustration courtesy of Peter Johnsson).

As has been noted in the discussion of Stalsburg's work on the 'Ulfberht' blades, there is little evidence to support the argument for the Church's control and oversight of sword production, in the Carolingian period or any other.[98] However, such control and oversight need not have been an essential factor in the adopting of geometry in sword design. Given the way in which the same principles of harmonious proportion are to be found in all aspects of medieval art, architecture, and material culture, shared by all sorts of craftsmen and artisans, it would be unsurprising if there should not have been a cross-fertilisation of ideas between the makers of weapons, and those who made other high-status decorated objects for both the Church and secular elites.[99] Since the hilt furniture of a sword would have been made by a different craftsman from the smith making the blade, and that it is likely that such men, skilled in casting, gilding, chasing and enamelling might well have been making a wide variety of high-status objects, including liturgical and decorative objects, sometimes for the same clientele, they would almost certainly bring the same aesthetic to their work no matter what the final object might be. The adoption of the new aesthetic and ideas of proportion and harmony would not have needed the direct intervention of priests. The craftsmen would not have needed a priest present to imbue his work with geometric harmony and spiritual strength. Just as with the inscribing of blades, the incorporation of those principles would have been enough to make the sword aesthetically beautiful and spiritually powerful.

A Mystical Sword for a Christian Age?

Sometime in the eleventh or twelfth centuries, there was a wholesale shift in the way that the sword was considered as an object of mysticism and a conduit of supernatural power. No longer was the power incorporated into the blade by mystical smiths. No longer did the blade have a *wyrd* – a fate – of its own. The sword became a more prosaic weapon.

This did not divorce the sword from all spiritual significance. The Church had, from a very early stage, adopted the sword as a metaphor and symbol, drawing on biblical references, especially from the Old Testament and Revelations, where the sword was a tool of divine authority, of chastisement, of victory over evil. In Hebrews 4: 12 the word of God is said to be 'sharper than any two-edged sword', and this image is repeated in Ephesians 6: 10–16, where Paul describes the 'armour of God'. The faithful are exhorted to put on this armour, each piece representing an aspect of their faith, and to take up 'the sword of spirit, which is the word of God'.

In Revelations this metaphor is taken further. In 1: 16 we read that the 'one like unto the Son of Man had in his right hand seven stars: and out of his mouth went a sharp two-edged sword: and his countenance was as the sun shineth in his strength'. In 19: 15 that image is repeated when the armies of Heaven are led by the one called

---

[98]   See above, pp. 18ff.
[99]   For the ubiquitous artistic style across different crafts and art forms, see *The Age of Chivalry: Art in Plantagenet England, 1200–1400*, ed. J. Alexander and P. Binski (London, 1987), *passim*.

Figure 4. The Word of God depicted as a sword issuing from the mouth of Christ.
The Queen Mary Apocalypse, first quarter of the fourteenth century.
(BL Ms Royal 19B xv, fol. 37r, by permission of the British Library Board).

'The Word of God', out of who's mouth 'goeth a sharp sword, that with it he should smite the nations: and he shall rule them with a rod of iron: and he treadeth the winepress of the fierceness and wrath of Almighty God'. Both descriptions were popular subjects for illustration, the description taken quite literally, with Christ being shown with a sword blade coming out of his mouth or the sword sitting across his mouth. The depiction of the Word of God in the fourteenth-century Queen Mary Apocalypse is particularly striking. Christ rides ahead of white clad knights, their swords drawn and displaying a red cross on surcoat and banner, in his hand is a folded quire or book and, across his mouth, as if clenched between his teeth, a small sword.[100]

It is tempting to see a correlation between this imagery and the desire to inscribe invocatory passages into sword blades, physically converting the sword into the word of God, so to speak. However, this would seem a tenuous connection to draw.

---

[100] BL Ms Royal 19B xv, fol. 37r.

A far more direct impact of the Church's appropriation of the sword lies in the doctrine of the Church's two swords.[101] The Papal Bull *Unum Sanctum* issued by Pope Boniface VIII in November of 1302 stated that

> We are informed by the texts of the gospels that in this Church and in its power are two swords; namely, the spiritual and the temporal. For when the Apostles say: 'Behold, here are two swords' [Luke 22: 38] that is to say, in the Church, since the Apostles were speaking, the Lord did not reply that there were too many, but sufficient. Certainly the one who denies that the temporal sword is in the power of Peter has not listened well to the word of the Lord commanding: 'Put up thy sword into thy scabbard' [Matthew 26: 52]. Both, therefore, are in the power of the Church, that is to say, the spiritual and the material sword, but the former is to be administered for the Church but the latter by the Church; the former in the hands of the priest; the latter by the hands of kings and soldiers, but at the will and sufferance of the priest.[102]

As we shall see in the next chapter, this metaphor for the supreme authority of the Church was made literal in the inauguration rites of kings, where the officiating prelate would invest the candidate-king with a sword as a mark of his wielding of material power.

Swords were still occasionally said to have been a direct gift from God, but when they were, they were passive conduits through which his power flowed, rather than powerful in their own rite. *Szczerbiec*, the coronation sword of the kings of Poland, supposedly was given by God for the vanquishing of the enemies of Duke Boleslaw, and a sword was said to have appeared to the English king Athelstan during his battle with the Scots at Brunnanburh in 937. In neither case did these swords hold any discernible magic properties.[103] They merely enabled the recipients to continue the fight; they did not in and of themselves guarantee victory.[104]

Whether by the integration of sacred geometric principles in their design, the protective inscriptions incised into the blades, the relics imbedded in their hilts, or simply the words said over them by a priest, swords could act as a vehicle through which God, Christ, the Virgin, or the saints could provide protection and power to its wielder. And it is in this latter point that the distinction must be made. The weapon itself had no intrinsic magic or power. As with all religious objects in the Middle Ages, they were not to be venerated themselves, but to act as conduits for God's Grace. It was not any spiritual strength within the weapon that protected the warrior, nor the inscription on it, but God acting through that inscription or weapon. It is this distinction that underpins the change in the mythic or magical properties attached to swords between the early and high Middle Ages. In traditions of the English and Norse literature, drawing more strongly on earlier cultural forms, the sword could

---

[101]   Michael Wilks, *The Problem with Sovereignty in the Later Middle Ages* (Cambridge, 1963), p. 261.
[102]   'Unam Sanctum: One God, One Faith, One Spiritual Authority', *Papal Encyclicals Online*, https:// www.papalencyclicals.net/Bon08/B8unam.htm (accessed 15 February 2022).
[103]   Biborski et al, 'Szczerbiec (the Jagged Sword)', p. 95. Lewis, '"Names of great virtue and power"', *passim.*
[104]   *Chronicon Abbatiae Rameseiensis*, ed. W.D. Macray (London, 1886), p. 16, cited in Clanchy, *From Memory to Written Record*, p. 40.

have agency. It acted of its own volition, as often to the detriment as to the benefit of their wielder. The swords of the epic and romance literature of central Europe shared something of this mystique but, since all spiritual power derived from God, could not share that same potency.

So why does the naming and description of the hero's sword persist in tales well after the magic of the blade had diminished?

Of course, to a certain extent, they are survivals of the earlier oral traditions. Textual artefacts are not uncommon in the retelling of ancient tales; the classic (and classical) example being the persistence of chariot warfare in Homer's *Iliad*. However, in the case of the romances these are not straight survivals; the names have been changed and adapted for the contemporary audience. In the case of *Excalibur*, the shift from the Welsh *Cadelfwch* to the French *Caliburn/Excalibur* is further complicated in the *Vulgate Merlin* by the invention of a (nonsensical) Hebrew etymology. There are a couple of potential motivations for the fabrication. As has been noted, Hebrew words were considered to have had magical properties, which is why they were often used in the wording on protective amulets. It is possible that the creation of a Hebrew etymology for *Excalibur* is intended to suggest that it have similar magical or apotropaic powers. More likely, however, the intention is to add a *gravitas* to a blade born of a biblical antiquity.

What holds an almost mystical significance for the princes of the high Middle Ages, the thing that sees them collecting the swords of the heroes, is not their magical properties or spiritual power, but their ties to the quasi-historical past. *Marmiadoise* once belonged to Aeneas, the Trojan hero of Virgil's *Aeneid*.[105] Arthur's return of *Excalibur* to the Lady of the Lake is not only an echo of the ritual deposition of arms and armour into water seen as far back as the Bronze Age, but might also be seen to reflect the idea that a sword was borrowed for the lifetime of the warrior, and that its fate and fame would continue on in the hands of another.[106] As we have seen, a number of the significant swords in the sagas were barrow finds, recovered from the burial mounds of great warriors to serve another (*Skofnung* being a key example). Although not taken from a tomb, *Excalibur*'s receipt from, and return to, the Lady of the Lake has something of this. The weapons of the heroes of the past – *Joyeuse*, *Durendal*, *Excalibur*, and the like – were sought, owned, and displayed by the princes and kings of high medieval Europe not because they were symbols of spiritual power, but because they were symbols of chivalric virtue and political legitimacy. And it is to that element of the sword's symbolism in medieval culture that we turn next.

---

[105] Warren, *History on the Edge*, pp. 202–11.
[106] A pedant might write that it is Sir Griflet or, in later versions, Bedivere who actually returns the sword but, as the Lady gave Arthur the sword it is equally valid to say that it was his to return, even if someone else was sent to do it, rather like a library book.

2

The Powerful Sword

AT AGINCOURT, IN THE midst of his near miraculous victory over the French, Henry V suffered what, on the face of it, should have been a great loss. A force of local nobility and peasants appeared behind the English lines and ransacked the baggage wagons. According to the *Chroniques de Ruisseauville*, the men of the nearby town of Hesdin, led by the knights Ysembert d'Azincourt and Robinet de Bournouville, carried away gemstones, two crowns, a fragment of the True Cross and 'the sword of King Arthur which was worth so much money that no one knew what to do with it…'.[1] Anne Curry has described the losses as 'a personal inconvenience but nothing more, since it had no effect on the outcome of the battle and was compensated for by the overwhelming nature of the victory'.[2] Surely the loss of *Excalibur*, Arthur's famous sword and symbol of British kingship, should have had more significance than that?

Henry was not the first monarch to have parted company with Arthur's sword, however. In 1191, on his way to join the Third Crusade, Richard *Coeur de lion* landed in Sicily. He met Tancred, the island's new king, and, on securing transport for his onward journey, made him a gift of 'the finest sword of Arthur, who was once noble king of the Britons. The Britons called the sword "Caliburn"'.[3]

Why were these monarchs so casual with their handling of such an important and iconic sword? In Richard's case the obvious answer is that it was the sword's intrinsic value that he chose to trade on. Perhaps, as Emma Mason suggested, the sword reflected Richard's chivalric prestige.[4] One might suggest that in giving the weapon to King Tancred, Richard was making a double statement of this position. As well as his ownership of the sword – a mark of his worthiness as an inheritor of Arthur's realm

---

[1] Anne Curry, *Agincourt: A New History* (London, 2005) p. 208. The sword was passed to the son of John the Fearless, Duke of Burgundy, in an unsuccessful attempt to avoid the repercussions of the raid, which had led to French prisoners being executed.

[2] *Ibid*, p. 209.

[3] *Gesta regis Henrici Secundi Benedicti abbatis / The Chronicle of the Reigns of Henry II and Richard I, A. D. 1169–92; Known Commonly under the Name of Benedict of Peterborough*, ed. William Stubbs, vol. 2 (London, 1867), p. 159.

[4] Emma Mason, 'The Hero's Invincible Weapon: An Aspect of Angevin Propaganda', *The Ideals and Practices of Knighthood: Proceedings of the Fourth Strawberry Hill Conference*, ed. C. Harper-Bill and R. Harvey (Woodbridge, 1990), pp. 121–38. See also Barber, 'Arthurian Swords I', pp. 15–16.

and legacy, Richard's gift was a deed of great *largesse*, and as such enhanced his status and reinforced his position within the chivalric community.

Christopher Berard suggests that the gift was far from a simple transactional one, but reflected a more nuanced political move, heavily imbued with Arthurian symbolism.[5] In negotiating the freedom of his sister Joan (who had been held by Tancred on the death of her husband who was his predecessor to the Sicilian Crown), Richard had promised the marriage of his nephew, Arthur of Brittany, to Tancred's daughter. Berard argues that the gift of *Excalibur* was made with the intent that Tancred would use it to knight Arthur at his wedding, returning the sword to the man Richard intended to be heir to the throne of Britain, and making Arthur of Brittany heir to his legendary namesake.[6] Why it should be Tancred that was chosen is not entirely clear, but Berard's suggestion that it would forestall Philippe of France from performing the ritual as Arthur's liege seems the most likely reason.[7]

We hear no more of the sword given to Tancred after the exchange. The King of Sicily died in 1194, and his throne was taken by Henry IV of Germany. Arthur was not destined to be Richard's heir. Too young at the time of Richard's death in 1199, it was his uncle John who took the throne, and Arthur was imprisoned and then disappeared. There is no record of the sword being returned to the Plantagenet dynasty, and we should presume it to be lost. There is no further mention of *Excalibur* in the hands of English monarchs until it is taken from Henry at Agincourt.

We should not be surprised by its disappearance from the historical record. In the early thirteenth-century cycle of romances Arthur's sword had already gone, returned to the Lady of the Lake upon Arthur's death. Thus, the sword was no longer in the world, and was unavailable, even to monarchs such as Edward I and Edward III who actively courted a link between themselves, their court, and that of Arthur.

So how did Henry V come to have it? The answer is almost certainly that he did not, and that the sword looted from his baggage was misidentified. The earliest reference to the sword being taken merely identifies it as the sword of King Arthur. It is only later commentators that specifically name it as *Excalibur*. As we have seen Arthur is identified with several swords in his tales; *Seure* in the Prose Lanceleot, *Clarent*, his sword of state, with which he is killed by Mordred in the version of the legend written around 1400 known as the *Alliterative Morte Arthure*, or *Marmiadoise*, the sword that Arthur covets enough to kill its original owner to possess.[8] It is neither the only named sword within the Arthurian tales nor the only one to be owned by an English monarch.

In 1207 King John receipted for the delivery of a collection of items brought from the Tower of London to his palace at Clarendon. These included 'a great crown that came from Germany, precious clothes and jewelry', and 'two swords, namely the

---

[5] C.M. Berard, *Arthurianism in Early Plantagenet England, from Henry II to Edward I* (Woodbridge, 2019), pp. 123 *ff*.

[6] *Ibid*, p. 126.

[7] *Ibid*, p. 126.

[8] See above, p. 11.

sword of Tristan, and another sword of the same royal'.[9] However John's connection with the sword of the Cornish Arthurian hero Tristan goes back further than 1207. Aurell has suggested that Henry II may have conferred the sword on his young son in 1185, when he knighted him and granted him the appanage (land to provide income as a younger son of the monarch) of Cornwall and Ireland, on the eve of John's first expedition across the Irish Sea as that country's lord.[10] If this was the case then Henry may have intended a piece of Arthurian theatre similar to the one his son Richard intended for Arthur, linking his son John with Tristan, the Cornish hero who travelled to Ireland and slew the Irish giant and champion Morholt, freeing Cornwall from the payment of tribute.[11]

Just as with *Excalibur*, Tristan's sword seems to disappear after the single mention in 1207. Given the way in which John's regalia and treasures were to disappear – famously 'lost in the Wash' as he fled the baronial faction and their French allies – we might assume that it was amongst those items that went beneath the waves of the estuary.

The sword would have been a distinctive one. According to the legend, when Tristan used it to kill Morholt a piece was broken off and remained lodged in the giant's skull. In the *Prose Tristan* romance this feature is used to give the sword a name and a pedigree. According to this story Tristan's sword, along with that of his fellow knight of the Round Table and rival Palamedes, was discovered in an abbey by Charlemagne on his conquest of England, 130 years after Arthur's death.[12] Charlemagne kept Palamedes' sword for himself but passed Tristan's blade on to Ogier the Dane. Ogier found it a little long and heavy and, because of the notch caused by Morholt's slaying, had the sword shortened, after which he found, with a certain inevitability, it a little short and so named the weapon *Cortaine*, or 'short'.[13]

This name offers another tantalising link between the sword delivered to John at Clarendon and his son Henry III. Matthew Paris records how, in the procession following the marriage of Henry III to Eleanor of Provence in 1236, John of Scotland, Earl of Huntingdon and Chester 'carried the sword of St Edward, which was called "Curtein", before the king, as a sign that he was earl of the palace, and had by right the power of restraining the king if he should commit an error'.[14] This sword – *Curtein*, *Courtain* or *Courte* – reappears amongst the English regalia through the rest of the Middle Ages, and right down to the present day.[15] Eventually it takes on a distinctive

---

9   'duos enses, sciliset ensem Tristami et alium ensem de eodem regali'. *Rotuli litterarum patentium in Turri Londinensi Asservati*, ed. Thomas Duffus Hardy, vol 1, part 1 (London, 1835), 77b, quoted in Berard, *Arthurianism*, p. 141.

10   Martin Aurell, *The Plantagenet Empire, 1154–1224*, trans. David Crouch (Harlow, 2007), p. 153, cited in Berard, *Arthurianism*, p. 141.

11   Berard, *Arthurianism*, p. 142.

12   *Ibid*, pp.197–98. As always, the romances play fast and loose with historical 'fact'.

13   *Ibid*, p. 198.

14   'Comite Cestriae gladium Sancti Aedwardi, qui Curtein dicitur, ante regem bajulante, in signum quod comes est palatii, et regem si oberret habet de jure potestatem cohibendi,' *Matthaei Parisiensis, monachi Sancti Albani, Chronica majora, vol. III (A.D. 1216 to A.D. 1239)*, ed. H.R. Luard (London 1876), pp. 337–8. *Matthew Paris's English History. From the year 1235 to 1273*, vol. 1, trans. J.A. Giles (London, 1889), p. 9.

15   The current version was made for Charles I and is one of the few pieces of the Crown jewels to have

form, having no tip, and is given the symbolism of being the 'sword of mercy'.[16] The name, and the lack of a tip has led to this sword being linked with the sword of Tristan, but it is not clear whether the connection between Ogier's sword *Courte* and Tristan's sword began with the Angevin dynasty's regalia or with the romance.[17]

There is another explanation as to why Tristan's *Courte* should become the royal sword of English monarchs. *Clarent*, according to the *Alliterative Morte Arthur*, was Arthur's Sword of State, a symbolic weapon which he did not use in battle, but which Mordred stole from him and used to strike the fatal blow that ended his life.[18] It seems unlikely, but one might suggest that, at some point, *Courte* and *Clarent* become confused or conflated within the minds of those commentating on the coronations and regalia of English kings, and thus Tristan's broken sword was substituted for Arthur's Sword of State.

From relatively early on the *Courte* of the English regalia was identified as the first and most important sword within the collection. Neither of the other two swords routinely used are named; although by the seventeenth century they had become identified with the monarch as dispenser of Spiritual Justice and Temporal Justice, whilst *Courte*, as noted above, is the 'Sword of Mercy'. Again, quite how Tristan's *Courte* might come to be seen as such is not obvious from its story. There is nothing especially merciful about either Tristan or Ogier's use of the weapon, nor is there a clear example of them choosing *not* to use it. Neither of the two heroes is a king, so they do not have the role as dispensers of justice, and the sword does not have an identity as a Sword of State in the tales (unlike *Clarent*). It would seem that the only reason that *Courte* has the connotation is because of its lack of a tip. Again, this is the assertion of modern commentators; without its tip the sword cannot be used to thrust and is therefore somehow representative of the sparing of life.[19] Its ability to cut is ignored (the current sword is not without an edge, nor is there anything to suggest that the previous versions of *Courte* were). A more likely derivation is its similarity with the executioners' swords of western and central Europe, whose blades uniformly have the same blunted profile, a clear mark that the weapon's sole purpose was decapitation.[20]

---

survived Cromwell's Commonwealth. The definitive discussion of these swords of state and their use is 'The Sword Catalogue', ed. Claude Blair, *The Crown Jewels: The History of the Coronation Regalia in the Jewel House of the Tower of London* (London, 1998).

[16] This may be as early as the reign of Henry VI, according to British Museum MS Harg. 497, fol. 30, which describes the procession of Henry VI to his coronation (according to L. Legg, *Coronation Records* (London, 1901), p. xxv.

[17] Berard, *Arthurianism*, p. 198.

[18] *Morte Arthure*, ed. G.G. Perry (London, 1865), lines 4190–207, and lines 4251–2.

[19] The Royal Collections Trust describes how *Curtana* 'has had its tip removed so that it no longer functions as a weapon, although in origin it was constructed in the same way as a practical sword.' (https://www.rct.uk/collection/search#/44/collection/31730/the-sword-of-mercy (accessed 1 August 2021)). This seems unlikely. There is nothing in the blade profile to suggest anything other than that it was forged this way.

[20] Given that the current *Courte*, made in the first half of the seventeenth century for James I, bears the running wolf makers mark of the Passau bladesmiths it is possible that the blade was intended as an executioner's weapon. For more on executioners' sword see below, pp. 71ff.

Given all this, it would seem quite likely that it was *Courte* and not *Excalibur* that Henry V was carrying in his baggage, and that it was misidentified by the French chroniclers; it was easy enough that a sword from the Arthurian myths in the saddlebags of an English monarch should be assumed to belong to Arthur himself and that it be Arthur's most famous sword, *Excalibur*.

The Sword of a King?

The English coronation sword is peculiar in western and central Europe in that it is not connected with a monarch, either fictional or historical. Whilst the coronation sword of English kings bore the heritage of the Arthurian and Carolingian heroes Tristan and Ogier, those of many if not the majority of other kingdoms were inextricably linked with historical kings or princes.

The French Sword of State was claimed to be Charlemagne's *Joyeuse*. It survives in the Louvre, Paris, and is clearly a mixture of forms and dates.[21] Its scabbard was remade for the coronation of Charles X in 1825, the blade is of a form datable to anywhere between the tenth and fourteenth centuries, and the ornate cross to the twelfth century (although the decoration would suggest earlier). The pommel, however, gilded and decorated with zoomorphic motifs and knotwork, could well be contemporary with the Holy Roman Emperor.[22] It is possible that a sword accepted as *Joyeuse* was used for the coronation of Philip Augustus in 1179, but its use is first formally attested in that of Philip III, *le Hardi*, in 1270.[23]

Ironically, the sword used in the inauguration of the Holy Roman Emperors was not connected to Charlemagne (perhaps because the French monarchs had already laid claim to it). By 1350 their Sword of State was identified as belonging to Saint Maurice, the Roman soldier-martyr who was the Empire's patron saint.[24] Dating the surviving sword and identifying its earliest use in an inauguration is difficult. Unlike the French *Joyeuse*, the *Reichsschwert* ('Imperial Sword') has not been altered in the modern era, and there is no clear record of when any changes were made. Just as with *Joyeuse*, however, the sword is not homogenous, and has been made up of several distinct parts of different dates, in order to provide a sword and scabbard that makes the correct statement for the occasion of an emperor's coronation. Thus, the pommel bears the arms of the Guelf emperor Otto IV (King of the Romans from 1198, and Holy Roman Emperor from 1209 to 1218), whilst the scabbard decoration of fourteen silver plates (seven each side) depicting the emperors from Charlemagne to Henry III (Emperor 1046–1056) suggests

---

[21] Joyeuse – 'Epée du sacre des rois de France', Musée du Louvre, Département des Objets d'art du Moyen Age, de la Renaissance et des temps modernes, MS 84.

[22] https://www.louvre.fr/en/oeuvre-notices/coronation-sword-and-scabbard-kings-france (accessed 1 August 2021).

[23] *Regalia: Les instruments du sacre des rois de France, les honneurs de Charlemagne* (Paris, 1991), pp. 91–2.

[24] The sword is held in the Imperial Treasury, at the Hofburg Palace in Vienna (Inv. No. XIII 17), alongside another sword connected with the imperial coronation, the so-called sabre of Charlemagne (Inv. No. XIII 6). Mechthild Schulze-Dörrlamm, *Die Salier Das Reichsschwert: Ein Herrschaftszeichen des Saliers Heinrich IV und des Welfen Otto IV* (Sigmaringen, 1995), p. 10.

Figure 5. *Joyeuse*, the supposed sword of Charlemagne, used in French royal coronations down to that of Charles X in 1824. Pommel 1000–1100, cross 800–1000, blade potentially 1300, scabbard and other fittings, 1825. (Musée de Louvre, accession no. MS 84. © RMN-Grand Palais (Musée de Louvre) / Daniel Arnaudet).

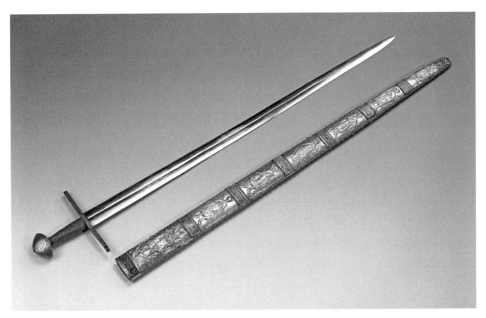

Figure 6. The *Reichsschwert*, or sword of St Maurice, used in the coronation of Holy Roman Emperors. Scabbard: 2nd half of the 11th century, sword: 1198/1218 (Schatzkammer, WS XIII 17, KHM-Museumsverband).

it was made for the coronation of Henry IV almost a century earlier.[25] Otto's selection of a scabbard with clear iconography relating to the early imperial houses must have been designed to make a statement about his and his Guelph family's legitimacy during the investiture disputes and the ongoing struggles with the house of Staufen (in the person of his rival Philip of Swabia) for the imperial Crown.

The Polish coronation sword, *Szczerbiec* (meaning 'the notched sword' or 'chipped sword'), now in Wavel Royal Castle, National Art Collection, Kraków, Poland (Inv. No. 137), seems to be of mid-thirteenth century date with only minor later additions.[26] This gives the lie to the origin myth of the sword, that it was given to the Polish Duke Boleslaw *Chrobry* ('the Brave', duke 992–1025, king from 1025 until his death in the same year) by an angel, gaining its name in 1018 when Boleslaw used it to strike the gates of the city of Kiev in celebration of his victory there.[27] The most likely origin for the sword is with another Duke Boleslaw, Boleslaw *Pobożny* ('the Pious', born c.1224–1227, died 1279).[28] It is highly decorated with a mixture of symbols and inscriptions, most of which are of contemporaneous date, including depictions of the *Agnus Dei* and the four Evangelists on plates on the grip and on ends of the

[25] Schulze-Dörrlamm, *Die Salier Das Reichsschwert*, pp. 35, 82.
[26] Biborski and Stępínski, 'Szczerbiec (the Jagged Sword)', pp. 93–148.
[27] Biborski and Stępínski, 'Szczerbiec (the Jagged Sword)', p. 95. There is no sign of a notch in the blade to support this story, however.
[28] *Ibid*, p. 137.

Figure 7. *Szczerbiec*, the coronation sword of the kings of Poland, note the inscription on the cross (before 1250–c.1325) (Royal Castle of Wawel, Kraków, Inv. No. 137. © Norman Barrett / Alamy Stock Images).

crosspieces.[29] The cross is inscribed with the inscription QUICUMQUE Hec + NOMI[N]A DEII SECUM TVLERI[T] NVLLVM PERICVL[VM] CN EI OMNIO NOC[E]BIT ("whosoever bears with himself these names of God, no danger will do him any harm") on one side and CON· CIOMON· EEVE SEDALAI· EBREbEL.[30] The latter is obscure, but appears to be derived from the Hebrew names for God.[31] As we noted earlier, the use of Hebrew and cod-Hebrew inscriptions were a regular feature of medieval protective amulets, one copied in the decoration of swords from the twelfth through the fourteenth centuries, and this would seem an extremely clear example of such practice.[32] This is reinforced by the Latin inscription on the other side of the cross. Whilst the sword has only minor additions it has been adjusted, and the hilt furniture has been reset at least once, with the result that certain pieces have been lost, namely two narrow plates on the side of the grip which, according to a drawing of 1764, bore the name of Duke Boleslaw.[33]

The most obvious feature of this sword is the slot that pierces the blade, 64mm long and 8.5mm wide in the fuller of the blade, just below the cross.[34] Whilst some had suggested that it was an intentional alteration, perhaps to hold a relic, the truth seems to be that it is the result of corrosion eating through the blade, leaving a hole that was then 'tidied up' some time before 1792.[35] The sword's scabbard, as with that of *Joyeuse*, is an eighteenth- or nineteenth-century replacement.[36] The ornate decoration of the hilt, especially the decorated metal grip with its rectangular cross-section, has led commentators to suggest that the sword may have been inspired by Iberian styles, but beyond this the link between the royal household of Poland and the Peninsula suggested by Biborski *et al*, via Hungary and Aragon, or with the Johannite or Templar orders are rather tenuous, as is the suggested connection with Roland's *Durendal*.[37]

A fourth coronation sword, another directly connected to a historical figure, is that of the kingdom of Bohemia, the sword of St. Wenceslas, currently kept in the Treasury of St. Vitus Cathedral, Holy Cross Chapel, Prague Castle. Its current form may be the work of Charles IV of Bohemia, who was responsible for the expansion of the treasury and the inclusion of relics of Wenceslas within the royal regalia. The sword seems to have been updated by Charles in 1346, when a contemporary cross and rock crystal pommel may have been added to the tenth-century blade.[38] As with

---

[29]   *Ibid*, pp. 112–13.
[30]   *Ibid*, pp. 112–22. Lewis, '"Names of great virtue and power"', p. 3*ff*.
[31]   *Ibid*.
[32]   See above, p. 24.
[33]   Biborski and Stępínski, 'Szczerbiec (the Jagged Sword)', p. 98.
[34]   *Ibid*, p. 106.
[35]   *Ibid*, p. 139.
[36]   *Ibid*, p. 100.
[37]   *Ibid*, pp. 130–8.
[38]   http://www.korunovacni-klenoty.cz/en/texts/st-wenceslas-sword.html (accessed 1 August 2021). As always, the dating of such changes is difficult if not impossible to pin down.

Szczerbiec there is a hole cut into the upper portion of the blade, although in this case it is clearly cruciform in shape. Whether or not this was a deliberate alteration or, as with the Polish weapon, a 'tidying up' of corrosion damage, is not clear.[39]

All the coronation swords discussed above were used because of their connection with a past monarch or dynasty. In the case of the Continental examples those individuals were historical figures, and the aim was to tie the new monarch with a dynasty more ancient or more prestigious, or simply to suggest a continuity between dynasties. The English case is rather different as the dynasty being referred to was one of mythical historicity.[40] The reason for this is twofold. Unlike many of the European monarchies, the English Crown from the Norman Conquest onwards had passed within a single line of inheritance. Even those one might consider usurpers – Stephen, Henry IV, Edward IV, and Henry VII – had claims that lay within the royal bloodline. As such there was less need to identify themselves symbolically with a preceding regime, as it were. The second lies in the politics of the Conquest and the way in which the Anglo-Norman monarchs and nobility sought to integrate themselves within England's story. As we discussed above, for the incoming Norman kings, the only preceding monarch with whom they could identify was Edward the Confessor, born of a Norman mother and an exile in the Duchy for twenty-five years. In the mid-thirteenth century the saintly monarch's cult was incredibly popular. This is why Matthew Paris, who Henry III had commissioned to write a new *Vita* of the Confessor, identified *Curtana* as Edward's sword.[41] However, for the early Plantagenets and for Edward III, it was Arthur and his court who dominated, providing a much more ancient and deep connection with Britain's past, and the work of Geoffrey of Monmouth, Wace and others in interweaving the mythical past of Britain with the incoming Saxon kings and thence to the Anglo-Norman dynasty meant that the need for a powerful, significant and unifying antecessor was best served by those most ancient (and least divisive) of kingly figures.

'Accingere gladio tuo super femur tuum, potentissime': Swords in Inauguration Rituals

The inauguration of western and central European kings comprised a series of rituals and ceremonies that all served to transform the king-elect into a king proper.[42] Whilst

[39] A temptation to suggest that this alteration is a case of one sword being remade in imitation of the other is to go well beyond the evidence.

[40] One might argue that, for a medieval audience, there was no difference between the documented history of a figure like Charlemagne or Wenceslas, and a mythic figure such as Arthur or Tristan.

[41] D. Carpenter, 'King Henry III and Saint Edward the Confessor: The origins of the cult', *EHR*, CXXII (2007), pp. 865–91.

[42] Johanna Dale notes that whilst we commonly use the term 'coronation' for the making of a king in fact this is just one part of the rite, and coronation ceremonies were repeated at various key points within a monarch's reign, and so 'inauguration' is a more appropriate term to cover the entire ceremony (*Inauguration Rituals and Liturgical Kingship in the Long Twelfth Century* (York, 2019), pp. 137 *ff*). Jacques le Goff prefers the term 'rite of passage' (J. Le Goff, 'A Coronation Program for the Age of Saint Louis: The *Ordo* of 1256', *Coronations: Medieval and Early Modern Monarchic Ritual*, ed.

there are differences in the nature of the rites across the different realms and indeed at different points in the medieval period, reflecting the development of concepts of medieval kingship, its relationship with the Church in particular and with the people who were to be ruled, there is an overarching commonality in that all drew on the inauguration rites of the Merovingian kings of the early Middle Ages.[43]

It is not always clear what the inauguration ritual contained. Most of the narrative sources are uninterested in the detail of the making of a king or queen. The key sources for the details of the inaugurations of monarchs are the *ordines*. These are framework documents for those involved in the organisation and performance of the inauguration, laying out the detail of actions and words to be used comprising, as Kantorowicz described them 'a magical thicket of prayers, benedictions and ecclesiastical rites'.[44] What we can see from the *ordines* is that one of the consistent acts within the inauguration of a monarch in any medieval realm and for the entire period under question was the presentation of a sword. Every surviving *ordo* includes instructions for the officiating bishop (or, in the case of the Holy Roman Emperor, the pope) to present the king-elect with a sword. Again, the exact manner by which the transfer happens changes with time and context, but in general terms it follows the following pattern.

The sword is amongst the regalia laid on the altar. It is taken from there and girded around the monarch's waist. It is then taken back, replaced on the altar, taken up again and presented, unsheathed, to the monarch-elect. The monarch brandishes the unsheathed sword, returns it to the officiating prelate who then gives it back to the monarch, who in turn passes it to a nobleman or member of the court who thereafter acts as sword-bearer, holding the sword, point uppermost, as the rite is completed, and carrying it before the new monarch as he and his court process away from the church.[45]

There is also a standard format for the prayers spoken during the presentation, in that they almost invariably draw on Psalm 44. The fourth verse of this psalm reads '*Accingere gladio tuo super femur tuum, potentissime*' ('Gird your sword to your thigh, oh thou most mighty'), and goes on to exhort its subject to 'ride forth victoriously in the cause of truth, humility and justice'. The preceding psalm makes clear that it is not the sword but God who grants the victory.[46] One of the most complete prayers we have from the *ordines*, from the Roman *curia ordo* of around 1200, announces that the sword is being given to the (in this case) Emperor in order that he use it to 'establish

János M. Bak (Berkeley, CA, 1990), p. 47). I am following Dale's usage, mostly because it is more grammatically flexible a term.

[43] The origins of the European coronation rites are uncertain, but the clearest link is with the Merovingian dynasty through Charlemagne's creation as Holy Roman Emperor. Dale, *Inauguration Rituals*, pp. 28 *ff.*

[44] Kantorowicz cited in Dale, *Inauguration*, p. 27.

[45] *Ibid*, p. 80, Le Goff, 'A Coronation Program', pp. 48 *ff*, Jeanne-Claude Bonne, 'The Manuscript of the *Ordo* of 1250 and its Illuminations' in Bak (ed.) *Coronations*, pp. 66–7. BnF Latin 1246, *Ordo ad Coronandum regem et reginam Francorum*.

[46] BnF Latin 1246, 26v; Dale, *Inauguration*, p. 80. R.A. Jackson, 'The *Traité du Sacre* of jean Golein', *Proceedings of the American Philosophical Society*, 113–114 (1969), pp. 305–24. This reinforces what was said above about the understanding of the function of apotropaic inscriptions on swords.

Figure 8. The same sword depicted three times within the Coronation of a French King. Detail from the *Ordo ad coronandum regem et reginam Francorum*, c.1240–1270. (Bibliothèque nationale de France, BnF Département des Manuscrits, Latin 1246, fol.17r).

equity and to curse and destroy the enemies of the Church'.[47] When Abbot Suger of St Denis crowned Louis *le Gros* as king of France in 1108, he took from him the sword of the *militia*, replacing it with the sword of the Church, in a physical representation of the doctrine of the Church's two swords, discussed above.[48]

The thirteenth-century *Ordo ad Coronandum regem et reginam Francorum* depicts this sword-wielding 'hokey-cokey' very neatly. The sword appears three times in an image depicting the anointing of the candidate-king on the forehead; on the left in the hands of a bishop, in the centre resting on the altar, and on the right in the hands of a layman.[49]

---

[47] *Ibid*, p. 80.

[48] Jean Flori, 'Les Origines de l'Adoubement Chevaleresque: Étude des Remises d'Armes et du Vocabulaire qui les Exprime dans les Sources Historiques Latines jusqu'au Début du XIIIe Siècle', *Traditio*, 35 (1979), p. 221. On the doctrine of the Two swords, see above, p. 32. The symbolism of these rites is almost identical to those intended in the gifts of swords (and caps) to princes in Europe by the pope himself, a practice which started in the fifteenth century, but continued through until 1823 – see Eugène Müntz, 'Les épées d'honneur distribuées par les papes pendant les XIVe, XVe, XVIe siecles', *Revue de l'art chrétien*, 32 (1889), pp. 400–11.

[49] BnF Latin 1246, fol. 17r. See Fig. 8.

The transfer of the sword back and forth reflects the fact that there are several separate rituals taking place. One already discussed is the passing of the temporal authority and responsibility for protecting the Church to the monarch. The other – where the prelate girds the sheathed sword around the waist of the candidate – is likely to be instantly recognisable to most as part of a knighting ceremony.

'Guy drew his sword, then he was a knight': The Sword in the Making of a Knight

The making of a knight, with the girding on of the sword and striking of the *collée* – the blow to the shoulders with the flat of the blade – is probably the most readily recognisable of medieval rituals involving a sword.[50] It seems obvious that the sword should be at the central symbol of the making of a knight, perhaps more than it should be expected as that of the making of a king.

There is a clear link between the inauguration rituals of kings and the *adoubement* of the knight, centred on the giving and girding on of the sword, and its blessing by a priest. The blessing, as Keen notes, had been standardised very early; it is first found in the Mainz Pontifical of the tenth century and is repeated thereafter almost verbatim in *ordines* for monarchic inaugurations and, later, for the creation of knights. This is most clear in the pontifical of Guillaume Durand, where every aspect of the inauguration ritual is repeated in the knightly ritual – the blessing, the girding, and the brandishing.[51]

That having been said, there was far more variety in the ceremonials necessary for the conferring of knighthood, even within the same period and realm, ranging from simple actions on the battlefield, consisting of little more than the striking of the *collée*, to lavish ceremonies involving the knighting of hundreds of candidates. However, they can all be seen as deriving from two ancient rites.[52] The first is the giving of arms by a lord to his military vassal. The roots of this practice can be seen in Roman and sub-Roman Germanic tradition (and indeed, in anthropological terms in a wide range of martial and masculine cultures).[53] It seems clear that by the middle of the eleventh century the gift of war-gear – helm, hauberk, shield, lance, sword, and horse – was the central (in some cases only) ceremony to mark the entrance of

---

[50] Whilst striking the shoulders with the flat of the sword has become the defining element of the knighting ceremony, in the Middle Ages the *collée* was not always delivered and, even then, was often a buffet or strike with the fist or the palm to the ear or the chest.

[51] Keen, *Chivalry*, p. 65.

[52] Here I am following Maurice Keen, *Chivalry*, pp. 64–82, D'A.J.D. Boulton, 'Classic Knighthood as Nobility Dignity: The Knighting of Counts and Kings Sons in England, 1066–1272', *Medieval Knighthood V: Papers from the Sixth Strawberry Hill Conference 1994*, ed. Stephen Church and Ruth Harvey (Woodbridge, 1995), pp. 41–100, and Flori, 'Les Origines de l'Adoubement', pp. 209–72. For a different interpretation of the early form of the knighting ritual, see Max Lieberman, 'A New Approach to the Knighting Ritual', *Speculum*, 20.2 (2015), pp. 391–423. For an overview of the historiography, see Peter Coss, 'The Origins and Diffusion of Chivalry', *A Companion to Chivalry*, pp. 7–38.

[53] Keen, *Chivalry*, pp. 66–7.

a man to the rank of *miles*. The second ceremony was a noble rite of passage, the *adoubement*, recognising the coming of age of a member of the nobility.[54] These two separate ceremonies – the first marking a man's entry into the profession of arms and the second his entry into a closed aristocratic elite, gradually fused as the knights became increasingly aware of themselves as a distinct caste and as the lines between knighthood and nobility became increasingly blurred.

As we have said, there is general agreement that the rite for creating a knight devolved from the royal inauguration rituals we have been discussing. As Boulton puts it, with much qualification, by

> 1189 the actual rite of initiation [to the rank of knighthood] may have begun to take the (possibly) classic form in which the (possibly) eleventh century *colée* and the (probably) early twelfth-century type of dubbing with sword-belt and spurs were joined by religious acts (including the blessing of the sword) ultimately derived, like the other elements of the nobiliary dubbing ceremony, from Carolingian coronation *ordine*.[55]

Note that he talks of the knight being made through the act of the 'dubbing of the sword belt'. Most commentators have recognised that it is the girding on of the belt, as much if not more than the sword, that was important within the ritual.[56] So important was this element that it became the defining term in England in the twelfth and early thirteenth centuries to distinguish between the noble knight who had undergone the *adoubement* (the '*miles accincti*') and the non-noble 'ordinary' knights (the '*miles gregarii*' or '*miles provinciales*') who had had their status marked solely by the gift of arms.[57] The belt was therefore a symbol of enhanced status. Any *miles* might bear a sword, but only a noble one had the belt to hang it from.

The *cingulum militia*, or military belt, is a symbol with a long history, dating back to classical Rome. From the earliest days of the professional Roman army the belt, along with the studded sandals or '*caligae*', were accessories worn to distinguish the soldier from the civilian.[58] Not only when on active duty but even in everyday wear or as a retired veteran, the soldier could be recognised as 'gentlemen covered in arms

---

[54] Brunning (*The Sword*, p. 37) has suggested that the Harley Psalter – an Anglo-Saxon manuscript of the first half of the eleventh century, but drawing on the ninth-century Utrecht Psalter – shows a king dubbing a retainer with a sword, but in fact it appears to be a lord with his sword across his knee (on the significance of which see below, p. 59), in the presence of two servants. BL Harley MS 603, Fol. 65r, http://www.bl.uk/manuscripts/Viewer.aspx?ref=harley_ms_603_f065r (accessed 1 August 2021).

[55] Boulton, 'Classic Knighthood as Noble Dignity', p.59.

[56] *Ibid*, p. 53; Flori, 'Les Origines de L'Adoubement', p. 217; David Crouch, *The Image of Aristocracy in Britain, 1000–1300* (London, 1992), p. 198. BL Royal 20 D XI, fol. 134v, an early fourteenth-century manuscript of the cycle of Guiallume d'Orange, shows four knights being belted (Fig. 5), with a similar scene in the statutes of the mid-fourteenth century *Ordre du Saint-Esprit au Droit Désir* (BnF MS 4274, fol.8v) (Fig. 6).

[57] Boulton, 'Classic Knighthood as Noble Dignity', p. 53. For more on the internal divisions between the ranks of knights, see Peter Coss, 'The Origins and Diffusion of Chivalry', pp. 17–18, as well as his monograph *The Knight in Medieval England, 1000–1400* (Stroud, 1993).

[58] Stefanie Hoss, ,Cingulum Militare: Studien zum römischen Soldatengürtel des 1. bis 3. Jh. n. Chr.', Unpublished PhD thesis (Leiden, 2011), and 'A Theoretical Approach to Military Belts', *Rimska Vojna Oprema U Pogrebnom Kontekstu* (Zagreb, 2010), pp. 317–26.

s 19 liliers ·N· fu ocis
E n la bataille des felone· sar̃3.
D iex en ait lame car il por dieu le fist
C omẽt vivien fu fais chevalierſ

eignoz biron p̃ dieu oz ẽtendez
I ceste eстoire· iames meillor vorrez
Cest de ·G· le mãrchiſ au cort nez
Le meilloz homẽ· q̃ de mẽ fuſt nez
R e qui des armes peuſt pluſ endurer
O nc ne fina la ceue granz bontez
C͛ 1 naiſt· pa · a ſou poor greuez

Figure 9. Three knights being 'belted'. Detail from an early fourteenth-century manuscript of the cycle of *Guillaume d'Orange*. (BL MS Royal 20 D XI, fol. 134v, by permission of the British Library Board).

Figure 10. The belting of a knight on induction into the *Ordre de la Satin-Esprit au Droit Désir*. Detail from *Statuts de l'ordre du Saint-Esprit au droit désir*, c.1353–1354.
(Bibliothèque nationale de France, BnF Département des Manuscrits, Français 4274, fol. 8v).

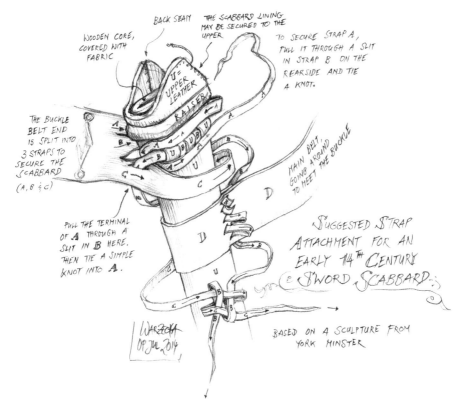

Figure 11. Reconstruction of the attachment of a belt to a scabbard,
based on an early fourteenth-century sculpture from York Minster.
(Reconstruction and Illustration by Roland Warzecha).

and encircled by belts', as Juvenal put it.[59] By the late Roman period the *cingulum*,
along with other trappings of military culture, had also been adopted by civil servants
as a mark of their service to the state, setting them and the solider apart from (and
superior to) the unarmed commoner and churchmen. In the post Roman period the
trappings of the imperial government were retained or adopted by the kings, nobles
and warriors who filled the vacuum left by Rome's collapse, and thus the *cingulum*
continued to be an emblem of status and (martial) power.[60]

Stefanie Hoss has argued that the martial symbolism of the classical Roman belt
may have been a status-transfer from the sword which hung from it, and that this

---

[59] *Ibid*, p. 321.
[60] This may be true for the francophone central and western European traditions, but does not appear
to be for the Anglo-Scandinavian one, which might explain why Brunning notes (*The Sword*, pp.
19–23 and 113–14) that the scabbard and sword belt receive very little attention in the sources that she
considers, to the extent that in some artistic depictions the sword seems to magically cling to the hip
of its bearer. For the use of the *cingulum* as symbols of authority by Frankish kings, see Lieberman,
'A New Approach to the Knighting Ritual', *passim*.

may have come about because the way in which the scabbard was attached to the belt made it difficult to remove the sword. As a result, they became integral to each other. If one were to disarm then one removed sword, scabbard, and belt in one piece.[61]

One could make the same argument for the sword and sword-belt of the late twelfth and thirteenth century. At this time, the belt for carrying a sword was threaded through the scabbard and tied with a complex series of loops and knots.[62] It would be possible to unthread the whole ensemble, but this would be a complicated and time-consuming task. This is perhaps why so many depictions of swords being carried or laid rest at this period have the belt wrapped around the sword.[63]

In the late fourteenth and fifteenth centuries the *cingulum militia* had evolved further, becoming increasingly wide, and studded with metal and enamelled plates. It had also become separate from the suspension system for the sword, which increasingly was attached with straps and buckles to a narrow leather belt. Arguably (just as Hoss has argued for the classical *cingulum*), it was still the significance of the sword as a mark of martial status that underpinned the belt's symbolism as the mark of a warrior, even though the two were no longer physically connected.

We should not be too quick to dismiss the place of the sword within the dubbing ritual, however. The famous scene in the Bayeux Tapestry showing William the Conqueror bestowing arms upon Harold Godwinson gives no prominence to the sword or the belt.[64] Harold is already wearing his sword, it pokes through a slit in his hauberk, rendering the belt invisible. Instead, it is the helm that William is setting upon Harold's head, and the banner denoting him as a leader of men, which are significant. But this image may well serve as a *terminus ante quem*. Certainly, by the middle half of the twelfth century the sword is integral to the knighting ritual, enough to be included in a wide range of sources. Jean de Marmoutier's description of the knighting of Geoffrey of Anjou in 1128, for example, makes specific mention of his being given a sword from the English royal treasury, with the provenance of having been forged by the mythical smith Wayland.[65] Richard's gift of *Excalibur*, and John's receipt of *Courte* are also gifts of arms in this sense, as well as being pieces of political theatre. The epic and romance literature – so often both the mirror and framer of chivalric behaviour – also put the sword at the heart of becoming a knight. When Chrétien de Troyes depicts the knighting of the Arthurian hero Percival in his *Conte du Graal*, we are told that Gornemant De Goort, the noble in whose court Percival is being knighted, not only ties on his right spur 'for the custom was that he who knights someone must tie on his spurs', but also girds him with a sword.[66]

---

[61] Hoss, 'A Theoretical Approach to Military Belts', pp. 321–22.

[62] This can be seen represented by a cross marking at the top of the scabbard in both Figs. 5 and 6. Fig. 7 is a reproduction based on surviving examples and an early fourteenth-century sculpture in York Minster.

[63] See for example Figs. 6, 8, 14, and 15.

[64] L. Musset, *The Bayeux Tapestry*, trans. R. Rex (Woodbridge, 2005), scene 21. *Bayeux Tapestry Digital Edition (revised edition)*, ed. Martin K. Foys (Saskatoon, 2011), Bayeux view, panel 55, http://www.sd-editions.com/Bayeux/online/index.html?facsimile=Bayeux&panel=55 (accessed 21 August 2022).

[65] See Keen, *Chivalry*, p. 65.

[66] Chrétien de Troyes, 'The Story of the Grail', pp. 401–2. Chrétien describes the knighting of pages

It is the sword which Gornemant says signifies Perceval's lifting to the 'highest estate that God has instituted and commanded'.[67] In *The Song of William*, one of a series of epic poems about the mythical hero William of Orange written at the end of the twelfth and beginning of the thirteenth centuries, we read of the William's nephew Guy, of whose diminutive stature and tender years much is made. He does not receive an *adoubément* as such. Having been placed in the care of his aunt as too small and young for war, he persuades her that he should be allowed to prove his prowess and honour, and is given knightly equipment before riding off to join the army. William himself needs only a display of Guy's horsemanship to be persuaded to allow him to join the host. Riding into battle he slays numerous Saracens with his lance, but it is only when he draws his sword that he achieves his true potential, for we are told 'Guy drew his sword, then he was a knight'.[68]

By the latter part of the thirteenth century, when the Catalan thinker Ramon Lull is writing his *Libre qui es de l'ordre de cavalleria*, the sword is not only central to the rite, but it has also become a sacred object, its blessing on the altar transforming it into a divine tool, given into the hands of the knight, its two edges reminding him to protect the weak, and uphold justice.[69]

The date for the establishment of the rites for the inauguration of both kings and knights accords nicely with the appearance of religious invocations on sword blades, discussed in the previous chapter. These inscriptions echo the *ordines* for dubbing knights or inaugurating kings. As we saw above, the nature of the inscriptions varies widely, but the series of swords bearing elements of Psalm 143 [144] is particularly significant, given that it also forms a central element of the litany used in the inauguration rites.[70] This adds weight to the argument that the inscriptions were not (or were not only) a general invocation but were inscribed specifically for the inauguration rites themselves.

The inscribed hilt of the *Reichsschwert* is perhaps the clearest indicator of the sword inscription's active role within the Imperial inauguration. The phrase BENEDICTVS. Do(minv)S. DE(v)S. QVI. DOCET. MANV(s) + – 'Praise My Lord God, who teaches my hands (to fight)' – taken from Psalm 143 [144] is inscribed around the circumference of the pommel and is oriented to be read when the sword is point downwards. The coats of arms on each side of the pommel are inverted compared to each other. The Imperial arms are on the same side as and matches the orientation of, the pommel's written inscription, whilst the personal arms of Otto IV

---

by Gawain and Queen Yguerne in similar terms – Joachim Bumke, *Courtly Culture: Literature and Society in the High Middle Ages* (New York, 2000), pp. 235–6.

[67] Chrétien de Troyes, 'Story of the Grail', p. 402.

[68] 'Gui traist l'espee, dunc fu chevalier', *La Chanson de Guillaume*, ed. Duncan McMillan (Paris, 1949), p. 76.

[69] Keen, *Chivalry*, p. 64. The slightly earlier anonymous *Ordene de Chevalerie* similarly accords the sword a mystical meaning, its two edges reminding the knight that justice and loyalty came together (*Ibid*, p. 7).

[70] See above, p. 47. Lech Marek, 'The Blessing of Swords', pp. 9–20.

on the opposite side are oriented so that it is correct when the point is uppermost. The triumphal statement + CRISTVS. VINCIT. CRISTVS. REIGNAT. CRIST'(vs): INPERAT (Christ Triumphs, Christ Reigns, Christ Rules) is inscribed twice, once on each side of the cross, and these are oriented to match that of the coats of arms on the pommel.[71] It seems clear that the sword decoration has been completed specifically for the two elements of the inauguration ritual, and reflects the different identities of the candidate. The sheathed sword, girded around the candidate's waist, must surely have had the Imperial arms, and the extract from Psalm 143, outermost. Then, when the sword was handed to the candidate for the second time, and passed to his sword-bearer, the candidate's personal, his secular identity, if you will, would have been outermost. This would suggest that the sword is being girded onto Otto IV as the Emperor, which makes sense as the girding on of the sword is the element of the ritual in which there is a transfer of power and authority, in this case from the Pope to the Holy Roman Emperor.[72] When the sword is being borne before the emperor the identity that is presented is that of the individual beneath the imperial Crown, Otto himself.[73]

As always, we must ask who is going to be able to read these inscriptions and symbols. Their size precludes them being for those at a distance. The inscribed passages are very small and could only have been read by those handling the sword. We have already suggested that such inscriptions might have been intended to be read and meditated upon by the candidate for knighthood, or may have served as an aide-memoire for the officiating prelate.[74] The same may well have been true in these royal inaugurations too (indeed, as the latter seem to have formed the basis for the former, it would seem that this has to be the case). Even if the decoration on the sword served no practical function during the rite, and was merely conspicuous decoration of a sword being used on a specific occasion, the fact remains that the designer/commissioner of the sword had thought about how it was to be used within the rite, and what it symbolised at different points.

The point at which the inauguration of a king and inauguration of a knight really differ is in the third and final passing of the sword, where it is handed to a designated sword-bearer.[75] When girded on the monarch or the knight, accompanied by psalms and prayers connected with King David and the Maccabees, the sword was symbolic of martial power and victory through God's intervention. With this second passing of the sword, it becomes the temporal sword of the Church, entrusted into the hands of the monarch so that they can defend the Church and dispense justice. In this final

---

[71]   Schulze-Dörrlamm, *Die Salier Das Reichsschwert*, pp. 16 and 20.
[72]   Flori, 'Les Origines de l'Adoubement', p. 218.
[73]   Of course, the fact that Otto changes his arms, impaling the Imperial eagle alongside his own family blazon, means that, iconographically, the two identities are already merged heraldically.
[74]   See above, p. 27.
[75]   Günter Krüger's "daz Swert ze tragen, ze furen und ze halden" Eine kleine Kulturgeschichte des zeremoniellen Schwerttragens.' (*Das Schwert – Symbol und Waffe*, pp.197–205) provides a brief overview on the topic of bearing swords.

phase the sword becomes a secular symbol of power and status. The sword is passed from the hands of the prelate or the monarch to an individual within the secular court.

It is indicative of the fact that this was a secular element of the rite that the individual selected for the honour varied widely from realm to realm. In France, the sword was passed to one of the officers of the royal household. In the *Ordo ad Coronandum regem et reginam Francorum* the appointed man is the Seneschal, the senior officer of the civilian household.[76] That position was suppressed in 1191, however, and the *ordo* for the inauguration of Charles V of France in 1364 records the sword being passed to the Constable, perhaps a far more fitting figure, as he was the senior military officer of the realm.[77]

In England the right to bear the king's sword fell to one of the great noble households rather than to a named officer of the court.[78] During the thirteenth century it seems to have been the Warenne earls who claimed the privilege. Certainly, William de Warenne was writing to Henry III to claim the rite from his sickbed in 1220:

> If I could be present in the right of my ancestors, which they had from your ancestors, I ought to bear your sword before you. And therefore I earnestly beseech you, as my excellent lord, that you will not allow my franchise to be lost or diminished through my absence.

He was to apply again in 1236, in anticipation of the coronation of Henry's queen Eleanor, but was unsuccessful.[79]

The Warenne claim may not have been as ancient as William pretended. The chronicler Roger of Hoveden records that for the coronation of Richard the Lionheart in 1189 the three noblemen who were to bear swords before the king were David, Earl of Huntingdon, John Count of Mortain (Richard's brother, and future king of England), and Robert Earl of Leicester.[80]

Only one, if any, of the swords being carried by the three great noblemen appear to have been used in the rite itself. Roger of Hoveden merely describes how the archbishop gave the king a sword 'to suppress the Church's enemies'.[81] It is possible that, as we have noted, if the modern rite resembles the medieval, then each sword symbolised different aspects of the king's authority and duty.

However, it is just possible that the swords that Roger describes being carried at Richard's inauguration are not those of the king at all, but of the earls themselves.

---

[76] BnF Latin 1246, fol. 16r. Le Goff, 'A Coronation Program for the Age of Saint Louis', pp. 49 and 54. Bonne, 'The Manuscript of the *Ordo* of 1250', p. 66.

[77] Jackson, 'The *Traité de Sacre*', p. 314.

[78] H.G. Richardson, 'The Coronation in Medieval England: The Evolution of the Office and the oath', *Traditio*, 16 (1960), pp. 111–202.

[79] *Ibid*, p. 134.

[80] 'Deinde venerunt David frater regis Scotiae comes Huntedun, et Johannes comes Moretonii frater ducis, et Robertus comes Leicestriae, portantes tres gladius regios sumptos de thesauro regis, quorum vaginae desuper per totum auro contectae errant; medius autem illorum ibat comes Moretonii.' Roger of Hoveden, *Chronica*, ed. W. Stubbs. Vol. III (Cambridge, 1870), p. 9.

[81] 'deinde tradidit ei idem archiepiscopus gladium regni, ad malefactores ecclesiae comprimendos.' *Ibid*, p. 10.

Crouch notes that there is a reference to earls having the duty to bear swords before the king as early as the reign of William Rufus.[82] Both he and Boulton observe that there was a practice in the Angevin period for the creation of counts and earls by an inauguration ceremony not unlike that of the regal or knightly ones, with the girding on of a sword, a practice that Crouch indicates had its origins in Normandy.[83] That such a ceremony should exist should not be a surprise; after all we have already seen how the royal rites of inauguration were adopted and adapted for the making of knights. The making of dukes and counts using the same rite would be the obvious middle step. Again, Roger of Hoveden records the act, this time in 1199 on the day of John's coronation. We are told that John girded William Marshal with the sword of the county of Striguil, and Geoffrey Fitz Peter with that of the earldom of Essex.[84] It is notable that the men are described being girded with the 'sword of the county'; this would suggest that the sword is tied to the title and not to the individual.

The comitial swords of England have their equivalents on the continent.[85] In the Bayeux Tapestry William of Normandy, Count Guy of Ponthieu, Robert, Count of Mortain and Harold himself are all depicted at certain points carrying swords (or having them held) whilst in civilian clothing. Those moments are quite telling. In the first example, where Harold is brought before Guy of Ponthieu, after being shipwrecked, the latter, sat on a throne with a footstool, holds his sword on his hip, point uppermost. Harold's sword, in contrast, is at first held by a Norman (recognisable by his short-cropped hair and lack of a moustache), and then by Harold himself, scabbarded, with the belt hanging loose around it and with the point all but resting on the ground.[86] In the scenes between William and Harold, William is always bearing his sword. In his first appearance, where Harold and William talk at Rouen, William leans on the sword, point down whilst Harold makes a statement to the duke.[87] In the third scene, where Harold swears the oaths, the sword is once more erect, point uppermost.[88] Unsurprisingly, a sword appears in the scene of Harold's coronation, with two men pointing to it. Musset identifies it as a symbol of temporal authority, balancing Stigand, the (flawed) spiritual authority behind Harold's kingship, but also, perhaps, a reminder of his duty to defend his realm.[89]

[82] Crouch, *Image of Aristocracy*, p. 194.
[83] *Ibid*, p.149; Boulton, 'Classic Knighthood as Noble Dignity', p. 64.
[84] 'Eodem die coronationis suae, Johannes rex accinxit Willelmum Marescallum gladio comitatus de Striguil, et Gaufridum Filium Petry gladio comitatus de Essex.' Roger of Hoveden, *Chronica*, ed. W. Stubbs. Vol. IV (Cambridge, 1871), p. 90.
[85] Crouch, *Image of Aristocracy*, p. 194 *ff*.
[86] L. Musset, *The Bayeux Tapestry*, scenes 8 and 9. *Bayeux Tapestry Digital Edition*, Bayeux view, panel 20, http://www.sd-editions.com/Bayeux/online/index.html?facsimile=Bayeux&panel=20 (accessed 21 August 2022).
[87] Musset, *Bayeux Tapestry*, scene 14. *Bayeux Tapestry Digital Edition*, Bayeux view, panel 37, http://www.sd-editions.com/Bayeux/online/index.html?facsimile=Bayeux&panel=37 (accessed 21 August 2022).
[88] Musset, *Bayeux Tapestry*, scene 23. *Bayeux Tapestry Digital Edition*, Bayeux view, panel 59, http://www.sd-editions.com/Bayeux/online/index.html?facsimile=Bayeux&panel=59 (accessed 21 August 2022).
[89] Musset, *Bayeux Tapestry*, scene 30. *Bayeux Tapestry Digital Edition*, Bayeux view, panel 72, http://www.sd-editions.com/Bayeux/online/index.html?facsimile=Bayeux&panel=72 (accessed 21 August 2022).

The next depiction of Harold, on his shaky throne being informed of the portent of Halley's Comet, does not feature the sword, but then neither do the two images of Edward the Confessor similarly crowned.[90] The sword was clearly a necessary element of the inauguration of a king, but it was not part of the image of sacral kingship.

William is once again displaying his sword when sat between his half-brothers, Odo and Robert Count of Mortain. Robert has his own sword, as we would expect of a man of comital rank, but he holds it horizontally across his lap, and appears to be in the act of drawing it. Some have suggested that this shows his keenness for battle, others that it leads the viewer forward into the next scene. Davidson, in her work on the Anglo-Saxon sword, notes that oaths of fealty made to a king with the sword resting on his lap, in the fashion depicted here.[91] However, this does not fit with the context of this image. Perhaps most importantly, he is displaying his sword in a neutral way in the presence of William his brother and lord, but not in a subservient or powerless pose, as Harold's was shown when brought captive before Guy.[92]

In essence, the sword is held by the nobleman (William, Guy or Robert) when he is in a formal situation, when he is acting as the Duke or the Count. It is clearly displayed, resting point uppermost in either the crook of his arm or on his knee, when he is the dominant figure, but when another character is gesturing to show they are making a statement (Harold in the image of the Duke and Earl at Rouen, and Odo in the scene of the ordering of the boats) the sword is rested point downwards in a neutral position.[93]

The one set of scenes where we do not see the sword being displayed as a symbol of authority are those of battle. In these Duke William is not depicted wielding a sword but a *baculum*.[94] His brother Odo is depicted with the same object, and this has traditionally been described as a club or mace carried because, as a churchman, he was prohibited from shedding blood.[95] This is patently a nonsense. Hitting someone whether with a sword or a club is going to cause the drawing of blood. The *baculum* is, in fact, a classical symbol of command, possibly connected with the vine staff of Roman centurions, and later developing into the 'wand of command', regularly

90   Musset, *Bayeux Tapestry*, scenes 33, and 1 and 25, *Bayeux Tapestry Digital Edition*, Bayeux view, panel 75, http://www.sd-editions.com/Bayeux/online/index.html?facsimile=Bayeux&panel=75, panel 1, http://www.sd-editions.com/Bayeux/online/index.html?facsimile=Bayeux&panel=1, and panel 65, http://www.sd-editions.com/Bayeux/online/index.html?facsimile=Bayeux&panel=65 (accessed 21 August 2022).

91   Davidson, *The Sword in Anglo-Saxon* England, p. 76.

92   Musset, *Bayeux Tapestry*, scene 44. *Bayeux Tapestry Digital Edition*, Bayeux view, panel 113, http://www.sd-editions.com/Bayeux/online/index.html?facsimile=Bayeux&panel=113 (accessed 21 August 2022).

93   This correlation between orientation and power has been noted by Brunning (*The Sword*, p. 37).

94   Musset, *Bayeux Tapestry*, scenes 16 and 51. *Bayeux Tapestry Digital Edition*, Bayeux view, panel 49, http://www.sd-editions.com/Bayeux/online/index.html?facsimile=Bayeux&panel=49, and panel 157, http://www.sd-editions.com/Bayeux/online/index.html?facsimile=Bayeux&panel=157 (accessed 21 August 2022).

95   On this see, Robert W. Jones, *Bloodied Banners: Martial Display on the Medieval Battlefield* (Woodbridge, 2010), pp. 134–5. See also Robert C Woosnam-Savage, 'Weapons', *1066 in Perspective*, ed. David Bates (Leeds, 2018), pp. 57–78 (pp. 72–5 regarding clubs and maces in particular).

recorded being carried by senior officers in command of troops. Edward III carried a white wand at Crécy, whilst at Agincourt Sir Thomas Erpingham, commanding the English archers, commenced their shooting by throwing his baton into the air.[96] It would appear that, at the points in the Tapestry's narrative when the Duke or the bishop are depicted carrying their *bacula*, it is their role as military commander, rather than as dispenser of justice or wielder of ducal or comital power, that are significant. In the first instance William and another figure (potentially Odo) are interrogating 'Vital' about the movements of Harold's army.[97] In the next panel William is exhorting his knights to fight bravely.[98] The next appearance of the baculum is in the hands of Odo as he 'urges on the young men'.[99] Again, in the following image – where William throws back his helmet to show that he is still alive – the duke is also holding his *baculum* up.[100] As well as having a classical origin, the use of a *baculum* rather than a sword to display martial authority is a practical one. On the battlefield, after all, many people would be waving swords about. Those being flourished as a symbol of power and authority would be lost in the general brandishing for practical purpose. In a group already distinguished by being sword-wearers, the wearing of a sword gave you no special authority.

The seeming exception to this would be those men who held the rank of Constable of France. They received a sword on their appointment, direct from the king. It was generally recognised to be *Joyeuse*, the famed sword of Charlemagne. That the same sword was presented to the king of France on his inauguration (at least from the 1270s) may seem a little confusing, but it is always possible that the sword of the king and of his constable was indeed the same weapon. It was the constable, after all, who received the king's sword and bore it before him during the latter stages of the inauguration ritual. The passing of the sword, a symbol of the king's right to wield

[96] Edward III at Crécy: 'Quant ces III batailles furent ordonnés et que chascun sçot quele chose il devoit faire, le roy d'Engleterre monta sur un petit palefroy, un blanc baston en sa main, a dextre de ses mareschaulx.' Jean Froissart, *Chronicles*, Book One. Besançon, Bibliothèque municipale, ms. 864, fol.136 v, transcribed Godfried Croenen, with the collaboration of Peter Ainsworth and Inès Villela-Petit (*The Online Froissart*. https://www.dhi.ac.uk/onlinefroissart/ apparatus.jsp?type=codi&node=Bes-1 (accessed 12 March 2022)). For Erpingham at Agincourt, see *La Chronique de Enguerran de Monstrelet: en deux livres, avec pieces justicatives 1400–1444*, ed. L. Douët d'Arcq, vol. 3 (Paris, 1859), p. 106.

[97] Musset, *Bayeux Tapestry*, scene 49. Bayeux Tapestry Digital, Bayeux view, panel 127, http://www.sd-editions.com/Bayeux/online/index.html?facsimile=Bayeux&panel=127 (accessed 21 August 2022). Vital has been identified as one of Odo's tenants, making it even more likely that it is the bishop who is the lead figure.

[98] Musset, *Bayeux Tapestry*, scene 50. Bayeux Tapestry Digital Edition, Bayeux view, panel 134, http://www.sd-editions.com/Bayeux/online/index.html?facsimile=Bayeux&panel=13 (accessed 21 August 2022).

[99] Musset, *Bayeux Tapestry*, scene 54. Bayeux Tapestry Digital Edition, panel 157, http://www.sd-editions.com/Bayeux/online/index.html?facsimile=Bayeux&panel=157 (accessed 21 August 2022). The Tapestry's caption names the cudgel at this point, although why it should feel the need to is unclear. Perhaps the inference is that he is driving them on with it.

[100] Musset, *Bayeux Tapestry*, scene 55. *Bayeux Tapestry Digital Edition*, Bayeux view, panel 160, http://www.sd-editions.com/Bayeux/online/index.html?facsimile=Bayeux&panel=160 (accessed 21 August 2022).

temporal power, to his lieutenant on the battlefield was, perhaps, a reflection of the delegation of power.

The depictions of the Constable's sword, of which there are many spanning the medieval period, are remarkably consistent, in that whilst the cross and pommel of the weapon are invariably in the latest style, the scabbard is almost always blue and decorated with *fleurs des lys*, the arms of the king of France. This, once again, makes one wonder if the sword is indeed that of the king, but even if it was not it would serve as a reinforcement of delegated authority. The scabbard's decoration is a heraldic display. The bearing of the king's heraldry by another makes a powerful statement. The Constable is bearing not only the king's sword but also his arms – he has, to all intents and purposes, become the king.

The surviving example of the Constable's sword, currently held in the *Musée de l'Armée* in Paris (J 26), is most certainly not *Joyeuse*, since it is clearly of fifteenth-century form in all its parts. It is also (obviously) not the *Joyeuse* that is currently held in the Louvre (which does appear to have been the sword used in royal inaugurations), but as we have seen, it was easy for people to play fast and loose with the identities of swords with mystical backgrounds, and it is quite possible that the two swords could share the same identity.[101] This sharing of identity would also accord with the idea of the sword as a symbol of delegated authority. The weapon might even be a surrogate. One could conceive of a situation whereby the Constable received the royal *Joyeuse* (the one taken from Reims and used in royal inaugurations) from the hand of the king at his own investiture but then that weapon was returned to the abbey with the rest of the royal regalia, whilst the Constable carried the surrogate as a symbol of his rank.

Again, the sword of the Constable is not a symbol of military command in itself, but of delegated authority. Just as, in a royal inauguration, the presiding bishop or archbishop delegated the Church's temporal power to the king by girding on the sword, so the king sub-contracted part of that temporal authority to his Constable. That the Constable exercised that delegated authority through the command of the king's armies was, as far as the symbolism of the sword was concerned, irrelevant.

B(e)aring a Blade: Swords of State as a Display of Authority

As we have seen, at the end of a royal inauguration ritual the sword that had been girded around the candidate and then placed on the altar, handed to the candidate and brandished by them, leads the procession of the new monarch out of the cathedral and back to their palace. The bearing of the sword in processions was not limited to the inauguration of the new monarch, however, but was an integral part of many ceremonial processions. In the fifteenth-century Beauchamp Pageant the illustrator included a figure bearing a sword in almost every courtly scene, whether it be at Beauchamp's knighting, his investment into the Order of the Garter, or his

---

[101] 'Épée d'un connétable de France', *Musée de l'armée*, inv. J 26, and 'Épée du sacre des rois de France', *Louvre: Département des Objets d'art du Moyen Age, de la Renaissance et des temps modernes*, inv. MS. 84.

meeting with the French Duc de Bar, Venetian Doge, the lieutenant of the Mameluke Sultan or the king of France.[102] Even the Earl himself is afforded a bearer when, towards the end of the manuscript, he is depicted as the 'lorde roial, the kynges lieutenant… which forms regent in the Frenche tong'. He is shown enthroned, robed, and crowned with his ducal coronet, every bit the princely figure, including, at his shoulder, a man bearing a sword.[103] Very often the sword-bearer is the only distinctive member of the court or the only individual to accompany their lord. The sword itself is invariably held point up, sheathed in a decorated scabbard.

The bearing sword was clearly conceived of as an essential symbol of power and authority. In two different depictions of the meeting between Richard II and Wat Tyler and his supporters, the king is depicted with his sword-bearer riding behind him, next to the royal banner, the sword – as always – point uppermost and sheathed.[104] In Wace's *Roman de Rou*, William Longsword, the second ruler of Normandy, sends out his sword with one of his barons to stop a quarrel between esquires. 'As soon as the man carrying it had brandished it above the Normans there was no one who dared strike or deal blows'.[105]

Alongside the swords of monarchs and the high nobility, there is a third category of men who were routinely accompanied by a bearing sword. Ironically, perhaps, this group, which represents the most current and actively used, is amongst the least well researched. The granting to the mayors of British towns and cities of the right to be preceded by a bearing sword is poorly understood, but equally poorly recorded in our sources.[106] There are no references to Swords of State in an English city before the reign of Edward III, although circumstantial evidence would suggest a much earlier adoption.[107] Part of the problem is that the recognition of the practice is often buried within a charter granting other rights and freedoms, or that the original charter does not survive, so that the right is only mentioned retrospectively. The earliest Sword

---

[102] *The Beauchamp Pageant*, ed. Alexandra Sinclair (Donington, 2003) at his knighting (pp. 56–7), his inauguration into the Order of the Garter (pp. 66–7), meeting the Duc de Bar (pp. 70–1), meeting the Doge (pp. 80–1), and Sir Baltirdam, lieutenant of the Mameluke Sultan (pp. 86–7), behind the king of France (pp. 106–7). Indeed, bearing swords appear on every formal occasion, behind those in authority.

[103] *Ibid*, pp. 152–3. The editor notes that Beauchamp is given a more elevated and princely title in the manuscript than he held in real life, and the depiction is clearly an attempt to portray the figure as a prince in all but name.

[104] The death of Wat Tyler in 1381, from Froissart's Chronicles (*Chroniques sire Jehan Froissart*. BnF MS Français 264, fol. 159v). See Fig. 8. The juxtaposition of the elegant – and relatively small – Bearing Sword and the out-sized and powerful looking falchion with which the Mayor of London strikes Tyler down is remarkable in both cases.

[105] 'Entre lez esculiers estoit ja la melee, par un de sez barons y envoia s'espee; dez que cil qui la tint l'a sor Normanz monstrée n'I out puiz qui osast donner coup ne colee.' Wace, *Roman de Rou*, p. 49.

[106] The only major work on the subject is Edward Barrett's *Ceremonial Swords of Britain: State and Civic Swords* (Stroud, 2017), and he draws heavily from C. Blair and I. Delamer, 'The Dublin Civic Swords', *Proceedings of the Royal Irish Academy*, 88C (1988), pp. 87–142. Whilst the work is an excellent catalogue of surviving Bearing Swords, its aim is to inform and instruct current holders of the office of Sword-bearer, rather than delve deeply into the medieval origins of the role. However, much of what follows draws on Barrett's monograph and Blair and Delamer's original article.

[107] Barrett, *Ceremonial Swords*, p. 49.

Figure 12. The death of Wat Tyler. Detail from a manuscript of *Les Chroniques de sire Jehan Froissart*, c.1401–1500. (Bibliothèque nationale de France, BnF Département des Manuscrits Français 2644, fol. 159v).

of State, unsurprisingly, appears to be that of the mayor of the city of London. We know that he had the right to a bearing sword by 1389, but only because the privilege is referred to in the grant of a sword to the mayor of the city of Coventry in that year.[108] That the right of London's mayor to be preceded by a bearing sword was being held up as a template for another city must surely mean that the privilege was well-established by that time, and therefore of earlier date. There is a reference to the mayor's sword-bearer, one John Blyton, accompanying the mayor William Walworth out to meet with Wat Tyler in 1381, and to his retirement in 1395; however, there is no further mention of the sword or its bearer until the sixteenth century, when the city rather than the mayor himself began paying the costs of the sword-bearer and his appurtenances.[109]

[108] *Ibid*, pp. 50–1.
[109] For Blyton, see *The Chronicle of London*, ed. H.N. Nicholas (London, 1827), p. 74, and *the Calendar of Letter-Books of the City of London: H, 1375–1399*, ed. Reginald Sharpe (London, 1900), p. 433. See

A number of other charters granting such swords to towns specify that they are to be held and used 'in the manner of London' even though they predate the first mention of a Sword of State in London by almost a decade.[110] In some cases, it is clear that the town or city received the honour not by charter but informally, as a gift from the monarch. These often appear to be granted on a whim, an act of largesse by a monarch touched by the loyalty of their subjects. This would appear to be the case when King John gave the sword from his hip to the mayor of Lynn (now King's Lynn, in Norfolk).[111]

Sometimes the gift was in thanks for a particular service, particularly loyalty at times of strife. Thus, Exeter's mayor was given a sword by Henry VII and the right to bear it in 1497 in recognition of the city's loyalty to Henry VII in resisting the siege of the Yorkist pretender Perkin Warbeck.[112] Similarly, Drogheda had received the right in 1469 in recognition of its resistance against Lancastrian-led Irish lords rebelling against Edward IV.[113]

The gift may have been made simply to elevate the status of the mayor and to 'increase his honour', as the grants refer to it. In the case of Waterford, their sword seems to have been given by Edward IV in 1461 as a way to prop up the authority of the mayor and burgesses at a time when the town was riven by factionalism between Yorkist and Lancastrian parties, with pressure from the rural families (and long-standing enemies of the town) the O'Driscolls and Le Poers.[114]

Petitioning the monarch could also be seen as an attempt to gain status. In 1392, Thomas Mowbray, the Captain of the Calais garrison, petitioned Richard II on behalf of the port for the right to have a bearing sword for its mayor. This coincided with the return of the Staple to the town, giving it a monopoly on English raw wool being exported overseas, and serving as a suitable spur for the burgesses to seek a recognition of their importance.[115]

Sometimes the petition might have a political connotation. In 1446 the town of Lynn petitioned Henry VI for the right of their mayor to be preceded by a sword. Within the month the Bishop of Norwich had protested to the king that the grant damaged his honour, on the grounds that he held lordship over the town, which

---

also P.E. Jones, 'The Surrender of the Sword', *Transactions of the Guildhall Association*, III (London, 1968), pp. 8–13.

[110] *Ceremonial Swords*, pp. 50–1. The first clear reference to London's Sword of State is 1395, but Coventry receives the right to a Sword-bearer 'in the manner of London' in 1387.

[111] *Ceremonial Swords*, p. 54. The provenance for this is highly questionable; there is no record for a bearing sword, nor even a mayor, for Lynn in this early date and, as we shall see, the town's status and the circumstances surrounding the documented granting of a bearing sword by Henry VI is both revealing and suggests that John was unlikely to have made such a grant.

[112] *Ibid*, p. 213. Blair and Delamer, 'The Dublin Civic Swords', p. 92.

[113] Blair and Delamer, 'The Dublin Civic Swords', pp. 91–2.

[114] Randolph Jones, 'How Waterford won its civic sword: the battle of Ballymacaw', *The fifth annual Dr. Niall Byrne memorial lecture*, The Medieval Museum, Waterford (4 November 2016), https://www.academia.edu/35007211/2016_How_Waterford_won_its_civic_sword_the_battle_of_Ballymacaw (accessed 12 January 2022).

[115] *Ceremonial Swords*, p. 52.

had been established by Herbert de Losinga in 1100.[116] Indeed, the burgesses and incumbent bishop had clashed repeatedly since the thirteenth century, as the bishop asserted his rights of lordship and suzerainty over the elected officials of the town.[117] This latest attempt on the part of the town to assert their independence was also to be thwarted, as Henry withdrew his grant, stating that he did not intend to damage the honour or authority of the Church. As a result, in formal processions the sword preceded the bishop, and the bishop preceded the mayor and the town officials, who followed behind in the same manner that members of the bishop's household would have processed.[118]

This dispute, and the use of a bearing sword as a means of bolstering of the position of the mayor of Waterford, would seem to infer that the right to a bearing sword was connected to the possession of authority and executive power within a town. This is supported by the evidence of the most frequent means by which a city or town was granted the right to a bearing sword; through a charter, at the same time as the wider rights, privileges and duties of the town and its corporation were being confirmed.

Not every town or city's mayor in England received the right to be preceded by a sword, indeed the vast majority did not. It is far from clear what the criteria for grants would have been, but there is enough circumstantial evidence for us to speculate a little. The town's economic or strategic importance may well have been a factor. Several of the written grants refer to the sword as increasing the honour of the town or city, the gift reinforcing the municipality's connection to the Crown. In the case of a number of others, including Bristol (in 1377), Chester (in 1394), Norwich (in 1404), Kingston-upon-Hull (in 1440), and Gloucester (in 1483) – all of whom were granted a bearing sword as part of a charter of rights – that right was connected to the establishment of the town as a county.[119] This new status seems to have given the mayor a number of royal prerogatives, including the office of escheator. Barrett has suggested that it was this latter title and role, which involved the sequestration to the Crown and management of lands belonging to those who died without an heir or who were convicted felons, that gave the mayor the right to be preceded by a sword.[120] However, I have not been able to identify any occasion where the escheator is said to have had the right to be preceded by a sword of state. What seems more likely is that these grants parallel the earlier practice of granting swords to those of comital rank, who,

---

[116] *Ibid*, p. 54.

[117] *The History of Parliament: the House of Commons 1386–1421*, ed. J.S. Roskell, L. Clark, and C. Rawcliffe (London, 1993), https://www.historyofparliamentonline.org/volume/1386-1421/constituencies/bishops-lynn (accessed 12 January 2022). Matthew Phillips, 'Urban conflict and legal strategy in medieval England: The case of Bishop's Lynn, 1346–1350', *Urban History*, 42.3 (August 2015), pp. 365–80.

[118] *Ceremonial Swords*, p. 54. William Richards, *The History of Lynn* (London, 1812), vol. 1, p. 387.

[119] *Ibid*, p. 50. Blair and Delamer argue ('Dublin's Civic Swords', p. 90) that all towns with county status had bearing swords, but also that some towns obtained their swords before they became counties, whilst other towns with bearing swords never gained that status.

[120] On the role of the Escheator as laid out in their oath of office see Bodleian Library, Ashmole MS 1146, f. 9v (the French language oath), and Ashmole MS 1147, p. 75 (the oath in English). For Barrett's assertion that the appointment of Escheator came with the right to be preceded by a sword, see *Ceremonial Swords*, p. 50.

as we have seen, had the weapon not in their own right, but by right of the county over which they presided.[121]

The connection of such 'county swords' with the right to administer justice is also reflected in the granting of a sword to the mayor of the town and county of Coventry. In 1384 the mayor was granted the right to a sword of state, but it was to be carried behind him 'because he did not do justice'.[122] Barrett has interpreted this to mean that the mayor was being shamed for failing in his duties or for an injustice, much as had happened to Henry le Despenser, Bishop of Norwich, following his impeachment in 1383. However, I would argue that the point that was being made was that the mayor, at the time of the grant, had no authority to administer royal justice within the city and that, as he 'did no justice' he was not entitled to be preceded by the symbol of royal authority. That only three years later, in 1387, the grant was changed, and the sword brought before the mayor rather than after him might suggest that the mayor's jurisdiction had caught up with the honours which he was being accorded.

The connection between a town's sword of state and the delegation of royal authority is made most clear in the instructions for what was to happen to the sword when someone of royal authority was present in the town. In the case of Calais, it was stipulated that it should be borne before the Mayor or his lieutenants 'for the honour of the town', point uppermost, *except* in a royal presence – that being the king (at the time of the grant Richard II), his uncles, or the Captain of Calais or his lieutenants – when the sword was to be carried point downwards.[123] The charters granting swords to York (1386) and Norwich (1403/4) both make similar stipulations. There were also provisions for the formal surrendering of the sword to the monarch on their arrival in the town, a ritual that can be traced in the city of London back to the reign of Richard II, and persists today.[124]

The evidence for, and research on, the use of bearing swords or swords of state in a continental context is, if anything, even more fragmentary than for the British Isles. The Mayor of Liège received 'une grande longe espée à dois mains', presumably for use as a bearing sword (since the Mayoral bearing sword became known as 'Le Nuremburg' thereafter), as part of a trade deal with the citizens of Nuremburg toward the end of the fourteenth century.[125] There is a reference to a ceremonial sword of over seven feet length in the 1420 inventory of Philip the Good, Duke of

---

[121] See above, p. 57.

[122] *Ceremonial Swords*, p. 51. Blair and Delamer, 'The Dublin Civic Swords', p. 89.

[123] *Ceremonial Swords*, p. 52. The Captain of Calais carried royal authority as a direct representative of the king charged with the defence of this English continental enclave.

[124] *Ibid*, pp. 61–3. Blair and Delamer, 'The Dublin Civic Swords', p. 93.

[125] N. Melville, *The Two-Handed Sword: History, Design and Use* (Barnsley, 2018), p. 12, citing Cl. Gaier, 'L'Apparition Précoce de l'Épée à Deux Mains dans l'est de la Belgique (XIIIᵉ -XIVᵉ siècles) d'Après Quelques Épitaphiers Liégeois', *Bulletin de Société de le Vieux Liège*, Tome VII, no. 159 (1967), pp. 226–30. This may not, of course, be considered a bearing sword *per se*, as it does not obviously indicate any devolved authority. Instead, it might be more akin to the practice of some modern British cities (such as Bath) who have assumed the privilege in order to process a weapon received as an honoured gift.

Burgundy.[126] Another example, from Leuuwarden in the Netherlands, is the so-called sword of 'Grutte Pier', 'Big Peter'.[127] He was a Frisian rebel leader at the end of the fifteenth and early sixteenth century, and something of a folk hero, said to possess superhuman strength. The sword that sits in the museum is almost certainly not the sword of a giant, but a bearing sword, recognisably similar in form to two other swords connected with the English king Edward III, one hanging in St George's chapel, Windsor, and the other, long associated with the king and displayed next to his tomb for centuries, is now on display in the Queen's Diamond Jubilee Galleries, at Westminster Abbey.[128] It is also comparable in scale to two others, held in the Royal Armouries' collection, under the accession numbers IX.1024 and IX.1025. Both are over two metres (6 feet) in length and six kilograms (13lbs) in weight, and have long been presumed to be swords of state for Henry IV and Henry V.[129] Yet another equally large sword is held by the National Museum of Scotland, although this one appears to date to the sixteenth century.[130] Swords of such scale (and especially weight) are unlikely to have been forged as practical weapons for combat, instead being made specifically for use as bearing swords; out-sized symbols of the authority and power of the man they preceded.

That is not to say that swords of this scale are all to be discounted as being purely ceremonial. Nickel describes the 'bearing sword' of the German nobleman Konrad Shenk von Winterstetten, Cup-Bearer and close member of the households of the Holy Roman Emperor Frederick II and his son Heinrich, weighing in at a hefty 4.3 kilograms (approximately 9 ½ Ibs), and 141 centimetres (55 ½ inches) long, as having a similar hilt to those described above.[131] A gift of either Frederick or Heinrich, its inscription ends with the exhortation to 'leave whole not a single iron hat' (LA. GANZ. DEHAINE. IISENHUT), suggesting that it was meant to be used.

The Great Swords of the Sixteenth Century

Whilst there had always been swords of exceptional size, by the sixteenth century a form had developed where blades of over a metre and a half were the norm.[132] For many these 'great swords' are the quintessential bearing sword, although they are

[126] Melville, *The Two-Handed Sword*, p. 12.
[127] https://www.friesmuseum.nl/collectie/een-greep-uit-de-collectie/zwaard-van-grutte-pier (accessed 1 August 2021).
[128] Whilst the sword in St George's Chapel is merely referred to as 'Edward III's sword', the one in the Jubilee Gallery at Westminster Abbey is accessioned 'Westminster Abbey 0864'.
[129] Both weapons are on display at the Tower of London. https://collections.royalarmouries.org/object/rac-object-122.html and https://collections.royalarmouries.org/object/rac-object-123.html (accessed 1 August 2021). All four swords are recorded in *Ceremonial Swords*, pp. 88–91.
[130] http://nms.scran.ac.uk/database/record.php?usi=000-100-002-238-C (accessed 1 August 2021). National Museums of Scotland, H.LA 45, 'Sword and Scabbard belonging to the Sempills of Elliestoun'.
[131] Nickel, 'A knightly sword with presentation inscriptions', pp. 209–10. Some of this weight and length is the result of a sixteenth-century alteration, during which the tang had to be extended to accommodate a new hilt.
[132] Melville, *The Two-Handed Sword*, pp. 25ff.

quite different in function from the examples we have just been discussing. These swords are not the symbol of authority of an individual mayor or monarch. With their ornate guards – long crosses, increasingly elaborate side-rings – often augmented by 'parrying lugs' (protuberances on the blade protecting the wielder's left hand when advanced on to the sword's ricasso), and flamboyant (literally) blades, these swords are synonymous with the equally larger-than-life landsknecht and Swiss soldiers of the period.[133]

They are often dismissed as being too large and unwieldy to be an efficient weapon, their battlefield use limited to wild charges by the *doppelsöldner*, supposedly paid double because of the risk of death, who would launch themselves suicidally at the enemy pike blocks to try and disrupt their formation before their own pikes engaged. Often, commentators and museums relegate them to the status of parade weapons, carried by the bodyguards of monarchs and nobles, no more than an outlandish symbol of rank, status, and power in an era of outlandish symbols.

Unlike the oversized bearing swords described above, the great swords of the sixteenth century belie their apparent unwieldiness. Whilst often a good two or three kilograms heavier than a longsword, they rarely weigh more than four or five kilograms, and their heft and balance are such that they are far from an inefficient or cumbersome weapon. Those that are grossly over this weight and do handle badly often turn out to be Victorian forgeries or have been re-hilted in that era, with a focus on making them look Renaissance rather than with a concern for, or understanding of, how to retain their proper heft. Thus, Royal Armouries IX.926, dating to between 1540 and 1560 and bearing the maker's name of Christoph Stantler of Munich, weighs a mere 3.3kg and is 1.73m in length and has a rather plain and workaday form but a comfortable heft, whilst IX.7 has a blade of similar date and profile, but has been re-hilted with an incredibly heavy, 'garden ornament' hilt that has completely unbalanced it as a weapon.[134]

It is true that the sixteenth-century great sword cannot be used in the same way as an arming- or longsword. The extra weight and length of the blade, countered though it is by the length of the grip, still means that it is primarily a weapon for big cuts. Two key fencing manuals that deal with its use – Diego Gomes de Figueyredo's *Memorial of the Practice of the Montante* (published in 1651), and Francesco Fernando Alfieri's '*L'arte di ben maneggiare la spada*' (published around 1640) – give plays that comprise a series of great sweeping arcs, with little opportunity for the use of the thrust.[135] It is unsurprising, therefore that historians should be happy to see it as a weapon for cutting the heads off pikes and halberds (although in reality this would

---

[133] *Ibid*, p. 1.

[134] My thanks to Bob Woosnam-Savage, former Curator of Armour and Edged Weapons, for giving me access to these weapons, and a number of others, and for the colourful description of IX.7's replacement hilt.

[135] Diego Gomes de Figueyredo, *Memorial of the Practice of the Montante*, trans. E. Myers & S. Hick (n.p., 2009). The original manuscript is in the Ajuda Library in Lisbon, MS49, III, 20, no.21) Francesco Fernando Alfieri, *L'arte di ben Maneggiare la Spada*, trans. James Clark. https://wiktenauer.com/wiki/Francesco_Fernando_Alfieri#Lo_Spadone_.28.22The_Greatsword.22.29 (accessed 1 August 2021).

Figure 13. The author handling a sixteenth-century two-handed sword, Royal Armouries IX.765, c.1530–1570. (Author's photo).

be far less easy than those historians seem to think), but cannot see how it could ever be a practical weapon for a bodyguard.

Yet this is exactly what the manuals for the use of such swords predicate their techniques upon. Both Figueyredo and Alfieri describe several plays specifically for use in urban situations. They include plays for fighting in narrow streets, for fighting in wide streets and for fighting opponents both in front and behind. Figueyredo includes one entitled 'the lady guard', in which it is presumed that the lady hides behind the swordsman's shoulder and he defends her, 'the cloak guard', a series of moves used to 'defend one who has fallen to the ground or who has deliberately cast themselves at your feet so as not to hinder you'.[136] These plays are unlike any other *fechtbüch* in this regard.[137] They are specific, and arguably reflect the kinds of situation faced by some sort of bodyguard. Alfieri reinforces this with an aside attesting to the effectiveness of the play against hafted weapons in a narrow street, saying that by making a simple or double *mollinelli* (literally 'a windmill' – performing a series of cuts in a figure of eight) in a narrow street 'you can advance against a shafted weapon, pike or halberd, and win it, as I myself have done, beholding the effect in actual practice more times at different occasions in the presence of gentlemen and grand princes'.

Whilst Figueyredo had a long military experience, we are less sure of Alfieri's practice. He does seem to be a fencing master, and we must accept that it is just as possible that the fights he wins against staff weapons took place in the fencing salle, as display fights for prospective patrons, as it is that he was guarding the gentlemen and grand princes. As we shall see, we need to be careful not to assume that just because a manual seems to indicate a way in which the sword is used, we should take it literally.[138] The plays in these texts may seem eminently practical, but their authors also recognise that this is not why their works are being read, instead focusing their introductory remark on how the perfection of these weapons' use is an excellent training tool, benefiting fitness and agility, rather than on its facility for personal defence.[139]

It can be difficult to judge the heft and therefore the efficiency of a weapon simply by eye. The massive bearing swords connected with Edward III have been struck with the running wolf mark of the Passau workshops, the foremost bladesmiths of the medieval period, which would suggest that they were made as functional blades, even if their dimensions would seem to make them impractical for even the most powerful of warriors.[140] As we have seen, other swords may have begun life as practical weapons even if they became ceremonial symbols. The swords of state of the cities of York, Dublin, and Exeter, whose mayors received them directly from the monarch, must surely have been weapons intended for their original owners' actual use.

Perhaps a better way of differentiating between those swords which had a practical function and those whose use was wholly ceremonial is to consider the decoration on the weapon, and particularly any inscriptions. As we have seen with the *Reichsschwert*, and indeed with those swords with 'mystical' inscriptions, the direction of the lettering should make us consider the way in which the sword was intended to be oriented when viewed. Those with inscriptions and markings which read 'right' when the blade is held point upward are likely to have been made with the intention of being used as a ceremonial weapon from the beginning and therefore are less likely

---

[136] Figueyredo, *Memorial*, pp. 13 and 14.

[137] For more on this, and the nature of the fencing manual or *Fechtbüch*, see below, pp. 125ff.

[138] See below, pp. 155ff.

[139] Alfieri, cap. 3. Figueyredo, *Memorial*, p. 16. The plays themselves have the feel of 'flourishes' – a series of cuts and thrusts that are combined as a display of skill with the weapon rather than as practical combat techniques.

[140] The 'running wolf' mark of the bladesmiths of Passau and Solingen have been a sign of quality from the thirteenth century through to the present day. Of course, this does assume that the Passauer bladesmiths *only* made practical blades for 'real' weapons.

to be 'practical'. Even here there is the caveat, and it is a vital one, that just because a weapon is highly decorated and appears to have a clear ceremonial function this should not preclude its use as a practical weapon. Work by James Hester for his doctoral thesis uncovered many supposedly ceremonial swords that show damage to the blade and cross that suggests that they had seen actual use.[141]

The Executioner's Sword

The swords we have been discussing thus far in this chapter were primarily symbols of delegated authority, and a mark of the bearer's right to wield power and judgement. There is another sword often discussed alongside civic bearing swords that has a much more direct relationship with the dispensing of justice.

The sword had been used as a means of execution throughout the Middle Ages, although for most of the period a normal sword was used. By the sixteenth century German executioners were utilising a weapon of peculiar design.[142] With a broad, heavy blade, short in proportion to its grip and with a squared or very short tip, it was a tool for one specific blow.[143] Nuremburg's executioner between 1578 and 1618, one Frantz Schmidt, had a sword made to his own specifications.[144] This would in part have been to ensure that the tool suited his own height, strength, and cutting style, but also because the weapon, with its unique and distinctive form, was a symbol of his trade and his peculiar place in society.

Indeed, it is possible to posit a correlation between the development of the distinctive form of the sword and the change in executioners' status. Throughout the Middle Ages the executioner had been a social pariah, condemned by the secular authorities and Church alike.[145] However, with the Reformation the Protestant and Catholic faiths both started to consider capital punishment as essential for the maintenance of order, and the role of the executioner essential. As a result, like the earlier doctrine of Just War, the executioner's actions were no longer deemed sinful providing he performed them under legitimate authority and without malice.

---

[141] James Hester, 'Battle Damage on Ceremonial Swords', *School of Mars*, 25 August 2020, YouTube https://www.youtube.com/watch?v=hn4qLxTUSFE (accessed 1 August 2021) and 'To Adorn the Great at Light of Mars', pp. 35–83. As Hester notes, one cannot be certain that such damage is a result of actual combat or from later custodians playing with them. See also Brunning, *The Sword*, pp. 85–6.

[142] For a brief overview of the executioner's sword, see Vilém Knoll, 'Executioners' Swords – Their Form and Development: A Brief Summary', *Journal on European History of Law*, 3.1 (2012), pp. 158–61.

[143] Joel F. Harrington, *The Faithful Executioner: Life and Death in the Sixteenth Century* (London, 2013), p. 42. There are many surviving examples see, for instance, Royal Armouries IX.728, which dates from 1674 (see Fig. 10). Some have holes bored through the tip, and there is a popular myth that weights were hung from these in order to add extra power to the cut. There is no evidence for such a function (indeed the addition of swinging weights would do more to inhibit a clean cut than aid one), but their true purpose remains obscure.

[144] *Ibid*, p. 42.

[145] See K. Stuart, *Defiled Trades and Social Outcasts: Honor and Ritual Pollution in Early Modern Germany* (Cambridge, 2006), p. 121ff, and Ilse Bogaerts, 'Representations of executioners in Northern France and the Low Countries', *ICOMAM Conference October 2009 Proceedings* (Leeds, 2012), pp. 149–65.

Figure 14. An Executioner's sword, decorated with scenes of execution. German, 1674. (Royal Armouries IX.728).

However, it was not until the passing of the *Constitutio Criminalis Carolina* by the Emperor Charles V in 1532 that executioners received clear secular support for their duties, alongside regulated wages, and guarantees of legal protection against retribution for his carrying out of his work.[146] Given that this is about the same time as we find the earliest examples of the executioner's sword in its distinct form, one can infer that the sword was reshaped as a result of the executioners' new-found legitimacy; a badge of office, if you will, as much as a tailormade tool.

The ceremonial aspect of these weapons is clear from the surviving examples, of which there are many. Almost invariably they are inscribed. Some strike a sacred note, such as the late seventeenth-century example in the Cleveland Museum of Art which bears the inscription, above an image of Justice, 'Wan ich Das Schwerdt thu auff heben so / Wunch ich Dem armen sunder das Ewege Leben' – 'If I raise the sword then so / I wish the poor sinner eternal life'.[147] A similar sword in the same museum has an image of the crucifixion and the Latin phrase 'VIAT JUSTICIDET VERBUM CARO FACTUM', 'That there might be Justice the Word was made Flesh'.[148] An example in the Royal Armouries, dated 1674 (IX.728), has depictions of various forms of execution (a man impaled upon a stake, another about to be beheaded, a third broken on a wheel and a fourth hung upon a hook), each with their own reflective exhortation.[149]

In all these cases the images, if not the text, is oriented to be viewed when the point of the weapon is uppermost, a clear indication that these swords were in their own way bearing swords. This decoration on the blade has led many to presume that these were purely ceremonial, with plainer examples being used for the actual act, or that the blades were decorated when the executioner and his sword retired. This makes some sense. A public execution was a ritualised act, the clear dispensation of justice by an individual delegated to the task, and the sword was the symbol of that authority. However, even after recognition under the *Constitutio Criminalis Carolina*, the executioner, and the tools of his trade, were tainted with dishonour.[150] Even those who came into contact with either the man or his implements could become tainted by association. As such, whilst the execution itself was a civic occasion, in which the judge, council representatives, and heads of the city guilds accompanied the condemned to the place of execution, it was the executioner, supported by his bailiffs and 'skinners' who oversaw the spectacle.[151] It is unlikely that the executioner, dishonoured as he was, would be a participant in any of the civic ceremonials and parades. As such the sword is unlikely to have been displayed other than during the

---

[146] Joel F. Harrington, *The Executioner's Journal: Meister Frantz Schmidt of the Imperial City of Nuremberg* (Charlottesville, 2016), p. 25.

[147] Executioner's Sword, late 1600s. Cleveland Museum of Art 1916.1620 (https://clevelandart.org/art/1916.1620, accessed 1 August 2021).

[148] Executioner's Sword, late 1600s. Cleveland Museum of Art 1916.1616 (https://clevelandart.org/art/1916.1616, accessed 1 August 2021).

[149] See Fig. 10.

[150] Stuart, *Defiled Trades and Social Outcasts*, p. 121*ff*. The situation in the sixteenth century had improved somewhat on the medieval period when the Executioner was both a social and religious pariah. (Harrington, *The Executioner's Journal*, pp. 27–8).

[151] Harrington, *The Faithful Executioner*, p. xiv.

process of execution, and therefore it is equally unlikely (though not impossible) that the executioner should carry two such weapons with him. It is more likely that the plain examples that survive were the tools of journeyman or itinerant executioners, or those of smaller less affluent towns.

Executioners' swords are also distinctive in being imbued with magical properties in the contemporary popular imagination. In some cases, the weapons were thought to vibrate in the presence of those destined for the gallows, or to chime to warn their owner of an impending execution. They were even accorded healing properties.[152] In the increasingly secular world at the end of our period it may seem surprising that we should see swords with more magical power than those famous heroic emblems discussed at the beginning of this chapter. But the executioner's sword was a symbol and tool of very particular power. The form of the executioner's sword was determined in part by its function, the breadth and length of the blade a result of the desire to make a powerful clean cut to severe the condemned's head. However, this form also served to symbolise that function and became a badge of the executioner himself. Like the other swords we have discussed in these first two chapters, the executioner's sword was both a tool and symbol of power and authority. In the next chapter we look at another example of how form could follow function and become imbued with a symbolic significance as a result.

---

[152] B. Ann Tlusty, 'Invincible Blades and invulnerable Bodies: Weapons Magic in Early Modern Germany', *European Review of History*, 22.4 (2015), pp. 664–5. Executioners often also served as unofficial healers and surgeons, their knowledge of anatomy and their ironic responsibility for keeping the condemned healthy enough for execution giving them invaluable knowledge (Harrington, *The Faithful Executioner*, p. 39).

3

The Falchion:
A Case Study of Form, Function, and Symbolism[1]

WHEN EDWARD II'S OFFICERS put together an inventory of the goods and chattels left by Roger Mortimer in his castle and the abbey of Wigmore after his rebellion in 1322, everything was catalogued down to bed linen, the cruets: even the peacock.[2] Amongst this collection of aristocratic bric-a-brac, in the keeping of Wigmore Abbey and sandwiched between 'four books of romances' and 'one coffer containing charters, deeds and other records', is listed 'one brass horn that with a certain falchion is said to be the charter of the land of Wigmore'.[3]

Such symbols of conveyance are not unusual. A wide variety of objects either have survived or are recorded as being used to mark grants. There is a long tradition of so-called 'tenure horns', such as the 'Pusey Horn' held in the Victoria and Albert Museum with its early fifteenth-century inscription recording it as a token of a grant by King Cnut to William Pusey.[4] Knives are also common tokens. Such objects served as a tag for a memory in the 'pre-literate' period, the transfer of the object being a physical act that could be watched and remembered at the same time as the words of the transfer were heard and remembered.[5]

Whilst knives seem to have been common symbols of conveyance, swords were not. Clanchy provides three examples of the symbolic use of swords in connection with land ownership. He repeats Walter of Guisborough's account of the Earl Warenne's display of a rusty sword before Edward I's *Quo Warranto* proceedings.[6] He recounts how in the 1130s the knight Thomas de Muschamps, becoming a monk at

---

[1] A version of this chapter was published as '".j. veel feble fauchon dil anxien temps.": The Selection of the Falchion as Symbol of Tenure: Form, Function and Symbolism' *The Sword: Form and Thought*, ed. Lisa Deutscher, Mirjam Kaiser, and Sixt Wetzler (Woodbridge, 2019), pp. 167–75.

[2] The series of inventories taken of Wigmore are held at the National Archives, E 163/4/48 (2e), E 101/333/4 and e 372/179 (22.d), and at the British Library Add.MS 60584. My thanks to Barbara Wright for permission to use her transcription work.

[3] 'Uno cornu eneo quod cum quoddam Fauchone est ut dicitur Carte terre de Wygemore.' In the initial inventory of 1322, E 154/1/11B and '.j. veel feble fauchoun dil anxien temps' in the inventory taken in 1324, E163/4/48 (2a).

[4] On tenure horns, see J. Cherry, 'Symbolism and Survival: Medieval Horns of Tenure', *The Antiquaries Journal*, 69 (1989) pp. 111–18.

[5] Clanchy, *Memory to Written Record*, pp. 35–43, 254–60.

[6] Clanchy, *Memory to Written Record*, pp. 36–8.

Durham shortly before death, laid his sword on the altar as a remembrance when he invested the house with his estate at Hetherslaw.[7] Finally, he records how the royal treasury held the sword that was miraculously provided by St Odo of Canterbury to the English king Athelstan at his victory over the Scots at Brunnanburh in 937.[8]

None of these examples are really what might be called a 'charter sword'. The sword Warenne brandished might have been a symbol of his status as earl as we discussed above, and therefore in some way a mark of the grant of land and territory, were it not for its rusted state. Instead, it served (whether in reality or just in Guisborough's narrative) as a symbol of the role of his ancestors in the Conquest, and the longevity and status of his family, rather than as a token of remembrance for the obtaining of a particular piece of land. De Muschamp's sword was primarily a symbol of the surrender of his status as *miles strenuus*, a reversal of the inauguration to knighthood we looked at earlier, not necessarily connected with the gift of Hetherslaw to Durham. Nor is the Athelstan sword symbolic of a specific land transfer. Rather it is a miracle story, and its presence in the royal treasury more akin to the collection of heroic mystical swords gathered by Angevin kings discussed earlier.[9] Another example, the sword, once held at Battle Abbey and now in the National Museums Scotland, Edinburgh (A.1905.633), purported to be that of William the Conqueror, who founded the institution in commemoration of his victory in 1066, cannot be dated any earlier than around 1417.[10] Even if the sword was that of the Bastard, it is still not being used as an object of tenure.

The sword as charter is in fact highly unusual. What is even more unusual with regard to the Wigmore inventory, however, is the type of sword being used.

The falchion has a very distinctive form.[11] It is generally shorter than a 'knightly' sword; the broad, single-edged blade is on average between eighteen inches and two feet (forty-five to sixty centimetres) in length. Traditionally, two distinct blade forms were identified; one – typified by the Conyers falchion we shall look at in detail below – has a straight-backed blade, which broadens away from the cross, in a similar way to a modern cleaver or machete.[12] The second has a curving blade and ends with a cusped point. It is often described as 'oriental', since it looks very much like a scimitar.[13]

---

[7]   *Ibid*, p. 39.

[8]   Clanchy, *Memory to Written Record*, pp. 40–1.

[9]   See above, pp. 37ff.

[10] Sir J. Noel Patton, 'Notes on the sword of Battle Abbey, formerly in the Meyrick Collection', *Proceedings of the Society of Antiquaries of Scotland*, 10 (1874) pp. 462–75 and plates XV and XVI.

[11] Relatively little work has been done on the falchion, and there is no single extensive treatment of it. For general overviews, see E. Oakeshott, *The Archaeology of Weapons*, pp. 235–8; Quentin Hawkins, 'The Meat Cleaver', *Military illustrated*, 112 (September 1997); William J. McPeak, 'The Falchion - Short Sword that Made Good', *Command*, 41 (January 1997); Claude Blair, *European and American Arms* (London, 1962) pp. 4–10; Heribert Seitz, *Blankwaffen*, vol. 1 (Braunschweig, 1965), pp. 188–97).

[12] See Fig. 11.

[13] See Fig. 12. C.C. Hodges, 'The Conyers Falchion', *Archaeologia Aeliana*, Series 2, 15 (1892), p. 214; Blair, *European and American Arms*, p. 5; Oakeshott, *The Archaeology of Weapons*, p. 238. As we shall see, the suggestion of an eastern European or Middle Eastern origin for the falchion is almost certainly erroneous.

Figure 15. The Conyers falchion; mid- to late thirteenth century in form
(Image by kind permission of the Chapter of Durham Cathedral).

However, recent work by J.G. Elmslie identifies five distinct types and seventeen sub-types. Survivals are rare, with maybe only forty extant examples.[14] The frequency of their appearance in period art belies this rarity, however. Yet it remains a distinctive weapon, and in the context in which it is found here, something of an oddity.

By itself, the Wigmore reference might be discounted as a mere curiosity; an aberration merely adding an extra layer of interest to a fairly common example of a tenure horn. But there are two other examples that can be produced of falchions appearing as 'charter weapons'.

The first is a well-known and indeed, uniquely well-preserved example of its type. The Conyers' falchion, now housed in the cathedral treasury of Durham, was owned by the Conyers family who presented it to the Bishop of Durham on his first arrival in the diocese.[15] In return they retained possession of the manor of Sockburn. Whilst the ceremony is first recorded in an inquest post-mortem for Sir

[14] I am most grateful to J.G. Elmslie for his comments on an early draft of this chapter, and for sharing, ahead of its publication in the catalogue, his typology.

[15] 'Conyers Falchion', 1260-70. Sword. (Durham Cathedral, DURCL: 18.2.1). Sir Edward Blackett and Baron de Cosson's letters *The Proceedings of the Society of Antiquaries of Newcastle-upon-Tyne* April and May 1891, bound as 'The Conyers Falchion' in *Armes and Armures* (Royal Armouries Library 03984); Hodges, 'The Conyers Falchion', pp. 214–18; J. Wall, 'The Conyers Falchion', *Durham Archaeological Journal*, 2 (1986) pp. 77–83.

Figure 16. A falchion of fifteenth-century form, found near the site of the battle of Castillon (1453). (Royal Armouries IX.5409).

John Conyers (the fourth of this name), dated to April of 1395/6, the sword itself is of a style of the mid-thirteenth century, dated by reference to similar sword forms seen in period visual depictions, including the mid-thirteenth-century Westminster Painted Chamber.[16] This dating is reinforced by the identification of the heraldic decoration on its pommel – *gules three lions passant gardant or* on one side and *or, an eagle displayed sable* on the other – as the arms of the Plantagenet kings of England after circa 1198 and Henry III's brother Richard of Cornwall as King of the Romans respectively.[17]

The legend attached to the sword, which was current in the early seventeenth century when the antiquarians were doing their rounds, says that in 1063 the first Sir John Conyers slew a 'wyrm' that had been terrorising the people of the area. The grateful bishop granted him and his heirs the manor in perpetuity, and the presentation of the sword to the incoming bishop which had slain the beast was a ritual reminder of the act. The truth of the matter appears to be that Bishop Ranulph Flambard granted the land to the Conyers family, sometime between 1099 and 1128. They are recorded as being enfeoffed with Sockburn in a confirmation charter dated to between 1128 and 1135 and may well have been the original Domesday tenants. By the 1170s they held land for $7^1/_2$ knights, making them major players in the Palatinate-Bishopric.[18]

The second example, known as the Pollard falchion (the actual sword is long lost), is very similar in many ways to the Conyers weapon. The Pollards were also a Durham family holding a collection of properties, the tenure for which was to present a falchion to the incoming bishop on the first occasion he crossed their lands.[19] As with the Conyers family a myth had grown up by the seventeenth century that an early scion of the family had killed the beast ravaging the region, although the beast

[16]   For the Painted Chamber, see J. Hewitt, *Ancient Armour and Weapons in Europe from the Iron Period of the Northern Nations to the End of the Thirteenth Century* (Oxford and London, 1855) plate 82, 313, taken from *Vestuta Monumenta*, vol. vi (London, 1883), plate xxxvi.

[17]   C.D. Liddy, 'Land, legend and gentility in the Palatinate of Durham: The Pollards of Pollard Hall', *North-East England in the Later Middle Ages*, ed. C.D. Liddy (Woodbridge, 2005), p. 91; Blackett and de Cosson, 'The Conyers Falchion', p. 2. Richard, Earl of Cornwall, was crowned King of the Romans in May 1257.

[18]   Hodges, 'The Conyers Falchion', pp. 214–18. W. Aird, *St Cuthbert and the Normans: The Church of Durham 1071–1153* (Woodbridge, 1998), pp. 207–13.

[19]   Blackett and de Cosson, 'The Conyers Falchion', p. 2; Liddy, p. 89.

was a great boar rather than a dragon.[20] Again, they were granted land by a grateful bishop, and the sword presented was the weapon that had slain the beast. Just as with the Conyers falchion, the Pollard sword is first attested to in an inquest post-mortem, this time of John Pollard's widow Dionisia in 1400, in terms strikingly like that of the Conyers record.[21]

The documentary evidence shows that the land connected to the falchion ritual – some fifteen acres next to Auckland Park – was in fact granted to the family by the Bishop of Durham sometime in the thirteenth century.[22] Unlike the Conyers, the Pollards were not a landed family from the time of the Conquest. Rather they appear to be serving in the episcopal household. They managed the bishop's estates in the Auckland area from a townhouse on the market square in Bishop Auckland itself, and acquired a patchwork of lands in the area as they became available.[23]

There is no similar myth attached to the Wigmore falchion, no Mortimer equivalent to the Conyers' or Pollard's illustrious dragon- or boar-slaying ancestors. The fourteenth-century Wigmore Chronicle, which sets out to establish the Mortimer pedigree, records that Ralph de Mortimer, seigneur de Saint Victor-en-Caux, was granted Wigmore by capturing the English landholder Eadric *Silvaticus* (Eadric 'the Wild', also known as Eadric Cild), who rebelled against William in 1070.[24] In actuality, Domesday records the castle of Wigmore as being built by William FitzOsbern, on 'waste' that had been held by Gunnfrothr TRE.[25] The sequence of events is wholly unclear; it may be that Ralph Mortimer was involved in defeating Eadric – he certainly received the latter's lands in Hampshire, Leicestershire and Warwickshire (although not those in Herefordshire and Shropshire). It is also possible that he was involved in subduing the 'Revolt of the Earls' of 1075, which included FitzOsbern's son Roger de Breteuil, Earl of Hereford. It seems most likely that it was after Roger's dispossession and imprisonment that Wigmore came into the Mortimer family's hands.[26] By the fourteenth century, the events had become conflated.[27]

So, we have three families, each of whom appear to have memorialised their acquisition of territory with a falchion. Why do these families choose to do so? Why a blade at all?

The answer to the latter question would appear a simple one. These are Conquest lordships; the land coming to the family's possession through a deed of arms. The Conyers' vanquishing of a dragon, the Pollards' slaying of a great boar and Mortimers' defeat of Eadric the Wild: all are tales of martial victory. Like the Earl Warenne,

---

[20] Liddy, p. 92.
[21] *Ibid*, pp. 89–90.
[22] *Ibid*, p. 77.
[23] *Ibid*, pp. 83–4.
[24] W. Dugdale, *Monasticon Anglicanum*, ed. J. Caley, H. Ellis, and B. Bandinel. Vol. VI (London, 1830), pp. 348–9.
[25] *Domesday Book: A Complete Translation*, ed. A. Williams and G.H. Martin (London, 2002), p. 506.
[26] My thanks to Carol Davidson Cragoe for the opportunity to read her chapter on the history of Wigmore prior to its publication in *Wigmore Castle, North Herefordshire: Excavations 1996 and 1998*, ed. S. Rátkai (Abingdon, 2017).
[27] Carol Davidson Cragoe, pers. comm. 19 April 2013.

they may have felt it was right and proper that their possession should be recorded by something more martial than just a knife, a cup, or horn. Even if we have to discount the dragon-slaying and giant boar stories of the former two as myths, one could easily propose that they are embroidered tales of half-remembered victories over Norse raiders or outlaw bands. It is tempting to extrapolate a dragon from dragon-prowed ships, and a boar from boar-topped helmets like those described in *Beowulf*, to rationalise the mythic tales.

Such ideas are overly romantic, however. Besides, such a theory ignores the fact that despite the myths, the Pollard and Conyers lands were not Conquest tenures at all but grants from a grateful bishop in recognition of service within the episcopal administration.

The Pollard falchion may quickly be accounted for. As Liddy suggests, the Pollards were never a top-flight noble family. Like so many of the gentry families who came to prominence in the late thirteenth and fourteenth centuries, they were episcopal clerks and administrators who had made good.[28] Although not of the same social class there are links between them and the Conyers family, unsurprising in the closed society of the Durham bishopric. It is almost certain that the two families knew each other; members of both families appear on the same witness lists.[29] It would appear that the Pollards' use of the falchion as a signifier of tenure was a conscious aping of the Conyers family, attempting to acquire a similar standing and status by creating for themselves an ancient and heroic genealogy.[30]

The Mortimer holding of Wigmore does seem to have been gained by right of conquest, although whether it can be tied to a defeat of Eadric the Wild or of the Earl of Hereford is less clear. If we can argue for the moment that it **is** Eadric's dispossession that sees the Mortimers in receipt of the land of Wigmore, then one might argue that this provides the key to the question of why the weapon used here, and in Durham, is not a knightly sword but a falchion.

Is it possible to accept for the moment that the weapon that becomes the charter of the lands of Wigmore is that of the Eadric *Silvaticus*? Might not the horn, examples of which are often seen as tenure objects connected to forest land and as badges of office connected with foresters, be a link to Eadric as *Silvaticus*, one of the 'wild men' who took to the forests and marshes in their rebellion against the Conqueror and his sons?[31] If so then it might be possible to argue that the 'falchion' recorded in the inventories was in fact a seax. These knives were of a distinctive shape, broad-bladed and single-edged, the larger ones often having a 'broken-back' form, in which the back of the blade curved or angled sharply toward the tip. They are found in the

---

[28] Liddy, p. 89. On the development of the administrative gentry, see M. Keen, *The Origins of the English Gentleman* (Stroud, 2002).

[29] Liddy, p. 91.

[30] *Ibid*, p. 91.

[31] Cherry, *passim*. There is an effigy of a forester-knight at Pershore in Worcestershire (see Coss, *The Medieval Knight*, p. 76. On the use of the suffix *silvaticus* for Norman rebels, see *The Ecclesiastical History of Orderic Vitalis*, ed. and trans. M. Chibnall, vol. 2 (Oxford, 1969), pp. 216–18 and Susan Reynolds, 'Eadric Silvaticus and the English Resistance', *BIHR*, 54 (1981), pp. 102–5.

archaeological record of northern Europe and Scandinavia from the sixth century through to the last decades of the eleventh. Whilst some are the size of ordinary knives, there is also a variant, inventively named the 'long seax', that has blades of up to two feet in length.[32] They are in many ways comparable to the later falchion and, indeed, a number of commentators have suggested that the mid-thirteenth-century falchion is in fact a descendant of the early medieval seax.[33] Such a derivation is unlikely, however. Elmslie's work shows that the falchion first appears in southern Europe around the 1240s, a good century and a half after the seax falls out of favour, and he argues for a form of convergent evolution rather than direct descent.[34]

One could possibly argue that the '*veel feble fauchoun dil anxien temps*', as the object is recorded in the 1324 Wigmore inventory, was perhaps the seax of Eadric the Wild; the weapon of the defeated Englishman being held by the Mortimers as a token of their role in the taking of the lordship, either directly from Eadric himself or because of their involvement in putting down the rebellion of the Earl of Hereford.[35] The change in terminology need not worry us; the old English word seax had fallen out of use well over a century before the inventories were penned. The clerk performing the inventory would have seen a broad-bladed, single-edged weapon (albeit in a poor state of repair) and recognised it as a falchion, a term in common use at the time.[36]

What of the Conyers falchion? The weapon that sits in the cathedral treasury is most definitely not a seax misnamed. It is neither the weapon that the fabled John Conyers used to slay the dragon, nor is it a token that Bishop Flambard might have been presented by the Conyers as a symbol of tenure in the early twelfth century. As has been said, it is clearly a weapon of the mid-thirteenth century or later.

The most obvious answer here is that it is a replacement for the original symbolic object: a bright, new shiny sword to replace a rusty and tarnished '*veel feble fauchoun dil anxien temps*'.[37] One can almost imagine Sir Humphrey Conyers, head of the family around 1260, preparing for the arrival of the new Bishop Robert Stitchell, saying 'We can't give the new bishop this old thing' and commissioning a new weapon to be made.

The arms displayed on either side of the pommel are also suggestive of this renewal of motifs. There is little indication that the arms are copied from an older exemplar; the leopards and the eagle on the other face are both executed in a distinctively

---

[32] Oakeshott, *The Archaeology of Weapons*, pp. 117–19. The two key typologies for these weapons are Wheeler, *London and the Saxons*, and Georg Schmitt, 'Die Alamannen im Zollernalbkreis' (PhD thesis, Stuttgart, 2005), pp. 33–5.

[33] Oakeshott, *The Archaeology of Weapons*, p. 235, Wall, p. 80, Blair, p. 5.

[34] Indeed, the weapon need not be a seax *per se*; around forty percent of 'Viking' swords are actually single-edged (Jan Petersson, *De Norrske Vikingsverd*, and Elmslie, pers. comm. 12 October 2015).

[35] '.j. veel feble fauchoun dil anxien temps'. TNA E163/4/48 (2a).

[36] On similar variations in the use of technical terms in a military context, see Andrew Ayton, *Knights and Warhorses: Military Service and the English Aristocracy Under Edward III* (Woodbridge, 1999), pp. 62–9.

[37] Liddy (p. 91) suggests that the falchion is a more prestigious artefact bearing the royal arms and those of the Holy Roman Empire, but not that the original token was also some form of sword.

thirteenth-century style, and the three leopards charge was not adopted by the English monarchs until the very end of Richard I's reign.

Whilst the lion decoration is quite clearly linked to the Plantagenet royal house, the eagle charge is a more difficult one to pin down. The suggestion which is generally accepted is that the arms are those of the King of the Romans (the title given to the Holy Roman Emperor prior to his coronation by the Pope) which, when combined with the stylistic evidence and the use of the English royal arms has been taken to indicate some form of link with Henry III's brother Richard of Cornwall.[38] Most commentators have simply suggested that the eagle's appearance is simply part of the Conyer's self-aggrandisement: the family displaying some notional link to Henry III and his family. Whilst it was common for families to display the arms of major noble and even royal houses alongside their own, in order to suggest a connection between them, basking in the reflected prestige, there is generally some tie of blood or service, no matter how tenuous.[39] As yet no-one has been able to draw a link between the Conyers family and either Henry III or Richard of Cornwall.[40]

Another suggestion has been that the eagle is in fact the attributed arms of Leofric of Mercia, grandfather of Morcar of Northumbria, and therefore of Morcar himself.[41] In this case the heraldry is not original – there was no such thing in the 1070s – but is attributed to the earl, in the same way in which we see the arms of Edward the Confessor and other figures from pre-heraldic antiquity being created in the thirteenth century.[42] If this interpretation of the arms is accepted, then the decoration on the hilt refers not to the family's current ties to the royal house but is instead an allusion to the pre-Conquest origins of the land they held. This in turn adds greater weight to the idea that the Conyers falchion too might have been a replacement for a much older weapon, possibly a seax.

Whether or not one can accept the idea that the Conyers' falchion is a replacement for an earlier seax, the question still stands: why a falchion? Why not a knightly sword more befitting one of the senior noble families in the Palatinate?

If the falchion is a replacement for an older weapon of similar form, then it is important that, as a visual cue for a particular memory, the new weapon retains something of the appearance of the old. We can go further than this, however. There is something in the shape of the falchion that suggests antiquity. In medieval iconography the falchion is routinely depicted in the hands of ancients, whether biblical or classical. This practice becomes more pronounced in the Renaissance, when artists began to depict their classical subjects *al antiqua*, in a classical style, rather than the medieval practice of imprinting contemporary fashions on the past. The costume is not always any more accurate, and indeed often tend towards the exotic and fanciful. The artists, to some extent, were looking for a weapon that was similar in look to the

---

38 Blackett and de Cosson, 'The Conyers Falchion', p. 2. Liddy, p. 91.
39 Coss, *The Medieval Knight*, p. 91.
40 Nor is there any clear evidence that Richard ever adopted the King of Germany's arms. He spent very little time in Germany, making only four visits between his election in 1256 and his death in 1272.
41 Wall, 'The Conyers Falchion', p. 78.
42 Charles Boutell and Arthur Charles Fox-Davies, *English Heraldry* (Whitefish, MT, 2003), p. 18.

Roman *gladius* – short and broad-bladed – but which also had an air of the exotic. The falchion was indeed short and broad-bladed. It also had the air of the exotic, because of another iconographical use to which it was put.

The falchion was routinely put in the hands of 'the enemy'. Most obviously they are seen in the hands of Islamic foes where they become caricatures of the eastern *shamshir* or scimitar, with exaggerated curved blades and spines. In fact, Islamic weapons through to the late fifteenth century had only a mild curve. The extremely curved, banana-shaped blade does not really appear until the sixteenth century and, even then, does not look remotely like the fat-bladed weapon beloved of Hollywood Harem guards and stereotypical 'oriental' cultists. It would seem that these owe more to the medieval depictions of western European manuscripts than to any actual weapons of the Islamic world.[43]

In a similar fashion, falchions can be seen in the hands of the forces of Hell. One of the clearest and most easily read examples of the symbolic function of the falchion lies within the thirteenth-century romance *Robert le Diable*, and its fourteenth-century English counterpart *Sir Gowther*.[44] In these tales the hero (or, perhaps more appropriately, anti-hero) is born after his mother makes a pact with the devil for a child or is impregnated by a devil who appears in the form of her husband, depending on the version of the story. His infernal origins soon come to the fore; he suckles nine wet nurses dry and grows at a prodigious rate. He becomes a nightmare version of Georges Duby's wild young knights, the *juvenes*.[45] By fourteen he is a handsome fellow (we are told that there is none more beautiful) and he bands together with some like-minded fellows and starts on the tournament circuit, causing destruction and mayhem wherever he goes. By twenty he has been excommunicated, having slaughtered priests, pilgrims, and merchants and burnt over twenty abbeys to the ground. In the French version he cannot restrain himself at tournament, wanting to kill everyone he unhorses, whilst in the English version he hangs priests from hooks and rapes wives and virgins.

Eventually, after the slaughter of an entire convent of nuns, he comes to realise his wickedness, learns of his diabolic origins and goes to the Pope for absolution. This he achieves by acting as a mute fool at the emperor's court, then defending Rome from the Turks disguised by three different coloured sets of armour given him by God. He dies as a hermit (according to the French version) or having married the emperor's daughter and becoming Emperor himself (in the English *Sir Gowther*).

What makes the tale particularly interesting is Robert/Gowther's sword. He bears a blade which only he is strong enough to wield, and with which he is able to slice

[43]   For a visual record of the form of non-European blades during the high Middle Ages, see D. Nicolle, *Arms and Armour of the Crusading Era, 1050–1350: Islam, Eastern Europe and Asia* (Cambridge, 1999).

[44]   'Sir Gowther', in *The Middle English Breton* Lays, ed. Anna Laskaya and Eve Salisbury (Kalamazoo, MI, 1995), http://d.lib.rochester.edu/teams/publication/laskaya-and-salisbury-middle-english-breton-lays (accessed 1 August 2021). *Robert le Diable: Roman d'Aventures*, ed. E. Löseth (Paris 1903). For a discussion of the religious understanding of the romances, see Neil Cartlidge, *Heroes and Anti-Heroes in Medieval Romance* (Cambridge, 2012), pp. 229–34.

[45]   Georges Duby, *The Chivalrous Society*, trans. C. Postan (London, 1977), pp. 112–18.

men and mounts in half in the grand tradition of medieval romance combat depictions. However, unlike Roland or Arthur or Ogier the Dane, Robert/Gowther forges his own weapon, from a mixture of iron and steel, and the form that weapon takes is a falchion.

The significance of the falchion has been imperfectly understood by those who have studied both *Robert le Diable* and *Sir Gowther*. Recognising the importance of the sword for the medieval knight, most have suggested that the falchion represents the hero's social status and his continued chivalric nature despite his distinctly un-chivalrous deeds.[46] This would be fine if the sword Gowther/Robert carried was a normal, 'knightly' sword, but it is not.

As with the Conyers and Wigmore falchions, the choice of the weapon is deliberate. The specification of a falchion as the weapon he forges and wields reflects a special symbolic significance and, given the hero's behaviour, that significance must be one of the monstrous and evil. This is reinforced by what happens to the sword when the hero comes to realise his misdeeds and embarks on his penitential transformation. In *Robert le Diable* the falchion is cast away. The weapon which has been used for evil deeds is discarded, cast off along with his evil past. In *Sir Gowther* there is a slightly different take on the story. Gowther confesses his past to the Pope and begs for advice on how he can gain absolution. The Pope tells him to cast away his falchion, but Gowther refuses, saying that he needs it, for he has few friends. The hero goes on to redeem himself, performing great deeds with his formerly diabolical falchion, which is now put to a holy, rather than diabolic, use. This connection between the anti-hero and his sword, and the way in which the purpose of the sword is tied into the purpose and fate of the wielder has echoes of the relationship between hero and sword that we see in the early medieval literature and reflected in the sagas, as emphasised in Brunning's work on early medieval sword culture.[47]

It is not just in literature that the falchion appears in the hands of the diabolical. In the Douce Apocalypse of around 1270, the horsemen, described in the Book of Revelations chapter 9, verses 16–21, are depicted as knights riding lion-headed horses.[48] Two of the knights wield falchions. The rearmost, leaning back over his horse to strike at the men behind him, carries a wickedly serrated blade that mimics the tooth-filled grin on his face. The link between demonic forces, the outsider or 'other' and Muslims in medieval art and literature is a common, well-known one.

The falchion is prominent in a number of other images. In two fifteenth-century manuscripts of Froissart's *Chronicles* the meeting of Richard II and the peasant rebels under Wat Tyler, and the death of the latter at the hands of William Walworth, the

---

[46] Muriel P. Cadilhac-Rouchon, 'Revealing Otherness: A Comparative Examination of French and English Medieval Hagiographical Romance', Unpublished PhD thesis (Cambridge, 2009), pp.153–7, https://www.repository.cam.ac.uk/bitstream/handle/1810/240568/Muriel%20Cadilhac-Rouchon%20PhD.pdf;sequence=1 (accessed 1 August 2021).

[47] See above, p. 15. Brunning, *The Sword*. Michael Uebel suggests that Gowther's refusal to give up the sword is because it remains a crucial token of his identity, but also his separation from society (M. Uebel, 'The Foreigner Within: The Subject of Abjection in *Sir Gowther*', *Meeting the Foreign in the Middle Ages*, ed. A. Classen (London, 2002), p. 104).

[48] Bodleian Library Ms. Douce 180, fol.28r, see Fig. 13.

Figure 17. Falchion-wielding, demonic knights from the Douce Apocalypse, c.1250–75. (Bodleian Library MS. Douce 180, 28r. © Bodleian Libraries, University of Oxford. Reproduced under Creative Commons licence CC-BY-NC 4.0).

mayor of London, are depicted.[49] In both manuscripts Walworth is shown wielding an oversized falchion, two-handed, raising it high above his head in preparation for the killing blow. Froissart's description of the event tells us that, after cursing Tyler as a 'gars puans' or 'stinking knave':

> he drew a great baselard which he was carrying, and struck Tyler such a violent blow to the head that it knocked him down at his horse's feet. As soon as he had fallen, he was surrounded on all sides and could no longer be seen by the crowd gathered there, who called themselves his people. Then one of the king's squires, named Ralph de Standish, dismounted and drew a fine sword which he was wearing and thrust it into Tyler's belly, and there he died.[50]

[49]   See Fig. 12. A similar image is to be found in Jean Froissart, *Chroniques*, vol. 2, BL Royal MS 18 E I, fol. 175r.

[50]   "il traït un grant bazelaire que il portoit, et lasche et fiert ce Tieullier un tel horion parmy la teste que il l'abbat aux piéz de son cheval. Sitost que il fut cheuz en piéz, on l'environna de toutes pars, par quoy il ne feust veüz des assemblés qui la estoient et qui se disoient ses gens. Adonc descendi un escuier du roy que on appelloit Jehan Standuich, et traïst une belle espee que il portoit et la bouta ou ventre de ce Tieullier, et la fut mort.' Taken from Besançon, Bibliothèque municipale, ms.865, Folio 76 v. English translation by Keira Borrill, from *The Online Froissart* (https://www.dhi.ac.uk/

Walworth is described as wielding a 'grant bazelaire' – a great baselard'. Like the falchion, a baselard is a very particular form of weapon, a large dagger or short sword, often with a hilt in the form of an inverted H. The weapon is most definitely distinct and different from a falchion. It may be possible that the illuminators' choice of weapon was accidental (the medieval usage of the term was somewhat loose), but the size and prominence of the weapon make it unlikely that it was an arbitrary decision. The illuminators are making a statement.[51]

A further recurring iconographic trope involving the falchion is St Peter's severing of the ear of Malchus, the servant of Caiaphas, in the garden of Gethsemane. Whilst early and high medieval depictions generally show Peter using a knife, from the latter half of the fourteenth century onwards it is a falchion that becomes more commonly shown. Indeed, so closely linked is the falchion with Peter's act that in late medieval Germany one of the words for a falchion is *malchus*.[52] The Poznan Archdiocesan Museum in Poland houses what is claimed to be St Peter's sword. First attested by the Polish chronicler Jan Długosz in 1475, opinion is divided on its actual date, and its form is an unusual one, with a steadily broadening blade and squared off, machete-like tip.[53] However, its most likely provenance is that it is some sort of high medieval falchion.

Falchions appear in other related biblical contexts. Numerous depictions of the beheading of John the Baptist, and of the execution of saints, such as Barbara or Catherine, show the executioner wielding a falchion, often of great size and two-handed, in a fashion similar to that of Walworth in Français 2644.[54] Many of

---

onlinefroissart/browsey.jsp?pbo=BookII-Translation_76v&imgo=&divo=ms.f.transl.BookII-Transla tion&panes=1&GlobalMode=facsimile&imgo=&dispo=pb&GlobalWord=0&GlobalShf=&pbo=B ookII-Translation_76 (accessed 1 August 2021).

[51] John Leland, in his essay on pardons on the grounds of self-defence during the reign of Richard II, 'briefly discusses how a baselard was seen as a 'more dangerous, probably larger, weapon' (John Leland, 'Pardons for Self-Defence in the Reign of Richard II: The Use and Abuse of Legal Formulas', *Creativity, Contradictions and Commemoration in the Reign of Richard II: Essays in Honour of Nigel Saul*, ed. Jessica A. Lutkin and J.S. Hamilton (Woodbridge, 2022), pp. 158–9. My thanks to Caroline Palmer for bringing this chapter to my attention.

[52] Heribert Seitz, *Blankwaffen*, p. 189. Egerton Castle suggests the term was used as synonym for the 'braquemar', 'a short, broad, and straight-bladed sword' (Egerton Castle, *Scholars and Masters of Fence: From the Middle Ages to the Eighteenth Century* (London, 1885), p. 229).

[53] http://muzeum.poznan.pl/zbiory/miecz-sw-piotra/ (accessed 1 August 2021), and Janusz Stępínski, Grzegorz Zabniski and Elzbieta Maria Nosek, 'Metallographic examinations of St Peter's Sword from the, Archdiocesan Museum in Poznan', *Waffen-und Kostumkunde*, 57.1 (January 2015), pp. 19–62.

[54] See, for example, the fifteenth-century wall painting depicting the execution of Saint Catherine on the south wall of St Peter and Saint Paul's church, Pickering North Yorkshire (Fig. 18). Also the same subject as depicted in the *Book of Hours of Simon de Varie*, dated to 1455 (National Library of the Netherlands Ms KB 74 G37a, fol. 14r); Benozzo Gozzoli, *The Feast of Herod and the Beheading of Saint John the Baptist*, 1461–62 (Samuel H. Kress Collection, National Gallery of Art, New York, NY, inv. 1952.2.3); Cologne Master, *Decapitation of Saint Catherine*, circa 1470–80 (Städel Museum, Frankfurt-am-Main, inv. SG 445); Giovanni Battista Biagio di Antonio, *Beheading of Saint Catherine of Alexandria*, circa 1480–90 (Bonnefantenmuseum, Maastricht, inv. 3413); Unknown Artist of the Flemish School, *The Beheading of Saint Barbara*, late fifteenth century (Victoria and Albert Museum, London, inv. P.15-1959); Lucas Cranach the Elder, *The Martyrdom of Saint Barbara*, circa 1510 (The

Figure 18. The Beheading of Saint Catherine in a fifteenth-century wall painting, Church of St Peter and St Paul, Pickering, North Yorkshire. (© Holmes Garden Photos / Alamy Stock Photo).

the images predate the development of the specialist executioners' swords described earlier, but not all. These events take place in the ancient past and in the Middle East, of course, so one might explain the depiction of the executioners' weapons as reflecting scenes of antiquity or exoticism, as we discussed above. However, many of the depictions do not show the executioner in antique or eastern dress, but as a contemporary western European.

The use of the falchion in the depiction of the ancient and exotic might explain the connection between the images of St Peter, John the Baptist, and the various other saints, since all of the executions are being committed by an ancient and/or pagan foe. It might also be that by the fifteenth century (when we get the greatest number of images of Peter wielding a falchion), the *messer*, or the stylistically-similar *bauernwehr* or *hauswehr*, is routinely seen on the belt of rural individuals in German and eastern European iconography.[55] These practical working knives, similar to the

Metropolitan Museum of Art, New York, NY, inv. 57.22); Hans Fries, *The Beheading of St John the Baptist by Hans Fries*, 1514 (Kunstmuseum, Basel).

[55] Sixt Wetzler (pers. comm.) notes that the *messer* and *bauern-* or *hausewehr* are not the same. The former is a dedicated fencing weapon, with a *nagel* (lit. 'nail') that projects at ninety-degrees from the cross to act as a 'parrying lug', and is carried also by the higher echelons of society. The latter can be any form of longer, simple, single-edged blade, assuredly fulfilling the role of an all-round 'machete'.

modern-day machete in both form and usage, seem to have been carried as a matter of course, and were more frequently depicted in illustrations of common folk as a result. *Messers* are very similar to falchions in that they share the same single-edge and cusped blade form, and can be near identical in size. It may be that what we see as a falchion in many of the late medieval and Renaissance depictions is in fact a *messer*. It would be unsurprising that central and eastern European artists, depicting the events of the past in the milieu of the present, should choose to show St Peter reaching for a *messer*, whereas in earlier years those who chose not to show Peter using a sword would depict him with a smaller knife, typical of the ones hanging on the belts of common men in that period.

This does not explain why the illustrator of the Froissart chronicles should have chosen a remarkably similar iconography for a near-contemporary and thoroughly European event. On this occasion it is not the location of the act, nor its antiquity, that is the link, but the motivation for that act. Instead the common link is that the motivation for the killing blow was one of wrath.[56] This is clearly the case with St Peter striking Malchus, and with Walworth striking Wat Tyler, but it can also be argued that the decollation of John the Baptist, the massacre of the innocents, and many of the executions of saints were done with the same sense of wrath.[57] The selection of the falchion as the weapon of choice for the wrathful blow takes us back to Elmslie's arguments for the weapon being perceived as somehow 'imperfect', and with Gowther/Robert's use of it in their diabolic rampages. The falchion's broad and cusped blade made it seem a brutal weapon, for hacking and hewing; more like a butcher's cleaver rather than a sword.

In the ways in which the falchion appears within our sources we can see how the form and function of a sword informed the symbolism with which it was imbued. It also shows how complex that symbolism could be. The broad-bladed form, single-edged and designed for hewing cuts, suggested power and brutality. Standing in contrast to the knightly sword, imbued with Johnsson's sacred geometry, and the 'austere perfection of line and proportion' that made the 'the very essence of beauty' in Oakeshott's eyes, the falchion could serve not only as the heirloom of a dragon-slaying hero, but also as the instrument of the wicked.[58] So strong is this imagery that down to today we perceive of curved and single-edged blades as being the weapon of the other, whether it is the stereotypical scimitar-wielding Arab in the first Indiana Jones movie *Raiders of the Lost Ark* (1981), or the elegantly curved two-handed weapons of the Elves and the crudely forged machetes of the Uruk-Hai in the *Lord of the Rings* movies (2001–2003).[59] This, and its similarity to the seax and the *messer*, means that

---

[56] I am grateful to Peter Johnsson for first suggesting this line of enquiry.

[57] It is interesting that medieval depictions of Judith's killing of Holofernes rarely show a falchion, even though she uses his sword, which would give the illustrator even more reason to depict it as a falchion – the exotic sword of the enemy. One might suggest that this is because Judith's blow is not seen as being struck in anger or against an innocent, but as a righteous act in protection of her (and God's) people.

[58] Oakeshott, *Records*, p.1.

[59] *Raiders of the Lost Ark*, dir. Stephen Spielberg (Paramount Pictures, 1981). *Lord of the Rings* series, dir.

it is rarely considered a chivalric weapon, instead often perceived as being that of the commoner. This was far from the case; in our visual sources the falchion is as often in the hands of the knight as it is in the hands of the commoner, and there is little difference in the quality of the surviving examples of the falchion and of the 'knightly' sword, and they were forged and decorated using the same techniques. However, the converse is true, and our understanding of the elite nature of the 'knightly' sword is also erroneous. In the next chapters we will start to move away from this view of the sword as a symbol for and of the nobility alone, and begin to uncover some of the other cultures of the sword that existed in the European high and late Middle Ages.

Jackson. Tolkien often specifies in both the *Lord of the Rings* novels and *The Hobbit* that the orcs and goblins carried curved swords and scimitars.

4

The Civilian Sword

IN THE SAME WAY that the modern fantasy genre has taught us to expect swords to have magical properties and names, it has also taught us to expect everyone to be carrying one. The fantasy novel, or game of 'Dungeons and Dragons', habitually has its heroes laden down with weapons, or with their ostentatiously significant sword strapped to their hip (or across their back) as they stroll from town to town. As the underlying theme for these stories is usually one of conflict and heroic combat, the hero's need to have his weapon close to hand is a necessary plot device. However, it has also led to a popular perception of the medieval world as resembling the wild west, with men carrying weapons as a matter of course, all too ready to use them. One of the occasions where this image is most resonant is in discussions of medieval towns. Pointing to the survival of bans and restrictions on swords in medieval towns in England and Germany, the analogy with American mid-west town ordinances demanding the surrender of weapons whilst within town limits is readily made.[1]

In fact, this view is wrong. There is little in the visual and written sources to suggest that the wearing of a sword was the norm in everyday life of the high and late Middle Ages; even for those whose status and function within society was built around the sword and its use, much less those who were not amongst the *pugnatore*. If we are to understand the cultural significance of the sword in the high Middle Ages, we need to be clear about who possessed swords and where they appeared outside the strictly martial context.

Discussions of the sword in a medieval civilian context rarely differentiate between the question of ownership, carriage, and use. This is problematic for understanding the place of the sword in civilian life. Just as with modern handguns, it might be

---

[1] The topic regularly surfaces in internet discussions of medieval swords and sword use, especially amongst HEMA enthusiasts. One of the very few people to have contributed with any authority and research is the HEMA practitioner and trainer Matt Easton. See Matt Easton, 'Sword Carrying Laws in Medieval England', *Schola Gladiatoria*, 11 November 2013, YouTube, https://www.youtube.com/watch?v=9rp3nve9CJk (accessed 1 August 2021). See also a conversation thread on the 'MyArmoury.com' site – 'Medieval Laws Concerning Weapons.' *myArmoury.com Discussion Forums*, 27 March 2011, http://myarmoury.com/talk/viewtopic.22719.html (accessed 1 August 2021). A number of works on gun control in the US have pointed out that legislation in the 'old west' was often stricter than today. See, for example, Adam Winkler, *Gunfight: The Battle over the Right to Bear Arms in America* (New York, 2011). The key academic work on this, albeit for the early modern period is B. Ann Tlusty, *The Martial Ethic in Early Modern Germany* (Basingstoke, 2011).

acceptable to own a sword, or indeed any weapon, but that did not mean that it was acceptable to take it out on the public street, whilst actually using it was a different matter altogether.

Sword Ownership

What do we know about the levels of sword ownership in the Middle Ages? We would expect kings, nobles, and knights to own them; they were, after all, symbols of their power and status and the tools of the martial trade. But what about those below them in the social scale?

There were a number of forms of legislation passed that required free men of all ranks to possess weapons and armour. In broad terms in most of western Europe in the high Middle Ages men were expected to have weapons for the defence of their community, whether at national level, like the 'Assize of Arms' issued by English monarchs from the 1180s onwards, or by local ordinance for the provision of watch and ward within a town or city. In most cases those weapons were kept at home, but even where they were held centrally at an arsenal their supply and use fell on the individual.

Henry II of England issued his *Assize of Arms* in 1181, alongside a version for his continental lands, known as the *Assize of Le Mans*.[2] Ostensibly, these documents laid out the martial equipment that every man was expected to possess for the defence of the realm or ducal holdings. The amount of equipment required was determined by income, with those earning the 'knights' fee' of £20 per year being expected to possess a coat of mail, lance, and shield, with gradations down through to those in the lowest income bracket, who were expected to carry gambeson, iron cap, and lance.[3] In neither of these documents, however, at whatever level, is anyone expressly expected to own a sword. Nor do they appear in the Florentine *libro di Montaperti*, a document of 1260 similar to the Assizes in that it details the equipment expected of citizens who made up the Florentine militia as they prepared for war with Siena. It states:

> that any free cavalryman of the Commune of Florence, both the city and the county of Florence, ought to own and is obligated to carry and have in the present army a saddle for his warhorse; a horse covering; either a breastplate or coat of mail; greaves or mail leggings; a steel cap; a coat of plates or coat of mail [for the thighs]; a lance; a shield, either a targe or a broad shield. And whoever disobeys this and thus does not carry and have in the army said arms… shall be condemned and fined, for the saddle 20 solidi of small florins; for the covering 60 solidi; for the breastplate or coat of mail 100 solidi; for the greaves or mail leggings 20 solidi; for the steel cap 20 solidi; for the lance 20 solidi; for the shield, either the targe or broad shield 20 solidi of small florins.[4]

---

[2]   For a broad comparison, and a discussion of Henry's intentions regarding the documents, see John D. Hosler, *Henry II: A Medieval Soldier at War, 1147–1189* (Leiden, 2007), pp. 115–19.

[3]   *Select Documents of English Constitutional History*, George Burton Adams and Henry Morse Stephens (London, 1906), p. 23.

[4]   'quod quilibet habens equum pro Communi Florentie, tam civitatis quam comitatus Florentie, teneatur et debeat portare et habere in presenti exercitu sellam ad destrarium, covertas equi, panzeriam sive asbergum, caligas sive stivalettos de ferro, cappellum de acciario, lamerias velcoraczas, lanceam, scutum sive targiam vel tabolaccium amplam. Et quicumque contrafecerit et ita non

Item, that any infantryman of the city of Florence, ought to own and is obligated to carry and have in the present army, a breastplate or coat of mail with plate gauntlets, or with plate gauntlets with mail sleeves; a steel cap or close-fitting helmet; a plate gorget or collar; a lance; a shield or large shield. And whoever disobeys this and does not carry or have in the army said arms… shall be condemned and fined, for the breastplate or coat of mail with gauntlets or gauntlets and mail sleeves 20 solidi in small florins; for the cap or close-fitting helmet 10 solidi; for the gorget or collar 10 solidi; for the lance 10 solidi; for the shield or large shield 10 solidi in small florins.

This is an exhaustive list of equipment, and very specific about both what should be carried, and the level of fine to be raised if it is not. The sword is noticeable by its absence, especially from the 'free cavalry', who would have been drawn from the consular aristocracy that formed the knightly caste within the city, and whom we might assume to be owners of swords.

We might infer from the absence of the sword from these lists meant that men were not expected to own them, but given that the upper tier were those earning a knight's fee then it is more likely that (at this level at least) the possession of a sword was taken for granted, and as such did not need to appear in the list of required equipment. This is of limited help, however, in determining sword ownership below the level of the knightly class, as it is then impossible to determine whether the weapon was not included because it was assumed that one would be worn, or because there was no expectation that one would be carried. The Assize of Arms was reissued by Henry III in 1252, and this does specify the possession of a sword, by those with goods valued between forty shillings and ten marks, all but the lowest rank in society.[5] This would suggest that the 1181 English document omits swords because they were a given rather than because men were not expected to own them.[6]

---

portaverit et habuerit in exercitu dicta arma, ut dictum est, puniatur et condempnetur, de sella in soldis viginti florinoram parvorum, de covertis in soldis sexsaginta, de panzeria sive asbergo in soldis centum, de caligis sive stivalettis de ferro in soldis viginti, de cappello acciarii in soldis viginti, de lameriis sive coraczis in soldis viginti, de lancea in soldis viginti, de scuto sive targia seu tavolaccio in soldis viginti florinorum parvorum. Item, quilibet pedes civitatis Florentie teneatur et debeat portare et habere in presenti exercitu panzeriam sive corictum cum manicis ferres, aut manicos ferreos cum coraczinis, cappellum de acciario vel cervelleria, gorgieriam sive collare de ferro, lanceam, scutum sive tabolaccium magnum. Et quicumque contra fecerit et non portaverit et habuerit in exercitu dicta arma, ut dictum est, puniatur et condempnetur, de panzeria sive coricto cum manicis sive de manicis cum coraczinis in soldis viginti florinorum parvorum, de cappello sive cervelleria in soldis decem, de gorgieria sive collare in soldis decem, de Iancea in soldis decem, de scuto sive tabolaccio in soldis decem florinorum parvorum.' *Il libro di Montaperti (An. 1260)*, ed. Cesare Paoli (Florence, 1889), pp. 373–4. My thanks to Kelly DeVries for highlighting the source and providing me with the translation, which also appears in *Medieval Warfare: A Reader*, ed. Kelly DeVries and Michael Livingstone (Toronto, 2019), pp. 71–2.

5   *Calendar of Close Rolls of the Reign of Henry III: AD 1237–1242*, ed. H.C. Maxwell Lyte (London, 1911), pp. 482–3.

6   A similar requirement was promulgated in Norway, the *Landslov* of 1274, the *bylov* of 1276, and the *Hirdskråa* (of 1273–7). (See Victor Hegg, 'English and Norwegian Military Legislation in the Thirteenth Century. The Assize of Arms of Norwegian Military Law.' Unpublished MA dissertation (Bergen, 2021)). Here, however, the sword was mandated for all categories down to those with chattels of six marks, and even those of the lowest category were required to have either sword or axe.

Turning away from the general expectation for military equipment laid out in government statute, we can look at what men appeared carrying. Several muster rolls recording the names and equipment of those with a duty to provide equipment survive. However, these can also be frustratingly unhelpful. The most widely referenced of these is the roll for the town of Bridport, Dorset, on England's south coast, taken on the fourth of September 1457.[7] Of the 146 individuals who are recorded as having appeared with military equipment (or whose entries are not illegible because of damage to the manuscript), half are described as bringing a sword alongside their other equipment, whether bow, spear or glaive. Of the rest, twenty more are described as appearing with only a dagger as their sidearm, with only five individuals bearing neither.[8] The apparent clarity of the document might lead one to make assumptions about sword ownership in a fifteenth-century town, but again there are some oddities that should cause pause for thought.

Firstly, whilst it is seems plausible that the equipment listed was owned by those who appeared at the muster, the fact that some individuals bring more than they could use themselves (a number of individuals are recorded as bringing two or more helmets, bows, or swords) and that at least four of those listed are women, should make us question whether the swords were the sidearm (for want of a better word) of the individual listed as presenting it, or if they were in fact part of the stored military equipment.[9] Secondly, the only two individuals recorded as turning out with 'whyte harnys' – that is to say a complete set of plate armour – are not recorded as bringing with them any swords. The name of the first individual is missing, that portion of the manuscript being damaged, but he appeared with 'hole whyte harnys, ii jackys, ii salette et ii arc[us] et ii shefe sagitt[arum], ii dagger' (a whole white harness, 2 jacks, 2 sallets, 2 bows, 2 sheaves of arrows and two daggers).[10] The name of the second individual is Robert Byrche, and he is only listed with 'a Whyte harnys wt a basenet' (that is a bascinet).[11] As with the 1181 Assize of Arms, there is a problem here in that one might equally well assume that swords are not mentioned for these two gentlemen because, given that they are of sufficient status to own a full harness, they would be expected to possess a sword in any case, and it need not be recorded. Similarly, one might suggest that the lack of swords amongst the equipment provided by the first individual, which must be that required for the outfitting of two archers, is either because the men who were to be given the equipment might reasonably be expected to possess their own swords, or because a sword was not considered a necessary or appropriate weapon for an archer. In both cases none of these interpretations answer

7   Thom Richardson analysed this document in 'The Bridport Muster Roll of 1457', *The Royal Armouries Yearbook, 2* (Leeds, 1997), pp. 46–52.
8   The numbers are based on the transcription in Thom Richardson's article.
9   Alis Hamel is the only one of the four women to have any equipment listed next to her name. She was recorded as bringing a jack, a sword, a buckler, ten arrows and a bow, and was 'instructed' (the Latin abbreviation is *ordinab*) to bring a sallet and a sheaf of arrows. Richardson, 'The Bridport Muster Roll', p. 49.
10   *Ibid*, p. 47.
11   *Ibid*, p. 51.

the question as to why, if the possession of a sword was a given, other men should be recorded as bringing swords whilst they should not.

There are similar issues with other militia rolls. A surviving roll for the city of Norwich, dating a hundred years earlier than the Bridport roll, has men in full harness and men in half harness listed without any mention of weapons, whilst the archers are recorded with their bow, arrows, sword, and dagger, and many men equipped with 'staff', sword, and dagger.[12] Again, we see that not all the men are recorded bearing swords, and those who we might most expect to possess them – those with the most armour, and the officers of the militia (the constables, *centenars* and *vintenars*) – are not recorded as possessing them, whilst those arguably further down the social order (at least, if we assume that an archer was inevitably the social and economic inferior of a man in armour) are.

A slightly different approach is to look at the weapons being held in the arsenals of major towns in the later Middle Ages, when many towns took up the responsibility for supplying its citizens with arms, rather than expecting them to provide their own. Here swords *do* appear. As a single example, the arsenal of the French city of Troyes in 1474 held 1047 swords, which equates nicely with the number of helmets held (1046), slightly more than the stores of either body armour (848 all types) or ranged weapons (871 guns, crossbows or bows), and slightly less than the number of other hand weapons (1532 partizans, guisarmes, pikes, maces and mallets, axes, javelins and other staff weapons).[13] What this suggests is that swords were an expected part of the martial equipment of a man serving in the militia, but that they were not required to possess their own. Of course, just because the town had swords (or indeed any other piece of equipment) does not mean that the men for whom they were being provided did not also have their own swords (or indeed other martial equipment) at home.[14]

In short, these documents specifying what men weapons men had for the defence of their community are of little more help in determining the level of sword ownership amongst the general population than those that that specified what they should possess for that purpose. Also, as these are documents relating to the equipping of men for war, they tell us nothing about the social norms for the day-to-day wearing of the sword.

If we turn our attention to lists of personal effects, whether inventories or wills, then swords do appear more often, and in greater numbers. The Privy Wardrobe accounts relating to the Tower of London include many swords and scabbards in various states of repair and of hugely varying quality and decoration, certainly not all

---

[12] 'View of arms in the leet of Conesford in the city of Norwich, carried out before J[ohn] Bardolf of Wormegay and his associates, the king's Justices of the Peace in Norfolk, on 27 July 1355', William Hudson, 'Norwich Militia in the Fourteenth Century', *Norfolk Archaeology*, 14 (1901), pp. 295–301. The *Centenar* was a man placed in charge of a hundred footsoldiers, whilst a *vintenar* had charge of twenty.

[13] Philippe Contamine, 'L'armement des populations urbaines à la fin du Moyen Âge: l'exemple de Troyes (1474)', *Pages d'histoire militaire médiévale (XIVe-XVe siècles)* (Paris, 2005), pp. 65–78. Again, my thanks to Kelly Devries for highlighting the source and providing the translation, which also appears in *Medieval Warfare: A Reader*, pp. 73–4.

[14] Nor does it mean that they were trained to fight with them, but that is a matter for later in the book.

for the king's personal use.[15] This means that some of these weapons must have been stored for issue to members of the *familia regis*, the king's military household, or to mustered field armies, which suggests that not every man who came to serve would be expected to come with his own weapons.

Inventories of great noblemen also list multiple swords. That of Raoul II de Nesle, Constable of France, who was to die on the battlefield of Courtrai in 1302, lists, amongst the martial equipment he owned, in one property ten swords without silver decoration valued at 100 shillings, one sword of Genoan manufacture garnished with silver, valued at ten pounds, another sword with one scabbard of velvet garnished with silver, valued at six pounds, another with a green silk scabbard 'strewn with escutcheons', valued at twenty shillings, one with a black scabbard with a green bag garnished with silver, valued at six pounds and a final one with a crystal pommel, valued at three pounds.[16] Meanwhile, in Paris he had twenty-eight more swords, including nine, each worth six shillings, bound in a long bag itself valued at nine shillings. There were fifteen swords bound in a silk bag, at a value of twelve shillings each, one sword garnished with leather valued at 100 shillings and a final one, garnished with embroidery of the arms of Nesle, valued at six pounds.[17] Raoul was one of the leading noblemen in the realm and, as Constable, one of its foremost military figures, so a large collection of weapons would be no surprise. Again, however, we should be wary of assuming that all of them were intended for his personal use and not for distribution to members of his household.

A sense of the ownership of weapons of someone of less exalted status and means comes from the account of losses of John Sampson, Constable of Stirling Castle, who was forced to surrender it to William Wallace in 1299. His personal losses were:

> two aketons which cost him more than 40s., two gambesons more than £4, one hauberk and one habergeon 40s., one pisan with the cape 10s., jambers and cuisses more than 8s., one chapel de fer 20s., one chapel of sinew 40d., iron gauntlets 5s., one pair of plates more than one mark, one pair of trappers two marks, three swords, one misericord, and two anelaces with grips of ivory 10s.[18]

What we appear to be seeing here is a description of the harness for a single knight. For the most part there is only one of everything, with extras of one or two items, the

[15]   On the Tower Armoury, see T. Richardson, *The Tower Armoury in the Fourteenth Century* (Leeds, 2014).

[16]   '*x espees sans argent C s' vne espee de gennes garnie dargent x l' vne autre espee a i fuerre vermeil garni dargent vi l' vne autre a fuerre vert de soie seme descuchons xx s' vne autre espee a i fuerre noire a Beug' v[er]t garni dargent vi l' vne aut' a pomel de cristal iiij l'*. Lille, Archives départementales du Nord, B450/4401, transcribed and translated by Ralph Moffat, *Medieval Arms & Armour: A Sourcebook. Volume I: The Fourteenth Century* (Woodbridge, 2022), Document 4, p. 40.

[17]   *Ibid.*

[18]   '*deux Aketons q[ue] lui custerent plus de xl s ij Gambesons plus de iiij li j hauberk & vn hauberion xl sol[i]d' j Pisane oue la Cape x s Jambers [et] quisoz plus de viij s vn chapel de feer xx s j chapel de Nerfs xl den' Gants de feer v s j peire de plates plus de vn marc' vn peire de Treppes ij marc' tres espeis vn misericord & deux Anlaces oue les maunches de Iuoir x s.*' Kew, TNA E 159/80, m. 50; published in Moffat, *Medieval Arms and Armour: A Sourcebook*, Document 12, p. 48. Again, I am grateful to Ralph Moffat for permission to use his transcription and translation.

hauberk, and the habergeon – both mail shirts, but the latter being longer and with full sleeves – a helmet of iron and one of sinew. From this we might infer that three swords was indicative of the number of weapons carried by a knight on campaign. Three swords were also left by Sir Fulk Pembridge of Tong in Shropshire when he wrote his will in 1325, one noted as being specifically for tourney and one specifically for war.[19]

What about further down the social order? Swords often appear in wills for men of the urban middle class, although seldom in the numbers owned by Raoul de Nesle or even Sir Fulk Pembridge. Richard Goldsmith, a goldsmith of Carlisle, left a sword in his will of 1379, as did Thomas Karlton, the Rector of Castle Carrock in Cumbria, in 1380.[20] John Cadeby, a mason from Beverley in Yorkshire who died around the middle of the fifteenth century, left a sword with scabbard and buckler valued at 2 shillings in his will, whilst John Carter, a tailor from the city of York, left a sword valued at ten pence, equal in value to his camlet doublet.[21]

None of these men are exceptional amongst their class. There is nothing to suggest that they were particularly belligerent or had second careers as military men. The value of their swords was less than any of those of Raoul de Nesle, as we might expect for the purchasing power of merchants compared to one of the great nobles of France.[22] That such men owned swords at all, however, speaks to their wide availability and ownership.

Carrying Swords in a Civilian Context

Owning a sword and carrying it as part of one's military equipment is one thing, but what can we say about the propensity for wearing a sword as part of everyday dress?

Geoffrey Chaucer's famous pilgrim party is often seen as a cross-section of medieval society, socially and morally. His description of their character and status is combined with descriptions of their mounts and their garb. In only three cases – the Yeoman, the Miller, and the Reeve – are the pilgrims described carrying swords, with two more – the Franklin and the Shipman – portrayed as possessing daggers.[23]

---

[19] London, British Library, Stowe Charter 622. *Ibid*, Document 34, p. 71.

[20] For Richard Goldsmith, see Carlisle Archives, DRC/1/2, pp. 303–4 (Moffat, *Medieval Arms and Armour: A Sourcebook*, Document 108, p. 174). For Thomas Karlton, see Carlisle Archives, DRC/1/2, p. 331 (*Ibid*, Document 117, p. 178)..

[21] *Testamenta Eboracensia, Or Wills Registered at York, Illustrative of the History, Manners, Language, Statistics, &c., of the Province of York from the Year 1300 Downwards*, vol. 3, ed. James Raine and John William Clay (London, 1865), pp. 98 and 302.

[22] We must be careful with such valuations, obviously, as we are not comparing like with like either chronologically or geographically

[23] Geoffrey Chaucer, *The Canterbury Tales*, trans. David Wright (Oxford, 2011). In the case of the Franklin the weapon is specifically described as an 'anlaas', or *anlace*, a narrow-bladed dagger (Line 357, from 'General Prologue, taken from *The Riverside Chaucer*', *Harvard's Geoffrey Chaucer Website*, n.d. https://chaucer.fas.harvard.edu/pages/general-prologue-0 (accessed 8 January 2021). Much more work needs to be done on the various types and forms of daggers, and this might shed more light on the symbolism attached to them.

The five craftsmen – the Haberdasher, the Carpenter, the Weaver, the Dyer, and the Tapestry Maker – all have knives with silver handles.

The surprise is that the two individuals we might most expect to carry swords – the Knight and the Squire – are *not* described as doing so. They are, after all, the two representatives of the military elite. The knight is a grizzled veteran, still dressed, famously, in his jupon stained by the mail of his habergeon. The squire, the quintessential fashionable young noble, is also martially experienced from his service in the military campaigns in France. It is possible, as we have suggested for the muster rolls, that their possession and carrying of a sword was taken for granted by Chaucer. But this seems unlikely, as it would mean him missing out on an opportunity to use the description of the weapon to reinforce his characterisation of the individuals. This is something he does for the three characters who do carry swords. The Reeve's rusty blade might reflect a careless character, but this is not borne out by other elements of Chaucer's portrait, such as his close-cropped hair and beard.[24] Instead the dominant feature of the Reeve, of which much is made in the prologue to the Reeve's tale, is his age.[25] As Brookes Forehand argued, the weapon is a reflection of the Reeve's age and of his clinging on to his violent and lusty youth, now past, noting a similar use of this symbolism by Chaucer in his piece 'Envoy to Scogan'.[26] The Miller's carrying of a sword and buckler, a combination which was connected with disorder, also reflects his character, as we shall see.

Less easy to rationalise in this way is the Yeoman's wearing of the same. Here however it is hard to ignore the prosaic answer, that the sword and buckler are, like the bow and arrows he also carries, the tools of his trade.[27] Yet, if that is the case, why is he the only one to be so fully equipped? Thompson argues that he was acting as a bodyguard for the Knight and the Squire, but that would seem to be an unnecessary role for individuals on so well-travelled a road as that to Canterbury. As all of Chaucer's other characters are to some extent archetypes, for Chaucer and his audience the bow, arrows, sword and buckler, and hunting horn served to define the yeoman-forester of medieval society.[28]

What Chaucer's pilgrim group suggests is that few people carried swords, even when travelling. The same seems to be the case if we look at visual depictions of daily life.

Depictions of scenes that are not military in nature rarely show men carrying swords. Whether it be fifteenth-century Italian frescos of urban life, such as those of the allegory of good and bad government in the Palazzo Populo in Siena or the Procession of the Magi in the Palazzo Medici Ricardi, or the thirteenth-century Morgan Picture bible, or the fifteenth-century *Trés Riches Heures de Duc de Berry*

---

[24] *Canterbury Tales*, p.18.
[25] Lines 3867–98, from 'The Reeve's Prologue and Tale', *Harvard's Geoffrey Chaucer Website*, n.d. https://chaucer.fas.harvard.edu/pages/reeves-prologue-and-tale (accessed 1 January 2021), lines 3867–98.
[26] Brookes Forehand, 'Old Age and Chaucer's Reeve', *PMLA*, 69.4 (1954), pp. 984–9.
[27] Kenneth J. Thompson, 'Chaucer's Warrior Bowman: The Roles and Equipment of the Knight's Yeoman', *The Chaucer Review*, 40.4 (2006), pp. 386–415.
[28] It is also possible that the falchion or *messer* was also used as a symbol of office. The fifteenth-century effigy of Jenkin Wyrall, Forester of Fee (in All Saints church in Newland, the Forest of Dean) depicts him in civilian dress, with hunting horn and a falchion on his belt.

Figure 19. A king and his courtiers sat in conversation, from a mid-fourteenth-century manuscript of *Guiron le Courtois*. (Bibliothèque nationale de France, BnF Département des Manuscrits Français 5243, fol.51r).

by the Limbourg brothers, men almost never appear with swords unless they are in military garb.

In a fifteenth-century prose version of the romance of *Regnault de Montauban*, there are numerous depictions of fifteenth-century French courtiers and courtly life.[29] In almost no case does an individual in civilian dress have a sword belted around their waist. The only exceptions to this seem to be when one of the characters has been travelling, but even then, it is not universal.

Another romance illustrated in high detail is the mid-fourteenth-century romance of *Guiron le Courtois*.[30] Just as with the fifteenth-century *Regnualt*, there are numerous depictions of the knightly hero meeting with others of his status, and his betters. In almost no cases are these nobles wearing swords unless they are in military garb or have been travelling.

In a rather different manuscript tradition, the *Codex Manesse*, a fourteenth-century book of songs and poetry depicts the *minnesänger* – nobles and knights who were also poets writing metrical verse in Germany – in a range of courtly and martial activities.[31] Leaving aside the twenty-seven martial images (of tournament, battle, or knights in full armour), where we would expect to see swords, only twenty-two of the 140 figures are depicted with a sword, and in the vast majority of cases the sword is being leant on or is hanging beside the individual. In two cases, that of King Wenceslas of Bohemia ('Wenzel von Böhmen') and the Landgrave Herman von Thüringen (named in the folio of Klingsor von Ungarland), the sword is displayed in a formal fashion.[32] King Wenzel's sword is borne scabbarded, the belt wrapped around the blade and point

[29] *Regnault de Montauban, Rédaction en prose.* BnF, MS Arsenal 5072–75.
[30] BnF, Département des Manuscrits. NAF 5243, *Guiron le Courtois.* See fig. 19.
[31] Große Heidelberger Liederhandschrift, Cod. Pal. germ. 848 (Codex Manesse).
[32] *Ibid*, fols. 10r and 219v. See Figs. 20 and 21.

Figure 20. King Wenceslas of Bohemia sitting in State. Detail from the Codex Manesse, c.1300–1340. (Universitätsbibliothek Heidelberg, Cod. Pal. germ. 848 Große Heidelberger Liederhandschrift (Codex Manesse), fol. 10r).

Figure 21. The Landgrave of Thüringen and his wife. Detail from the Codex Manesse, c.1300–1340. (Universitätsbibliothek Heidelberg, Cod. Pal. germ. 848 Große Heidelberger Liederhandschrift (Codex Manesse), 219v).

uppermost by an individual standing next to throne, whilst the Landgrave is sat next to his wife, holding his weapon upright, also scabbarded and with the belt wound around the blade. Both are serving as a symbol of power and authority, in the fashion of the bearing swords we considered earlier.

In only five cases is the *minnesänger* wearing a sword in civilian garb. Four of them – Graf Conrad von Kirchberg, Sir Rudolf von Rosenberg, Der von Wildonie, and von Stamheim – are depicted outside of a tower or castle, receiving either a parchment or a circlet.[33] The fifth figure, Rubin von Rüdeger, is shown, sword and buckler belted at his waist, seemingly leading a lady into a forest.[34] For all of these examples one might posit that they are travelling or even questing, given the subject matter of the scenes. Whilst one might argue that the Codex Manesse is not the most naturalistic depiction, calling into question how far we can rely on the detail of the scene, the situation is replicated in any number of visual sources.

In the Beauchamp Pageant, the wearing of a sword is far more common, but on every occasion the individual is either in a military context, and armoured, or acting in a formal capacity. This could be greeting a noble guest (as do the Duke de Bar, the Doge of Venice, and Sor Baltirdam, the Sultan's lieutenant – the last depicted with a heavily curved and clip-pointed falchion, as befits his foreign nature).[35] It might also be at court, where the noblemen are denoting their rank, or are receiving a commission from the king.[36] It is possible that the depiction of sword wearing has a more specific connotation, the nuance of which is lost. Certainly, where Beauchamp is depicted as Henry VI's guardian, he is the only one to be shown wearing a sword, perhaps indicating his role as the boy-king's protector.[37] When the Earl is depicted as 'lord roial' in France, he is shown enthroned at court, the two men at the front left have swords on their waists, whilst those on the right have purses, which might betoken something of the Earl's role, or indicate that his court is made up of the merchants and the nobility.[38] There are no swords being carried by those who are dining at the formal meals, nor in any of the coronation scenes (save by the sword-bearer himself, when present) nor in scenes of religious services (which again should not come as a surprise). Thus, whilst swords are more commonly shown, the illustrator is not including them as a matter of course.

Obviously, these examples are very far from exhaustive, but they are representative examples of depictions of nobles and courtiers, who of all people we might expect to be routinely wearing a sword. Where a sword appears in the hand or on the hip of someone not in armour, then the sword is either because the individual is involved in some formal task or duty, or because they are expecting or intending violence.

Another approach for understanding the carrying of weapons by the civilian population is to look at examples of when the weapons were used. The surviving

---

[33] *Ibid*, fols. 24r, 54r, 201r, and 261r respectively.
[34] *Ibid*, fol. 395r.
[35] Fols. 5v, 8r and 11r, and 9v. *The Beauchamp Pageant*, pp. 70–1, 80–1 and 86–7.
[36] See fols.12v, 13r, 14r, 14v, 16v, 26r. *Ibid*, pp. 98–101, 104–5, 114–15.
[37] Fol. 23r, *Ibid*, pp. 140–1.
[38] Fol. 26r, pp. 152–3. The clergy are noticeable by their absence.

medieval Coroners' rolls are of great interest here. These record instances of people who died 'other than their natural deaths', including those dying by suicide and accident. When such a death was reported the coroner would call together a jury of local men, and he and they would investigate what had happened. The coroner would determine the time of death and record the injuries sustained, and the instrument or weapon which caused the same. The jurors would identify the deceased, determine the cause and circumstances of the death, and name any other individuals connected with it. The coroner would then arrest any suspects or direct the sheriff or constable to do so; he would seize the suspect's chattels and arrange for him to be jailed. These details were then written up for presentation at the next appearance of the King's justices. Survival of such rolls are patchy, and the process of enrolment equally so. Even so some conclusions can be drawn.

When Barbara Hanawalt looked at the rolls of Northamptonshire, London, and Oxford in her study of violent deaths in the fourteenth century, she found the percentage of unnatural deaths caused by cutting or piercing weapons was seventy-three percent.[39] Knives accounted for forty-two percent of all deaths, whilst those caused by a sword was roughly comparable in London and Oxford at eleven and ten percent respectively, but somewhat lower in the Northamptonshire records, at six percent.[40]

Leaving aside the question of why there should be twice as many sword-related deaths in towns as in the countryside for the moment, the low frequency of such deaths in all three samples is very clear, as is the contrast with the high number of those caused by knives. Given that the context in which most of these homicides occurred was during an argument (Hanawalt puts the number at sixty percent for rural Northamptonshire and as high as eighty percent for London and Oxford), it seems that most fatal attacks were not premediated, but spontaneous acts of violence. By definition, these spontaneous attacks will have been made with whatever weapon was most readily to hand, and this would suggest that whilst medieval men and women might readily have a knife or dagger on their belt, a sword was far less likely to be to hand in the heat of the moment.[41]

Looking at the details of cases where swords are being used, it is far more often the case that when a sword is involved the wielder carried it with intent to use it. William Rose, a mariner, was killed by John Loveryk and Robert de Dyeghere, who

---

[39] B.A. Hanawalt, 'Violent Death in Fourteenth- and Early Fifteenth-Century England', *Comparative Studies in Society and History*, 18.3 (1976), pp. 300–1. On the difficulties of assessing the homicide rates of historical societies (including a critique of Hanawalt's own calculations), see Robert R. Dykstra, 'Lies, Damned Lies, and Homicide Rates', *Historical Methods: A Journal of Quantitative and Interdisciplinary History*, 42.4 (2009), pp. 139–42. The proportions are consistent across Europe, see P. Spierenburg, *A History of Murder: Personal Violence in Europe from the Middle Ages to the Present* (Cambridge, 2008), pp. 34ff.

[40] Hanawalt, 'Violent death', p. 319, Appendix IV.

[41] *Ibid*, p. 311. Hannah Skoda states that much of the violence recorded was performative – done with the intention of it being witnessed – however, the rolls suggest that the majority of murders were spontaneous acts (Hannah Skoda, *Medieval Violence: Physical Brutality in Northern France, 1270–1330* (Oxford, 2013), p. 78)

sought him out in the London streets following a quarrel, for example.[42] Sometimes the deaths occurred in what might best be termed a gang fight. In November of 1325, John atte Vise, a saddler, was killed by a sword blow from John de Wynestone, a goldsmith, during a fight between members of their respective guilds.[43] In 1339, a group of apprentices of the Bench (a group of junior lawyers) assaulted two clerks of the Chancery with swords and *balghstafs*.[44]

In Oxford the basis for dispute was more commonly one of 'town versus gown', the most famous example being the St Scholastica Day riot, when a dispute over the quality of a tavern's ale escalated into a three-day running battle between townsmen and scholars that saw a hundred deaths.[45] A smaller altercation took place in the city in 1306, between a group of clerks and scholars, with both sides deploying swords and bows.[46]

A number of the killings involving swords occurred during robberies, either by the robbers themselves or by others coming out as part of the 'hue and cry', the pursuit of a criminal by able-bodied men of a community. In 1325, Gilbert de Mordoen and seventeen companions set out to abduct the daughter of one Robert Pourte (who was Gilbert's ward) with 'stones in their hoods, swords, knifes and other weapons'.[47] In August 1265, William the Shepherd was struck down with a blow to the head delivered by John, Richard Herbert's son, who was one of the robbers that William had been pursuing as part of the hue and cry.[48] In London in 1328 John de Glemham, another Apprentice of the Bench, was killed when answering a local hue and cry, not by the original assailant, but by a third man – William le Taverner – who appeared with a drawn sword.[49] Quite why William should have struck John is not clear. The rolls rarely explain the motivation of those causing death, except in the most general sense, so we rarely hear the cause of a quarrel and often there is just a sense that there was a longer tale lying behind the bare bones recorded.

Some men appear more likely to have carried a sword by dint of their status. In October of 1321, John de Harwe, a porter, had the affrontery to remonstrate with Thomas atte Chirche, an esquire to the Earl of Arundel, for nearly riding down a woman and child as he and a companion rode towards the Tower of London.[50] Thomas drew his sword 'in a fit of anger' and struck John down. Likewise, Francis de Vilers, knight quarrelled with John de Wodenhaly, a church rector, and both drew

[42] *Ibid*, p. 228.
[43] *Calendar of Coroner's Rolls of the City of London, A.D. 1300–1378*, ed. Reginald Sharpe (London, 1913), p. 132–3. A *balghstaf* is generally thought to be a stout staff or cudgel, based on Shakespearian use.
[44] *Ibid*, p. 226.
[45] Carl Hammer, 'Patterns of Homicide in a Medieval University Town: Fourteenth-Century Oxford', *Past and Present*, 78.1 (1978), pp. 3–23.
[46] *Records of Medieval Oxford Coroners' Inquests, the Walls of Oxford etc*, ed. H.E. Salter (Oxford, 1912), pp. 15/16.
[47] *Calendar of the Coroner's Rolls of London*, p. 115.
[48] *Select Cases from the Coroner's Rolls, AD 1265 – 1413, with a Brief Account of the History of the Office of the Coroner*, ed. Charles Gross (London, 1896), p. 1.
[49] *Calendar of Coroner's Rolls of the City of London*, p. 135.
[50] *Ibid*, pp. 34–5.

their swords, John striking Francis in the head.[51] It may not be unexpected that a squire such as Thomas, or a knight such as Sir Francis, would bear a sword, but that a church rector would draw in response may come as a surprise. Servants even further down the social order also appear with swords more frequently than, say, tradesmen. John de Pastone, a servant of Matthew de Essex, struck off the hand of the goldsmith Robert Denys, following a quarrel.[52] In February 1325 two servants of the same master, Richard de Dancastre and William de Tutbere, quarrelled and drew swords on each other.[53]

Whilst all the above examples may seem a rather disparate collection, what they have in common is that the wielders of the swords are carrying them with a specific purpose in mind, either nefarious or legitimate. On those occasions when the sword is drawn and the blow struck in anger during a quarrel without premeditation, rather than with malice aforethought, then it is normally the case that the sword is being carried because the individual is travelling. Occasionally, the records describe men who have quarrelled going home to collect a sword, as happened in Oxford in April 1306, when a disagreement over the closing of a tap room escalated when three clerks returned to their lodgings to fetch 'swords and bucklers and other arms' and broke back into the house, assaulting the owner and his wife.[54]

Swords are still rare as weapons drawn to resolve a quarrel. Far more common in such circumstances is that one of the protagonists draws a knife, and the most common knives to be drawn are described as *trenchour* knives, the knife used to eat with, or *twytel* or 'whittle', referring to the tang and one of the cheapest forms of construction: in other words, the sorts of knives that common men and women had hanging from their belt as a matter of course and were, therefore readily to hand.[55] The instances of deaths caused by knife wounds are so much higher than those caused by sword blows that one can only conclude that swords simply were not worn as a matter of course by the medieval population. Again, this does not mean that swords are not owned or possessed.

It is notable that many of those wielding swords are either clerks or students. As we shall see, there is a clear connection between the formal teaching of swordplay and these groups of men.[56] Many of the sources make them appear to behave much like the *tiros* of George Duby's eleventh- and twelfth-century chivalric class; young men, without responsibility, existing within a closed society made up almost exclusively of other young men, and able to act with near impunity, protected by their nobility.[57]

---

[51]   *Ibid*, p. 91.
[52]   *Ibid*, p. 42.
[53]   *Ibid*, p. 52.
[54]   'Records of Medieval Oxford', p. 16. The Saint Scholastica Day riot escalated in a similar fashion.
[55]   Other forms of knife, such as the 'Irish knife' or daggers such as the 'baselard' (which we discussed briefly with regards the death of Wat Tyler, above), 'anlaas', 'misericord', and 'falchion' (which, as have we said, is strictly speaking not a knife but a sword), are far less frequent. This is also noted by Leland, 'Pardons for Self-Defence', pp. 158–9.
[56]   See below, pp. 134ff.
[57]   Georges Duby, 'Les "jeunes" dans la société aristocratique dans la France du Nord-Ouest au XIIe siècle,' *Annales: Économies, Sociétés, Civilisations*, 19.5 (1964), pp. 835–46.

They formed a community distinct from but within the town, in a wholly young male environment, protected by the separate jurisdictions of Church and College. Such men often had a connection with the nobility, either because they were younger sons of knights and nobles, because they were serving or destined to serve as clerks within noble or royal households, or as clerics within a Church whose hierarchy was also dominated by those of noble birth. As such they were already on the fringe of the chivalric community and, as Skoda says, sought to connect with the chivalric milieu, including through the ownership and carrying of swords.[58] It was these sorts of men that were at the heart of the riots in Oxford and Paris. It is perhaps no surprise therefore that the university authorities made attempts to control weapon carrying, similar to those we see in the towns of which they were a part, with bans on scholars and professors carrying weapons in the street.[59]

Attacks with a sword were rare, and generally premeditated when they did occur. Even where we might expect an individual to own a sword, there is little to suggest that they were wearing them continuously, carried as a matter of course. Unlike the early modern period, when the sword was a fashion accessory constantly on the hip of a gentleman, one carried a sword in the high Middle Ages because it was functionally necessary for the job one was doing, or because one intended (or expected) violence.

Why do we see bans on the carriage of weapons in city streets? If we turn our attention back to the bans on weapon-wearing in the city streets of Europe, again we see that things are not as straightforward as they are often portrayed.

Weapon Bans in Medieval Towns

What is the evidence for weapons bans in European cities at this time? There is clear evidence for restrictions in the towns of the Holy Roman Empire. There are surviving examples of knife-shaped measures, supposedly hung from chains at the city gates to allow men to gauge whether their weapons needed storing. There is an undated instruction published in the town of Zwolle that 'no-one shall carry knives or other weapons longer than the city measure that hangs in front of the city hall and at the gates, on penalty of a five-pound fine'.[60] Similar restrictions appear in fourteenth-century Augsburg and fifteenth-century Rothenburg.[61] However, as Tlusty notes, these restrictions were not universal, neither within Germany nor within Europe as a whole.[62]

[58] Skoda, *Medieval Violence*, p. 154. Ruth Karras makes the same such assertions in From *Boys to Men: Formations of Masculinity in Late Medieval Europe* (Philadelphia, PA, 2002).
[59] *Statuta Antiqua Universitatis Oxoniensis*, ed. Strickland Gibson (Oxford, 1931). Heidelberg University had similar ordinances, see Lynn Thorndike, *University records and Life in the Middle Ages* (New York, NY, 1975), p. 291.
[60] *Thuis in de late middeleeuwen: het Nederlands burgerinterieur 1400–1535* (Waanders, 1980), p. 73, quoting A. Telting, *Stadboeken van Zwolle* (Zwolle, 1897), p. 302.The work also shows an image of one of these measuring knives, from the collection of the Museum de Waag (inv # 2732.3).
[61] Tlusty, *The Martial Ethic in Early Modern Germany*, p. 61.
[62] *Ibid*. She notes that in the thirteenth century the city of Freiburg permitted all citizens to bear arms of all kinds, including pikes and crossbows.

As we have already noted, that London banned the carriage of weapons has been widely commented upon. However, a closer inspection of the evidence suggests that the city never had a blanket ban on the carrying of weapons in public. Whilst certain ordinances, such as the clearing of filth from the streets and the ditches, are passed year on year and are clearly part of the regular business of the mayor and his council, the same is not true for restrictions on the carriage of weapons. Survival of the ordinances passed within the city, both issued by the Crown and by the municipal authorities, is very good, and they show quite specific criteria accompanying the restrictions on weapons. Some are rather obvious and straightforward. Controls on 'nightwalkers' – those who go about armed after curfew with malicious intent – are found on several occasions.[63] There are usually exemptions, for example, for those acting as the city's officers performing watch in the wards, but also for 'great lords', 'respectable persons of note' or their 'acknowledged retainers', provided they carry a light and are going about after dark with a good purpose.[64] The ban promulgated in January 1327, which exempted the watchmen, extended that exclusion to 'the Hainauters of the Queen, who are accustomed to go armed in the manner of their country'.[65] This contextual-isation might be taken to indicate that 'going armed' was not the custom of retainers in England, but given that the occasion for this ban was the promulgation of the Parliament that was to see Edward II deposed in favour of his son, it would seem the exclusion was less a recognition of cultural difference and more a recognition of the coercive power of Isabella's Hainauter troops who, under Jean de Beaumont, had accompanied her and Roger Mortimer back from the Continent in September 1326. In most other cases foreigners are picked out for particular attention in weapons bans at times of international tension. The fear of the French and Flemish sailors and merchant communities acting as a fifth column in English port towns was almost constant through the fourteenth century, reinforced by the reality of French raids

[63] Most of the ordinances are to be found in *The Calendar of Letter Books of the City of London*, ed. Reginald R. Sharpe, 11 vols. (London, 1899–1912). A compilation of some of the ordinances was put together by the HEMA practitioner Dave Rawlings in a discussion on the online forum of 'Schola Gladiatoria' (No Swords and bucklers in London Please', *Schola Gladiatoria Forum*, 25 April 2006, http://www.fioredeiliberi.org/phpBB3/viewtopic.php?f=4&t=447&start=0& and 'No fencing Schools in London Allowed, c. 1300', *Schola Gladiatoria Forum*, 4 April 2006, http://www.fioredei-liberi.org/phpBB3/viewtopic.php?f=4&t=231& (accessed 1 August 2021).

[64] An exemption for the officers of the City is to be found dated 2 January 1327 (*Calendar of the Plea and Memoranda Rolls of the City of London: Volume 1, 1323–1364*, ed. A.H. Thomas (London, 1926), Roll A 1b: (i) Dec 1326–Oct 1327. *British History Online* http://www.british-history.ac.uk/plea-mem-oranda-rolls/vol1 (accessed 1 August 2021). Exemptions for a 'great lord, or other respectable person of note, or their acknowledged retainer' appear in an undated thirteenth-century memorandum of royal articles (Folios xvb, *Calendar of Letter-Books of the City of London: C, 1291–1309*, ed. Reginald R. Sharpe (London, 1901), pp. 15–20. *British History Online* http://www.british-history.ac.uk/london-letter-books/volc/pp15-20 (accessed 1 August 2021). Other similar exemptions for knights and nobles appear elsewhere in the memoranda, and to the Mayor of Coventry's proscription of weapons in the city dating to 1421 (*The Coventry Leet Book; or Mayor's Register, Containing the Records of the City Court Leet or View of Frankpledge, A.D. 1420–1555, with Divers Other Matters*, trans. and ed. Mary Dormer Harris (London, 1907), p. 30).

[65] *Calendar of the Plea and Memoranda Rolls* cited above.

on the south coast, such as that which resulted in the burning of Southampton.[66] In 1362, at the height of the Breton civil war – one of the proxy wars fought by England and France during the Hundred Years war – London enacted a specific ordinance 'that no Fleming, Brabanter or 'Selander [sic for Zeelander] carry arms or a knife, small or large, with a point, secretly or openly, under penalty of forfeiture'.[67]

The 1326 ban on carrying weapons within the city of London was issued because of the calling of the Parliament for that year. A similar ban, 'restricting the carrying of arms and forbidding horse-play in the City of London and Palace of Westminster', was instituted during the session of the 1351 Parliament.[68] Likewise, there was a ban for the three days around the coronation of Richard II in 1377, and in 1416 a ban was put in place on the occasion of the visit of Sigismund of Luxemburg, the King of the Romans, and his retinue.[69] On all these occasions there would have been a greater than normal number of men in the city, including the household retainers of knights and nobles, carrying weapons as a reflection of the lord's honour and puissance. The possibility of conflict between them, or between them and the men of the city was very real. Indeed, the predations of these large bodies of liveried retainers was so great that, by the time of Richard II's reign, Parliament was passing laws to try and restrict their recruitment.[70] A weapons ban within the city would be a sensible precaution at such charged times, but aimed less at the citizens themselves than at the incoming armed retainers.

The fear of armed disorder within the city could be a real one. In 1281 Edward I issued a writ demanding the punishment of 'all bakers, brewers and other misdoers walking the City by night with swords and bucklers and assaulting those they met…'.[71]

---

[66] On the defence of Southampton, see Randall Moffett, 'The Military Organisation of Southampton in the Late Medieval Period, 1300–1500', Unpublished PhD thesis (Southampton, 2009).

[67] Fol. cviii, *Calendar of Letter-Books of the City of London: G, 1352–1374*, ed. Reginald R. Sharpe (London, 1905), *British History Online* http://www.british-history.ac.uk/london-letter-books/volg (accessed 1 August 2021).

[68] Folio ccviiib, *Calendar of Letter-Books of the City of London: F, 1337–1352*, ed. Reginald R. Sharpe (London, 1904), pp. 232–49. *British History Online* http://www.british-history.ac.uk/london-letter-books/volf/pp232-249 (accessed 1 August 2021).

[69] On the occasion of the coronation of Richard II – fol. lxix, *Calendar of Letter-Books, G, British History Online* http://www.british-history.ac.uk/london-letter-books/volg/pp88-101 (accessed 1 August 2021). On that of the visit of the King of the Romans, fol. clxxvii, *Calendar of Letter-Books of the City of London: I, 1400–1422*, ed. Reginald R. Sharpe (London, 1909), *British History Online* http://www.british-history.ac.uk/london-letter-books/voli (accessed 1 August 2021).

[70] N.E. Saul, 'The Commons and the Abolition of Badges', *Parliamentary History*, 9 (1990), pp. 302–15. Philippe, Duke of Burgundy, passed similar legislation in March 1432 for the County of Hainault, where the growth of noble retinues was causing similar issues for order. His restrictions included bans on the wearing of armour and the carrying of arms (Item, que aucuns d'ores en avant ne porte armures, c'est assavoir : grans coutiaulx à claux et à crois, makes creltelëes et escanlellées d'ollec-quins, plonmées et aufres basions mourdriers et non raisonnables, sour enkéir ceux qui feroient au contraire en LX sols d'amende et les bastons conficquiez.' *Cartulaire des comtes de Hainaut, de l'avènement de Guillaume II à la mort de Jacqueline de Bavière [1337–1436]*, ed. L. Devillers (Brussels, 1881), p. 139).

[71] Fol. 127, *Calendar of Letter-Books of the City of London: A, 1275–1298*, ed. Reginald R. Sharpe (London, 1899), pp. 207–30. *British History Online* http://www.british-history.ac.uk/london-letter-books/vola/pp207-230 (accessed 1 August 2021).

Such disorders were more than once the cause of instructions being issued.[72] Again, we should be careful not to take this as an indication of general lawlessness. The reference to specific guilds may suggest specific issues or rivalries between different factions within town, such as the fight that broke out on in Walbrook and Bridge Street on 2 August 1340 between members of the Fishmongers and Skinners Guilds.[73] This may also be the reason for the restrictions placed by John Leeder, the mayor of Coventry in 1421, that

> no boche, ne non othur man of Craft, ne no nygh neighborgh of contre, ber no billys, ne gysamez, ne no grett stauys within the Cite, up the peyn of forfatwre of the same wepons, and hut boodyes to prison and pay xx s. at euery trespas.[74]

Leeder's proclamation goes on to instruct innkeepers to remind their guests to leave their weapons in their rooms, a measure we see in London and on the continent. He also provides an exemption for nobles and knights, something else that we have seen is common to such ordinances. These exemptions have been used to suggest that weapons bans were class-based, designed to prevent the lower classes and 'peasants' from rebelling. However, like the bans, the wording of such exemptions tends to be rather particular, and suggests a rather more nuanced purpose. The ban of November 1327 instructs that the prohibition did not apply 'to the servants (*valettis*) of earls and barons of the realm, *viz.* each earl and baron is allowed to have his servant carrying his sword in his presence'.[75] Again, in the summer of 1372, the exemption was made for 'servants of lords or knights carrying their masters' swords'.[76] It would seem that the exemption was not made because a nobleman was expected to carry their sword at their hip, nor with the intent that the nobleman or knights should have a sword ready for use (although it is clear that the households of noblemen would often accompany their lord armed as a statement of power), but rather to permit the carriage of bearing swords, the symbol of the nobleman's rank and status discussed above. As we saw in the previous chapter, the bearing sword served to indicate the possession and wielding of devolved power. If the bans were promulgated for events such as coronations and the opening of parliaments, then

---

[72] There was a proclamation against arms-bearing in the city in December of 1393, 'because of disturbances of the King's Peace by armed bands'. (Fol. cclxxxix, *Calendar of Letter-Books of the City of London: H, 1375–1399*, ed. Reginald R. Sharpe (London, 1907), pp. 396–408. *British History Online* http://www.british-history.ac.uk/london-letter-books/volh/pp396-408 (accessed 1 August 2021).

[73] 'Roll A 1 (1338–41)', *Calendar of the Plea and Memoranda Rolls of the City of London: Volume 1, 1323–1364*, ed. A.H. Thomas (London, 1926), pp. 100–42. *British History Online* http://www.british-history.ac.uk/plea-memoranda-rolls/vol1/pp100-142 (accessed 8 January 2021).

[74] 'no butcher, nor other man of craft nor near neighbour of the district, bear no bills, nor guisarmes, nor great staves within the city, upon pain or forfeiture of the same weapons, and their bodies to prison and to pay 20 shillings at every trespass'. *The Coventry Leet Book*, p. 29.

[75] 'Roll A 1b: (ii) Nov 1327 – July 1328', *Calendar of the Plea and Memoranda Rolls of the City of London: Volume 1, 1323–1364*, ed. A.H. Thomas (London, 1926), pp. 37–65. *British History Online* http://www.british-history.ac.uk/plea-memoranda-rolls/vol1/pp37-65 (accessed 1 August 2021).

[76] fol. cclxxxixb, *Calendar of Letter-Books of the City of London: G, 1352–1374*, ed. Reginald R. Sharpe (London, 1905), pp. 288–95. *British History Online* http://www.british-history.ac.uk/london-letter-books/volg/pp288-295 (accessed 1 August 2021).

we should expect noblemen to be on the street displaying all the formal insignia of their rank, and so it makes sense for a caveat to the ban be included in order to allow them to do so without falling foul of the law. Such a display of authority would certainly be appropriate for attendance at parliament, but might also have been a social convention in general.

The so-called 'Merciless Parliament' of 1388 ruled that:

> no Servant of Husbandry, or Labourer, nor Servant [or] Artificer, nor of Victualler, shall from henceforth bear any Baselard, Sword, nor Dagger upon Forfeiture of the same, but in the Time of War and for the Defence of the Realm of England.[77]

That does seem to be a wholly class-based restriction. Indeed, it was part of a wider statute reinforcing earlier laws controlling the labour of such men and women, restricting their freedom to leave or change their employ, fixing their wages ('because that Servants and Labourers will not, nor by a Long Season would, serve and labour without outrageous and excessive Hire'), and is immediately followed by a clause instructing them to practice with the bow and arrow on Sundays and holy days, rather than playing 'importune Games'.[78] This makes it much closer to the popular perception of a general ban, but it is, once again, specifically on the carriage of arms in a specific context (since it allows for the bearing of arms 'in Time of War and for the Defence of the Realm'), responding to a very particular perceived threat, in this case of a labour force (many of them returned veterans from England's wars with France) rising up in armed protest against their betters.

A closer reading of the various prescriptions on weapons reveals that there is no evidence for central government, or even individual cities, instituting blanket bans on the carriage of weapons in the street. Instead, what we see are pieces of legislation that served as added precautions around politically charged events, or were carefully targeted at specific elements within society: the retainers of noble households, and the young men of the guilds, law schools, and universities. Where there is a more general condemnation of the carrying of weapons, it is in connection with social and moral outrage, and that outrage is being directed at a very particular and distinct culture of swordsmanship.

Buckler-play: Non-Noble and Ludic Sword Culture

On 10 August 1339, John de Shirborne, Coroner, William de Pontefract, and Hugh le Marberer, Sheriffs of the city of London were informed of the death of Richard de Bulkele.[79] He and William de Northamptone had been fighting in the Earl de Warrene's close in Bishopsgate, when William stabbed Richard through the arm with

---

[77] Ric. II. C. 4-6, *Great Britain, The Statutes of the Realm*, vol. 2 (London, 1963), p. 57.
[78] *Ibid*, p. 57. Just as with the city of London bans, those 'travailing by the Country with their Master, or in their Master's Message' are exempt, which not only allows the maintenance of armed retainers, but would also allow them to bear weapons as a symbol of their official status and service of a lord.
[79] *Calendar of the Coroner's Rolls of London*, pp. 229–30.

a short knife. William fled to a local church, pursued by Richard who collapsed and died outside it. What makes this case interesting for us is that the victim and his killer are both described as 'boklerplaiers'. There are numerous references to buckler-players and buckler-play in a wide variety of contexts. Amongst those excluded from the grace of Parliament in 1381 for their part in the Peasants' Revolt was one Johannes Turnour 'boclerplaier de Stistede'.[80] A political poem lauding the victories of Edward III over the French describes the campaign of Robert, 2nd Baron Morley, one of Edward's leading commanders, as 'Dare lered the men þe Normandes at buckler to play'.[81] 'Buckler-play' also appears in a fifteenth-century religious poem, 'The Mirror of the Periods of Man's Life'. It has Reason tell Man that 'in the age of.xx. ʒeer, Goes to Oxenford, or lerne lawe'.[82] Lust retorts that 'harpe and giterne þere may y leere, And pickid staffe and buckelere, þere-wiþ to playe'. In a late fifteenth-century English-Latin word book dated to 1483 the terms 'buckler-player' and 'buckler-playing' are recorded as being synonymous with the Latin 'gladiator' and 'gladiatura'.[83]

These references to 'buckler-play' reveals a culture of civilian swordsmanship that is unfamiliar to most of us today. They also show a different approach to swordsmanship, one that was neither elite nor noble, military nor (intentionally) mortal.

The sword and buckler were a common weapon combination throughout the Middle Ages. Whilst rarely mentioned in twelfth- and thirteenth-century sources, they are ubiquitous from the fourteenth century onwards.[84] They appear frequently in visual sources, and although they are depicted in the hands of full-armoured men-at-arms in a battlefield context, they are predominantly found with lower-status combatants and, more significantly for our focus, individuals in a non-military context. Men fighting with sword and buckler are also very common within marginalia, again almost invariably in civilian dress. Craig Hambling has suggested that they are most readily found in depictions of the lower and middle classes, and those engaged in criminality.[85]

We have already seen the sword and buckler as the weapons of the boorish miller in Chaucer's *Canterbury Tales*, but the poems referred to above and the coroners' rolls and city ordinances suggest that it is the urban middle class, frequently guildsmen and students, who are most likely to be found wielding the combination of weapons.

[80] 'Richard II: November 1381', *Parliament Rolls of Medieval England*, ed. Chris Given-Wilson, Paul Brand, Seymour Phillips, Mark Ormrod, Geoffrey Martin, Anne Curry, and Rosemary Horrox (Woodbridge, 2005), *British History Online* http://www.british-history.ac.uk/no-series/parliament-rolls-medieval/november-1381 (accessed 1 August 2021).
[81] *The Poems of Laurence Minot*, ed. John Hall (Oxford, 1914), p. 15, and *Political Poems and Songs Related to English History*, vol. I, ed. Thomas Wright (London, 1859), p. 70.
[82] The poem is recorded in Lambeth MS 853, and appears in *Hymns to the Virgin and Christ, the Parliament of devils, and other religious poems*, ed. F.J. Furnivall (London, 1865), p. 61.
[83] *Catholica Anglicanum: An English-Latin wordbook dated 1483*, ed. S.J.H. Heritage (London, 1881), p. 46.
[84] Herbert Schmidt, *The Book of the Buckler* (Berlin, 2015). Schmidt's work is primarily a typology and discussion of manufacture of the buckler, in much the same vein as Oakeshott's *Records of the Medieval Sword*.
[85] Craig Hambling, 'Posh Bucklers: The Noble Use of Ignoble Objects' paper presented to the International Medieval Congress 2021 (online), 5 July 2021.

That Johannes Tourner, Richard de Bulkele and William de Northamptone could all be termed 'buckler-players' indicates that the use of sword and buckler was seen as a trade or craft. This reinforces the non-noble aspect of sword and buckler, but also begs the question as to what that trade might have been. They do not appear to have been judicial champions. Such men seem to have fought with peculiar weapons, a pick or cudgel, and their role is normally very clearly elucidated in the references to them, making them distinct from our 'players'.[86] The term 'players' make it unlikely that they were a special form of bodyguard, or a particular type of soldier.[87]

The city and university ordinances hint at their actual role. The customaries of the *Liber Albus* record two prohibitions on the holding of schools of fencing or buckler-play, prohibitions that seem to have dated back to at least the thirteenth century.[88] Buckler-play and fencing seems to have been synonymous. As Olivier Dupuis has noted, 'escremie' – 'skirmishing' – was the medieval French term for fencing: literally to 'defend' or 'protect' oneself.[89] He also notes the connection between *eskermyes* – 'skirmishing' – and the prohibition on the establishment or participation in schools of fence and of buckler-play within the limits of a number of European cities. The link is made again in the records of the trial of Roger le Skirmisour, prosecuted in 1311 for running a school of fence.[90] According to the prosecution he and his school were considered to be sources of moral corruption, 'drawing young men together, sons of respectable parents, to the wasting of their property and injury of their own characters'.[91] Here then we see, once again, the connection between 'skirmishing', 'buckler-play', young men and antisocial behaviour.

Students and apprentices seem to have been particularly susceptible to the allure of the activity. We have already noted the writ of Edward I against the bakers and brewers 'walking the City by night with swords and bucklers and assaulting those they met'.[92] The universities regularly passed legislation in much the same terms, attempting to restrict members of the colleges from going about with weapons by day or by night, and establishing boards of enquiry to investigate those 'disturbers

---

[86] M.J. Russell, 'Accoutrements of Battle', *Law Quarterly Review*, 99.3 (1983), pp. 432–6. M.J. Russell, 'Hired Champions', *The American Journal of Legal History*, 3.3 (1958), pp. 242–59. Medieval illustrations of such men are plentiful, for example on the funerary brass of Robert Wyvil, Bishop of Salisbury, whose use of a professional champion is mentioned above (p. 25)

[87] Medieval soldiers are rarely identified as such, in the way that tradesmen are and, even when they are, it is usually with the epithet being used to denote social status rather than tactical role. On medieval terminology around soldiers, see S. Morillo, 'Milites, Knights and Samurai: Military terminology, comparative history, and the problem of translation', *The Normans and their Adversaries at War*, ed. R. Abels and B. Bachrach (Woodbridge, 2001), pp. 167–84.

[88] 'Qe nulle teigne Escole deskermerye de Bokeler deinz la cite.' (D.158). 'Qe nul teigne Escole de Eskermerye ne de Bokeler deinz le cite.' (Custum. 217), *Munimenta Gildhallae Londoniensis: Liber Albus, Liber Custumorum et Liber Horn*, ed. H. Riley (London, 1859), pp. 640 and 643.

[89] O. Dupuis, 'The Roots of Fencing from the Twelfth to the Fourteenth Centuries in the French Language Area', *Acta Periodica Duellatorum*, 3.1 (2015), pp. 37–62.

[90] 'Memorials: 1311', *Memorials of London and London Life in the 13th, 14th and 15th Centuries*, ed. H.T. Riley (London, 1868), pp. 81–93. British History Online http://www.british-history.ac.uk/no-series/memorials-london-life/pp81-93 (accessed 1 August 2021).

[91] *Ibid.*

[92] See above, p. 107.

of the peace, public taverns, those who practice the art of sword and buckler, and those who keep women in their rooms, which can give rise to scandal and infamy'.[93] In July 1313 the authorities within Oxford university sought to restrict the creation of 'nations' – affinities of students from particular geographical regions – in order to prevent factional conflict and bloodshed. They called on the college denizens to inform on anyone they suspected of being in such a league, 'or to disturb the peace of the university, or to exercise the art of the sword and buckler, or to keep a whore in his house, or to bear arms, or in any way to foment discord…'.[94] In the latter half of the fifteenth century the 'aularian statutes' prohibited members of the halls from engaging 'in games with boards or dice, handball, the art of the two-handed sword or of the sword and buckler, or any other improper game which disturbs the peace and distracts from study', fining malefactors fourpence.[95] The issue was not peculiar to English universities. In the university of the northern Italian city of Ferrera students would routinely engage in games and 'boyish pursuits' to divert themselves from their studies, including jousting and prize fighting. The latter, in medieval terms, was not restricted to fisticuffs, as it was to be by the late eighteenth century, but it was rather a number of forms of armed and unarmed combat pursued to win a purse of money.[96] The same attitudes are to be found in Germany and France in the same period, although the sources are less explicit.[97]

Olivier Dupuis records the death of an English fencing master in Paris in 1331, killed by his pupil. The official account of the investigation notes that the pupil inflicted a small wound on his teacher 'not from a movement of anger or hatred but only the playing of the said game, as he had been accustomed to do so'.[98] The use of the word 'play' here and in the general description of fencing suggests a ludic quality to this type of sword combat.[99] Everything about how it was practiced, and by whom, emphasises this. It is condemned by civic and university authorities alongside gambling, playing dice, drinking, and hiring prostitutes, as a game that 'that distracts from study', or as the cause of disorder and disputes, similar to the condemnation of Roger le Skirmisour, as leading the young men of London to waste their property'. This echoes the bans and prohibitions on tennis, football, and numerous other games, all of which were also seen as distractions from more serious pursuits, such as archery, which were of the benefit of the wider community or realm.

---

[93] *Statuta Antiqua Universitatis Oxoniensis*, pp. 88–9.
[94] *Ibid.*
[95] *Ibid*, p. 576.
[96] Thorndike, *University Records and Life*, p. 338.
[97] See Olivier Dupuis, 'Organization and Regulation of Fencing in the Realm of France in the Renaissance', *Acta Periodica Duellatorum*, 2 (2014), p. 233–54, and 'The roots of Fencing', *passim*, and 'Timeo Clipeos et Plagas Ferentes, or the Accidental Death of a Fencing Master in 1331', *Martial Culture in Medieval Town*, 20 April 2020, https://martcult.hypotheses.org/926 (accessed 1 August 2021).
[98] 'ipsum Jaquemardum vulnerauerat plagam odicum faciendo eidem ut dicitur |9| non motus ira vel odio, sed solummodo dictum ludum prout consueuerat exercendo'. Dupuis, 'Timeo Clipeos et Plagas Ferentes'.
[99] This has been recognized by, among others, Brian R. Price, 'The Martial Arts of Medieval Europe', Unpublished PhD thesis (Denton, TX, 2011), p. 47 *ff.*

Chaucer's ploughman, although very far from the being in the same class as the students and clerks, shares much of the same boorish, disorderly, 'laddish' behaviour we would expect to see from his social betters. That he too should be wearing a buckler with his sword reflects this and reinforces the image of the sword and buckler as a less noble form of combat.

A further indicator of the low and questionable moral standing of buckler-play and buckler-players is the connection between the fencing master and entertainers on the margins of society, such as jugglers, acrobats, and dancers.[100] Even as late as the sixteenth century fencers and fencing bouts were depicted as one of the activities of the carnival and fair, 'esbattermenten' or 'frivolous activities' as the Flemish called them.[101] Sword dancers and jugglers appear in a number of illustrations of both common and court entertainments. An Italian 'master of the sword, the battle-axe, the short dagger and all other weapons and the buckler' from Lucca was recorded as arriving in Metz, performing tricks and dancing on a tightrope.[102] In the fifteenth-century depiction of a fencing school by the German engraver 'the Master of the Banderolles', we see men practising or fighting with longsword and spear, as well as lifting rocks, and one individual performing an acrobatic feat by flexing backwards over a pair of crossed swords.[103] In 'The Littlemore Anslem', a late eleventh- to early twelfth-century collection of prayers and meditations, Salome is depicted in a similar manner, dancing before Herod, tumbling between four swords.[104] One might consider the actions of Taillefer, the Norman jongleur who rode between the English

[100] Sydney Anglo, *The Martial Arts in Renaissance Europe* (New Haven, CT, 2000).

[101] Bert Gevaert and Reinier van Noort, 'Evolution of Martial Tradition in the Low Countries: Fencing Guilds and Treatises', *Late Medieval and Early modern Fight Books: Transmission and tradition of Martial Arts in Europe (14th to 17th centuries)*, ed. Daniel Jaquet, Karin Verelst, and Timothy Dawson (Leiden, 2016), p. 382. Daniel Jaquet, 'Fighting in the Fightschools, late XVth, early XVIth century', *Acta Periodica Duellatorum*, 1.1 (2013), pp. 56–9.

[102] 'quant ledit maistre ytalliens vint à juer, il paissoit tout les aultre de bien juer et faisoit chose incredible et non à croire à gens qui ne l'airoie veu, tent sus la petite corde laiche comme sus la grosse. Et n'y ait homme qui sceust raiconter les tour qu'il faisoit sus la dite petite corde, et sambloit qu'il ne touchait ny à_ciel ny à terre de legiereté qui estoit en lui. Et estoit ledit maistre cy bien acoustré qu'il n'y_ait seigneurs en Mets qui eust de plus belle roube qu'il avoit, et estoit maistre jueulx d'espees, de la haiche d'airme, de la courte daigue, de toutte airmes et du bouclier.' Paris, BnF, nouv. Acq fr. 67120, edited by Fanny Faltot, 'Les Mémoires de Philippe de Vigneulles', Unpublished PhD thesis (Paris, 2015), pp. 128–29, quoted in Daniel Jaquet, 'Dancing on the rope, swallowing knives, juggling with daggers. Sword players in the 15th century', *Martial Culture in Medieval Town*, 15/04/2021, https://martcult.hypotheses.org/1240 (accessed 24 February 2022)

[103] Anglo, *The Martial Arts in Renaissance Europe*, p. 14.

[104] Bodleian Library MS. Auct. D. 2. 6, fol.166v. See Fig 21. There are also sword dancers amongst the acrobats and entertainers in the depiction of the adoration of the golden idol in the eleventh-century 'Bible of Roda' (BnF Latin 6 (3), fol. 64v), whilst a woman balances on the points of two swords, to musical accompaniment in the fourteenth-century 'Smithfield Decretals' (British Library Royal 10 E IV, fol. 58). Jaquet reproduces images of the Nuremburg Cutlers' Guild sword dance of the sixteenth century, and a banner depicting acrobats balancing swords and jumping over them in the fifteenth-century 'Wolfegg hausbuch' (Jaquet, 'Dancing on the rope'). The use of the sword in dancing and acrobatics has a very long history, but is now poorly understood, and there has been no recognition amongst dance historians or folklorists of its potential connection to sword play or early fencing masters. See Stephen D. Corrsin, 'The Historiography of European Linked Sword Dancing', *Dance Research Journal*, 25.1 (1993), pp. 1–12, and *Sword Dancing in Europe: A History* (Enfield Lock, 1997).

Figure 22. Salome performs a sword dance before Herod. From 'The Littlemore Anselm'
(late eleventh or early twelfth century. Bodleian MS Auct. D.2.6, fol. 166v.
© Bodleian Libraries, University of Oxford. Reproduced under
Creative Commons licence CC-BY-NC 4.0).

and Norman armies at Hastings, singing the song of Roland and juggling with his
sword, in a similar light.[105]

By the fifteenth century there was some formal recognition of fencing, with
the establishment of brotherhoods of fencers and the licensing of schools of fence,
although, as with all things pertaining to non-knightly swordsmanship the evidence
is sparse.[106] The Holy Roman Emperor recognised the *Marxbrüder* – a collection of
fencing masters – as a guild of fencers in 1487, but they appear to have been well-established a decade before then. There are ordinances governing fencing from as early
as 1355, suggesting that the *Marxbrüder* were not necessarily anything new, and there
were similar bodies in Flemish cities at around that same date.[107] Contemporaneously,
in France, one finds certificates documenting the right of fencing masters to run
events and schools, although the first royal ordinances available are sixteenth century

---

[105]   Histrio cor audux nimium quem nobilitabat
   Agmina praecedens inumerosa ducis
   Hortatur Gallos verbis et territat Anglos
   Alte proiciens ludit et ense suo. *Carmen de Triumpho Normannico*, trans. Kathleen Tyson (Scotts
   Valley, CA, 2013), p. 66.

[106]   On schools of fence, see below.

[107]   Dupuis, 'Organisation and Regulation of Fencing', pp. 235*ff*. Gevaert and van Noort, 'Evolution of
   Martial Tradition in the Low Countries', pp. 376–409.

in date.[108] It was not until the reign of Henry VIII that fencing guilds were established in England, with a monopoly granted to the London Masters of Fence in 1540. However, there had been illicit schools since the thirteenth century. None of these professional organisations, however, seem to have had the same legitimacy as other martial guilds, such as the civic archery and crossbow guilds established in Flemish towns in the thirteenth century, whose patrons included the Duke of Burgundy himself.[109] Indeed the role of these late medieval and early Renaissance guilds seem to be more about the regulation of the men running schools of fence, calling themselves 'masters', rather than encouraging the urban community to learn the fighting arts to assist in the defence of the polity, as was the case with the Guilds of St. George (for crossbowmen) or St. Sebastian (for archers).[110]

It would appear, then, that Richard de Bukele, William de Northamptone, and John Tourner were, like Roger le Skirmisour, professional teachers of sword and buckler fighting, masters of fence. The fact that this could be recognised as their trade speaks to how lucrative this otherwise disreputable career could be, and therefore how popular a pastime it must have been within medieval towns and their young urban professional communities. The popularity of the sport, however, should not be seen as evidence for such men carrying swords in the street as a matter of course, any more than the popularity of sports fencing in the nineteenth century through to today sees men wandering around with foils and sabres. Nor, though, should we see the various bans on fencing schools as part of a general prohibition on the owning of weapons.

There was never a blanket ban on swords in the Middle Ages. References to such bans are inevitably connected to particular fears about peace and order, whether that was the predations of 'nightwalkers', or the potential for insurrection brought about by the arrival of noblemen and their armed retainers. Most of the time, once should imagine, the general rule of law would be sufficient deterrent for most people to strike out with a blade. Besides, few were carrying swords as part of their everyday attire; that was a development of the sixteenth century, when the rapier – a sword made specifically to be worn alongside civilian clothing, and as much a symbol of gentlemanly status as a weapon – became *de riguer* amongst the middle and upper classes. Given what we have seen of the popularity of swordplay amongst the clerks and students of medieval cities, it is perhaps no wonder that, when the rapier comes along, they are amongst the most vociferous about their right to carry them as a mark of their dignity.[111]

Whilst men might not have been wearing swords as a matter of course, that did not preclude them owning them, or knowing how to use them. The prohibitions on

---

[108] Dupuis, 'Organisation and Regulation of Fencing', pp. 236–7.

[109] Laura Crombie, *Archery and Crossbow Guilds in Medieval Flanders, 1300–1500* (Woodbridge, 2016).

[110] See Jean Chandler, 'The Guild and the Swordsman', *Acta Periodica Duellatorum*, 2.1 (2014), pp. 27–66. There is much more work to be done on this subject, tracing the development of the fencing guilds through the late Middle Ages into the Renaissance and trying to understand the relationship between them and the other urban guilds.

[111] Tlusty, *The Martial Ethic in Early Modern Germany, passim.*

buckler-play and schools of fence passed by civic and university authorities tell of a popular pastime of swordsmanship amongst those who were not of knightly rank, one pursued for entertainment rather than military necessity. As we shall see in the next chapter, it is an irony that it is this non-knightly and ludic culture of swordsmanship that provides us with some of our strongest evidence used as a source for understanding swordsmanship – the actual use of a sword – in the high and late Middle Ages.

5

Learning the Sword

WHEN IT COMES TO understanding the way in which the medieval military elite learnt to use their weapons, and particularly the sword, we have precious little information. The common understanding is that at a young age a nobleman would become squire to a knight, usually a family member, serving a kind of apprenticeship by acting as a servant whilst also learning the craft of war. Such a statement leaves a lot unexplained, however. Who undertook this training? Were there formal classes run by a 'master-at-arms' as is often depicted in the Hollywood epics like *Prince Valiant* or *The Black Shield of Falworth*, both of which depict rows of uniformed squires receiving bellowed instructions from a grizzled veteran, with all the precision of modern military drill?[1] What of royal children, who were not farmed out to be squires? Who within the household looked to their training?

Our sources are almost silent on the subject. The biographies of individual knights tend to skip over their childhood years, unless to pronounce them as prodigies of strength or maturity.[2] Sir John Hardyng, a fourteenth-century chronicler and knight, does outline the education of a young nobleman, but all he has to say about war is that at sixteen he is 'to werray and to wage'...

> To juste and ryde, and castels to assayle,
> To scarmyse als, and make sykur courage;
> And every day his armure to assay
> In fete of armes with some of his meyne,
> His might to preve, and what that he may do may
> Iff that we were in such a jupertee
> Of were by falle, that by necessite
> He might algates with wapyns hym defende:

---

[1]   *Prince Valiant*, dir. Henry Hathaway (Twentieth Century Fox, 1954). *The Black Shield of Falworth*, dir. Rudolph Maté (Universal Studios, 1954).

[2]   The biographer of William Marshal ignores his subject's eight years as a squire, saying 'I do not wish to continue to devote my skill not narrating the time during which William was a squire' (*History of William Marshal*, ed. A.J. Holden, trans. S. Gregory, vol. 1 (London, 2002), pp. 40/1). On what material culture can (and cannot) tell us about the training of youths for war, see Robert C. Woosnam-Savage, '"He's Armed Without that's Innocent Within" A Short Note on a newly Acquired Medieval Sword for a Child', *Arms & Armour: Journal of the Royal Armouries*, 5.1 (2008), pp. 84–95

> Thus should he lerne in his priorite
> His wapyns alle in armes to dispende.[3]

This suggests that the boy effectively learns by doing, by taking part in battle and campaign. But how was he taught the basic skills?

Romance and epic literature rarely dwell on the childhood and youth of their heroes either. In the romance of Perceval, where the wild and untamed protagonist is taught knighthood by Gornament, we get an impressionistic image of a knight's training. Gornament's pedagogical approach is to demonstrate techniques, watched by the young Perceval, and then to get the young man to copy him. This Perceval is able to do without difficulty for, whilst Gornament has perfected his technique by 'practising since boyhood', the techniques come naturally to Perceval 'since Nature was his teacher and his heart was set upon it, nothing for which Nature and his heart strove could be difficult'.[4]

Interestingly, whilst Perceval is ignorant of riding, and handling lance and shield, but has a natural ability, the young Welshman confidently tells Gornament that none knows more about defending themselves with a sword 'because I often practiced, hitting pads and shields at my mother's house until I was weary from it'.[5] Given that Perceval's mother has been trying to shield him from his knightly heritage, his ability to train at her house reinforces what we saw in the last chapter of swordplay; that it was not a peculiarly chivalric skill. It also seems to suggest that swordplay was not something that even the naturally-gifted Perceval could master without practice.[6]

Perceval's reference to 'hitting pads and shields' reflects one of the most repeated pieces of written advice on training with the sword outside of the high and late medieval *fechtbücher* traditions. A number of general texts of instruction on chivalry and princely conduct make reference to training for combat as being an important part of being a good lord, and encourage their readers to train at the 'pell', a wooden post, about man-height. The advice is generally that the pell is attacked using a wooden sword and a wicker shield of double weight, to strike it in the 'head' or the 'legs' and advancing and retreating around it as if it were a real opponent.

The advice, however, is not new. Their source is the fifth-century military commentator Vegetius.[7] His *De Re Militari*, dealing with everything from the selection of men of the right temperament to logistics and strategic planning, was widely read in the Middle Ages, and used as the classical authority on military matters.[8] Often these medieval renderings of Vegetius' wisdom are dismissed as being

---

[3] John Hardyng, quoted in R.P. Dunn-Pattison, *The Black Prince* (London, 1910), p. 17.
[4] Chrétien de Troyes, 'The Story of the Grail (Perceval)', pp. 399–400.
[5] *Ibid*, p. 400.
[6] This need for heroes to diligently practice their swordsmanship is something seen in Anglo-Scandinavian heroic literature. See Sixt Wetzler, '*Combat in Saga Literature: Traces of martial arts in medieval Iceland*', Unpublished PhD thesis (Tübingen, 2017), pp. 105–6.
[7] Vegetius discusses the use of the pell in training legionaries in Book One of his *De Re Militari* (*Vegetius: Epitome of Military Science*, trans. N.P. Milner (Liverpool, 1996), p. 12).
[8] On the use of Vegetius' text in the Middle Ages, see Christopher Allmand, *The De Re Militari of Vegetius: The Reception, Transmission and Legacy of a Roman Text in the Middle Ages* (Cambridge, 2011).

of no practical value, simply a medieval author cribbing a classical authority for an air of *gravitas*. However, closer readings show that many of these works do add their own glosses, theories, and innovations applicable to their own circumstances. The fifteenth-century English verse translation of *De Re Militari*, titled *Knyghthode and Bataile*, is an example of this, with new material being added to reflect the primacy and sacred nature of chivalry and the chivalric class.[9] The author's description of the use of the pell, however, is only marginally different from that of Vegetius.[10] Like his classical authority, the use of sword and shield weighing twice that of that used in combat is advised, as is practising making cuts to head, arms, hands and legs, and advancing and retreating and attacking flanks, as if against a real enemy. The author also infers the primacy of the thrust over the cut, as does Vegetius. The only slight variation is that whilst Vegetius says that the recruit attacked the pell 'as though it were an armed opponent', *Knyghthode and Bataile* declares 'It is the Turk: though he be sleyn, noon harm is', which Steven Bruso suggests is an admonition to have the correct psychological frame of mind, but which also reflects a fairly typical demonisation of the infidel.[11] Similarly, the *Konungs Skuggsjá* – 'The King's Mirror', a Norwegian text from around 1300 which provides instruction to young men seeking a career at court or in the Church – repeats the Vegetian advice to practice against a pell, but also tells them to go and find a well-trained 'foreigner or compatriot' to practice sword strokes with.[12]

Perhaps the most oft-used example of a medieval knightly training regime lies in the biography of Jean le Maigre, the Marshal Boucicaut. This fifteenth-century paragon of knightly prowess not only trained with double-weight weapons, but in full harness would run a mile every day, vault into the saddle from a standing start, climb hand-over-hand the underside of a ladder or the space between two close-built walls by bracing himself against them.[13] Whilst such feats are quite achievable, they were included by the Marshal's biographer to show an extraordinary physical prowess, beyond the norm for most of the chivalric community. As Craig Taylor has rightly

---

[9]   *Knyghthode and Bataile* survives in three manuscript versions – Pembroke College, Cambridge, MS 243; London, British Library, MS Cotton Titus A.xxiii; and Oxford, Bodleian Library, MS Ashmole 45.1. See *Knyghthode and Bataile*, eds. Roman Dyboski and Z.M. Arend (London, 1935) and *The Earliest English Translation of Vegetius De Re Militari*, ed. G. Lester (Heidelberg, 1988). The latest edition is *Of Knyghthode and Bataile*, ed. Trevor Russell Smith and Michael Livingston (Kalamazoo, MI, 2021). See too Catherine Nall, *Reading and War in Fifteenth-Century England: From Lydgate to Malory* (Cambridge, 2012), pp. 11–47 and 114–38.

[10] J. Clements, 'On the Pell', *ARMA: The Association for Renaissance Martial Arts*, n.d. http://www.thearma.org/essays/pell/pellhistory.htm#.XpHlfchKjDY (accessed 1 August 2021). Steven Bruso, 'Bodies Hardened for War: Knighthood in Fifteenth-Century England', *Journal of Medieval and Early Modern Studies*, 47.2 (2017), pp. 255–77.

[11] Bruso, 'Bodies Hardened', p. 269.

[12] 'hvart sæm hælldr er ut lænndzkr eða herlænzkr.' *Speculum Regale: Ein altnorwegisher Dialog, nach Cod. Arnmagn. 243 Fol. B*, ed. O. Brenner (Munich, 1881), p. 99. Brent Hanner, 'The King's Mirror as a Medieval Military Manual', *De Re Militari*, n.d. https://web.archive.org/web/20110805101755/http://www.deremilitari.org/resources/articles/hanner.htm (accessed 1 August 2021). See also Wetzler, 'Combat in Saga Literature', pp.105 *ff*.

[13] *The Chivalric Biography of Boucicaut, Jean II le Meingre*, trans. Craig and Jane H.M. Taylor (Woodbridge, 2016), pp. 30–31.

Figure 23. A sword designed for hunting boar, c.1530–1570. (Royal Armouries IX.5391).

pointed out, the biography was never intended as a treatise on knightly conduct or martial training, but was, in fact, part of a carefully orchestrated campaign to depict Boucicaut as a paragon of knightly virtue at a time when his career had seen some major setbacks.[14] What is being described is not weapons' handling or combat techniques, but what one might consider exercises for physical conditioning.[15]

Two further chivalric pastimes are often cited as serving as training for combat. Hunting provided experience and practice in horsemanship, and encouraged an appreciation of terrain, both in terms of moving across it as well as some tactical understanding. It encouraged courage and physical fitness too. Hardyng suggested that at fourteen a noble's son should:

> to the felde… At hunte the dere, and catch an hardynesse.
> For dere to hunt and slea, and se them blede,
> Ane hardyment gyfffith to his corage,
> And also in his wytte to takyth hede
> Ymagininge to take thaym at avauntage.[16]

Whilst it may be claimed that the act of hunting, and the ritual butchery of the prey that followed served to accustom the individual to killing and death, it is also the case that the killing of animal is a different proposition from killing a man.

Hunting also offered familiarisation with weapons, obviously. The main hunting weapons were bows and crossbows and spears, but swords might also be used. Gaston Phoébus, the Count of Foix, who wrote a treatise on hunting in 1387, suggested that slaying a boar with a sword was the greatest of all hunting feats, suggesting that the sword used should have a four-foot blade, with a long *ricasso* to prevent the hunter cutting their own leg.[17] By the fifteenth century *estocs* – stiff and narrow bladed swords designed for the thrust – were being used, and by the opening of the sixteenth century a form had been developed specifically for use against boar, with a tip that widened into a leaf-shaped spearhead, and lugs to prevent the blade embedding too deep into the beast, keeping it at 'safe' distance from the wielder, and requiring a

[14] Craig Taylor, *A Virtuous Knight: Defending Marshal Boucicaut (Jean II Le Meingre, 1366–1421)* (Woodbridge, 2019).

[15] Brusso, 'Bodies Hardened', p. 266.

[16] John Hardyng, in Dunn-Pattison, *The Black Prince*, p. 17.

[17] Gaston Phoébus, *Livre de la chasse*. BnF MS 616, fol. 94r–94v.

different skillset from regular swordplay to use it effectively.[18] Again, it must be said that no matter how dangerous hunting boar was (and indeed still is) there was a difference between wielding a sword against a boar and wielding it against a human opponent with a sword or spear of their own. Hunting might serve as some preparation for the rigours of campaign and combat, but it was *not* campaign or combat.

The other method by which the knight supposedly learnt his trade was the tournament. Almost every historian who talks about the tournament or joust will at some point indicate either that its purpose was training for war or, at the very least, that its origins lay in such a purpose.[19] Similarly, Richard the Lionheart's overturning of his father's ban on tournaments in 1194 is often explained as being a response to the poor quality of English knighthood, who lacked the opportunities to train available to their continental counterparts who were active on the tournament circuit.[20] Some have even suggested a link between the tournament and the so-called 'cavalry games' – the *hippika gymnasia* – of the classical Roman cavalry.

The line between the medieval tournament and the classical Roman *hippika gymnasia* is a tenuous one, and even if the tournament was a relatively safe (but not wholly risk-free) environment in which knights such as William Marshal could hone their skills, it is not where they would have learnt those skills in the first place. From their earliest appearance tournaments were spectacles for the chivalric elite, and a place to show one's individual prowess, that elite's currency.[21] To appear unprepared and lacking in ability not only put the fighter at risk of capture, injury, or death, but also might result in his forfeiture of horse and harness, at great expense, as well as damage his reputation. It certainly was not the place at which one learnt to ride, or to use the lance, much less the sword. Roger de Hoveden wrote that 'A youth must have seen his blood flow and felt his teeth crack under the blow of his adversary and have been thrown to the ground twenty times. Thus, will he be able to face real war with the hope of victory'.[22] To my mind, Hoveden is describing the tournament field as a place where youths learn to endure the physical exertions and pain of being in combat. It is a place to test their mettle, harden themselves for the realities of war. This is not the same as learning martial skills. Crouch argues that the individual joust

---

[18]   A prime example of such a sword is in the Royal Armouries, dating to the middle third of the sixteenth century (Royal Armouries IX.5391). See Fig. 16.
[19]   See, for example, Keen, *Chivalry*, p. 83; R. Barber and J. Barker, *Tournaments: Jousts, Chivalry and Pageants in the Middle Ages* (Woodbridge, 2000); Nigel Saul, *For Honour and Fame: Chivalry in England, 1066–1500* (London, 2011), pp. 15–16; Steven Muhlberger, *Jousts and Tournaments: Charny and the Rules for Chivalric Sport in Fourteenth-Century France* (Union City, CA, 2002), p. 19; Alan V. Murray, 'Introduction: From Mass Combat to Field of Cloth of Gold', *The Medieval Tournament as Spectacle: Tourneys, Jousts and Pas d'Armes, 1100–1600*, ed. Alan V. Murray and Karen Watts (Woodbridge, 2020), p. 1. For a slightly more nuanced view, see David Crouch, *Tournament* (London, 2005), pp. 3 *ff.*
[20]   Keen, *Chivalry*, p. 88. The truth is that Richard's primary concern was securing a lucrative revenue stream for the Exchequer and ensuring royal oversight of an event that was often the locus for unrest and intrigue, rather than a desire to see the quality of English knighthood (many of whom were travelling across the Channel in pursuit of tournament action).
[21]   Almost everyone cited in note 19, above, will make this point too.
[22]   Roger of Hoveden, *Chronica*, ed. W. Stubbs, vol. 2 (London, 1869), pp.166–7.

developed as a means of better showcasing individual skill in front of an audience, but also to enable younger knights to demonstrate their prowess without becoming easy prey to more experienced warriors, again indicating that the tournament was no place to 'learn the trade'.[23] When William Marshal's biographer describes his first engagement, it is clear the hero does not lack martial skills, just the judgement to hold on to his captives once he subdues them.[24]

Of course, there was no clear-cut distinction between training and sport, and the two intermingled. Every combat helped the knight to improve.[25] A clear merging of the two is to be seen in a passage from the remarkable writings of the fifteenth-century King Duarte I of Portugal. In his *Livra da Cartuxa* he writes that:

> On certain days at the hour of tierce we do training, and the training is as follows. The trainee gets fully armed and runs up a slope for a goodly distance as hard as he can. Then he returns home, and there we have good iron armor for visitors to use, and spears, axes, and swords of wood: and when the trainee wants to spar with someone, he gets equipped with arms half again as heavy as those he would actually use on the day of battle. The sparring that he does with these people allows him to learn techniques, defences, and attacks that others know. And if nobody comes for eight or ten days to train with him, he can train with whomever he will. This practice allows him to develop good breath, and to learn from various people in feats of arms.[26]

Whilst this does seem to indicate a collective and regular exercise, and echoes something of Boucicault's practice, the reference to sparring against visitors and that one of the benefits is 'to learn from various people in *feats of arms*' (my emphasis) suggests that there was also an element of competition and display of prowess, something ludic and of the tournament, about the activities.[27]

One might argue, of course, that all the various forms of martial 'play' served as a means of practising martial skills in the same way that a 'friendly' sports match is played not only for the prestige of winning but also to help iron out any issues before the commencement of the campaign season proper.[28] This is undoubtedly true. What it does not do, though, is to 'train' the knight in either new tactics or new individual combat skills. There is no formal learning in these activities. There is no teaching of new skills, nor any sense of *praxis* – a cycle of theory, action, and reflection – indicative of a structured process for embedding and improving martial technique.

Another indication of the training regime of late medieval noblemen comes from the *Flos Duellatorum* of Fiore de'i Liberi. In his *Fechtbuch* written at the very end of the fourteenth century, this north Italian fencing master lays out his credentials. Fiore

[23] Crouch, *Tournament*, p. 115
[24] *History of William Marshal*, vol. 1, pp. 42–61.
[25] At least every combat he was able to walk away from.
[26] Duarte, *Leal Conselheiro*, ed. M.H. Lopes de Castro and A. Botelho (Lisbon, 1998), p. 270, quoted in *The Book of Horsemanship by Duarte I of Portugal*, trans. Jeffrey Forgeng (Woodbridge, 2016), pp. 41–2. There is a similarity here with the advice in the *konungs skuggsjá*, discussed above.
[27] On the 'feat of arms' (*pas d'armes*) as a form of chivalric combat, see the work of Steven Muhlberger, *Deeds of Arms: Formal Combats in the Late Fourteenth Century* (Union City, CA, 2005).
[28] As Caroline Palmer has pointed out (pers. comm.) income is also a factor in such 'friendlies'. It was almost certainly a consideration in the Middle Ages too.

claims that in his youth he studied under a number of masters from Germany and Italy, especially one 'Master Johane, called "Suveno", who was a student of Nicholai of Toblem in Mexiniensis diocese', as well as learning from 'many princes, dukes, marquises, counts, and from countless others in diverse places and provinces'.[29] That he was learning not only from formal masters but also from the nobility in general may be the best intimation we have of informal learning amongst the martial elite in the manner encouraged by Duarte I and the writer of the *Konungs Skuggsjá*.

He tells us that having learnt the art of fighting from many German and Italian masters, he was then retained by many 'great lords, princes, dukes, marquises and counts, knights and squires' to teach them the art of fencing and combat at the barriers, and that he did so for 'many Italians and Germans and other noblemen who were obliged to fight at the barrier, as well as to numerous noblemen who did not actually compete'.[30] He goes on to name six of them: Piero del Verde (an italicisation of the name Peter von Grünen, a German *condotierro*), Niccolo Voriçilino (possibly Nicholas von Urslingen, an unknown figure but potentially related to another German *condotierro* Werner von Urslingen), Galeazzo de capitani da Grimello, or da Mantova (Galeazzo Gonzaga, an Italian *condotierro* whom Fiore records as having fought a combat against Boucicaut), Lancilotto Beccaria, Gioanino de Bavo (possibly the French knight Jean de Bayeux), and Sir Açço da Castell Barcho (Azzano Francesco di Castelbarco, another *condotierro*).[31]

In all six cases, Fiore was training them '*combater in sbara*' – 'combat in the barriers' – that is to say, in each case he was training them for a formal *pas d'armes*, or duel of honour, not for warfare. Each of the men listed seems to have been an experienced warrior already. Fiore was not being retained to teach any of them the basics for sword play, but in order to train them in the 'wondrous secrets' of the art of combat that he had learnt, 'at great personal cost and expense' that, knowing them, 'make you invincible, for victory comes easily to a man who has the skill and mastery [of the temper of iron, and the qualities of each weapon for defence and offence in matters of mortal combat]'.[32]

The 'system' that Fiore lays out in his text, beginning with grappling and proceeding through a range of weapons including dagger, sword, lance, and axe, unarmoured and in armour, dismounted and mounted, lays out techniques for this same, particular style of combat. They deal with combat against a single opponent, making no reference to needing to be aware of the wider situation around the combatants, or any suggestion that the pupil might be fighting alongside a comrade.[33]

[29] Translation of the Pisani Dossi manuscript by Michael Chidester, https://www.wiktenauer.com/wiki/Fiore_de%27i_Liberi#Preface (accessed 1 August 2021). Neither Johane "Suveno" nor Nicholai of Toblem can be identified.

[30] Translation by Colin Hatcher of the 'Getty manuscript' (J. Paul Getty Museum MS Ludwig XV 13) of Fiore de'I Liberi's *Fior di Battaglia*, taken from https://www.wiktenauer.com/wiki/Fiore_de%27i_Liberi#Preface (accessed 1 August 2021).

[31] *Ibid.*

[32] *Ibid.*

[33] On the five occasions where more than one opponent is depicted – 2 swordsmen against a master with a dagger, 3 against the master using the sword in one hand, 3 against the master using the

The employment of a fencing master specifically for the purpose of training for trial by battle or a duel of honour appears to have been a common one by the fifteenth century. The fifteenth-century German master Hans Talhoffer is recorded in several cities in southern Germany, Austria, and Switzerland, as having been contracted to train men in preparation for judicial combats.[34] All four of his *fechtbücher* reflect fighting in a variety of such combats, again in armour and unarmoured, mounted and on foot.[35] Alongside techniques for fighting with the *messer*, he provides techniques for fighting with sword (both single-handed in combination with a buckler, and the longsword), dagger, spear, pollaxe, and flail.[36] He also has instructions for fighting with full length and spiked shields, which seem to have been a form of judicial duel, and a series of plates depicting a husband and wife combating each other; the husband up to his waist in a hole and wielding a club, the wife standing on the ground above him, with a stone wrapped in a veil.[37] Talhoffer incorporates this advice on the practicalities of combat with instructions relating to the ritualised nature of the engagements, specifying the diet and training regime to be held to in the weeks leading up to the fight.[38]

In London in the autumn of 1446 three men – Philip Treher, Master Hugh Payne, and John Latimer – were appointed by the Privy Council to prepare armourer William Catour and his apprentice John Davy for a trial by combat to determine the truth of an accusation of treason made by Davy against Catour.[39] These three men were to teach 'certain pointes of armis' to the two appellants. Interestingly Philip Treher, who was appointed Davy's trainer, had served in a similar role for the Prior of the Hospitaller Abbey at Kilmainham, a man named Thomas FitzGerald, in the combat he was to undertake in support of his claim of treason against the Earl of Ormonde, and was to be one of a number of men assigned as counsel to John Lyalton ahead of his combat against Robert Norreys, who he had accused of treason, in 1453.[40]

---

sword in two hands, 2 wielding spears against a master with staff and dagger, and 3 mounted combatants against the master on foot with a spear – the aim is to show how the same defence can be used against a range of different blows rather than to suggest how the master can defeat multiple opponents at once.

[34] Hans-Peter Hils, *Meister Johann Liechtenauers Kunst des langen Schwertes* (Frankfurt-am-Main, 1985), p. 176.

[35] There are a small number of images directed at fighting mounted spear against crossbow, and two where an individual with sword and buckler faces two opponents, neither of which would suggest a duel or tournament bout, but these are very much the exceptions rather than the rule.

[36] https://en.wikipedia.org/wiki/Hans_Talhoffer#Works (accessed 1 August 2021).

[37] Det Kongelige Bibliotek MS Thott.290.2°, Fols. 80r–84r. https://wiktenauer.com/wiki/Hans_Talhoffer#First_Manuscript_.281448.29 (accessed 26 March 2022). Talhoffer, *Medieval Combat*, pp. 242–50.

[38] See Daniel Jaquet, 'Six weeks to prepare for combat: Instructions and practices from the fight books at the end of the Middle Ages, a note on ritualised single combats', *Killing and being Killed: Bodies in Battle*, ed. Jörg Rogge (Mainz, 2018), pp. 131–64.

[39] Jacob Henry Deacon, '"Falsely Accused by the Villain"? A Fishy Trial by Combat in Fifteenth-Century London', *Martial Culture in Medieval Town*, 20/11/2019, https://martcult.hypotheses.org/404 (accessed 1 August 2021). *Proceedings and Ordinances of the Privy Council of England*, ed. Sir Harris Nicolas. Vol. VI (London 1837), pp. 56, 59 and 129–30.

[40] *Ibid.*

Unlike Fiore's clients none of these men appear to have had a martial background, so it is less of a surprise that the court should seek to support them with some technical know-how, lest the proceedings become a farce.[41]

What Fiore, Talhoffer, and Treher were employed to do was not to teach men how to sword fight. They were there to prepare men for a specific engagement in a particular format. In Fiore's case his *condotierri* clients must have had a solid grounding in skill at arms – they had made their careers in combat. What they wanted from him was specialist training, pre-fight conditioning, perhaps, something that would give them an edge (if you will excuse the pun). Similarly, Treher was being employed by the courts specifically to prepare litigants for judicial combat. His clients, however, had no obvious martial training, and so would have needed a greater degree of preparation, mental and physical. It is questionable just how much of this Treher would be able to provide in the short time he had between being employed and the combat taking place, especially as he was not a professional swordsman, but recorded by the court as a 'fyshmonger' by trade.[42]

The employment of Treher and, to a lesser extent, Fiore, as a fencing master might make us reconsider what we have assumed about the urban fencing community that we met in the last chapter. Treher was undoubtedly part of the same culture as Roger le Skirmisour, John Tourner, Richard le Bulkele, or William de Northamptone, but his employment by the Privy Council offers a counter-narrative to that of the antisocial buckler-player. Rather than being perceived of as an enemy of law and order, and a bad influence on society, his expertise (for which he was being paid the handsome sum of twenty pounds) was being used within the legal system at the highest level.[43] Fiore, on the other hand, sits closer to the more traditional view of noble swordsmanship: a professional like Roger le Skirmisour, but with noble roots and a noble clientele. What connects him to the non-noble, urban culture of swordsmanship (and, by association, those non-noble masters of fencing schools) are the manuscripts he produced on the subject.

The Fechtbücher Tradition

Thus far we have merely touched upon the one source that would seem the most obvious for an understanding of how swordsmanship was taught: the fight manuals or *fechtbücher*.

The term *Fechtbuch* (literally 'fight-book') is generally used as a catch-all for any manuscript that includes material of instruction on the practice of martial arts in medieval and early modern western Europe. Some 300 or more have been catalogued

[41] As it happened, in the case of Catour and Davy a farce was indeed what it became. Catour arrived too drunk to put up a proper fight, and was killed by Davy, stripped of his armour and left in the lists overnight until his formal 'execution' for treason – his body was drawn through the streets, and strung up before being decapitated, the head being placed on a spike on London bridge, whilst the rest of the corpse was displayed outside the Tower. (*Ibid.*)
[42] *Ibid.*
[43] *Proceedings and Ordinances of the Privy Council of England*, p. 59.

Figure 24. A leaf from I.33, the earliest of the *fechtbücher* (late 13th or early 14th century), showing a female fighter named Walpurgis (on the left) sparring with a priest (on the right). (Royal Armouries RAR 33).

at the present time, from the fourteenth to the eighteenth centuries.[44] Within this corpus is a huge variety of sources, varying immensely in composition and purpose. There is a marked difference between Fiore's full-blown system of fighting, written as he himself attests in his introduction from a desire to be remembered and as a statement of his credentials, and the pieces and fragments of swordplay found in commonplace books like that of 'the Pol Hausbuch' (Germanisches Nationalmuseum, HS3227a), the fifteenth-century English *fechtbücher* fragments, which are copied alongside recipes, magic rituals, astrological information, bits of poetry, and romance.[45] Different again is Gregor Erhart's sixteenth-century compilation of fighting texts, drawn from eighteen distinct works spanning nearly two centuries of practice.[46] ,

The earliest work to be given the epithet *fechtbuch* is Royal Armouries MS I.33, also called 'the Tower Fechtbuch', 'Walpurgis Fechtbuch' or 'Luitger Fechtbuch'.[47] There is an inevitability about the study of I.33. It has an almost gravitational pull, drawing researchers towards it like a moth to a flame. It is the earliest of the *fechtbücher* by nearly 100 years, true, but that is something of an excuse. It is opulently illustrated in a style that is quintessentially of its period and, unlike any other fight-book has the feel of an illuminated manuscript. The figures are characterful and detailed in a way that Fiore or Talhoffer's figures are not. Their stooping, 'hip-hinged' figures, swathed in pleated gowns with voluminous sleeves, and their playful expressions, give them an air of whimsy that belies the serious nature of the subject matter – combat with sword and buckler. The individuals have personality. The student, the priest, and the woman Walpurgis stand out as distinct characters in a work that has a narrative quality. This has led people to weave stories around the manuscript, using its contents to fill in for the absence of any solid knowledge of its origins or purpose. Thus, the priest becomes the manuscript's creator, and a biography is woven about him. He had once been a knight but, at the end of a long military career had retired to a monastery. However, he was unable to give up his martial past and so taught swordplay to maintain his skills.[48] The appearance of a woman – who appears to be named Walpurgis – inevitably fuels the debate about whether medieval women could or did fight with swords, although no-one, as yet, has presented a clear and compelling narrative as to who she might be.[49]

---

44 Daniel Jaquet, Audrey Tuaillon Demésy, and Iason-Eleftherios Tzouriadis, *Historical European Martial Arts: An International Overview* (Chungcheongbuk-do, 2020), pp. 10–13, indicate that the actual number is almost impossible to judge, despite several attempts to list the corpus of material available. *Late Medieval and Early modern Fight Books* has a (already outdated, as the authors recognise themselves) list of some 74 individual manuscript works and 35 printed ones from 1305 to 1630.

45 For HS3227a, see Eric Burkart, 'The Autograph of an Erudite Martial Artist: A Close Reading of Nuremberg, Germanisches Nationalmuseum, Hs. 3227a', *Late Medieval and Early Modern Fight Books*, pp. 451–80. There are three recognised English manuscripts that deal with fencing: 'The *Man Who Wol*' (BL Harl. Ms 3542), BL Add. Ms 39564 and BL Cotton MS Titus A. XXV.

46 Erhart's manual is in the collection of the Glasgow museums, Ms 1939.65.354.

47 The newest and most authoritative edition of this work is *The Medieval Art of Swordsmanship: Royal Armouries I.33*, ed. Jeffrey Forgeng (Leeds, 2018).

48 This was the belief of Heinrich von Günterode, writing in the sixteenth century (*De Veris Principiis Artis Dimicatorie.* (Wittenberg, 1579), C3rv), and this line of argument has been followed by others.

49 See Fig. 23. For discussions of Walpurgis, see Valerie Eads and Rebecca L.R. Garber, 'Amazon,

I.33's attractiveness belies its practicality. Despite being a popular resource for the HEMA community, I.33 is not easy to learn from. There is no obvious structure to the series of plays (which is not helped by the fact that, at some point in its history the manuscript has been rebound out of order and with quires missing).[50] It contains no fundamentals of the art. Indeed, at various points the text suggests that it offers techniques for combating the 'ordinary fighters', or *generales dimicatores*.[51] At another it tells us of a technique that 'will be quite rare, as no-one uses it except the Priest or his young protégés, i.e. his students'.[52] Throughout, the work is littered with technical terms particular to swordplay, without explanation.[53] From this we must conclude that the manuscript's creator assumed its audience would already have the fundamentals, and could concentrate on the advanced techniques which distinguished his method from that of ordinary fencers. For the modern practitioner seeking to follow the approach to swordsmanship of I.33 this leaves them at a disadvantage, the more so because its fighting style is different and distinctive from most later forms of sword and buckler combat, precluding the use of the latter to fill in the gaps in the older 'system'.[54]

For all the focus upon it, I.33 remains an outlier in the canon of *fechtbücher*. By dint of its age, the approach it takes to combat, and its terminology it does not fit easily with those works of the late fourteenth century and beyond (all of which seem to be connected parts of a common tradition of medieval martial arts). However, its format does fit with that tradition, and the choice of the scholar, the cleric and the woman provide a foundation stone on which to build an understanding of where these texts drew inspiration for their pedagogy and, as a result, offers some answer to the question of how swordplay was learnt and by whom.

The illustrations that have served to make I.33 so iconic have also caused scholars the most problems. As has been noted, they dominate the manuscript and their vibrancy and character make it all too easy to try interpreting them literally. Perhaps, counterintuitively, this makes them less important to the text. If they are really the author and his pupils (or his pupil and a benefactress, as Forgeng suggests Walpurgis

allegory, swordswoman, saint? The Walpurgis images in Royal Armouries MS I.33', *"Can These Bones Come to Life?" Insights from Reconstruction, Reenactment and Re-creation*, ed. Ken Mondschein (Wheaton, IL, 2014), pp. 5–23, Julia Gräf, 'Fighting in women's clothes. The pictorial evidence of Walpurgis in Ms. I.33', *Acta Periodica Duellatorum*, 5.2 (2015), pp. 47–71, and 'Walpurgis: The first lady of traditional Fencing', *Cote du Golfe School of Fencing*, 10 October 2018, https://traditionalfencing.wordpress.com/2018/10/10/walpurgis-the-first-lady-of-traditional-fencing/ (accessed 1 August 2021).

50 James Hester, 'A few leaves short of a quire: Is the "Tower Fechtbuch" incomplete?' *Arms and Armour*, 9 (2012), pp. 20–4. Fanny Binard and Daniel Jaquet, 'Investigation on the collation of the first fight book (Leeds, Royal Armouries, Ms I.33)', *Acta Periodica Duellatorum*, 4.1 (2015), pp. 3–21. *The Medieval Art of Swordsmanship*, pp. 23–6.

51 Royal Armouries Ms RAR.33, fols. 27 and 49. *The Medieval Art of Swordsmanship*, pp. 86, 130.

52 Royal Armouries Ms RAR.33, fol.7. *The Medieval Art of Swordsmanship*, p. 46.

53 Forgeng writes that 'Some parts of the text will probably never be comprehensible, as they assume a readership possessing a technical knowledge that is no longer available to us'. *The Medieval Art of Swordsmanship*, p. 27.

54 *The Medieval Art of Swordsmanship*, p. 18.

might be) then, it might be argued that, beyond visually demonstrating a technique (something they do imperfectly), they have no purpose in the text other than vanity.[55] If, however, the two male figures are taken as archetypes of learning – the teacher and the pupil – then they become much more integrated into the pedagogical approach of the manuscript, reinforcing its scholastic approach to the subject.

The choice of characters used in the illustrations places the work in the tradition of scholastic disputation. The *sacerdos* teaches the *scolaris* (or, as he may also be termed *cleintulus* or *discipulus*).[56] They are engaged in a disputation, a series of exchanges – play and counterplay: a dialectic of steel if you will.[57] There is a metaphorical element to the manuscript's protagonists, and its creator has chosen to couch its teachings in academic terms. This is reinforced by the language in which the manuscript is written. The bulk of it is Latin, but the technical terminology is given in German. This would suggest that the language of the fencing master (and of the art of swordplay) was the vernacular.[58] The use of Latin, then, becomes a becomes a deliberate choice, part of what Jeffrey Forgeng has called, 'the fictive appearance of serving as tools for learning the art', and placing it within a tradition of formal pedagogy.[59]

That choice of language also served to restrict access to the text, by making it comprehensible only to those who had a formal education.[60] This not only prevented it being understood by commoners, but also, arguably, by the nobility, who were often only functionally literate in Latin, and more used to a secular literature that was invariably written in the vernacular.[61]

One of the tropes in the writings of fencing masters is that their art was to be kept secret, not only from their competitors but also from commoners. Fiore writes in his treatise that the knowledge it contains should be kept secret, especially from the '*rurales*', the country folk who, having been created by Heaven 'of obtuse sense and inadequate of agility, to carry loads like beasts of burden' were not fit to learn such

---

[55] *Ibid*, p. 8.
[56] All three terms are used to describe the scholar, and all three are contemporary terms for a student, which is significant for reasons we shall see below.
[57] Forgeng expands on this in the introduction to his translation of I.33. (*Ibid*, p. 19).
[58] On the technical terminology of the *fechtbücher*, see Jan-Dirk Müller, 'Bild—Vers—Prosakommentar am Beispiel von Fechtbüchern. Probleme der Verschriftlichung einer schriftlosen Praxis', *Pragmatische Schriftlichkeit im Mittelalter. Erscheinungsformen und Entwicklungsstufen*, ed. H. Keller et al. (Munich, 1992), pp. 251–82, Matthias Johannes Bauer, 'Fechten Lehren, mitt verborgen vnd verdeckten worten', *Das Schwert – Symbol und Waffe*, and 'Teaching How to Fight with Encrypted Words: Linguistic Aspects of German Fencing and Wrestling Treatises of the Middle Ages and Early Modern Times', *Late Medieval and Early Modern Fight Books*, pp. 47–61.
[59] J. Forgeng, 'Owning the Art: The German Fechtbuch Tradition', *The Noble Art of the Sword: Fashion and Fencing in Renaissance Europe 1520–1630*, ed. Tobias Capwell (London, 2012), p. 170.
[60] It is ironic that today the reverse is true, and it is easier to decipher the Latin than it is the German vernacular.
[61] This is not to suggest that the knightly class were wholly ignorant of Latin. As Martin Aurell has argued, the knightly class had access to and contact with clerks and clergy, and a few would have had some formal education. See Martin Aurell, *The Lettered Knight: Knowledge and Aristocratic Behaviour in the Twelfth and Thirteenth Centuries*, trans. Jean-Charles Khalifa and Jeremy Price (Budapest, 2017).

skills.[62] A similar attitude is present in a number of the manuscripts drawing on the supposed teachings of the German master Johannes Liechtenauer, where the reader is told that the art is recorded in 'hidden and secret words' so that not everyone will understand it, in order to prevent the art from becoming common, and not held with the respect that it is due.[63]

Fiore himself was particularly circumspect about his teaching. He taught privately or swore to secrecy those few he allowed to watch, and fought duels against other masters who, jealous of his secrets, questioned his ability.[64] In part this made sensible business practice. The techniques he taught, and the manner in which he taught them were his stock in trade. In the relatively small world of the north Italian martial aristocracy, he might very quickly lose his market were his techniques to be broadcast to even a few friends of his pupils or picked up by rival masters.

The statements about keeping the swordplay out of the hands of commoners might be taken to suggest that the likes of Fiore were talking to the nobility and upper echelons of society in their works. They seem to be concerned about keeping the noble and chivalric art of swordsmanship out of the hands of those boorish and low-born, the commoners who might be perceived as a threat were they to be trained in fighting arts. However, this requirement for secrecy does not appear in the genre of chivalric literature. There is no request to keep the contents of the *Konungs Skuggsjá* secret, nor does Christine de Pisan ask that her readers take a vow of silence on the contents of her 'Book of Deeds of Arms and of Chivalry'. In fact, this desire for secrecy, and dismissal of the lower orders, is far more typical of the way in which the aspiring 'middle class' (for want of a better term) – the urban elites, government officials, and newly-landed – sought to distinguish themselves from those below, having aspired to and gained some of the respect and trappings of their aristocratic betters. It also fits within the tradition of maintaining the secrets of a trade or profession common to the trade and craft guilds, unsurprising for those whose works were the distillation of their profession as teachers of swordplay.

I.33 is remote in date, in language (the vast majority of later *fechtbücher* are wholly in the vernacular), in style (the way in which the work shows the use of sword and buckler is not one seen in later teachings of this weapon combination), and in provenance (we are generally able to trace a lineage of manuals and masters through the fifteenth and sixteenth centuries, but I.33 has only the most tenuous of ties to any of these). What it does share with the later fight-books, however, is the sense of formal education and pedagogy.

Whilst not personifying them in quite the same way, Fiore's *Flos Duellatorum* uses the same conceit of 'masters' (depicted in the manuscripts as fighters wearing a crown) in exchanges with 'scholars' (who are depicted wearing a garter) to depict

[62] https://wiktenauer.com/wiki/Fiore_de%27i_Liberi#Preface (accessed 1 August 2021).
[63] This comes from Christian Tobler's translation of the 'Starhemberg Fechtbuch' (Cod.44.A.8, Accademia Nazionale dei Lincei, Rome, Italy). https://wiktenauer.com/wiki/Johannes_Liechtenauer (accessed 1 August 2021).
[64] https://wiktenauer.com/wiki/Fiore_de%27i_Liberi#Preface (accessed 1 August 2021).

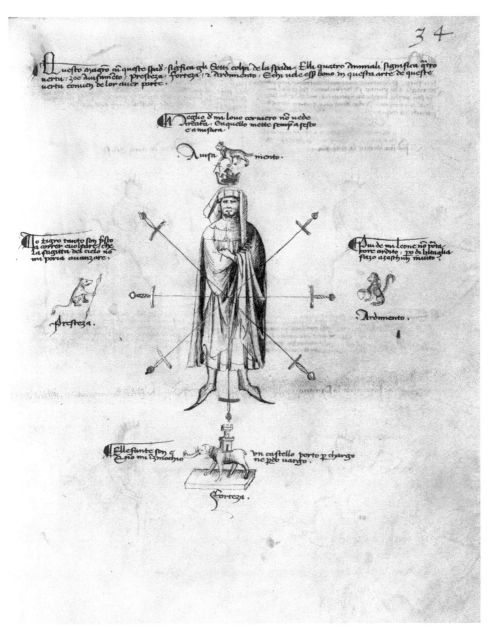

Figure 25. The 'segno' from Fiore de'i Liberi's *Flos Duellatorum*, c.1410 (Getty Ms. Ludwig XV 13 (83.MR.183), fol. 32. Digital image courtesy of the Getty's Open Content Program).

a series 'guards', 'remedies', 'counters' and 'counter-counters'.[65] Fiore also includes a visual representation of the principles of the art of swordplay; what he calls a '*segno*'. A man stands, arms folded, his body intersected by seven swords, equidistantly spaced, indicating the seven lines of attack. At his head, his feet and on both sides are four animals, representing the four principal virtues of swordsmanship: above his head a lynx symbolising prudence, at his feet an elephant surmounted by a tower, symbolising fortitude. At his right hand is the tiger, representing celerity, and at his left, the lion representing audacity.[66] Throughout his manuscripts, alongside the depiction of the techniques being described, there are many visual metaphors which serve to reinforce key points and concepts.

This visual mnemonic is backed up through his manuscript, and indeed that of almost all the *fechtbücher* traditions, by numerical and literary ones. In I.33 we are told that there are seven guards (but in fact the manuscript describes many more than that). Seven is a number that frequently occurs in western society; we might immediately think of the seven deadly sins or seven cardinal virtues. In Fiore the number of guards is given as twelve, another number with an immediate resonance in a Christian culture. In the German manuals of the fifteenth and sixteenth centuries there are four key guards, again a number easy to remember, and with cultural significance.

Except for I.33, whose guards are described in terms of where the sword begins, most of the medieval works give the guards names that seem illustrative in some way. Thus, Fiore's twelve guards have such evocative names as '*posta di donna*' (the woman's or lady's guard), '*porta di ferro*' (the iron door – where the blade is held with the tip away to the wielder's right, an invitation to an attack, like an open door), '*posta di fenestra*' (window guard – where the blade is held at head height, point at the opponent's face and the cross parallel to the eyes. The left arm of the swordsman can be said to form a window through which he can peer), and '*dente di zenghiar*' (boar's tooth – where the sword is held low at an angle forty-five degrees, with the point downwards but ready to rip upwards, just as would a boar's tusk). In the German tradition there are similar (though not identical) positions: '*vom tag*' ('of the day', although the sword is held more upright and can be above the head as well as at shoulder-height), '*alber*' (the fool's guard, because the lowered point of the blade appears unthreatening, although the German position has the blade in a straight line from the right hip, like the Italian variant *mez(z)a porta di ferro*), '*ochs*' (because the blade's position is reminiscent of the horns of an ox), and '*pflug*' (the plough, because the angle of the sword is reminiscent of a ploughshare).

The German *fechtbücher* tradition is predominantly based on the teachings of Johannes Liechtenauer. This nebulous figure may have lived sometime in the late fourteenth century: he does not appear in the historical record, and none of his original writings survive. Instead, his teachings come down to us as rhyming couplets – so-called *zedel* (literally 'notes') – which his self-proclaimed pupils then gloss in

---

[65] https://wiktenauer.com/wiki/Fiore_de%27i_Liberi (accessed 1 August 2021).
[66] See Fig. 25. https://wiktenauer.com/wiki/Fiore_de%27i_Liberi#Preface (accessed 1 August 2021).

their own works.[67] These *zedel* are ostensibly another means of restricting access to his teachings by the uninitiated. It seems ironic that we only have knowledge of these couplets because Liechtenauer's initiates felt it necessary to unpack the learning encoded within them. However, the *zedel* were not solely written to be obscure. They also served as aphorisms of swordplay, and mnemonic devices for Liechtenauer's pupils. Thus:

> Before and After, these two things,
> are to all skill a well-spring.
> Weak and Strong,
> Always remember the word Instantly.
> So you may learn
> to work and defend with skill.[68]

was a reminder of Liechtenauer's concepts of the *vor*, *nach*, and *inndes* which are the three 'tempos' in which one can act (that is to say the moments before the opponent's strike, after the opponent's strike, or in the same instant as the opponent's strike) that formed the core fundamental (the 'wellspring' as the *zedel* has it) of his system.

Such mnemonic devices were all part of the *ars memoriae* or 'art of memory', a long-standing classical and medieval method for organising and recalling knowledge, commonly used within medieval education.[69] However, the use of verse, descriptive names and significant numbers to encode important facts and information are not the only ways in which Liechtenauer's work shows evidence of its grounding in Aristotelian scholasticism. The *zedel* not only suggest that Liechtenauer taught within a rhetorical structure, sharing the same dialectical approach seen in I.33, but it can also be argued that many of the principles expounded within them, including concepts of motion and stability, of agency and passivity, the division of time into three parts, and the concept of separation and contact, were derived from an understanding of and adherence to Aristotle's *Physics*.[70]

Later followers of the teachings ascribed to Liechtenauer's teachings, including the seventeen masters who were identified by Paulus Kal as being members of the '*Gesellschaft Lichtenawers*' – the 'Company', 'Order', or 'Fraternity' of Liechtenauer – all

---

[67] Martin Wierschin, *Meister Johann Liechtenauers Kunst des Fechtens* (Munich, 1965) (for the *zedel*, pp. 1–22 and 127 *ff*). Hans-Peter Hils, *Meister Johann Liechtenauers Kunst des langen Schwertes*. See also https://www.wiktenauer.com/wiki/Johannes_Liechtenauer (accessed 1 August 2021).

[68] Vor und nach dy zway ding
Sind aller kunst ain vrsprinck
Swech vnd sterck
Inndes |Das wort do mit mit merck
So magstu lernen
Mit kunst arbaitten vnd weren. *Starhemberg Fechtbuch* (Biblioteca dell'Accademia Nazionale dei Lincei e Corsiniana, Cod.44.A.8), fol. 3v, transcribed Dierk Hagerdorn, trans. Christian Tobler. https://wiktenauer.com/wiki/Johannes_Liechtenauer (accessed 2 March 2022). On the language of the German tradition, see Matthias Johannes Bauer, 'Teaching How to Fight with Encrypted Words'.

[69] For more on this, see Frances Yates, *The Art of Memory* (London, 1966) and, specific to the *fechtbuch* tradition, Sean Hayes, 'Memory and Performance: Visual and Rhetorical Strategies of Medieval Martial Arts Texts', *"Can These Bones Come to Life"*, pp. 62–9.

[70] *Ibid*, pp. 141–87.

shared his pedagogical approach. The earliest references to these principles are not to be found in the writings of a named master, however. Instead, they appear in the so-called 'Pol Hausbuch' (Nürnburg Germanisches Nationalmuseum manuscript HS3227a), a German manuscript of the fourteenth or fifteenth century.[71] A *hausbuch*, or commonplace book is a private notebook in which its owner would collect a variety of snippets of information of interest to them.[72] The information collected could be quite eclectic. HS3227a contains, alongside the Liechtenauer material, material from other fencing masters, prayers, poetry, astrological, and alchemical writings. The English commonplace book Harleian Ms3542, one of only three middle English works to contain material on fencing, shows a similar heterogeneity, with its passages on fencing with the two-handed sword juxtaposed with a mixture of medical works, alchemical recipes, and other writings. A second English manuscript, Cotton Ms Titus A XXV, combines sections on fighting with the longsword and with the staff with a collection of chronicles, including Geoffrey of Monmouth, prophesies of the fourteenth-century English saint John Twenge, and a series of legal formulae.[73]

Although the origins of such texts were, like the *ars memoriae*, classical, used as a tool by scholars including Marcus Aurelius, and miscellanies compiled around a theme are extant from pre-Conquest England, the specific form of the commonplace book has been recognised as an invention of the fifteenth century. It stems from the burgeoning literate middle class, and draws on techniques learnt in school and university.[74] The compilers of these texts were unlikely to have been fencing masters themselves, but must surely have been their pupils, in order to have access to the original 'secret' material which was copied.

In every case, whether the source be a lavishly illustrated treatise of the likes of I.33 or extracts written into a commonplace book as in HS3227a, there is a direct connection with the techniques of learning and memory used by the academic community. In each work, practical swordplay is interpreted and codified for an audience that understood and appreciated an academic and literate form of learning. As such they, and the masters and schools out of which their content was distilled, must have shared that culture and understanding. Even those masters whose works are dedicated to noblemen and princes, such as Fiore or Vadi, show themselves to have been versed in the pedagogical techniques of the medieval school and university. This puts their works in a different oeuvre from the 'didactic' texts normally written by and for the nobility. None of these instructional materials, whether Gaston

---

[71] The dating of this manuscript is fraught with problems, hence the hundred-year span for its creation. For an outline and study of HS3227a, see Burkhart, 'The Autograph of an Erudite Martial Artist'.

[72] On commonplace books, see Earle Havens, *Commonplace Books: A History of Manuscripts and Printed Books from Antiquity to the Twentieth Century* (New Haven, CT, 2001). On middle class writing, see Malcolm Richardson, *Middle Class Writing in Late Medieval London* (London, 2016).

[73] https://wiktenauer.com/wiki/Man_yt_Wol_(MS_Harley_3542) and https://wiktenauer.com/wiki/Cotton_MS_Titus_A_XXV (accessed 1 August 2021). All three of the English texts (the third being BL Add MS 39564) have been transcribed, translated and published in B. Bradak and Brandon Heslop's *Lessons on the English Longsword* (Boulder, CO, 2010).

[74] David Parker, 'The Importance of the Commonplace Book: London 1450–1550', *Manuscripta*, 40 (1996), pp. 29–48.

Phoébus' *Livre de Chasse*, René of Anjou's *Traictié de la Forme et Devis d'ung Tournoy* (more commonly referred to as his 'Tournament Book'), or Duarte of Portugal's *Livro da Ensinança de Bem Cavalgar Toda Sela* ('Book of Teachings on Riding Well in Every Saddle'), shares the same approach or tone. They, and the chivalric 'manuals' of the likes of Ramon Lull, Geoffrey de Charny, or Christine de Pisan, are discursive in form, seeking to inform rather than teach. They have no requirements for secrecy, voice no fears that the knowledge might be passed down to those who were undeserving or who might use it for ill. There are no mnemonic devices nor is there a pupil/scholar dialectic (although de Charny's *Livre de Chevalerie* comes close in that it sets questions to serve as a talking point between equals).[75] In spite of their chivalric pretensions, the works the Italian masters or of the students of Liechtenauer are not chivalric texts in any form.

Cultures Within Cultures?
Legitimate 'Swordplay' Amongst the Urban Community

The *fechtbücher* and the masters who wrote them offer a solution to the apparent contradiction between the attitude of the authorities towards a master such as Fiore dei Liberi, and one like Philip Treher, or one like Roger le Skirmisour.

One of the common themes within the manuscripts is that they differentiate between the techniques of their authors and those of 'common fencers'. As we have seen, I.33 makes regular reference to techniques that are unknown to the 'common' (*generaliter*) fencer. Fiore asks his pupils to take special care to keep his techniques out of the hands of commoners, and the glosses of the Liechtenauerar *zedel* are likewise designed to prevent access to his teachings by those who had not been his pupils. Rather than assume that these injunctions were simply part of a sales pitch, offering secret methods guaranteed to defeat your untutored opponent, or to prevent the spread of sword use amongst the lower classes, it is possible that the distinction was being made between legitimate fencing masters and those who were not. This would accord with the trend in the late fifteenth and sixteenth centuries for fencing masters to be recognised by the authorities and to teach in a given city or area, to set up fencing schools or to establish professional guilds. It suggests a search for legitimisation, and recognition of fencing as worthy of incorporation, just as other urban professions had been, with intellectualism and scholastic principles serving as the defining element. In effect, the fencing masters who were producing and teaching in a scholarly way were seeking, to some extent, to mirror the universities by providing seats of martial learning.

If this is the case, then we might be wrong to consider the 'buckler-players' and 'masters of fence' as being part of the same culture of swordsmanship. Instead, we

---

[75] Ramon Lull, *The Book of the Order of Chivalry*, trans. Noel Fallows (Woodbridge, 2013); *The Book of Chivalry of Geoffroi de Charny: Text, Context, and Translation*, trans. and ed. Richard Kaeuper and Elspeth Kennedy (University Park, PA, 1996); Christine de Pisan, *The Book of Deeds of Arms and of Chivalry*, trans. Sumner Willard, ed. C.C. Willard (University Park, PA, 1999).

should perhaps think of the fencing masters as the legitimate face of what might be termed 'civil swordsmanship': that legitimacy coming out of the increased standing and self-awareness of the urban professional and mercantile class, and being given shape by utilising the same frameworks of guilds and fraternities that were present in other aspects of respectable urban life. The 'buckler-players' of the likes of Roger le Skirmisour can then be understood as the 'disreputable' side of the coin. This would tie in with the suggestion by some that we should understand the term 'schools' not as formal places of learning, but rather as a reference to any place where 'buckler-play' was conducted.[76]

There is, perhaps, a useful comparison to be made between the development and aspirations of the fencing masters and of the heralds.[77] There are many similarities. Like the earliest appearances of fencing masters, the heralds are first to be seen amongst entertainers, the troubadours, 'jugglers, gleemen, and minstrels of doubtful reputation', an itinerant, even vagabond figure, scraping together a living from the largesse of the knights and lords whose praises they sang at the tournament's edge.[78] By the late thirteenth century these entertainers might be part of noble house-holds. Jacques Bretel, the troubadour who recounts the events of the tournament of Chauvency, Lorraine in 1278, is clearly part of the household of the Lord of Chiny, who organised the event.[79] He and the other heralds who are in the stands show an informal familiarity with the ladies and other watchers of the tournament, suggesting both their integration with this elite society and, at the same time, the licence given to those who were outside of that hierarchy.

There is little in these scenes of the *gravitas* that one sees in the role in the fourteenth and fifteenth centuries.[80] As heraldry became more established and systematised, the nobility (and, from the late thirteenth century, by the aspirational gentry) increasingly saw it as a means by which individuals and families could display their individual identity, their family heritage, as well as interconnections with other noble families. The herald could fill a niche within chivalric society as the experts in this new field.[81] Thus heralds became employees of the noble houses. However, this process seems to have been a very piecemeal one, and it was not until the fifteenth century that heralds became wholly respectable and necessary officers within European chivalric society. By this date the herald (or those heralds employed

---

[76] See Olivier Dupuis, 'Organization and Regulation of Fencing in the Realm of France', pp. 233–54.

[77] My thanks to Eric Burkhart for suggesting this line of enquiry.

[78] Franck Vilart and Henri Simonneau, 'City Heralds in the Burgundian Low Countries', *The Herald in Late Medieval Europe*, ed. Katie Stevenson (Woodbridge, 2009), p. 95. David Crouch, *Tournament: A Chivalric Way of Life* (London, 2005), p. 63. Keen, *Chivalry*, pp. 135–6.

[79] *The Tournaments of Le Hem and Chauvency*, trans. Nigel Bryant (Woodbridge, 2020), pp. xxi–xxix and 61–121

[80] *Ibid.* Bryant notes that Bretel is scathing of the heralds for their bickering, pomposity, and acquis- itiveness, collecting the scraps of harness from the tournemant field like carrion, which suggests that we should not necessarily consider heralds to be of the same ilk as the troubadours and other chivalric wordsmiths. *(Ibid*, pp. xxviii–xxix).

[81] On the purpose and development of heraldry, see Robert W. Jones, 'Heraldry and Heralds', *A Companion to Chivalry*, pp. 139–58.

by the highest echelons of noble European society at least) seem to have formed a supranational organisation who were not only recorders of heraldic achievements (indeed this was in some ways the least important of their roles) but also messengers, ambassadors, and servants of the courts.[82] No longer the itinerant chancer, the herald was now a respected member of the noble court.

This change in status was not only a result of the importance of heraldry to the nobility. It was also a reflection of the move towards the incorporation of the professions in this period.[83] In a manner similar to craftsmen and tradesmen, physicians and surgeons, lawyers, and musicians all sought to gain 'a modicum of social acceptance and legal protection' through the formation of confraternities or brotherhoods.[84] Across Europe in the fourteenth century heralds began to adopt titles, and a hierarchy of sorts appeared, with 'pursuivants' at the bottom, 'heralds', and 'kings of arms' at the top. In the fifteenth century they formed themselves into corporations, known as colleges of arms.[85] Given the links that heralds had with both *jongleurs* and lawyers, it is reasonable to presume that their process of incorporation served as a template. It is interesting to note that one of the earliest references to a minstrels' guild in England, at Tutbury in 1380 gives precedence and authority over musicians to a 'king of minstrels' appointed by the Duke of Lancaster, under whose lordship Tutbury came.[86]

As part of royal and baronial courts, heralds were actively engaged therein, working alongside lawyers and clerks. Like them, these later medieval heralds (where they can be identified) seem to have been of gentry or common origins, but versed in court etiquette, literate, and holding some formal education.[87] Given that one of the functions they performed was to record arms, and the number of surviving illustrated rolls, many if not all heralds must also have had some artistic training too. Brault has noted how the language of heraldry is also that of the medieval artistic community, reflecting how the need for an unambiguous description of a shield started with those who were expected to replicate the designs on banners, shields and other material culture, and the close association of the heralds with those working in the decorative arts.[88] Again, this would have offered them examples of professional organisation and

---

[82] Katie Stevenson, 'Introduction', *The Herald in Late Medieval Europe*, p. 7.

[83] Jackson Armstrong, 'The Development of the Office of Arms in England', *The Herald in Late Medieval Europe*, p. 25.

[84] Kay Brainerd Slocum, '"Confrérie, Bruderschaft" and Guild: The Formation of Musicians' Fraternal Organisations in Thirteenth- and Fourteenth-Century Europe', *Early Music History*, 14 (1995), p. 258. Nancy G. Siraisi, *Medieval and Early Renaissance Medicine: An Introduction to Knowledge and Practice* (Chicago, 1990), pp. 17ff. James A. Brundage, *The Medieval Origins of the Legal Profession: Canonists, Civilians, and Courts* (Chicago, 2008).

[85] Stevenson, 'Introduction', *The Herald in Late Medieval Europe*, p. 4.

[86] Slocum, '"Confrérie, Bruderschaft" and Guild', p. 261. The same title was used in a statute passed by Charles VI of France establishing new statutes for the *confrérie* of minstrels of Paris in 1407 (*Ibid*, pp. 267–8).

[87] Stevenson, 'Introduction', *The Herald in Late Medieval Europe*, p.7. One of the issues with understanding the position and origins of heralds is that few of them are identifiable, because of the paucity of evidence for their role, and because, when they do appear in the sources, they are generally referred to by their title rather than by their name, making a prosopographical study almost impossible).

[88] Gerard J. Brault, *Early Blazon: Heraldic Terminology in the Twelfth and Thirteenth Centuries with*

behaviours, encouraging a corporate framework somewhat at odds with the chivalric ethos of which their expertise made them a part.

Armstrong has suggested that the increasing importance and social standing of the heralds was driven not by the nobility but by the gentry.[89] It was this aspirational class who needed the support of professional genealogists to affirm and uphold their position in society, through support in the courts, the establishment of pedigrees, and also to advocate for nobility being a product of honourable service rather than blood and birth, through tracts like Battolo di Sassoferatto's *De Insginiis et Armis Tractatus*, written around 1313, one of the most influential works on this subject.

Heralds and fencing masters shared their origins amongst entertainers, and the early perception of them as uncouth and immoral, at odds with the nobility of the activities in which they were engaged. A desire for noble patronage, achieved by some was also common.[90] One can see the masters of fence of the fifteenth and sixteenth centuries gaining their respectability in a similar way to the heralds, and with support from a similar quarter. When the fifteenth-century German master Paulus Kal listed the members of the 'Fellowship of Liechtenauer' (*Gesellschaft Lichtenawers*) in the early 1400s, this may have been in his mind, but it is may also be a memorial to deceased masters with a direct lineage, so to speak, to Johannes Liechtenauer, whose *zetteln* are the well-spring of the so-called German tradition.[91] The sixteenth-century creations of the German Marxbrüder and the English Corporation of the Masters of Defence can also be seen to mirror the process of incorporation amongst heralds, albeit quite some time afterwards. Both the heralds and the fencing schools had clear links with the universities, and the clerks and lawyers who studied at them. Many of the fencing masters had the same bourgeois origins, and aspirations of nobility, as their pupils, and as the heralds.

There is some evidence to suggest that not all heraldry specialists were full-time professionals. Before the battle of Evesham between Simon de Montfort, the leader of the baronial opposition to Henry III, and Prince Edward in 1265, it was his barber, an expert in heraldry, who provided the essential heraldic knowledge to warn that it was a royal army and not his son who were appearing before the castle. It is tempting to draw a parallel between de Montfort's barber and the fishmonger-cum-fencing instructor Philip Treher, although it should be said that their situations are not exactly cognate.[92]

---

[89] *Special Reference to Arthurian Heraldry* (Woodbridge, 1972), pp. 5–8.
      Armstrong, 'The Development of the Office of Arms in England', p. 16.
[90] Katie Stevenson, 'Introduction', *The Herald in Late Medieval Europe*, p. 6.
[91] Christian Henry Tobler, *In St George's Name: An Anthology of Medieval German Fighting Arts* (Wheaton, IL, 2010), p. 7.
[92] O. de Labrodorie, J.R. Maddicott, and D.A. Carpenter, 'The Last hours of Simon de Montfort: A New Account', *English Historical Review*, 115.461 (2000), p. 399. Identifying Prince Edward and the Duke of Gloucester's arms before Evesham was not the only herald-like service that de Montfort's barber carried out. He was rewarded with the sizable sum of 40 shillings for carrying news of the birth of Eleanor de Montfort's child to Queen Eleanor in the autumn of 1252 (J.R. Maddicott, *Simon de Montfort* (Cambridge, 1995), p. 42). This might suggest that, despite his title, he was in fact regularly acting in a formal capacity as herald.

It is also tempting to draw parallels between the written outputs of each. They both used technical terminology rarely found outside of their fields. In both cases that terminology was in the vernacular; the language of the artists who had to recreate the arms in the case of the heralds, and that of the pupils being taught to fence in the case of the fight masters. Both heralds and fencing masters wrote texts in Latin (for example the aforementioned *De Insginiis et Armis Tractatus* and the early sword and buckler manual commonly referred to as I.33) and produced works that fitted within particular literary formats.

It is here that we should draw a distinction between the two. The treatises produced by heralds fit within the wider body of chivalric literature. They are similar in style to the works of chivalric theory by the likes of Ramon Lull, Geoffrey de Charny, or Christine de Pisan. They handle more than just the practical matters of heraldic design, but also philosophical questions on the nature of honour and nobility.[93] There is more of the court than of the classroom about them. Their tone is discursive, without any of the mnemonic tricks of the didactic, often cryptic *fechtbücher*. The matters which we find bound alongside rolls of arms and *fechtbücher* also reflects this difference. Whilst both share the habit of collecting materials on different matters within a single text, undoubtedly picked up from the common literate and intellectual culture in which they mixed, *fechtbücher* tend to be bound with other treatises on combat or with matters of scientific interest and the ephemera of a middle class university-based education. Heralds rolls are to be found alongside works of military law, genealogy, ceremony, and diplomacy, matters directly connected to their professional function.

This distinction speaks to the difference between the herald and the fencing master. Whilst both may have considered themselves as part of chivalric society, both were, in fact, outsiders. However, the herald was tolerated, even included within the chivalric and courtly fabric, both in terms of function and pretension. They provided a specialist knowledge useful to chivalric society but lying outside of their expertise.[94] The fencing masters and their art remained, on the whole, ignoble, and outside of the chivalric culture even though they often couched their introductions in chivalric terms, because their expertise was already possessed by those within chivalric society, with the exception of specialist knowledge of single combat in a judicial context, to provide which the likes of Fiore or Treher might well be hired.[95]

The *fechtbücher* may seem to offer us the best indication of how swordplay was taught in the Middle Ages. However, it is important to sound a note of caution. As has been said, these works are a heterogeneous collection and most, if not all, cannot serve as training manuals and were never intended to be so. Some of them are certainly

---

[93] Stevenson, 'Introduction', p. 6.

[94] This position was a precarious one. By the end of the fifteenth century, across Europe, there was a decline in the number of heraldic officeholders (*The Herald in Late Medieval Europe, passim*).

[95] Fiore speaks of learning the art from knights and nobles, Sigismund Ringeck talks of the '*Ritterlich kunst*', or knightly art of the sword. Paulus Kal (who saw military service in the households of Ludwig IV Count Palatinate of the Rhine, Ludwig IX Duke of Bavaria –Landshut, and of the Archduke of Austria and Tyrol) wrote of dealing with 'all knightly weapons'.

practical *aides-memoire*, but others, including the copies of Fiore's *Flos Duellatorum* or Filippo Vadi's *De Arte Gladiatoria Dimicandi* were almost certainly gifts by the authors to their patrons, or perhaps an attempt to secure patronage.

Even where the text was intended as a means of transferring knowledge of the fighting, we should not presume that the practical lessons on which they were based shared the same scholastic method. In transferring the teachings to a written format, it is always possible that they were converted into a format most befitting written knowledge. At the very least something must have been lost (and possibly gained) in the translation from physical act to written word.

We certainly should not assume that the *fechtbücher* represent the only method by which swordsmanship was taught. Whilst the nobility would not have been ignorant of the book learning of the universities and professionals, and some of them may have embraced it, it was not a form of literature that was really part of their cultural experience. Even though the Liechtenauer *zetteln* include an exhortation for the young knight to fight bravely, and Fiore's preface refers to the knightly art of the sword, there are no allusions to chivalric literature or indications suggesting familiarity with chivalric texts, nor is there any clear cross-over between the *fechtbücher* and instructional literature like the *Konungs Skuggsjá*, or *Knyghthode and Bataile*. It seems that, just as with other aspects of the aspirational gentry and urban elites, they retained a distinctive yet allusive culture of swordsmanship that drew on that of their chivalric betters, but also reflected their distinctive professional and educational background and, perhaps, a more playful attitude towards the use of the sword.[96]

Whilst our sources seem to offer us an image of regular training and structured pedagogy, we are in the end viewing those processes through a distorting lens. The scholasticism of the *fechtbücher*, the lauding of martial virtue and discipline of Vegetius, and the physical conditioning regime of Boucicault; all these approaches may reflect actual practice, but they are also, to a greater or lesser extent, literary tropes that hide the reality of how men learnt to use the sword. The same, unfortunately, is true when we come to look at how the sword was used in combat.

---

[96] On the cultural interests of the high and late medieval gentry, see *Gentry Culture in Late Medieval England*, ed. R. Radulescu and A. Truelove (Manchester, 2006), P. Coss, *The Origins of the English Gentry* (Cambridge, 2003), M. Johnston, *Romance and the Gentry in Late Medieval England* (Oxford, 2014), and R. Radulescu, *The Gentry Context for Malory's Morte Darthur* (Cambridge, 2003).

6

Using the Sword

THIS BOOK HAS FOCUSED very much on the sword as a cultural artefact and symbol. We have looked at the spiritual and mystical significance with which it was imbued, its role as a totem of power and authority, even its role as a plaything of the urban and academic elite. It is all too easy, when approaching the sword in this way, to ignore that it was a tool developed for killing.[1] Men used swords to kill other men. Anything else they used them for – sport, symbol, gift, thing of beauty, euphemism, or metaphor – stems from this one simple, brutal fact. If we are to understand why the sword was such a significant weapon, and study it as a cultural artefact, then we should also attempt to understand this aspect of its culture. We should try and understand what swords do.

There has been relatively little work done on the sword as a tool for killing.[2] However there has been an increasing amount of work done on the question of medieval violence but focusing very much on its cultural and social context, particularly (and perhaps inevitably) by the martial, chivalric elite.[3] As a result we have a much clearer understanding of when it is appropriate to engage in violence and against whom, but less about the how. The analysis of what violence was done on individuals and by individuals has been the preserve of archaeologists. The study of skeletal remains, particularly of those from known battlefield graves, has given insight

---

[1] Some have argued that it is the only tool designed primarily for killing other men, all other weapons having an origin as a tool for hunting, farming, or building (Brunning, *The Sword*, p. 158).

[2] There is a very good exposition of what we can and cannot tell about weapon use in the Roman world by Simon James, 'The point of the sword: what Roman-era weapons could do to bodies – and why they often didn't', *Waffen in Aktion. Akten der 16. Internationalen Roman Military Equipment Conference (ROMEC), Xantener Berichte 16*, ed. A.W. Busch and H.J. Schalles (Xanten, 2010), pp. 41–54. There is to date no equivalent for the sword of the Middle Ages.

[3] For an overview of approaches, see Wetzler, 'Combat in Saga Literature', pp. 8–14. The foremost works on chivalric attitudes to violence in the Middle Ages are by Richard Kaeuper (*Chivalry and Violence* (Oxford, 2001)), but see also Samuel A. Claussen and Peter Sposato, 'Chivalric Violence', *A Companion to Chivalry*, pp. 99–118, and D. Crouch, 'The Violence of the Preudomme', *Prowess, Piety and Public Order in Medieval Society*, ed. C. Nakashian and D. Franke (Leiden, 2017), pp. 87–101. Joanna Bourke, *An Intimate History of Killing* (London, 1999) and *Deep Violence: Military Violence, War Play, and the Social Life of Weapons* (Berkeley, CA, 2015) considers the psychology of violence and combat in the modern military, whilst David Grossman's *On Killing: The Psychological Cost of Learning to Kill in War and Society* (New York, NY, 2009) and *On Combat* (Mascoutah, IL, 2012), and Rory Miller's *Meditations on Violence* (Wolfeboro, NH, 2009) are indicative of what might be thought of as a modern 'warrior' perspective.

into the brutality of battle and hand-to-hand combat.[4] Further individual finds have increased our knowledge and understanding of such wounds, as has the integration of the field of anthropology and forensic science. The former has been used to inform our understanding of the context of violent conflict, particularly outside of formal warfare, whilst the latter has been suggestive of ways of interpreting the use of weapons and of wounding in an historical context.[5] The approach of historical martial artists and reenactors, looking to use the written sources to physically recreate the use of the sword (and indeed a variety of other weapons), also offer another avenue for understanding the use of the sword and its effectiveness. However, achieving such an understanding remains a difficult process.

Whilst the medieval commentators, illustrators, and administrators, all of whom at one time or another have described armed violence, had fewer qualms about the graphic depiction of violence than most modern historians, their depictions must be treated carefully. The most frequent descriptions of violence are to be found in the epic and romances. Combat lies at the heart of all such tales, whether they be massed battles, more typical of the epic, or individualised martial exchanges more common in the later romances. They are full of detailed and graphic descriptions of wounds and death. Helmets are split, hauberks sliced apart, and men slain by the hundreds. At first glance they seem plausible enough, and one might argue that they must have had enough verisimilitude to convince a knowledgeable audience and keep them engaged. Some have argued that this gives us evidence enough of the medieval warrior's expectations of what combat was like, and the sorts of wounds that might be inflicted in it.[6] However, the descriptions of violence are also full of extremes and hyperbole.[7] Like the modern action hero movie, the heroes of the romance and epic are supermen, capable of feats far greater than normal men. They can withstand great blows, but their own blows are always deadly. At the same time the heroes' armour and weapons protect them from their enemies. Thus, Roland and Oliver can hack

---

[4] The three key sites of battlefield mass graves are Wisby in Gotland (fought in 1361) for which the key work is Bengt Thordeman, *Armour from the Battle of Wisby, 1361* (Highland Village, TX, 2010), Aljubarrota, Portugal (fought in 1385), for which the key work is E. Cunha and A.-M. Silva, 'War Lesions from the Famous Portuguese Medieval Battle of Aljubarrota', *International Journal of Osteoarchaeology*, 7 (1997), 595–99, and Towton, England (fought in 1461) for which see V. Fiorato, Anthea Boylston, and Christopher Knusel, *Blood Red Roses: The Archaeology of a Mass Grave from the Battle of Towton, AD 1461* (Oxford, 2000). See also Robert C. Woosnam-Savage and Kelly DeVries, 'Battle Trauma in Medieval Warfare: Wounds, Weapons and Armour', *Wounds and Wound Repair in Medieval Culture*, eds. L. Tracy and K. DeVries (Leiden, 2015), pp. 27–56.

[5] J.M. Dittmar, P.D. Mitchell, C. Cessford, S.A. Inskip, and J.E. Robb, 'Medieval injuries: Skeletal trauma as an indicator of past living conditions and hazard risk in Cambridge, England', *American Journal of Physical Anthropology* (2021), pp. 1–20. See also Piers D. Mitchell, *Medicine in the Crusades: Warfare, Wounds and the Medieval Surgeon* (Cambridge, 2004), pp. 137–83.

[6] See Rachel Kellett, 'Guts, Gore and Glory: Representations of Wounds Inflicted in War in Medieval German Literature' and Helen Neat, 'Depictions of violence in Floriant et Florete: Inter- and inter-textual patterns', both n *Battles and Bloodshed: The Medieval World at War*, ed. Lorna Bleach and Keira Borrill (Newcastle upon Tyne, 2013), pp. 161–76 and 177–98.

[7] Wetzler, 'Combat in Saga Literature'. Catherine Hanley, *War and Combat 1150–1270: The Evidence from Old French Literature* (Cambridge, 2003). Kaeuper, *Chivalry and Violence*, pp. 139–49.

their way through thousands of the infidel with barely a scratch (until it comes time for them to make their final, heroic sacrifice). When the heroes are pitched against each other, as we see in the twelfth-century epic of *Girart of Vienne*, depicting the first, bellicose meeting of Roland and Oliver, or regularly in the Arthurian tales, they will fight each other to a standstill, crushing and shattering armour, causing multiple wounds and absolute exhaustion, but never enough to kill.[8] Far from accepting such depictions as a true reflection the medieval audience, as Catherine Hanley has pointed out, was able to willingly suspend their disbelief, much as does a modern audience of action hero movies, recognising that it was an exaggeration for both the purposes of entertainment, and a means of emphasising the strength and prowess of a particular character, or the ferocity of a combat.[9]

She also notes that the same was true of the 'historical' and factual narratives of the chroniclers and historians. Certainly, biographies of the likes of *L'Histoire de Guillaume le Maréchal*, the *Chronique de Bertrand Guesclin* or the *Livre des fais du bon messire Jehan le Maingre*, all seek to laud their subjects, depicting them as the flower of chivalric knighthood, powerful, brave, and strong. Giving their subjects something of the air of the epic hero would suit their purposes excellently. After all, chivalric culture already blurred the boundaries between fact and fiction through the Round Table tournaments, where kings and nobles took the identities of Arthurian heroes in pageants of martial skill. Many chroniclers acted in the same way, and for much the same reason.[10] Whilst they might not have single individual as the focus of their narratives, they still had favourites and patrons who were to be lauded, and the audience for their reports were the same chivalric elite that listened to the romances. When looking for exemplars on which to base their descriptions of battle these historians, lacking direct experience of combat themselves, and rarely being eyewitnesses of the engagements on which they write, would have been drawn to the dominant chivalric literature describing combat.

There are relatively few examples of battlefield reportage or descriptions by knights themselves of the experience of battle. Even here we must be cautious in taking them too literally, as the influence of romance and epic can be seen within them as much as within the chroniclers' second-hand accounts. When the gloriously bloodthirsty Bertran du Born, a late twelfth-century Occitan noble, wrote how he loved Easter because it presaged the start of the campaigning season – with its sieges and battles, of warhorses throwing all into confusion, of knights thinking of nothing but breaking heads and arms and the sight of dead men with pennoned lances jutting from their

---

[8]   Bertrand de Bar-sur-Aube, 'Girart of Vienne', *Heroes of the French Epic*, trans. M. Newth (Woodbridge, 2005), pp. 437–45. Their fight only ends when an angel comes down from heaven to put a stop to it. On the use of armour as a symbol, and the problems of understanding the effectiveness of armour see Jones, *Bloodied Banners*, pp. 85–96.

[9]   Hanley, *War and Combat 1150–1270*, pp. 6, 162, 230.

[10] Ian McInnes, 'Heads, shoulders, knees and toes: Injury and death in Anglo-Scottish combat, c. 1296–1403', *Wounds and Wound Repair in Medieval Culture*, eds. L. Tracy and K. DeVries (Leiden, 2015), pp. 102–27, and '"One man slashes, one slays, one warns, one wounds". Injury and Death in Anglo-Scottish Combat, c. 1296–c. 1403', *Killing and Being Killed: Bodies in Battle: Perspectives on Fighters in the Middle Ages*, ed. Jörg Rogge (Mainz, 2021), pp. 61–78.

ribs – he was certainly playing on the epic trope.[11] Such sentiments, and the violent imagery that goes with them are part of the same performative masculinity that lies behind the depictions of violence in the romances. Others seem to have been more sanguine about the dangers of battle, and the injury one could expect to suffer. Jean de Joinville, Seneschal to Saint Louis, who accompanied his king on crusade in 1249, is one of the few men to report the detail of their experience of battle.[12] In his memoir of the crusade he records how in one engagement where he and his knights became trapped in a house:

> my Lord Hugh of Ecot receive[d] three lance wounds in the face, and my lord Raoul: and my Lord Frederic of Loupey received a lance wound between the shoulders, and the wound was so large that the blood flowed from his body as from the bung-hole of a cask. My lord Everard de Sivery was struck by a sword in the middle of the face in such sort that his nose fell over his lip.[13]

Although de Sivery was able to ride off to get aid, he was to die of the wound.

Whilst the description is a vivid one, it gives us very little of the context of the fight, which will be a recurring issue with understanding the use of the sword through such descriptions. The same is true of the accounts of judicial combat. Take, for example, the descriptions of the fight between Jacques le Gris and Sir Jean de Carrouges, fought in 1386, famous for being one of the last judicial combats fought in France.[14] Each of the accounts is different, not just in detail but even in the generalities.[15] Froissart has the combatants exchanging lance-thrusts, before killing each other's mounts with axes and then fighting with swords.[16] The Monk of Saint Denis has the two opponents immediately dismounting.[17] All agree that Carrouges was wounded, receiving a thrust to his thigh, but Le Gris' death is also described in different ways. The Monk of St Denis says that once he had Le Gris on the ground, Carrouges still found it very difficult to kill him with his sword, because le Gris was in full harness.[18] However, Froissart suggests that, after making repeated fruitless blows against his fallen opponent with his sword, Carrouges broke open his visor and stabbed him through the neck with his dagger.[19]

---

[11] For a prose translation, see J.F. Verbruggen, *The Art of Warfare in Western Europe During the Middle Ages*, trans. Sumner Willard and R.W. Southern (Woodbridge, 1997), p. 37.

[12] Jean de Joinville, *Vie de Saint Louis*, ed, and trans. Jacques Monfrin (Paris, 1998). Jean de Joinvile, 'The Life of Saint Louis', *Joinville and Villehardouin: Chronicles of the Crusades*, trans. M.R.B. Shaw (London, 1961).

[13] Joinville, 'The Life of St Louis', p. 221.

[14] It was the subject of the book *The Last Duel: A True Story of Crime, Scandal, and Trial by Combat in Medieval France*, by Eric Jager (New York, NY, 2004), adapted into a movie of the same name directed by Ridley Scott in 2021.

[15] Sydney Anglo had similar difficulties with the accounts of a combat between Anthony Woodville and the Bastard of Burgundy fought in Smithfield in 1467 (S. Anglo, 'Anglo-Burgundian Feats of Arms: Smithfield, June 1467', *Guildhall Miscellany*, 2 (1965), pp. 271–83).

[16] *Oeuvres de Froissart*, trans. Baron Kervyn de Lettenhove, vol.2 (Paris, 1871), pp. 36–7.

[17] *Chronicle of the religious of Saint-Denys: containing the reign of Charles VI, from 1380 to 1422*, vol.1, ed. and trans. M.L. Bellaguet (Paris, 1839), p. 464.

[18] *Ibid*, p. 466.

[19] *Oeuvres de Froissart*, p. 37.

The problem for us with these sources is that, whilst the descriptions seem full of detail, they are actually quite vague. Rarely are we told how the swords were used; most often it is only the end result that is of interest. There is no description of the exchange of blows leading up to Carrouges receiving his first wound, and nothing to describe *what* blows Carrouges struck against Le Gris' armoured body. For anyone attempting to understand how the sword was used in such a combat, there is very little to be gained. The same is true of Joinville's account. Whilst the injury suffered by de Sivery is graphically described, and his death from it remarked, we have no description of the fight that caused it; not how his opponent struck the fatal blow, nor whether de Sivery was able to defend himself and how he did. To make a rather banal comparison, it is like trying to understand the shape of a sports match purely from the score-line.

What of the coroner's rolls that we used earlier to get a sense of how frequently swords were used? The forensic nature of these reports, with the need to record all the events leading to an individual's death, must surely hold more detail, not only of the wound but how it was inflicted.[20]

It is true that we get a detailed record of the wound or wounds inflicted, their location and size, and the weapon that was used to inflict them. This encourages us to speculate as to the use of the weapon. Looking again at the enrolled reports that we considered earlier, we see two things. The first is that where swords are used the wounds tend to be longer than they are deep. Most sword wounds are between three inches and seven inches (7 ½ to 17 ¾ centimetres) long but, where a depth is indicated, is only an inch or two deep.[21] The blow dealt to William the Shepherd by John, son of Richard Herbert in Bedfordshire around 1 August 1265, which 'cut away a portion of the head with the brain and right ear' reinforces this and suggests a steeply angled blow.[22] Like William, the vast majority of those receiving sword wounds were struck in the head.[23] When James de Shoreditch killed Thomas de Walpol in June 1326, three blows were struck; the first was one-and-a-half inches long and penetrated to Thomas' brain. There was another to the right side of his head, four inches long and two inches deep, and a third on his left arm, seven inches long and a half inch deep.[24]

By comparison, the wounds recorded as being made by knives (of which there are many more) are invariably narrow (maybe only an inch or two wide) but several inches deep. For example, Richard de Dancastre received a wound from a

---

[20] See above, p. 102.
[21] For example, see the *Calendar of Coroner's Rolls of the City of London*, pp. 92 (a wound five inches long and one inch deep), 102 (seven inches long and three inches deep), and 135 (four inches long and two inches deep).
[22] *Selected Cases from the Coroner's Rolls*, ed. Gross, p. 2.
[23] Even where the location of the wound is not explicitly mentioned reference to a cut being 'down to the brain' is obviously sufficient to ascertain that it is a head wound. See *Records of Medieval Oxford's Coroner's Inquests*, ed. Salter, pp. 14–15, 18, 19, and 43, and *Calendar of Coroner's Rolls of the City of London*, pp. 58, 117, 146, 158, 164, 228, 2237, and 270.
[24] *Calendar of the Coroner's Rolls of the City of London*, p. 158.

'misericorde' an inch wide and six inches deep.[25] They also tend to be made to the chest or abdomen, as was the case for John son of John of Lyncoln, a cordwainer, stabbed and robbed by an unnamed groom in Blackheath in 1322, or Robert Cuteys stabbed in the chest by John Pope during an argument between the two of them, or Thomas, clerk of the church of St. Dionis Bakcherche, who received a stab wound in the left breast an inch wide and seven inches deep from John de Kirkeby, again as a result of an old argument.[26]

Can we reconstruct the events leading to a death from the account of the wounds inflicted? In the case of single wounds, the answer would seem to be a simple 'yes'. Where multiple wounds are caused, it is tempting to create a narrative around the blows. James de Shoreditch's assault on Thomas de Walpol seems to be quite clear. The first blow to the brain, the killing blow, was swiftly followed a second blow as the assailant swung the sword back around. That the wound to the left arm was a defensive wound, as Thomas tried in vain to protect himself from James' assault seems obvious; we can see similar wounds in other reports, such as the ones received by Thomas Hosebonde (whose arm was broken) and John Mason (whose arm was 'well-nigh cut off').[27]

Can we be certain, however? These wound patterns accord with the most natural way to strike with either the sword or the knife. Holding a sword, the most obvious and immediate blow is a strike down from the right shoulder downwards into the head of the target. The first blow described in almost all the *fechtbücher* is this very one, given from the left shoulder along a line from the target's left collarbone and through their right knee. Similarly, a thrust to the chest or stomach is the most likely strike with a knife or dagger, especially by someone who is not trained or is acting in the heat of the moment, which is the case for most of the protagonists in the coroners' records. However, there are multiple ways in which a man might be wounded in the hand or the arm without his having to raise it in defence, and a dagger wound to the chest might well have been aimed at the face or the head and gone astray. We are also presuming that the list of wounds is being given in the order they were struck, rather than in the order in which they were observed, or arbitrarily, according to a perceived severity.

The plea of Robert Essington's widow, made to the Court of the King's Bench in July 1314, offers us another complexity.[28] She testified that Robert had been attacked by a dozen assailants, causing seven wounds with seven different weapons, including bows, knives, a sword, and a staff. Three of these – a wound three inches deep and two inches wide from a 'cloth arrow', a sword blow that severed Robert's left foot at the ankle, and a six-inch long and two-and-a-quarter inch wide wound that went down to the brain inflicted by a blow from a 'Kentish staff' – are given as blows 'of which he died in her arms'. All of the wounds he received would have contributed to

---

[25] *Ibid*, p. 52.
[26] *Ibid*, pp. 52–3, 55, and 72.
[27] Both wounds were inflicted by John Coughwhel, who went on the rampage with a two-handed sword in August of 1389. *Records of Medieval Oxford's Coroner's Inquests*, p. 54.
[28] TNA KB 27/220/105-7d.

Robert's death, and any one of the three wounds 'whereof he died' might have been sufficient. One cannot help but suspect that the purpose of his widow's testimony was to identify individuals that the court could try for his murder, and that the men and the mortal wounds they struck were picked out for this purpose rather than because their wounds were more fatal than the others.[29]

The eyewitness testimony on which the enrolled accounts were made do not often contain any more detail than the chronicles and histories, and we should be mindful that they may be no more accurate. The enrolments are a digest of the original records, often made up well after the event. The coroners' records themselves would be a summary of the testimony of the jurors and witnesses, and the facts subject to their interpretation. Leland highlights how the coroners' rolls can be less detailed than the reports of inquests, and that, where self-defence was being claimed, it was quite the norm for the details of a death to be changed when it came to plead the king for clemency, with both the wounds and the weapons that inflicted them being manipulated in order to make that narrative of self-defence more plausible.[30] In some cases it is possible that wounds that were not fatal might not be noted or recorded at all. The purpose of the coroner's inquisition was to determine the cause of death, after all, not to provide a full forensic report as to how that death came about.

Using Forensic Archaeology to Understand Combat

One of the most exciting new approaches in the field of battlefield archaeology has been the introduction of the techniques of forensic science. The detailed analysis of wounds on the remains of those who have suffered trauma provides a new window into their lives and deaths. Studies of wound patterns allow identification of the type of weapon used, sometimes the order in which blows were struck, even evidence of past trauma, something that has then been used to flesh out (so to speak) the martial career of some individuals.[31]

Our expectations of forensic studies are often very high. This is in part, undoubtedly, a result of the popular portrayal of pathology. Modern crime dramas have become increasingly focused on the evidence that can be garnered from scientific forensic study. In the UK and the US shows like *Silent Witness*, *Waking the Dead*, or *CSI: Crime Scene Investigation*, *Bones*, and *Body of Proof* the pathologists and scientists take centre stage, the physical evidence allowing them to describe in minute detail the nature of

---

29 The Killing of Robert Essington was part of a land dispute with the Swynnerton family, who raided Staffordshire in the early fourteenth century, murdering and poaching game from regional rivals. See Peter Sposato, 'A Local Feud in the midst of National Conflict: The Swynnerton--Staffords of Sandon Feud, Staffordshire 1304–34', *Staffordshire Studies*, 19 (Spring 2010), pp. 15–42.

30 Leland, 'Pardons for Self-Defence', pp. 151–65. He does suggest that the coroners' rolls are likely to provide a more accurate account of what occurred (*Ibid*, p. 165.)

31 *Blood Red Roses*, pp. 94–95. See also Jo Appleby, Guy N. Rutty, Sarah V Hainsworth, Robert C. Woosnam-Savage, Bruno Morgan, Alison Brough, Richard W. Earp, Claire Robinson, Turi E. King, Mathew Morris, and Richard Buckley, 'Perimortem Trauma in King Richard III: a Skeletal Analysis', *The Lancet*, 385.9964 (January 17–23, 2015), pp. 253–9.

the crime committed, the weapon used, the assailant and even their motivation.[32] The reality is that such leaps of deduction are incredibly rare, and the programmes inevitably play fast and loose with the science in the name of a good story.

Equally, this fictionalised version of what a pathologist can achieve has been tapped into in order to popularise the fields of forensic and battlefield archaeology, through programmes such as *The Medieval Dead* (billed as 'CSI meets Time Team').[33] Just as with the TV pathology drama, there is often a dramatic recreation of the original act, identifying the wound and weapon, before building a narrative around the remains, and the tell-tale signs on the bones. Whilst there is no doubt that forensic archaeology can shed light on past conflicts, the interpretation of such evidence is not without problems.

Medieval remains indicating trauma related to interpersonal violence are not uncommon.[34] Almost all the remains are skeletal, and this means, inevitably, that only those wounds that leave their mark on bone remain to be seen, whilst those caused to soft tissue and organs, which might have been equally fatal, inevitably, do not appear at all. Thus, a sword blow might be struck that was debilitating or fatal, and yet still not leave its mark on the bone, whilst a thrust might miss bone altogether, or merely nick it leaving only the tiniest of marks – a thrust between the ribs that pierced the heart, for example, or a blow to the stomach – belying its significance and undetectable on skeletal remains. Equally, weapons might leave the most remarkable and significant trauma, and yet not be fatal, as is the case with the individual known as 'Towton 16'. This man had received a cut across the left side of his jaw which removed teeth and bone but, by the time of his death at Towton, had completely healed.[35] Had this man died at the time of the original set of wounds, we might very easily have assumed that such massive trauma would have proved fatal, or be expected to cause his death later through secondary infection.

Determining what sort of weapon inflicted a wound can also be difficult. A study by Jason Lewis has suggested that it is possible to distinguish between a cut mark made with a sword, an axe, or a knife.[36] Indeed, his experiments (which involved striking cattle bones with different types of blade and then analysing the resulting marks) suggested that it is possible to distinguish between different types of sword

---

[32]   *Silent Witness*, created by Nigel McCrery (BBC, 1996–). *Waking the Dead*, created by Barbara Machin (BBC, 2000–2011). *CSI: Crime Scene Investigation*, created by Anthony E. Zuiker (Jerry Bruckheimer Films, 2000–2015). *Bones*, created by Hart Hanson (Josephson Entertainment, 2005–2017). *Body of Proof*, created by Christopher Murphy (Matthew Gross Entertainment, 2011–2013).

[33]   'Medieval Dead', *Yesterday*, n.d. https://yesterday.uktv.co.uk/shows/medieval-dead/ (accessed 1 August 2021).

[34]   See M.R. Geldof, '"And describe the shapes of the dead." Making sense of the archaeology of armed violence', *Wounds and Wound Repair in Medieval Culture*, pp. 57–80.

[35]   *Blood Red Roses*, pp. 94–5.

[36]   Jason Lewis, 'Identifying sword marks on bone: Criteria for distinguishing between cut marks made by different classes of bladed weapons', *Journal of Archaeological Science*, 35 (2008), pp. 2001–8. See also Wenham, 'Anatomical interpretations of Anglo-Saxon weapon injuries', pp. 123–39, where microscopic analysis of weapon marks on Anglo-Saxon remains was made to create diagnostic criteria for the identification of such marks.

blade, opening up the intriguing possibility of a somewhat *CSI*-style connection between a particular blade mark and a particular blade profile from Oakeshott's typology.[37] Such close analysis is not easy, however, and one must wonder how much distinction there is between some blade types. Wounds caused by other parts of the sword might not be so easy to distinguish. Most of the *fechtbücher* at some point advocate striking the opponent with the cross or the pommel, and a *mortschlag* (literally a 'murder strike') where the sword is reversed and the opponent struck in the head with the pommel might not leave a wound that distinct from a similar blow with a mace, poll-axe or -hammer, or even a piece of wood.

Partial evidence left on the remains is only part of the issue for understanding the nature of weapon use. Context is significant for understanding how an individual died, and how a particular weapon was handled. Whilst we may have a solid situation for some of the dead – the battlefield graves at Aljubarrota, Wisby and Towton, and the skeleton of Richard III, for example, where we can be certain that the individuals interred were killed during or immediately after the battle – for those individuals excavated away from such sites it can be far more difficult to determine whether a wound was received because of deliberate violence, or accident.[38] For example, how would the archaeological record differentiate between the wounds inflicted on Richard de Strivelyn, who died after accidentally running onto the sword of Adam de Crofton outside the Caldewgate, Carlisle in 1301, from the very deliberate stab wounds suffered by any number of victims recorded elsewhere in the coroners' rolls?[39]

It is also impossible to determine definitively the state of mind of the wielder of the weapon from the wounds inflicted on his target.[40] Another example of how unusual circumstances might give the lie to the osteoarchaeology is that of the death of Robert Bays of Papworth, page of John de Blyton, 'from a blow struck by the latter with the hilt of his sword in throwing it to him in its sheath to catch'.[41] If one presumes that Robert was killed by a blow to the head, any wound made by the sword hilt would not reveal that tragic mischance that led to his death, and would be more likely to lead an investigator to determine murder rather than accident.[42]

Geldof notes that there is tendency to use the number and severity of wounds as a quantitative measure of violence.[43] Where an individual has received many perimortem blows, it is generally interpreted as indicative of a 'frenzied' attack.

---

[37] 'Future research may develop and implement methods to accurately and precisely quantify many more aspects of cut mark morphology, such as overall depth, channel angle, and possibly shape. These data could then be used to more rigorously predict sword class from marks, perhaps in combination with statistical techniques such as discriminant function analysis or canonical variance analysis.' Lewis, 'Identifying sword marks on bone', p. 2008.

[38] Geldof, "And describe the shapes of the dead", pp. 60, 75.

[39] Richard de Strivelyn's death is recorded in TNA C 47/2/64.

[40] Geldof, "And describe the shapes of the dead", p. 76.

[41] TNA C 47/75/1.

[42] This, of course, presumes that the narrative recorded was the truth, and that Robert Bays death was indeed a freak accident, and not, in fact, a fabrication worthy of a medieval version of an Agatha Christie novel.

[43] Geldof, "And describe the shapes of the dead", p. 76.

Such an interpretation is based on similar interpretations made in modern cases and modern forensics, occurring in the context of modern western European society, where such violent assaults more often than not *are* the result of someone in a 'frenzied' state. Geldof suggests that such a context is not always analogous to that of medieval Europe, 'in which knives were as common as house keys'.[44] He also points out that, in situations where such blows occur on the battlefield or in mortal combat, and where a killing blow might not be immediately fatal, such a 'frenzied' attack might actually be a measured and proportionate response, ensuring that an opponent was no longer a threat. Alternatively, it could be that the multiple wounds were in fact the actions of several combatants striking almost simultaneously.[45]

There is, then, a danger in trying to retrofit later descriptions of violence and sword use as evidence for its nature in the Middle Ages. A particular source that has often been cited in this way is Hugues Ravaton's *Chirurgie d'armée*.[46] In 1768, when his work was published, Ravaton was the Surgeon Major at the Landau Hospital in Bavaria, with over three decades' experience as a military surgeon. His treatise provides one of the earliest catalogues of wounds caused by melee weapons, each description and observation of the wound itself, the effect on the recipient and the prognosis for recovery, being based on his direct experience.

As Chouinard notes, Ravaton's work provides an important insight into the effect of swords on the human body, with far more examples than might be offered by a study of modern trauma surgery, or indeed modern warfare.[47] There is much of potential interest. For example, Ravaton states that thrusts are more difficult to treat and more likely to cause fatal wounds, with cuts tending to be more superficial, but larger and therefore more easy for the surgeon to spot and treat, whilst thrusts tend to be far deeper, but narrower, making them more difficult to locate, and they also damage viscera and blood vessels which are much more difficult to repair.[48] Sword thrusts to the heart were invariably fatal, as were those to the spine. He tells us that thrusts to the skull rarely cause death unless they manage to find one of its openings (the eye socket, for example, or the mouth or nasal passage), but that a solid thrust

---

[44] *Ibid.* See also Eric Burkart, 'Body Techniques of Combat: The Depiction of a Personal Fighting System in the Fight Books of Hans Talhoffer (1443–1467 CE)', *Killing and Being Killed. Perspectives on Bodies in Battle*, ed. Jörg Rogge (Bielefeld, 2017), pp. 105–7.

[45] *Ibid*, pp. 73 and 76. 'Chapter 13: Combat techniques', *Blood Red Roses*, pp. 148–54

[46] Hugues Ravaton, *Chirurgie d'armée, ou, Traité des plaies d'armes à feu, et d'armes blanches: avec des observations sur ces maladies* (Paris, 1768). A summary is given by Maxime Chouinard, 'Very Perilous: A sword wounds compendium by the surgeon Ravaton', *HEMA MISFITS (I don't do longsword)*, 2 April 2020, https://hemamisfits.com/2020/04/02/very-perilous-a-sword-wounds-compendium-by-the-surgeon-ravaton/#_ftn1 (accessed 1 August 2021).

[47] *Ibid.*

[48] 'Les coups tranchants sont en général moins dangereux que les coups de pointe, parcequ'ils forment des plaies plattes plus ou moins superficielles, que l'entrée est large, et qu'on voit du premier coup d'oeil ce qu'il y a à faire. Les coups de pointe au contraire doivent être regardés comme plus fâcheux, parcequ'ils s'introduisent profondément dans nos parties; que l'entrée en ☒t étroite; qu'ils intéressent souvent des visceres et des vaisseaux sanguins, auxquels le Chirurgien le plus éclairé ne peut porter que des secours incertains.' Ravaton, *Chirurgie d'armée*, p. 418.

could cause major damage to the brain.[49] He goes on to talk about the dangers of peritonitis from wounds to the abdomen, and of the damage done to ligament and nerves in cuts and thrusts to the limbs. In almost every case he offers examples where he treated the wound, along with the victim's recovery or not.

Ravaton's insights are compelling and complement our other sources, adding further (and graphic) detail to the rather dryer more factual reports of the coroner, and allow us to suggest a prognosis for the wounds described by the chroniclers. That being said, his work is not without its limitations, both for our own purposes and more generally. Inevitably in a book which is written to provide advice to other surgeons, Ravaton focuses on those wounds which were non-fatal. Given that he is a surgeon, those who had not survived their wounds rarely came into his care nor are they the focus of his attention; he laconically tells us that the immediately fatal thrusts to the heart 'are never brought to the attention of surgeons, and by consequence do not merit any details'.[50] He is also describing wounds that are made in an eighteenth-century military context. Some are in battle, many are in duels, and some are in play. Occasionally it is not clear what the circumstances are. We do not get a description of the passage of combat, nor the type of sword used to inflict the wound.

Given the period, and the preponderance of injuries received in duels, we can be fairly certain that most of the weapons used were of the smallsword or spadroon form, weapons with slim, stiff blades primarily designed to be elegant accompaniments to a gentleman's wardrobe, but whose needle-like blade made it an effective weapon.[51] In battle a heavier blade with both cutting and thrusting potential may have been used, and some may have been using sabres, curved weapons with a blade made for cutting. The blade profiles and heft of these weapons are different from those of medieval weapons, and the way in which they were wielded will have differed as a result. A medieval sword blade, for example, had a blade too wide to cause a wound so narrow as to be invisible to observers, nor to allow, as happened to one of a pair of duelling officers, a blow that passed into the eye next to the nose, leaving a wound so small that none thought it was the killing blow, but which proved to have punctured right through the brain.[52]

Ravaton's descriptions give some indication of the body's ability to survive wounds (this is the primary purpose of his work) but the focus is on the end result – the wound itself – and not on the passage of events that leads to its infliction. Similar comparisons of modern wounds and medieval descriptions pose the same problems.[53] They can suggest the body's ability to survive and recover from a variety of different

[49] Chouinard, 'Very Perilous'. Ravaton, *Chirurgie d'armée*, p. 422.
[50] Chouinard, 'Very Perilous'. 'Les coups d'épée de la poitrine qui ouvrent les ventricules du creur, ou les gros vaisseaux, ne viennent jamais à la connoillance des Chirurgiens, et ne demandent par conséquent aucun détail.' Ravaton, *Chirurgie d'armée*, p. 423.
[51] A.V.B. Norman, *The Rapier and Smallsword*. The spadroon was a slightly heftier military equivalent of the smallsword.
[52] Chouinard, 'Very Perilous'. Ravaton, *Chirurgie d'armée*, pp. 421–2.
[53] There are a few web sources that have discussed this, often with rather graphic depictions of modern wounds. For an example, see 'The Realities of Combat', *netvike.com*, n.d. https://www.netvike.com/wounds-from-combat.html (accessed 1 August 2021).

wounds, but the connection between this evidence and the medieval world is often a thinly tenuous one, lacking the contextual connection with the period that would allow for a true reconstruction of how the weapon had been used.

A study of the wounds caused by weapons, whether descriptions or from an analysis of historical or modern weapon pathologies leaves a huge gap in our understanding of how those wounds were inflicted. More than other descriptions of combat, which themselves have a tendency to be laconic, they rarely tell us of the exchange of blows. As a result, there is a risk that we build that narrative for ourselves, and ascribe motivations and intent to the giver and receiver of the blows that the evidence simply cannot support.

Evidence of Weapon Use on Weapons

There are similar problems if we look for evidence of use on the weapon rather than the victim. The edges of swords might be expected to show marks, nicks, and deformations caused by their striking a hard object, such as another sword or bone.[54] Such diagnostic evidence has been used quite widely in the study of Bronze Age weapons, modern replicas being used to try and replicate the marks on originals, in order to better understand the way in which blades were used against each other.[55] A similar approach has been taken by James Hester with regards medieval weapons.[56] His process entails a close examination of the blades surface, with particular attention to its edge, as well as to the cross, looking for marks and nicks that might indicate use. In his extensive study, which took in a substantial number of original examples in a range of collections and museums, Hester found that such marks were rare. This need not indicate that the swords he was looking at (many of which were high-status objects) were not used in combat. Indeed, as we noted above, Hester identified distinctive marks on a number of swords previously dismissed as 'ceremonial' weapons. Nor does it prove that blade-on-blade contact did not occur in medieval swordplay (as some HEMA practitioners, most notably John Clemens have argued).[57] Damage to blades is routinely described in both epic and romance literature, as well as in historical narratives. For example in the fifteenth-century biography of the knight Don Pero

---

[54] On the question of sword blades meeting edge on edge, see below.
[55] One of the latest studies is Raphael Hermann, Andrea Dolfini, Rachel J. Crellin, Quanyu Wang, and Marion Uckelmann, 'Bronze Age Swordsmanship: New Insights from Experiments and Wear Analysis.' *Journal of Archaeological Method and Theory*, 27 (2020), pp. 1040–83, but see the work of Barry Molloy, especially 'Martial Arts and Materiality: A Combat Archaeology Perspective on Aegean Swords of the fifteenth and Fourteenth Centuries BC', *World Archaeology*, 40.1 (2008), pp. 116–34.
[56] James Hester completed much work on this topic for his unpublished PhD, '"To Adorn the Great at light of Mars": Armed Fighting Techniques of the Late Middle Ages', Unpublished PhD thesis (Southampton, 2018). A summary of his work is available in two videos – 'Battle Damage on Arms and Armour', *School of Mars*, 15 April 2020, YouTube. https://www.youtube.com/watch?v=HSDS-p88Fyk (accessed 1 August 21) and 'Battle Damage on Ceremonial Swords', cited above.
[57] See, for example, Clemens, John, 'The Myth of Edge-On-Edge Parrying in Medieval Swordplay', https://www.thearma.org/essays/edgemyth.htm#.YyiOZXbMLD4 (accessed 19 September 2022). Clemens' argument carried far more weight than it should have within the HEMA community, but is now rejected as being an inaccurate interpretation of medieval swordplay based on flawed premises.

Nino, we are told that one combat was so violent that 'his sword had its gilded hilt almost broken and wrenched away and the blade was toothed like a saw and dyed with blood'.[58]

Hester suggests several prosaic reasons why there might be a lack of marks. Swords were well-maintained during their lives, and owners (or their servants) would have had the nicks removed after use. Those swords that were very heavily damaged were likely repurposed or discarded, and so do not survive to appear in modern collections. Finally, he proposes that some weapons may have had any marks of use and wear removed by collectors and curators in the eighteenth or nineteenth centuries out of a what we would consider today a wholly misguided sense of preservation.

The next stage in his approach is to determine the cause of damage to the blade, differentiating between corrosion, accidental damage from mishandling, damage caused by later owner's 'playing' with their collections, and those caused 'in combat during the object's actual working life'.[59] As well as clear marks of blade contact – kinks or bends in the edge of the weapon, or notches – there might be found wear marks from repeated grinding or honing, or even repairs (although these were a rare occurrence in Hester's examples). As all such damage and work is undatable, this is a difficult process (unless one has a provenance that would suggest that they were unlikely to have been taken out for a knockabout!)

Having identified these marks, Hester started to look at interpreting them over a range of different weapons. What he found were consistent damage patterns across the swords, with marks concentrating on both the strong and the weak of the blade; the latter being inflicted as the sword was used in attack, whilst the former more likely indicated the use of the sword to engage the opponent's blade defensively, whether as a parry or as a bind to control the opposing blade as part of an attack. The location of the marks on both edges of the blade, Hester argues, indicated the use of techniques using the false edge of the sword, as described in several of the *fechtbücher*.[60] Indeed the marks correlated very closely with the techniques of swordsmanship described in various manuscripts contemporaneous with the swords he was looking at. That there was no difference in these marks whether the sword was fourteenth, fifteenth, or sixteenth century in date, nor its geographical origin, nor whether the sword was a high-status example or a workaday one suggested not only that the style of swordplay was more or less homogenous across Europe in the high and late Middle Ages. It also indicated that, in Hester's opinion, such techniques were not specialist knowledge from the treatises or fencing masters, but were also being used by 'run-of-the-mill soldiers' wielding 'munitions' grade, commoners' weapons',

---

[58] De Gamez, Gutierre Diaz, *The Unconquered Knight: A Chronicle of the Deeds of Don Pero Niñó, Count of Bucha*, trans. Joan Evans (Woodbridge, 2004), p. 23

[59] Hester, 'Battle Damage on Arms and Armour'.

[60] Sixt Wetzler (pers. comm.) points out that it may also be the case that the sword, being two-edged and to all intents and purposes symmetrical, may have been turned around. One way of resolving this possibility would be to look at the pommel and hilt to determine if there is a 'front/ and 'back' side to the sword, as Brunning has argued for early medieval swords (see Brunning, *The Sword*, pp. 62–77), as this will indicate the preferred orientation for the sword and thus the edge more likely used as the 'true' edge.

who were picking up their swordsmanship as they went along.[61] However, he also recognised that the identification of an exact technique as the cause of a particular mark was near impossible, and so the commonality of damage across weapons of a broad range of statuses also made it impossible to suggest whether this meant that the techniques in the *fechtbücher* were more commonly applied than we might think, or that, when battle was joined and life was at stake, the more complicated techniques taught by the Masters were forgotten in favour of more straightforward ones which were easier to recall.

Hester's appraisal of blades is a similarly forensic approach to that of the osteo-archaeologist considering wound patterns, and he returns very similar results. He identifies the most common locations for marks on the blade and gives an indication of frequency. He differentiates between kinds of damage and makes some suggestions as to what type of impact may have caused it. Just as with the study of wounds, however, there are limits to what the study of such marks can tell us. Just as with wounds (indeed more than with wounds) there is no way of saying in what order the damage was inflicted, nor if it all happened in a single bout. Hester notes that there is no way of identifying the specific technique that caused the damage, nor the context in which the weapon was being used, whether it was against an armoured or unarmoured opponent, on horseback or on foot. Once again, it cannot provide the broader context. A sword used in play in a fencing school will be damaged in much the same way as it would were it to be used in a judicial combat or in pitched battle.

Hester's linking of damage on swords to the techniques outlined in the *fechtbücher* leads us to another approach that one can take towards gaining an understanding of the use of the sword as a weapon: looking at the *fechtbücher* themselves. These are, after all, sources that deal with the practicalities of wielding a sword. With their descriptions of strikes and counterstrokes, discussions of the timing of attacks, and (occasionally) accompanying illustrations, they are an obvious candidate for providing clear evidence of how a sword was used, the different types of cut and thrust that could be executed, and the injuries that these blows were expected to cause and defend from. This analysis can then be used as a cross-reference with the sources we have already discussed, either, as in the case of the narrative sources, as a check on the realism of the descriptions (although, as we shall see, this rather assumes that the *fechtbücher* are themselves realistic depictions of combat) or, as with Hester's approach and the osteoarchaeological evidence, to help provide some better context for the evidence that can be seen.[62]

---

[61]   *Ibid.*

[62]   Such an attempt to correlate descriptions of combat in the romances with the practices described in *fechtbücher* has been undertaken by Rachel E. Kellett. See *Single Combat and Warfare in German Literature of the High Middle Ages Stricker's Karl der* Grosse *and Daniel von dem Blühenden Tal* (London, 2008) and 'Royal Armouries MS I.33: The judicial combat and the art of fencing in thirteenth- and fourteenth-century German literature', *Oxford German Studies*, 41.1 (2012), pp. 32–56. See also Katherine Rose Hager's MA thesis, 'Endowed with Manly Courage: Medieval Perceptions of Women in Combat'. *All Theses* 2841 (Clemson, SC, 2018), https://tigerprints.clemson.edu/all_theses/2841 (accessed 1/8/21), and (for the Scandinavian literary tradition) Wetzler, 'Combat in Saga Literature'.

Sword Use and the *Fechtbücher*

At first sight the *fechtbücher* do appear to give us a much better sense of how the sword was used in combat. Unlike the narrative sources, which are often too laconic, too formulaic, or too fantastical in their descriptions of combat, the *fechtbücher* appear to provide detailed descriptions of the succession of blows, parries, and counterblows within a combat, generally with a fatal outcome for one or other party. As practical treatises, it might seem reasonable to assume that the techniques being explained are themselves practical and effective, without the hyperbolic exaggeration of the epic or romance. The type of weapon used is clearly defined. Unlike the 'fictional' narratives, the combats envisaged are short exchanges, where the opponent's blade is defeated as quickly as possible and a thrust or cut is made that kills or having incapacitated the opponent, is followed by a killing stroke. In Fiore's work each play ends with the opponent receiving a killing blow. In his section on the longsword ('the sword in two hands'), for example, the first play explains how the swordsman, having come into a bind with his opponent, brings the sword around to strike deep into the other side of the opponent's head. In the next, the reader is instructed to set aside the opposing blade, before bringing the point in line and thrusting into their opponent's face. The third has him disengage to cut his opponent's hands or thrust to his chest (preferably both, in succession).[63]

From the examples given in Fiore, or indeed the other masters, we can see that most strikes are to the head, face, and throat, the chest and the arms.[64] Cuts to the leg are far less common, and Fiore explains why, saying that:

> [w]ith a two handed sword it is unwise to strike to the knee or below, because it is too dangerous for the one striking. If you attack your opponent's leg, you leave yourself completely uncovered. Now, if you have fallen to the ground, then it is all right to strike at your opponent's legs, but otherwise it is not a good idea, as you should generally oppose his sword with your sword.[65]

Very often a single blow is not sufficient, and the treatises indicate multiple blows are to be given. Fiore, for example, describes a play in which, having pinned his opponent's sword to the ground with his foot, the reader is instructed to cut upwards

---

[63] https://wiktenauer.com/wiki/Fiore_de%27i_Liberi#Sword_in_Two_Hands (accessed 1 August 2021).

[64] Fiore's plays with the sword in one hand and in two hands list forty-six strikes, eleven each to the face and neck, eight to the head, five each to the chest and the arms and one to the back. There is also a kick to the knee and one to the groin. Eight references are to strikes in general (usually after a bind or disarm which leaves the opponent incapable of retaliating), but the images connected to these invariably show the blade aimed at the face or head. 'Fiore dei Liberi', *Flos duellatorum*. Getty MS Ludwig XV 13, trans. Colin Hatcher. https://wiktenauer.com/wiki/Fiore_de%27i_Liberi#Sword_in_Two_Hands and https://wiktenauer.com/wiki/Fiore_de%27i_Liberi#Sword_in_One_Hand (accessed 1 August 2021).

[65] 'che cum spada a doe mane non se de trare dello genochio in zu, perche e tropo grande pericolo aquello che tra. Che lo romane tuto discoverto quello che tra per la gamba. Salvo che se uno fosse cazuto in terra, ben se poria trar per gamba. Ma altramente non stando spada contra spada.' Getty MS Ludwig XV 13, 26r.

with the false edge under his beard or into his neck, before immediately returning with a downwards strike to his arms or hands.[66] This is not needless violence or cruelty, nor is it a frenzied attack, as understood by modern commentators. The cut up to the chin or neck may be a killing blow, but there is a danger that, in the moment, the attacker may lose control of the opponent's blade which would itself be brought up in a cut towards his groin and stomach. By cutting back down towards the arms and hands the risk from such an after blow is negated, whether through damage to the arms or wrists, or by covering the blade as it comes up. There are other occasions where the *fechtbücher* instruct that several bows should be struck in succession. Fiore tends to suggest multiple blows following a disarm, or when the opponent has been grappled and thrown to the ground. On one occasion, having wrapped his arms around an opponent's own, thus immobilising him and his sword, Fiore says that he can now 'strike multiple times until I am exhausted'.[67] Even if the line reads as a comic aside, the point being made is a serious one.

The Königsegg-Aulendorf Collection MS XIX.17-3, a *fechtbuch* produced some time between 1446 and 1459 by the German master Hans Talhoffer, includes the depiction of a trial by combat between Luitpold III von Königsegg, lord of the castle of Marstetten in Baden-Württemberg, and an unnamed opponent.[68] From folios 9r through to 23r the duel plays out step by step, from a depiction of Talhoffer himself helping Luitpold into his armour, through the approach to the lists, the two armoured opponents sat on chairs, hidden from each other by cloth screens held by servants (with their coffins resting on a bier behind them), to the start of combat with spears being thrown. There is then a fight with longswords, both protagonists half-swording. They each grab their opponent's blade, before Luitpold is thrown to the floor, his opponent kneeling on his back, holding his left arm in a lock as he draws his dagger. In the next image Luitpold has rolled so that his opponent is now underneath him. Both men rise and this time it is Luitpold who throws his opponent onto his back. Both men then draw daggers, Luitpold is stabbed in the thigh as he works his dagger under his opponent's sallet. The combat ends with Luitpold driving his dagger into his opponent's uncovered throat. The body is stripped, shrouded, and placed in its coffin, whilst Luitpold kneels and gives thanks to God for preserving his life.

---

[66] 'Lo scolaro che m'è denanzi à rebatuda la spada del zugador a tera, e io complisco lo suo zogho per questo modo. Che rebatuda la sua spada a terra io gli metto cum forza lo mio pe' dritto sopra la sua spada. Overo che io la rompo, o la pigio per modo che più non la porà curare. E questo non me basta, che subito quando gl'o posto lo pe' sopra la spada, io lo fiero cum lo falso de la mia spada sotto la barba in lo collo. E subito torno cum lo fendente de la mia spada per gli brazzi o per le man come depento.' Getty MS Ludwig XV 13, 26v.

[67] 'Quando io son incrosado io vegno al zogho stretto. Ello elzo de la mia spada entra le toy mane metto. E levo le toy brazze cum la tua spada in erto. Ello mio brazo stancho buterò per sopra li toy a man riversa e fererò li toy brazi cum la tua spada sotto lo mio brazzo mancho. E de ferir non ti lassarò in fin che sarò stancho. Lo zogo che m'è dredo che fa lo scolaro, ello è mio zogo e quello te voglio fare.' Getty MS Ludwig XV 13, 28v.

[68] For the manuscript see https://wiktenauer.com/wiki/Talhoffer_Fechtbuch_(MS_XIX.17-3) (accessed 1 August 2021). On Luitpold III von Königsegg, see Jens P. Kleinau, '1440 – 1459 Luithold III of Königsegg', *Hans Talhoffer*, 11 July 2011, https://talhoffer.wordpress.com/2011/07/11/who-was-lu-ithold-of-konigsegg/ (accessed 1 August 2021).

The depiction of the fight is realistic and, occurring in the middle of a *fechtbuch* between plates that seem didactic in purpose, might be considered based on a real event. As such it would offer an insight into the progress of a judicial duel, giving a far more detailed account than those of the judicial combats or battlefield engagements discussed above.

Unfortunately, there is no evidence that such a duel ever took place. The court records for the jurisdiction under which Luitpold came record no such event, and it is unlikely that these formal proceedings would not have been written up.[69] It appears that what we are reading is in fact a fictional duel designed by Talhoffer to place a series of techniques in the context of a real fight.[70] This does not mean that it is useless as a depiction of combat. It might be argued that what we have in effect is Talhoffer's description of how a judicial combat *should* occur if one or both of the combatants follow his methods. However, we should be careful not to presume that it was the normal way in which a judicial combat progressed. If the aim was to show a range of techniques, then Talhoffer may have padded the combat somewhat to ensure that he included all that he wanted. We should also not rule out the possibility that Talhoffer was following the literary tropes of combat descriptions, building tension by having Luitpold fall first, before regaining his feet to win the fight.

Talhoffer's works are one of the few *fechtbücher* where we see wounds being inflicted. They can be every bit as extreme as the graphic descriptions in our epics. In the folios dealing with unarmoured combat, chests and groins are stabbed and skulls cleaved down to the chin. On folio 90 verso a man receives a pommel strike to the face, on folio 79 verso a man loses a hand to a blow from an arming sword. The same injury is sustained from a falchion or *messer* blow on folio 123 recto, whilst on folio 76 verso a man is decapitated by a longsword blow.[71] None of the armoured combat sequences show the armour being defeated by a sword cut or thrust. In every case the opponent is dispatched once on the ground, using a dagger to pierce the space between the visor and bevor (the armour that protects the throat and chin).[72]

The depictions and descriptions of technique and combat in the *fechtbücher* seem to support the evidence we have from our other depictions of combat, and the forensic evidence on weapons and bone. If we take the likes of the *Flos Duellatorum* as teaching resources, then we should accept them as being wholly realistic. However, as we have already noted, they were not do-it-yourself manuals, but at best *aides-mem-oires*, or in some cases display pieces, presentations, and adverts for the masters. Given this we must ask were these techniques practical? How likely was it that, in the heat of combat a fighter, no matter how experienced, would be able to beat down his opponents' blade and place his foot firmly enough upon it to allow him to strike

[69]   Kleinau, '1440–1459 Luithold III of Königsegg'.
[70]   This is certainly the opinion of Burkart ('Die Aufzeichnung des Nicht-Sagbaren. Annäherung an die kommunikative Funktion der Bilder in den Fechtbüchern des Hans Talhofer', *Das Mittlealter*, 19.2 (2014), pp. 282–3.
[71]   See Det Kongelige Bibliotek, MS Thott.290.2°. https://wiktenauer.com/wiki/Talhoffer_Fechtbuch_ (MS_Thott.290.2%C2%BA) (accessed 1 August 2021).
[72]   *Ibid*, fols. 136r and 137v.

upwards? How often would it be possible to grab an opponent's blade and wrench it from his grasp? Even if it were to be possible, could it be carried out safely? Was the risk of getting a complex technique wrong really worth it?

The answer will, as always, depend on context. As Hester suggests there would have been techniques that were perfectly acceptable in the fencing school, or in a demonstration bout for the benefit of the court, but one would not dream of attempting it in mortal combat against a foe whose sole object was to kill you as quickly as possible. If we look at the *fechtbücher* not as simple 'how-to' manuals, but as showcases for the master's skill, an opportunity to present techniques that the potential pupil could learn if only they would give him a job, then we need to be more questioning of the validity of the techniques shown. The fancy disengages and footwork might look good in a grand book, and can be fun to learn (most HEMA practitioners will admit that disarming one's opponent, or using a bind to tie them up with their own sword blade, gives great satisfaction), but to manage that in the lists, against an opponent who is actively resisting you? Even if the technique might be perfectly safe in single combat, it might be utter folly on a battlefield, where one needed to be aware of multiple threats and differing weapons. The *fechtbücher* provide evidence for the style of combat within the context for which they written, but we should resist the temptation to apply their evidence to too wide a range of experiences of violence with the sword.

Non-Lethal Swordsmanship?

Throughout this chapter we have been working on the assumption that all combat was fought with the aim of killing or maiming an opponent. That simply was not the case. It is safe to say that most combats in the high Middle Ages were not fought with lethal intent. The whole culture of buckler-play was one of competition and sport; gladiatorial, yes, but not with the same connotation of deadliness. The medieval tournament was not fought with the aim of killing opponents, even in its earliest of forms, when it was indistinguishable from real battle. The chivalric *pas d'armes*, 'deeds of arms', in which small numbers of knightly combatants arranged fights to prove their honour and prowess, in part to while away the pauses in campaigning, were rarely fought to the death.[73] Even on the battlefield, an opponent's death was not necessarily something that was actively sought. One of the most widely recognised of the core principles of chivalry was that opponents (at least chivalric opponents) were to be captured rather than killed. Orderic Vitalis famously reported how, at the battle of Brémule in 1119, only three knights were killed out of some 900 combatants, because they were clad in armour, but also because they 'spared each other on both sides out of fear of God and fellowship in arms; they were more concerned to capture than to kill the fugitives'.[74] The process of capture and ransom became incredibly complex, so

---

[73] See Stephen Muhlberger, *Deeds of Arms, passim*.
[74] *The Ecclesiastical History of Orderic Vitalis*, ed. and trans. M. Chibnall, vol. 6 (Oxford, 1978), pp. 240–1.

that by the fourteenth century men were able to make their fortune speculating in a futures market based around the ransoming of noble captives in battle.[75]

Whilst the intent of the combatants may have been less than lethal, in very few of these forms of combat did this change the weapons being used. There is nothing to indicate that buckler-players were using anything other than real swords, and it would not be until the end of the fifteenth century that we start to see *federschwert* – 'feather swords' (as they have become known in modern terms); a training weapon with a thin blade, wide ricasso, and spatulate tip. Widely used in fencing schools through the Renaissance, these '*feders*' were designed to have the same weight and heft as a real sword, but to reduce the impact of either a cut or a thrust on an opponent, and the risk of causing serious injury.[76] It was quite common to use the same weapons in battle as in tournament, although there was increasing specialisation in forms of both weapons and armour. The combats known as *béhourt* were impromptu fights, often using little armour and non-metal weapons of leather, wood, or whalebone. At a tournament they may, perhaps, have been limited to non-knightly combatants. Whilst deeds of arms might also be fought with blunted weapons, just as often they were fought with the weapons of war, even in a combat *à plaisance*, where the objective was not to kill or capture an opponent but merely to make a decent show of prowess.[77]

There were no chivalric concessions made to restrict the lethality of weapons in open war. As armour got more sophisticated and better able to protect the wearer, new weapons, like the pollaxe, were developed with the aim of defeating it. Despite the supposed ban on crossbows *and* bows under auspices of the Second Lateran Council, no real attempt was made to limit their use in European warfare, nor against opposing nobility (nor indeed, as Richard the Lionheart learnt to his cost, against opposing royal blood either).[78] Both continued to be used in war, and to be developed with increasing power, whilst bolts and arrowheads were shaped, and in some cases hardened in order to pierce armour.

If the intent of combat was less than lethal, but the weapons were not, then it was the way in which those weapons were being used that prevented unwanted death and injury. A combatant would need to be skilled and controlled enough to strike his opponent in such a way that the hit was recognised, or that it persuaded the opponent to stop fighting, but without causing death or lasting injury. Not only

[75] Rémy Ambühl, *Prisoners of War in the Hundred Years War: Ransom Culture in the Late Middle Ages* (Cambridge, 2013).

[76] A good overview of these weapons is Roger Norling, 'A Call to Arms!' *HROARR*, 4 July 2012, https://hroarr.com/community-news/a-call-to-arms/ (accessed 1 August 2021).

[77] Keen, *Chivalry*, p. 86, and Crouch, *Tournament*, pp. 113–15. The exact nature of a *béhourt* does not seem to have been clear even in the fifteenth century – see Juliet Barker, *The Tournament in England, 1000–1400* (Woodbridge, 2003), pp. 148–9. On deeds of arms, see Will Mclean, '*Outrance and Plaisance*', *Journal of Medieval Military History*, 8 (2010), pp. 155–70.

[78] 'Artem autem illam mortiferam et deo odibilem ballistariorum et sagittariorum adversus christianos et catholicos exerceri de cetero sub anathemate prohibemus.' Canon 29, taken from *Decrees of the Ecumenical Councils*, ed. Norman P. Tanner, cited in https://www.papalencyclicals.net/councils/ecum10.htm (accessed 30 August 2022).

would blows need to be pulled to reduce their force, but also techniques would have to be modified, and some avoided entirely, as being too dangerous. Joachim Meyer, a fencer who compiled his *Gründtliche Beschreibung der Kunst des Fechtens* ('A Thorough Description of the Art of Fencing') in 1570, decried the use of the thrust (although his system did include 'plunging' strikes), noting that fencers of earlier generations not only used the point ('which is not the custom today') but also that they used much more of the sword (by which he may mean the cross and the pommel), and 'fenced sharply with both strikes and stabs'.[79]

This has often been taken as recognition that Meyer was using the sword in a different context to the earlier generation of fencing masters. That he and his fellows fought in schools and salles as a sport and exercise, rather than in earnest defence of their honour, and that he is contrasting the ludic fencing of the sixteenth century with the earnest combat depicted in the fifteenth-century manuscripts of men such as Fiore or Talhoffer, for whom combat was about bloodshed and killing. There is a subtext here which suggests that the thrust, which gave less opportunity than a cut for an opponent to see it and defend against it, was not only too dangerous for play but also somewhat dishonourable.[80]

That is not to say that this form of swordplay was without risk. Tlusty notes that the law recognised that the pursuit was inherently risky, and so rarely held those who caused injury or even death in such bouts at fault.[81]

The same was true on the tournament field. Whilst deaths might be 'regrettable and exceptional', injuries were an accepted part of participation.[82] There is little in the descriptions of them to suggest that the participants sought to restrain themselves in any way. There is the famous, and humorous, tale of how William Marshal, being sought out to claim his prize as the best knight of the tournament was found with his head on an anvil, a blacksmith hammering at his helm, as it had been so battered the knight was unable to take it off.[83] Jacques Bretel, the eyewitness reporter of the 1285 tournament of Chauvency, describes the *melée* – the massed combat highlight of the event – emphasising the power of the blows. When Renaut de Trie and the Count of Luxembourg found each other in the press:

> They made ready to defend themselves, and exchanged tremendous blows on arms and heads and necks, making their helmets ring out loud as they smashed and stove them; they joined so close that they were pounding each other's nasal with their pommels. When their blows were done they wrestled, seizing each other round the helm and

79 'Dieweil zwischen dem Schwerdt Fechten zu unsern zeiten, wie bey unsern vornfahren und uralten im gebrauch gewesen, ein grosser underscheid, das ich an diesem ort nur was jetzund gebräuchlig unnd so viel zum Schwerdt gehörig von häuwen erzelen, so vil der alten gebrauch aber belangt, wie sie beide mit Hauwen unnd stechen scharpff gefochten,' Joachim Meyer, *Gründtliche Beschreibung der Kunst des Fechtens* (Strasbourg, 1570), vol I, 10v. Transcribed Michael Chidester, trans. Mike Rasmusson. https://wiktenauer.com/wiki/Joachim_Meyer#Sword (accessed 1 August 2021).
80 On the connection between the thrust and dishonourable sword play see Tlusty, *The Martial Ethic in Early Modern Germany*, p. 100.
81 *Ibid*, p. 77.
82 Crouch, *Tournament*, pp. 98–101.
83 *History of William Marshal*, lines 2875–3164.

pulling and heaving with such force that they almost dragged each other down; but once they'd broken free they struck out again with their blades of steel, delivering massive blows to their hardy helms.[84]

It seems to be the case that someone had to be beaten into submission for the assaults to stop; the onus was on one of the combatants to admit that they had had enough, rather than on their assailant deciding that they had doled out enough punishment.

As night fell, the fight petered out, the combatants at Chauvency withdrawing to their lodgings 'weary and worn, for they'd battled long... high in spirits but battered, cut and bruised, covered in wounds on body and face as is the way after combat'.[85] Such injuries were not only accepted as part and parcel of performing in the tournament, they were also marks of courage and honour. As we have seen, Roger of Hoveden felt that for a young knight to distinguish himself in battle he must have at tournament:

> have seen his blood flow, heard his teeth crack under fist blows, felt his opponent's weight bear down upon him as he lay on the ground and, after being twenty times unhorsed, have risen twenty times to fight.[86]

In similar vein, Bertran de Born wrote that 'no one is respected until he has taken and given many blows'.[87]

For the chivalric classes, the desire to be a *preud'omme* – a man of prowess – meant participating in violence, and dealing out blows, *and* enduring blows of great power.[88] At its most extreme, the wounds and hardship suffered by knights were seen as being akin to Christ's suffering on the cross and, as such, something to be lauded and even desired.[89]

This approach towards violence and combat, the acceptance of a level of risk and injury as part and parcel of a martial pursuit, even when done as entertainment, adds yet a further complication in trying to understand how swords were used in combat. We cannot assume that even in a 'friendly' bout, all attempts were made to avoid injury, but equally we must recognise that there was, somewhere, a line drawn between the acceptable and unacceptable blow.[90] As with so much of what we have discussed in this chapter, it is hard for us to know, and our sources are very hazy on, exactly where that line lay in any particular case.

---

[84] Jacques Bretel, 'The Tournament at Chauvency', *The Tournaments at Le Hem and Chauvency*, trans. Nigel Bryant (Woodbridge, 2020), p. 111. As always, we should be aware of the potential for hyperbole in any of our narrative sources.

[85] *Ibid*, p. 115

[86] Roger of Hoveden, *Chronica*, pp. 166–7.

[87] Quoted in Verbruggen, *Art of Warfare*, p. 37.

[88] Kaeuper, *Chivalry and Violence, passim*.

[89] Richard Kaeuper, *Holy Warriors: The Religious Ideology of Chivalry* (Philadelphia, PA, 2009), pp.120–9.

[90] On the removing of an opponent's helmet as an indicator of the end of a fight, see Robert Jones, 'þen hentes he þe healme, and hastily hit kisses: The symbolic significance of donning armour in medieval romance', *Battles and Bloodshed*, pp. 25–38.

When we try to understand the way in which the sword was used, whether we rely on sources fictional, factual, or forensic, we find ourselves hampered by the same issues: a lack of detail. Whether it is the weapon and techniques used, the context and course of the fight, or the number, experience, and intentions of those fighting, these gaps in our knowledge can inhibit our understanding of the combat, or worse, encourage the invention of narratives around the few facts that are offered, shaped by sensibilities and assumptions that are wholly modern. It is to these modern assumptions, and the modern culture of medieval swords that we turn to next.

7

Recreating 'Medieval' Swordsmanship

THE 16 MAY 1894 edition of *Le Figaro* published a description of 'a lively event' to be held at the *Théâtre de la Monnaie* in Brussels; a presentation of 'Fencing through the Ages', with a series of scenes and dialogue depicting sword fights from the fifteenth to the eighteenth century.[1] The scenes were to have a musical score, and dialogue was provided by actors from the theatre's company, but the swordplay itself was to be enacted by 'M. et Mme Gabriel' of Paris, as well as 'several English fencers, the best blades in the United Kingdom, belonging to the London Rifle Brigade', and including amongst their number 'Captain Alfred Hutton, a scholar at the same time as a practitioner, who has made a specialty of historical fencing'.[2] The event was arranged by the press but under the auspices of the president of the *Cercle d'Escrime de Bruxelles* (the Fencing Circle of Brussels) Monsieur Albert Fierlants.[3] It had been inspired by a similar event in Paris a few months earlier. Organised by the Parisian 'Society for the Encouragement of Fencing' (*la Société d'Encouragement à l'Escrime*) this display had featured many of the same scenarios that were to be enacted in Brussels, including Monsieur and Madame Gabriel's smallsword fight.[4] These scenes were created by Monsieur Adolphe Corthey, whose research was lauded in *La Grande Dame*: 'The careful and difficult reconstruction, a result of research which has certainly been laborious, does M. Corthey the greatest honour'.[5]

These two events, and the men most directly connected with them – Alfred Hutton, Adolphe Corthey, and Albert Fierlants – along with the fencer and antiquarian Egerton Castle (whose 1885 work *Schools and Masters of Fencing: From the Middle Ages to the Eighteenth Century* Fierlants translated into French) were the leading lights in the nineteenth-century movement to rediscover and recreate the swordplay of the past. Their search for an authentic medieval swordplay makes them worthy of the title

---

[1]   Sylvius, 'Lettre de Belgique', *Le Figaro* (16 May 1894), p. 3.
[2]   'Figureront dans cette série de joutes historiques: m at mme gabriel de paris, et plusiers escrimeurs anglais, les meilleures lames de royaume-uni, apartenant a la london rifle brigade, entre autres le capitan alfred hutton, un érudit en même temps qu'un praticien, qui s'est fait une spécialité de l'esrime historique.' *Ibid*.
[3]   *Ibid*. Henri de Goudourville, *Escrimeurs Contemporains* (Paris, 1899), p. 199.
[4]   Jean de Mitty, 'La Société d'Encouragement a L'Escrime', *La Grande Dame: revue de l'élégance et des arts / publiée sous la direction de F. G. Dumas*, ed. F.G. Dumas (Paris, 1894), pp. 97–100.
[5]   'Cette restitution, minutieuse et difficile, due à des recherches qui certainement ont été laborieuses, fait le plus grand honneur à M. Corthey'. *Ibid*, p. 99.

of the progenitors of a modern fascination with historical swordsmanship. This has developed in several different directions since then, with a focus on entertainment, competition, and most recently, academic study. Whilst all of them seek to place themselves as 'authentic' in their approach, how close they come is dependent on many factors, including the compromises made to ensure participants' and audiences' safety, the nature of the source material used as a basis for the recreation, the weapons available or constructed, and the backgrounds and assumptions made by those wielding them, and their audience. In some cases these modern interpretations and reinterpretations have helped to shape our understanding of the medieval cultures of the sword that we have been discussing but, more often than not, they actually form a new, distinct, and modern culture of the medieval sword.

'Kernoozing' and the Victorian Understanding of Medieval Swordplay

Who were these founders, and why were they so interested in the swordplay of the past?

Hutton was a military man, having served as an officer in the 79th (Cameron) Highlanders, 7th Hussars, and the 1st King's Dragoon Guards. An avid and accomplished fencer, he established fencing societies for the officers of his regiments throughout his career and, on retiring, continued his studies. He also published numerous works on the subject from a military context, as well as on contemporary sports fencing, and historical swordsmanship.[6] Around 1859 he became connected with the City of London Volunteer Rifle Brigade, one of a number of volunteer units that formed as tensions with France rose. There he established a club devoted to historical modes of fencing amongst its officers; somewhat ironically these were the men who were to travel to Brussels and be recognised as 'the best blades in the United Kingdom' in the French *Le Figaro*.

Egerton Castle was one of his compatriots. Another officer, this time in the Second West India Regiment and the Royal Engineers militia, Castle was foremost an antiquarian and writer, as well as an accomplished fencer. In the 1908 Olympics he captained the English épée and sabre teams. He and Hutton were close friends, though Hutton was twenty years Castle's senior.[7] Castle's 1885 book *Schools and Masters of Fence from the Middle Ages through to the Eighteenth Century* was based on his reading of Hutton's 'magnificent collection of books treating of the sword and its use, ranging in date from the sixteenth century to the present day', although he notes, somewhat acerbically, that his friend Hutton seemed now 'inclined to neglect the sabre and the foil for the brush and the maul-stick'.[8] Both were members of the 'Kernoozers' – a dining club for collectors of arms and amour, who would discuss

6 Tony Wolf, *Ancient Swordplay: The Revival of Elizabethan Fencing in Victorian London* (Wheaton, IL, 2012), pp. 9–11.
7 *Ibid*, p. 9.
8 Egerton Castle, *Schools and Masters of Fence*, p. xi.

their latest acquisitions over drinks and dinner, often with a demonstration of swordplay by Castle and Hutton.[9]

These two Englishmen participated in numerous demonstrations of historical swordplay, at private clubs, for royalty, and to the general public. Using rapiers, singly and with the accompaniment of dagger or cloak, as well as sword and buckler, great swords, and small swords they used the fencing manuals of the sixteenth through to the eighteenth centuries as the basis for their studies and expositions, which they then played out both in modern fencing gear and historical costume.

Adolphe Corthey's background was slightly different. Although a noted sportsman – a shooter, canoeist, and archer, as well as fencer – he was first and foremost a playwright, producing satires for the Parisian stage.[10] It was this combination of interests that led him to be engaged in researching, choreographing, and writing the vignettes of historical fencing by Ernest Molier as one of the acts in his very successful Parisian circus.[11] These performances were the precursors of the Paris event that, in turn, spawned the Brussels display of which Hutton was a part. Like Hutton and Egerton Castle, Corthey published his research on historical swordsmanship in *L'Escrime à Travers les Âges* (*Fencing Through the Ages*) in 1892.[12]

All three men reflected the same attitude towards historical swordsmanship. For them true fencing came about in the sixteenth century, whilst the swordsmen of the Middle Ages did not 'fence' but, as Corthey put it:

> were content to shield themselves like ships at a breakwater. More akin to the sea turtle than the desert lion, it was for them only a matter of being capable of receiving strikes which do not harm too much. And the greatest warrior was he on whom one could beat the hardest and for the longest time without result.[13]

Hutton was slightly more nuanced. He wrote that:

> There are those who pretend that previous to the sixteenth century, the age of the rapier, fencing did not exist except among the lower orders, and that the great ones of the earth, the nobles and knights, despised it altogether and trusted only to the brute force of their strong right arms and to the splendid temper of their plate armour, and this they did to a very considerable extent…

However, he notes that they were also prepared to make use of the shield, and that 'wherever we see the attack warded by any kind of defensive weapon we have to recognise the art of fence albeit in archaic form'.[14]

[9] *Ibid*, pp. 13–21. The name of the club was born out of a mispronunciation of 'connoisseurs'.
[10] Adolphe Corthey, *Fencing Through the Ages*, trans. Chris Slee (Brisbane, 2015). Corthey's sole engagement with military matters seems to have been a letter in *Le Moniteur Officiel de la Gymnastique et de l'Escrime* of 20 November 1886, extolling the superiority of, and natural inclination for the use of the *armes blanche* by the French, over the German's use of gunpowder (Adophe Corthey, 'Français et Allemands: Armes Blanches et armes à feu, apropos de grandes maneouvres.' *Le Moniteur Officiel de la Gymnastique et de l'Escrime*, Third Year, Number 42 (20 November 1886), p. 7.
[11] Corthey, *Fencing Through the Ages*, p.14.
[12] *Ibid*.
[13] *Ibid*, p. 19.
[14] Sir Alfred Hutton, *The Sword and the Centuries* (London, 1901, reprinted Barton under Needwood,

Egerton Castle provided a more fully developed explication. He argued that two forms of medieval swordplay existed. The first, cultivated by the noble warrior, encased and secure in his steel armour, was based on brute force. He learnt 'little of what would avail him were he deprived of his protecting armour'.[15] Combat between knights was resolved, he argues, 'by the resistance of their armour and, ultimately, by their power of endurance'.[16] A contrasting school developed amongst those who Castle saw as not having the benefit of the chivalric elite's steel carapace:

> The other school, on the contrary, which was adapted to the weapons of the villain or burgess, was much more practical; it induced him to rely to a certain point on his weapons, as well as general activity, for defence, instead of on the artificial resource of armour.[17]

Castle recognised that fencing and fencing schools were a middle class and urban phenomenon, distinct from the knightly classes' learning of weapons, in much the way we have discussed above. Whilst he reached the same conclusion, however, he placed too much distinction on the swordsmanship of each group, did not consider that the knightly class, too, might fight in situations without armour, and was dismissive of the skill required to fight in armour.

These Victorian commentators reflected attitudes similar to other contemporaries who were collectors and curators of medieval weapons. Men who routinely described their medieval swords as being cumbersome, awkward, and crude. The remarks of sword-maker John Latham regarding a sword said to have belonged to Edward III, that had been bequeathed to the Royal United Services Institute, serve as a typical example. In answer to a question following his lecture on the subject of the shape of sword blades, he suggested that:

> from its tremendous weight that it was intended for a time when swordsmen had to deal with iron-plated men, as we have with iron-plated vessels, and you see how they solved the very question we are debating now. They got the heaviest weight they could, and they put as much force behind it as they could possibly give exactly the same thing we are now doing in our experiments with artillery against iron plated ships.[18]

As late as the 1930s the curator of the Royal Armouries, Sir Charles ffoulkes, could state that the sword of the medieval knight was 'lacking in every quality which a sword should possess. The grips are small, the blades are heavy and ill-balanced and the points of little or no use for the thrust'.[19]

This attitude towards medieval swordsmanship may seem a curious one for men who were professing to study the historical roots of their fencing culture. However, we should not judge them too harshly. There was a very good reason that Hutton's

---

2003), p. 1.
[15] Egerton Castle, *Schools and Masters of Fence*, pp. 18–19.
[16] *Ibid*, p. 19.
[17] *Ibid*.
[18] John Latham, 'The Shape of Sword Blades', *Journal of the Royal United Service Institution*, vol. VI (London, 1863), pp. 421–2).
[19] Charles ffoulkes and Capt. E.C. Hopkinson, *Sword, Lance and Bayonet: A record of the arms of the British army and navy* (Cambridge, 1938), p. xvi.

'magnificent collection' of books of swords and swordsmanship began in the sixteenth
century. The fifteenth-century masters were at the time unknown, their manuscripts
undiscovered in a myriad of private collections. These Victorian gentlemen's understanding of medieval swordplay was not based on fencing manuals, but on the
descriptions of combat in the medieval chronicles (Egerton Castle cites, as the sources
for his description of knightly combat being about endurance of man and armour,
'Olivier de la Marche, Froissart and other chroniclers'.)[20] As we have seen, these
narrators of medieval combat rarely gave more than a cursory description of combat,
and were, by nature of their genre, liable to play up the need for physical strength
and endurance. Reading heroic descriptions of Arthur's knights laying about them,
severing limbs and splitting heads, how could the Victorians think otherwise?

Furthermore, there was little obvious continuity between the styles of swordsmanship of the nineteenth-century French *salle* and the fifteenth-century fight-school.
To swordsmen used to the light and nimble fencing foil, sabre, or épée – all designed
to be manipulated at the wrist and finger with extreme speed and deftness – an
arming sword, let alone a longsword, must inevitably have seemed cumbersome and
slow.[21] By comparison there was a clear tradition and evolution of swordsmanship
from the Italian school of rapier fighting, through the development of the smallsword
down to the French school of fencing of the nineteenth century. A continuity in
the terminology, and a similarity in the heft (although the rapier was heavier than
the nineteenth-century foil, it handled much more like one than any high or late
medieval sword), meant that it was easier to understand the Renaissance weapons
than their medieval precursors.

Without the benefit of knowledge of or access to the earlier manuscripts, building
on a general tradition of historical study that saw the Middle Ages as a cruder, less
refined time, and – significantly – failing to recognise that knightly swordplay was
not confined to the battle- or tournament-fields, nor to combat in armour, it was
inevitable, that the Victorian revivers of historical swordsmanship should seem to
serve the medieval period so badly.[22]

The revival of historical swordsmanship that Hutton, Egerton Castle, and Corthey
began was not to last.[23] Their passion was neither carried on by their pupils nor

[20] *Ibid*, p. 19.
[21] A point made by J. Clements in his online article for ARMA: The Association for Renaissance
Martial Arts, 'What did Historical Swords Weigh?', *ARMA: The Association for Renaissance Martial
Arts*, n.d. http://www.thearma.org/essays/weights.htm#.YHQBT-hKjDA (accessed 1 August 2021).
[22] As J. Christoph Amberger put it, 'Few […] fencing historians […] can resist the temptation to put
current fencing phenomena into a simplistic evolutionary context in which the present is considered
a superior product of 'weedin' out the weak'. (J. Christoph Amberger, *The Secret History of the Sword:
Adventures in Ancient Martial Arts* (Burbank CA, 1996)). See too Ken Mondschein, 'Daggers of the
Mind: Towards a Historiography of Fencing' (https://www.whitman.edu/fencing/Articles/dagger-
softhemind.htm, accessed 28 March 2022), and Sixt Wetzler, 'Überlegungen Zur Europäischen
Fechtkunst', *Das Duell : Ehrenkämpfe vom Mittelalter bis zur Moderne*, ed. Ulrike Ludwig, Gerd
Schwerhoff, Barbara Krug-Richter (Konstanz, 2012), pp. 61–76.
[23] Similar movements to 'rediscover' historical swordsmanship also occurred in Germany, with the
work of Karl Wassmansdorff – *Sechs Fechtschulen (d.i. Schau- und Preisfechten) der Marxbrüder und
Federfechter aus den Jahren 1573 bis 1614; Nürnberger Fechtschulreime v.J. 1579 und Rösener's Gedicht:*

embedded itself within the wider fencing community, and the First World War almost wholly removed a generation of young, martially inclined young men who might otherwise have continued the practices of the London Rifle Brigade fencers. However, the attitudes of these men towards medieval swordplay were to endure. When the modern-day sports fencer looks for a history of the origins of his contemporary sport, they turn, quite naturally, to those nineteenth-century historians. As a result, they are similarly dismissive of medieval swordplay. The Olympic fencer Charles de Beaumont writes, in his 1978 book *Fencing: Ancient Art and Modern Sport*, that 'in the Middle Ages, the general use of armour required weapons, such as the battle-axe and the double-handed sword, to be heavy and clumsy', which seems to directly draw on the attitudes of Hutton and Castle.[24] Similarly, and more recently, the *Encyclopaedia Britannica*'s entries on 'swords' and 'fencing', both written by sports fencers, claim that proper swordsmanship developed as a result of the decline in armour. That on 'fencing' states:

> Among the nobility of Europe during the Middle Ages, the adept handling of a sword was hindered by the use of armour, which was virtually the only means of protection. Swords were heavy and used primarily to breach protective armour. With the introduction of gunpowder in the fourteenth century, however, armour fell into disuse... The demise of armour required that the wearer learn to manipulate a sword skilfully'.[25]

The similarity of this to the opinions of Hutton, Egerton Castle, and Corthey is immediately obvious. Indeed, so close are they that one of these gentlemen must surely have been the source.

Swords on Screen and Stage

Whilst these Victorian swordsmen and women have been recognised as historians of early swordsmanship, their demonstrations were as much to entertain as they were to inform. The public demonstration of swordplay seems to have been very popular and well attended. In recent times, most peoples' exposure to swordsmanship comes through the television, and movies.

Hollywood's fascination with swordplay arrived in the so-called 'swashbucklers' of the nineteen-twenties, thirties, and forties. Movies set in a historical past, with a clear good guy and bad guy; the core of such films was the fight scene. Very early on there was a desire for these sequences to have a realism to them, and specialist coordinators and choreographers were employed to stage them.

Ehrentitel und Lobspruch der Fechtkunst v.J. 1589: eine Vorarbeit zu einer Geschichte der Marxbrüder und Federfechter (Heidelburg, 1870)) and Gustave Hergsell's *Talhoffers Fechtbuch aus dem Jahre 1467; gerichtliche und andere Zweikämpfe darstellend* (Prague, 1887). In Italy the key individuals were Francesco Novati, *Flos Duellatorum, Il Fior di Battaglia di Maestro Fiore dei Liberi da Premariacco* (Bergamo,1902) and Guiseppe Cerri, *Trattato teorico pratico della scherma di bastone* (Milan, 1854).
[24] C.L. de Beaumont, *Fencing: Ancient Art and Modern Sport* (Worthing, 1978), p. 143.
[25] Nick Forrest Evangelista and Elijah Granet, 'Fencing', *Encyclopedia Britannica*, 30 April 2019, https://www.britannica.com/sports/fencing/ (accessed 1 August 2021).

The first of these were two Belgians – Henry Uyttenhove and Fred Cavens – and the American Ralph Faulkner. Henry Uyttenhove worked with Douglas Fairbanks in the 1920 movie *The Mark of Zorro*.[26] Cavens was employed for the 1923 comedy *The Three Must-Get-Theres* (a pastiche of Dumas' 'The Three Musketeers'), and worked on Fairbanks' movies *Don Q, The son of Zorro, The Iron Mask*, and *The Black Pirate*.[27] Faulkner worked with Basil Rathbone and Errol Flynn in many of their movies from 1935 onwards. All three men had a background in sports fencing; Uyttenhove was Professor of Fencing at the Belgian Normal School of Fencing, Cavens trained at the Belgian Military Institute for Physical Education and Fencing, whilst Faulkner learnt the sport after being injured in a stunt, becoming a national champion and member of the US Olympic team in 1932. Famously, Basil Rathbone was a competition-quality fencer, having been twice the British Army fencing champion during his service in the Great War.[28] These backgrounds were to shape the nature of the swordsmanship depicted in the movies of the day. No matter what period was being depicted, the swordplay remained firmly based on modern sports fencing, in its form, bladework, and athleticism. The fights were invariably linear, with the actors working back and forth, exchanging a rapid series of thrusts, parries, and ripostes, even when using the set and props to leap on and off. However, there was some recognition of the requirements of the medium in which they worked. Cavens said:

All movements, instead of being as small as possible as in competitive fencing, must be large but nevertheless correct. Magnified is the word.

The routine should contain the most spectacular attacks and parries it is possible to execute while remaining logical to the situation. In other words, the duel should be a fight and not a fencing exhibition, and should disregard at times classically correct guards and lunges. The attitudes arising naturally out of fighting instinct should predominate. When this occurs, the whole performance will leave an impression of strength, skill, and manly grace.[29]

By the end of the fifties swashbuckling was going out of fashion and the sixties saw few movies in the genre. In the seventies, however, Richard Lester directed *The Three Musketeers*.[30] Starring Michael York, Oliver Reed, Richard Chamberlain, Frank Finlay, and Christopher Lee, the movie staged several fight sequences, including one-on-one and mass combats. The choreographer for these was William Hobbs, who worked alongside Lester to provide a more realistic and accurate look, although some critics

[26] *The Mark of Zorro*, dir. Fred Niblo (Douglas Fairbanks Pictures, 1920)
[27] *The Three Must-Get-Theres*, dir. Max Linder (Max Linder Productions, 1922). *Don Q: The Son of Zorro*, dir. Donald Crisp (Elton Corporation, 1926). *The Iron Mask*, dir. Allan Dwan (Elton Corporation, 1929). *The Black Pirate*, dir. Albert Parker (Elton Corporation, 1926). For more on these three early fight arrangers, see Richard Cohen, *By the Sword: Gladiators, Musketeers, Samurai Warriors, Swashbucklers, and Olympians* (London, 2002).
[28] Richard Van Emden and Vic Piuk, *Famous 1914–1918* (Barnsley, 2009), p. 132.
[29] Quoted in Jeffrey Richards, *Swordsmen of the Screen: From Douglas Fairbanks to Michael York* (London, 1977), p. 44.
[30] *The Three Musketeers*, dir. Richard Lester (Momentum Pictures, 1973).

suggested the sequences were too elaborate and heavily scripted, lacking spontaneity.[31] Hobbs was dismissive of the swashbuckler approach to swordplay, preferring a gritty realism, where fighters made mistakes and scrambled to recover, and where the fear of death was real.[32] He was interested in the narrative of the fight, making it every bit a part of the storyline of the play or film in which it occurred.[33]

Hobbs was also the choreographer for Ridley Scott's 1977 movie *The Duellists*, noted for the historical accuracy of its setting, costumes, and the duelling sequences.[34] These movies more accurately represent the swordplay of their respective periods – the seventeenth and nineteenth centuries – as did the others with which Hobbs was connected, including *Cyrano de Bergerac* (1990), *Rob Roy* (1995), and *The Man in the Iron Mask* (1998).[35] By comparison, however, the movies with a medieval theme in which he choreographed the fights do not show the same level of historical accuracy. The swords in *Robin and Marian* (1976), *Excalibur* (1981), or *Ladyhawke* (1985) are used to make great, sweeping blows, blocked solidly by sword or shield, with little of the sophistication of fights from movies with Renaissance or early modern settings.[36]

It is intriguing that the same fight director who espoused a more authentic approach to his fight scenes, and who produced such nuanced and accurate combats, should seem to ignore the available evidence for the medieval period, producing sequences that lacked not only authenticity but also fencing skills. It is not simply that Hobbs lacked knowledge that swords were used differently at different periods of history. If that were the case, then we would see the same forms of swordplay in all his movies, just as happened in the thirties or forties, based on the principles of modern sports fencing. Nor can we claim that the simplicity and crudity of the swordplay is a lack of fencing skill on the part of the actors. It is true that the actors of the golden age of swashbucklers very often had some training in sports fencing whilst later actors, who invariably had to be willing to play a larger range of roles, have been less likely to have the leisure to specialise in the same way. Yet often we can see that an actor has skills in fight choreography on one film, but these are not replicated in another. Orlando Bloom, for example, showed great skill and ability with the choreographed smallsword fights in the *Pirates of the Caribbean* trilogy, but his handling of a sword in *Kingdom of Heaven* (in common with the other actors) is the stereotypical big, hewing

---

[31]   Vincent Canby, 'Spirites "Three Musketeers" (no 6)', *The New York Times*, 4 April 1974.

[32]   Mike Barnes, 'William Hobbs, Fight Director on Swashbuckling Classics "The Duellists" and "Rob Roy", Dies at 79', *The Hollywood Reporter*, 20 July 2018, https://www.hollywoodreporter.com/ news/william-hobbs-dead-fight-director-swashbuckling-classics-duellists-rob-roy-was-79-1128567 (accessed 1 August 2021).

[33]   Hobbs' fight arranging philosophy is best expounded upon in his books William Hobbs, *Fight Direction for Stage and Screen* (London, 1995) and the earlier, *Techniques of the Stage Fight: Swords, Firearms, Fisticuffs and Slapstick* (London, 1967).

[34]   *The Duellists*, dir. Ridley Scott (Paramount Pictures, 1977).

[35]   *Cyrano de Bergerac*, dir. Jean-Paul Rappeneau (UGC, 1990). *Rob Roy*, dir. Michael Caton-Jones (United Artists, 1995). *The Man in the Iron Mask*, dir. Randall Wallace (United Artists, 1998).

[36]   *Robin and Marian*, dir. Richard Lester (Columbia Pictures, 1976). *Excalibur*, dir. John Boorman (Orion Pictures, 1981). *Ladyhawke*, dir. Richard Donner (Twentieth Century Fox, 1998).

blows, albeit with a clear sense of timing, distance, and the tempo of the fight far from some of the bang-the-swords-together sequences in other movies.[37]

In part the contradiction lies in Hobbs' approach. He wanted a real fight, one that had a storyline of its own. As we shall see, this is not the same as portraying a historically authentic fight. More importantly there is a seeming failure to understand the weapons and fighting techniques of the medieval period, and to follow the traditional view that medieval swordsmanship was crude, and the weapons cumbersome and heavy. This is understandable when so many fight directors can trace their ancestry back to the sports fencers of the twenties and thirties, either as participants in the sport themselves, or via the stuntman and fight choreography industry. The legacy of Egerton Castle and Corthey would appear to be a long one.

Of course, fight directors only work within the confines of the rest of the movie. They are not the only individuals to have a role in the shaping of a fight.[38] As we have already suggested, the ability of the actor will have some part to play in how complex and authentic a fight will look. The overall director will have his own vision for how the fight should play out, and how it fits in the wider context of the piece. If they are enamoured of the flow and aesthetic of eastern martial arts (as has been fashionable for the depiction of hand-to-hand combat over the last thirty years) then their fight scenes are likely to follow. The editors will then cut and paste the sequence, adding sound and music to increase the drama and excitement.

Another major factor in the determination of the way in which the combat is played out lies in the props used. Very often prop swords are made without consideration or understanding of how a real sword is weighted and should feel. A prop sword for a particular production might have to last months of regular beatings, and often would be made thicker and heavier to ensure that it would not break, and so that nicks and gouges could be ground out. With props that are heavy and unbalanced it is inevitable that the combat will be slow and unbalanced. Alternately, they might be made lighter in order that the actor can lift it. The actor and the choreographer might then be led by the feel of the weapon; a heavy and cumbersome prop leads to a heavy and cumbersome fight. In the case of *the Lord of the Rings* trilogy, for example, the heroes' swords were made in two versions. Those for close-ups, (known as 'hero swords'), were made as 'real' swords, out of high-quality sprung steel and bronze, whilst those for actual combat scenes were made of light-weight aluminium with urethane hilts. The swords of the hundreds of extras, which were neither to be seen up close nor used in combat, were all plastic, formed from urethane.[39]

One of the fight choreographers who offered a very different attitude towards medieval swordplay was John Waller. Waller's background, unlike so many of his contemporaries, was not in sports fencing nor in stunt work and stage combat.

[37] *Pirates of the Caribbean*, dir. Gore Verbinski (Walt Disney Pictures, 2003). *Kingdom of Heaven*, dir. Ridley Scott (Scott Free Productions, 2005).

[38] I'd like to thank Mike Loades for his insights; they inform much of what follows.

[39] R. Woosnam-Savage, 'The Material of Middle-Earth', *Picturing Tolkien: Essays on Peter Jackson's The Lord of the Ring Film Trilogy*, ed. Janice Bogstad and Philip Kaveny (Jefferson, NC, 2011), pp. 139–67.

Instead, Waller came to the subject with a passion for medieval history and a desire to understand the weapons and armour of the period.[40] He built reproduction weapons, was a founding member of one of the earliest re-enactment societies – 'The Medieval Society', created in 1963 – before moving into fight choreography for the stage and screen. When the Royal Armouries opened its purpose-built museum in Leeds, it was John Waller who recruited and trained their interpretation team, a group who performed choreographed fights in costume, to show the use of the weapons of the past, bringing the museum's artefacts to life.

Having one foot on the stage and another (more firmly planted) in the museum and archives, Waller was one of the first European fight choreographers to try and understand the reality of the historical weapons.[41] He researched extensively, looking at original weapons, and reading and analysing the historical fencing manuals, using them to better understand the body mechanics of the fight. He made his own weapons, with an eye to giving the props a weight and heft more approximate to the originals he had handled. Unlike Cavens, who advocated ignoring the correct techniques in favour of the depiction of strength, skill, and manly grace, or Hobbs, for whom the story of the fight predominated, Waller advocated for staging that followed the principle of 'reality first, theatricality second':

> No action should be choreographed which does not have its basis in the realistic opportunities open to the combatants at any given point in the fight using the weapons at their disposal. The only exceptions are those techniques which may be judged too dangerous for combatants and visitors during public performances... I believe that attacks should be made with the weapon followed by the body and defenses by the body followed by the weapon. Blows should be avoided (with or without a time-hit) or blocked according to the realistic opportunities afforded the defender at any given point in the combat.[42]

As his friend and contemporary fight director Mike Loades argues, combat on the stage should have every bit the same search for truth as the dialogue, the movement, or any other element of the actors art. Combat on the stage should have three central truths: the authenticity of the weapons (the heft of the weapon informs the way in which you should move with it and use it), 'martial reality' (the moves choreographed for the performers should be a realistic move that would work in practice), and 'authenticity of historical style' (the fight should look correct for its period, in terms of the techniques used and the body shapes adopted by the fighters).[43]

---

[40] Guy Wilson, 'John Waller – A Life Remembered', *Arms and Armour*, 15.2 (2018), pp. 113–21. Again, I am also grateful to Mike Loades, a longstanding friend of Waller and a fellow fight choreographer, for his insights into the man and his approach to medieval swordsmanship.

[41] Mike Loades, pers. comm. 17 April 2021.

[42] John Waller, 'Thoughts & Ideas: John Waller, Head of Fight-Interpretation, Royal Armouries, Leeds, UK', *ARMA: the Association for Renaissance Martial Arts*, n.d, http://www.thearma.org/spotlight/JohnWaller.htm#.YHRs3uhKjD4 (accessed 1 August 2021). See also Waller's book, with Keith Ducklin, *Sword Fighting Techniques: A Manual for Actors and Directors* (London, 2001).

[43] Mike Loades, per. comm. 17 April 2021.

The approach of Waller and Loades to the recreation of historical swordplay came from a spirit of historical enquiry, as opposed to other fight directors who asked questions of theatrical effect. It was a holistic one, considering not only the fight and the weapons, but also the clothing of the combatants, the impact of being in armour both for the range of movement and visibility, and for the target areas that were available to cause an effective wound. The skills developed by those they trained and worked with were very much those of the fighter. The combats they choreographed and taught were to all intents and purposes real, the only difference being that they were choreographed (which served to keep the actors alive).

Re-enactment Swordplay

Waller carried his approach to medieval swordplay beyond the realm of stage and screen, into the newly burgeoning hobby of re-enactment. As well as being a founding member of 'The Medieval Society', he worked with Brigadier Peter Young, the founder of another early organisation, 'The Sealed Knot', dedicated to recreating the English Civil War, and was instrumental in the development of the combat aspect of this new hobby.[44]

Re-enactment combat presents a different set of challenges to combat for the stage or camera. Not only does it have to be historically accurate, but it also must balance the safety of the participants (and audience) against the spectacle of massed combat. This it must do without the benefit of extensive choreographing and rehearsal, and allow for a competitive element amongst the participants. Unlike a stage or movie fight, which is choreographed and rehearsed, re-enactment fights are unscripted engagements, whose participants will not have rehearsed, and will also be seeking to 'win' the fight. The lack of a script or rehearsed sequence, and the inherent dangers of 'freeplay' combat even with blunted weapons, are ameliorated by the imposition of rules of engagement that restrict the techniques that can be used. The exact nature of these restrictions varies from group to group, based around a perceived level of risk to the combatant and their equipment, the manufacture of the weapons being used (which are invariably 'rebated'), the number of participants (which can range from single combats between individuals to massed battles involving hundreds). Generally, the larger the number of combatants the more restrictive the rules. There is often an expectation of a minimum level of protective equipment (generally a helmet and hand protection), and there will usually be formal training and assessment, and a requirement that combatants enter the fight with consideration and control.[45] Strikes are generally limited to five or six target areas, with restrictions on strikes to particularly vulnerable areas, including joints and the head, and the prohibition of thrusts

---

[44] Wilson, 'John Waller – A Life Remembered', p. 117.

[45] For example, the Medieval Combat Society's *Code of Safety for Combat Activities* states that 'Anger, lack of consideration, an excessively competitive or aggressive attitude (other than that simulated) or an uncontrollable urge to "win regardless" is to be avoided'. 'Code of Safety for Combat Activities', *Society for Creative Anachronism*, n.d. http://www.themcs.org/documents/MCS%20 2012%20Code%20of%20Safety%20for%20Combat%20Activities.pdf (accessed 1 August 2021).

and grappling techniques. Combatants are expected to be capable of 'pulling' their blows, so as not to land them heavily, preventing injury to the 'opponent' or damage to their equipment.

Re-enactment combat is aimed at entertaining a paying audience, much like stage combat. However, it also has an element of entertaining the participants as well. The free-form and unscripted nature of the combat allows for an air of friendly competitiveness. In most re-enactment hits are registered by the recipient and combats are 'won' and 'lost' by mutual agreement.

In the American-based 'Society for Creative Anachronism' (SCA) – an organisation established in 1966 for the 'recreation of the arts and skills of pre-seventeenth-century Europe' – we see a more formalised competitive approach, that seeks to reflect the formal 'deeds of arms' of the medieval period.[46] Engagements are one-to-one. The weapons and armour used are regulated. For armoured fighting, weapons are made of rattan or foam, rather than steel, allowing blows to be laid on with force against opponents in a mixture of armours, metal, leather, or padded cloth. Fighters are expected to judge for themselves whether a strike would have been a wounding or killing blow, and to respond accordingly.[47] A blow to the arm will render the arm 'incapacitated', and the fighter may not use it for the remainder of the bout. A strike to the leg requires the combatant to continue the fight whilst 'kneeling, sitting, or standing with their legs together'.[48] Marshals observe the fights, but their role is one of monitoring the safety of the combatants and spectators, rather than to act as judges.[49]

A rather different form of competitive re-enactment combat developed in Eastern Europe and spread across the world in the late nineties and early 2000s. This is 'Historical Medieval Battles' (HMB), often referred to as 'buhurt' (a name taken from the medieval *béhourt*, the impromptu tournaments described above).[50] Originating in the re-enactment organisations of Russia, Belarus, and the Ukraine in the late 1990s, the key differences between HMB and the SCA's competitive bouts is that the former is exclusively armoured combat, with competitors using steel weapons, and wearing metal armour that is aesthetically similar to historical examples. In HMB combat the aim is either to land a set number of blows on an opponent (in one-to-one competitions) or to disarm or force to the ground all opponents in team competitions (in which teams can be as large as 150 strong).[51] A much wider range of blows is acceptable. Strikes are permitted to any part of the body, excepting the feet, knee joint, back of the knees, groin, back of the neck or base of the skull, and can include

---

[46] On the origins and culture of the SCA, see Michael Cramer, *Medieval Fantasy as Performance: The Society for Creative Anachronism and the Current Middle Ages* (Lanham, MD, 2009).

[47] 'Society for Creative Anachronism Newcomer's Portal: Armored Combat', *Society for creative Anachronism*, n.d. http://welcome.sca.org/armored-combat/ (accessed 1 August 2021).

[48] *The Society for Creative Anachronism Inc. Fencing Masters' Handbook* (Milpitas, CA, 2020), p. 18.

[49] *Ibid*, p. 23.

[50] See above p. 159.

[51] This is one of the categories of the 'Battle of the Nations', one of the leading international competitions of HMB. Other categories have included one-to-one duels with swords or polearms, and team 'buhurts' of 5, 12, and 30 combatants per side. http://new.botn.info/botn-story/ (accessed 1 August 2021).

strikes with swords or polearms (so long as they are not used to thrust), the shield, hands, legs, head, shoulders, or body.[52] Grappling (but not those techniques designed to painfully lock or break limbs, or chokeholds), throws and trips are all permitted, as are techniques aimed at taking a weapon from an opponent (as disarming them is also considered to have 'removed them from battle').[53] These rules, especially the 'last man standing' victory condition, the use of steel weapons, and armour that is heavier than that used in the SCA, results in a combat that is quite brutal, and injuries are far from uncommon.

HMB bouts very much resemble medieval armoured combat as imagined by Hutton or Corthey, with the victor being the warrior best able to withstand the heaviest blows for the longest period. Because the aim is to land blows and/or drive an opponent to the ground, there is a tendency for HMB fights to look a bit like a game of 'British Bulldog' in armour, and combatants will often bring in the techniques of other martial arts traditions, especially those of so-called mixed martial arts or 'MMA'.

The nature of HMB has also had an impact on shaping the armour and weapons used in the lists. Great emphasis is placed on the authenticity of the arms, armour, and clothing of participants. There should be no mixing of styles from different dates and different regions within a single harness, and primary source evidence for any style of equipment carried and worn is required.[54] As with regular re-enactment, that authenticity is balanced against the need to keep the combatant safe, so that armour is modified from the original form to provide extra protection for the face, and especially the eyes. Likewise, the weapons used are rebated. These protective measures invariably increase the weight of the blade and of the armour which, in turn, changes their heft and the combatant's ability to move, and thereby the nature of the combat.[55]

The major issue with all forms of armoured combat in re-enactment and HMB is that participants fight as if they were unarmoured. The armour does what it was always designed to do – protect the wearer from the blows of an opponent, but that opponent is making no attempt to defeat the armour. They are prevented from using the medieval techniques of locks and throws, and half-swording to deliver thrusts to vulnerable areas between the armour plates, by the rules of the governing bodies of the hobby and, hopefully, a desire not to do their opponent any lasting damage. In many ways, this is no more accurate than the 'knife sharpening' clash of blade on blade of the early days (and not-so-early days) of Hollywood or the theatres.[56]

---

[52] 'Battle of the Nations: Rules for Buhurt Categories', *Battle of the Nations*, 1 October 2010, http://www.new.botn.info/wp-content/uploads/2019/10/Rules-for-BUHURT-CATEGORIES_v1.0.2-1.pdf (accessed 1 August 2021).

[53] *Ibid*. In the individual 'tournament' competitions wrestling techniques are forbidden.

[54] 'BotN Authenticity Committee', *Battle of the Nations, n.d.* https://botn.info/organization-group/en-authenticity-committee (accessed 1 August 2021).

[55] That having been said, armourers for HMB have begun forging armour in titanium, which is easier to maintain as it does not rust and it is also some 40% lighter than the steel equivalent. Obviously, this has an impact on the fighter's ability to move.

[56] The term 'knife sharpening' is to be found in Jeff Palmer, 'The Golden Years of Hollywood', *The Fight Master*, 1.1 (April 1978), p. 8.

Learning by Doing? Historical European Martial Arts

Another approach to the recreation of historical swordsmanship is Historical European Martial Arts or 'HEMA'. It is best defined as the pursuit of martial arts of European origin that have died out or evolved into significantly different forms, the basis of study for which are the *fechtbücher* of the fifteenth century that we have discussed above, and various treatises of the sixteenth and seventeenth centuries.

It differs from re-enactment or stage combat in that fighters do not wear period clothing, but modern protective gear, including masks, gauntlets, and other body protection. This allows for a full range of blows to be landed with power and intent, including strikes to the head and face, and thrusts. It has a competitive element, like HMB, with tournaments being held across the globe, but there is a far greater focus on authenticity of method (in some cases the scoring system rewards combatants for the use of correct and 'authentic' techniques), and also on the need not to get hit, through the use of rules on priority, as are found in modern sports fencing.[57] In some regards it has similarities to the nineteenth-century 'kernoozers', in that there is often a spirit of academic enquiry, and information exchange. Indeed, some have suggested that HEMA's roots lie with those Victorian proponents of historical swordsmanship. However, there is no continuity between the pursuits and demonstrations of Egerton Castle and Hutton, and the modern HEMA community. As we noted above, with Hutton's death in 1910, and that of the French proponent of rapier and dagger fighting Georges Dubois in 1934, there was no-one to continue the practice which, at any rate had always been something of an antiquarian eccentricity.

The modern practice of HEMA is really a child of the late 1990s, born from the developments we have already described within stage combat and re-enactment. Members of the SCA looking to improve the quality of their historical swordplay gained access to sixteenth-century rapier treatises, many of which were shared by Professor Patri Pugliese, dance historian and collector of fencing manuals. Others had come across historical swordplay independently, and came to the SCA looking to practice it. In the UK the innovators were often fencing instructors, like the Scottish national coach (and another academic with a passion outside of his field) Professor Bert Bracewell, who taught both classical sports fencing and Victorian singlestick at Edinburgh Napier University, and whose pupils formed one of the earliest HEMA organisations, 'the Dawn Duellists'.[58] This group also benefited from the work of John Waller and Mike Loades. The latter's instructional video – *The Blow-by-Blow Guide to Swordfighting in the Renaissance Style* – was an inspiration to many within

---

[57] 'Priority' or 'Right of Way' is a process whereby an attack has to be successfully parried or avoided before a counterattack can be made – 'Priority (Right of Way) in Foil Fencing', *London Fencing Club*, n.d. https://www.londonfencingclub.co.uk/news/106-priority-right-of-way-in-foil-fencing (accessed 1 August 2021).

[58] 'The History of the Modern HEMA Movement', *Historical European Martial Arts Resources*, 30 May 2020, http://www.historicaleuropeanmartialarts.com/2020/05/30/the-history-of-the-modern-hema-movement/ (accessed 1 August 2021). It should be said that the origin stories for HEMA are already cloaked in myth and legend, but these seem to be the most concrete elements within them.

the re-enactment community to look again at how they portrayed historical swords-manship.[59] Alongside the re-enactors looking for a more authentic experience of historical swordsmanship, and sports fencers with an interest in historical combat, others came to the hobby, including practitioners of eastern martial arts looking for new challenges or disciplines from their own culture.

Initially, the groups formed were small and isolated, interpreting the manuals and techniques in very different ways. However, a few key connections were made, and collaborations begun. Practitioners started publishing their thoughts, transla-tions, and interpretations of the manuals. HEMA benefited from the fact that it was developing alongside an ever-increasing reach of the internet. This provided opportunities to create effective web forums, allowed for the creation of an inter-national community, and enabled a huge expansion in the exchange of sources, knowledge, theories, and practice. The growth of the HEMA community has seen the identification, transcription, translation, and interpretation of an enormous corpus of *fechtbücher*, both in physical print and online, as well as the establishment of professional 'masters' – instructors who are able to make a living from the teaching of HEMA.[60]

The equipment used also developed rapidly. In less than a decade practitioners went from training and sparring with wooden wasters or steel swords made for re-en-actment, protected by an array of improvised forms of body protection, including motorcycle and ice hockey armour and sports fencing defences, to being able to buy nylon wasters, steel *feders*, and protective equipment designed and manufactured specifically for HEMA by leading manufacturers of sports fencing equipment.

Despite its exponential growth in popularity, and the strong lines of communi-cation and structure between practitioners, the community remains a disparate one. There are a great many national and international umbrella organisations, such as the 'Academy of European Medieval Martial Arts' (AEMMA), the 'Historical European Martial Arts Coalition' (HEMAC), 'British Federation of Historic Swordplay' (BFHS), the 'Association for Renaissance Martial Arts' (ARMA) and the 'Deutscher Dachverband für Historisches Fechten' (DDFH). Each of these shares the aim of popularising and promoting the hobby, as well as protecting the interests of its members with regards to legislation regarding weapons, and the provision of the sort of formality necessary to obtain recognition as a legitimate sport (vital for practitioners to purchase personal injury and public liability insurance). Not every HEMA club or society is affiliated to one of these organisations nor is every HEMA

---

59 Mike Loades, *The Blow-by-Blow Guide to Swordfighting in the Renaissance Style*, dir. Mike Loades (Running Wolf Productions, 1991). Robert Brooks, 'The truth, the half-truth & nothing like the truth', *Hotspur School of Defence*, 22 October 2019, https://www.hotspurschoolofdefence.com/blog/the-truth/ (accessed 1 August 2021).

60 Many of those published sources have already been cited, but one of the key scholars to publish in paper is Jeffrey Forgeng. See, in particular, his work on I.33 (already cited), and on the manual of Johannes Lecküchner, published as *The Art of Swordsmanship by Hans Lecküchner* (Woodbridge, 2015). As we have noted, there is now a bewildering amount of material available freely online, of varying quality, but the website *Wiktenauer* (https://www.wiktenauer.com) stands apart as the most comprehensive and scholarly online collection and analysis of *fechtbücher* and later fencing manuals.

practitioner a member of a club or society. Many remain independent (some fiercely so), whether as small informal groups meeting in a village hall or someone's back yard, or as large schools with regular meetings held in their own fencing *salles*.

This variety of backgrounds from which practitioners of HEMA are drawn result in a wide range of approaches to the practice, prioritising different aspects, and emphasising different skill sets and interests. These differing flavours and foci shape the preoccupations, discussions, and debate between practitioners, and are the fuel for the fires of forum discussions, and published secondary material within the field.

For some enthusiasts sparring and competition lies at the heart of their practice. They may argue that as the sources were designed to teach men to fight and kill each other, free-play, sparring and competitive bouts should lie at the heart of the recreation. Combat is the purpose of the art. They may point to the manuals of Meyer and his like, which describe sword combat as a form of play within schools of fence (as we have seen). They can argue that only sparring and free-play, with unchoreographed techniques and blows being executed at speed towards an opponent, allows period techniques to be understood in context, and delivered correctly. For others, whilst sparring is a useful tool, and competition is fun, there is a concern that a focus on these activities become a distraction from the pursuit of historical accuracy, and that the adrenaline and excitement of free-play can lead to a loss of technique, especially amongst less experienced practitioners.[61]

Invariably, any formal competition requires rules to determine who has scored a point and 'won' a bout. These rules are often contentious, based on an interpretation of the original manuscripts and an assumed effectiveness of the techniques they teach. A key example are the debates over whether glancing blows and *schnitte* – light cuts to the fingers and wrist – should be considered legitimate attacks. Such strikes are often discounted from scoring, either on the grounds that hits to the hand are considered dangerous (even with protective gloves there is the chance of badly bruised or broken fingers) and should be discouraged, or because such hits would have been inconsequential in a real fight. They are, however, an integral aspect of some (but not all) of the *fechtbücher*, and to ignore them as a legitimate target, it could be argued, not only means that you are not replicating historical techniques, but that it also encourages people to be careless of their hands which results in a greater chance of them being hit and injured.[62]

Equally contentious is the question of 'double hits', that is to say who should 'win' in the case of both combatants striking each other simultaneously. This was a debate sports fencing had in the nineteenth century, and which resulted in the foil and sabre

---

[61] See three articles by HEMA coach Keith Farrell, 'The development of historical technique in modern HEMA tournaments', 27 August 2018, https://www.keithfarrell.net/blog/2018/08/the-development-of-historical-technique-in-modern-hema-tournaments/, 'Sparring and Fighting', 21 May 2018, https://www.keithfarrell.net/blog/2018/05/sparring-and-fighting/, and 'Trying to Simulate a Real Fight', 24 April 2017, https://www.keithfarrell.net/blog/2017/04/trying-simulate-real-fight/ (accessed 1 August 2021).

[62] See Keith Farrell, 'Attacking the Hands in Sparring', 17 September 2018, https://www.keithfarrell.net/blog/2018/09/attacking-the-hands-in-sparring/ (accessed 1 August 2021).

disciplines making use of the system of 'priority' or 'right of way' and the introduction of electronic scoring apparatus, where hits are registered through conductive
suits and weapons. Such rules ensure that a fighter who ignores his opponents' attack
so as to score his own 'hit' is punished, on the grounds that whilst he may have 'killed'
his opponent, he is still just as 'dead' himself. The counter argument is that both hits
should be scored, on the grounds that, in a real fight, both combatants would have
been wounded or killed. Those who are not supportive of competitive play argue that
all such rules encourage practitioners to develop techniques that capitalise on them to
score quick and easy points at the cost of remaining faithful to the use of techniques
drawn from the source material.

The question around the place of free-play in HEMA impacts on the equipment
that is used. The more intense the play the less control the fighter has, and a greater
amount of protection is required to keep combatants safe. The more restrictions
regarding the landing of blows or techniques that can be used, the greater the control
and the less important protection is to avoid injury. With mask, body, arm and leg
defences it is possible to spar at almost full intensity when using either nylon 'wasters'
or modern copies of the late medieval *feder*.[63] The armour, however, can inhibit
movement, vision, and sensation, whilst no matter how well designed they are nylon
wasters and *feders* do not behave in the same way as a sharp sword.[64]

By concentrating on controlled training in particular techniques, the practitioner is able to do away with much of the padding and use weapons that are more
analogous to the weight and heft of original swords. It is even possible to train with
a sharp sword; however, no amount of protection could make sparring with one of
these weapons safe. As we discussed in the last chapter, it is possible to use a 'real'
sword against an opponent and not kill them, but they must be prepared to accept a
level of risk and potential injury. Those levels, even amongst sixteenth-century fencers
using *feders* or *dusacks*, were far higher than most modern HEMA practitioners (or
their clubs and insurance companies) are prepared to take.[65] Any sparring with such a
weapon must be done at a much lower intensity, and with a far greater deal of control.
Training with sharp weapons, it is argued, gives a proper feel for the behaviour of
swords, as well as teaching a level of respect for not only the blade of one's opponent
but also one's own.[66] The cost of this is that whilst 'windings' of the blade (where the
edges of the two blades connect and the friction between them allows for swords to

---

[63] Some practitioners are now saying that the current level of protection, in particular for hands and
head is still insufficient to prevent injury.

[64] Nylon wasters have a habit of flexing around a parrying blade, with the result that in competition
hits may be called even when the parry has been a good one, something that a steel blade would
not allow.

[65] The 'dusack' is, many ways, to a *messer* what a *feder* is to a longsword, and was developed around
the same time. Originally made of wood or leather, with a broad, curving 'blade' and a simple oval
grip, modern examples are also produced in nylon plastic.

[66] Guy Windsor, 'Why you should train with sharp swords, and how to go about it without
killing anyone', *Chivalric Fighting Arts Association*, 18 February 2014, http://www.chivalricfighting.
wordpress.com/2014/02/18/why-you-should-train-with-sharp-swords-and-how-to-go-about-it-
without-killing-anyone/ (accessed 1 August 2021).

be twisted over and around each other without sliding off) can be performed much more effectively, blows cannot be landed, and some techniques – the hewing blows, thrusts, and *schnitte* – are almost impossible to do safely.

Most HEMA commentators suggest using a mixture of all of these approaches – solo drills, paired practice, cutting practice with sharp blades, and free-play, each with appropriate levels of protection and control, and at the appropriate level of expertise, as each develops different skills and aspects of swordsmanship.[67]

HEMA is not just a sport or a martial art. More than any of the other ways in which the use of the medieval sword has been recreated, HEMA has promoted the considered and critical study of the historical sources. There are an increasing number of 'scholarly practitioners', academics who combine traditional methods of historical research and HEMA practice.[68] They have built a sophisticated corpus of research around the *fechtbücher*, seeking to set them in their historical context, to better understand their function, and the situation of the fencing masters who wrote them.[69] Whilst not every HEMA practitioner feels the need to engage with the works as historical sources, or to understand their wider context beyond what one can do with a sword, many now have a more nuanced understanding of the source materials of their practice, and their limitations.

These scholars recognise that it is not simply enough to interpret the techniques by reproducing them in modern practice (indeed, Eric Burkart, one of the leading HEMA scholars, now argues that there simply is not enough information contained within the sources for this to be done), but that they must form part of a wider study of what Burkart calls a 'culture of fighting'.[70] The techniques only make sense within the context of the culture in which they were to be used, and the situation for which they were developed. As we have noted, few if any of the *fechtbücher* were composed as technical manuals in the way that the majority of modern HEMA practitioners seek to use them today. The missing elements required to bring the plays to life must come from the interpreter and they, as Burkart points out, are modern individuals with only modern experiences to draw on.[71]

Burkart compares the study of HEMA to the movement within musicology of 'historically informed performance'. Attempting to applying a historically accurate technical and stylistic approach to the music and using instruments that are either originals from the period or modern reproductions, 'HIP' performers sought to produce a historically authentic performance. However, they faced many of the same

---

[67] See Guy Windsor, 'How to spot the bullshit in any martial arts drill, and what to do about it', 8 October 2013, https://guywindsor.net/2013/10/how-to-spot-the-bullshit-in-any-martial-arts-drill-and-what-to-do-about-it/ (accessed 1 August 2021).

[68] Eric Burkart, 'Limits of Understanding in the Study of Lost Martial Arts: Epistemological Reflections on the Mediality of Historical Records of Technique and the Status of Modern (re-) Constructions', *Acta Periodica Duellatorum*, 4.2 (2016), pp. 5–30.

[69] Daniel Jaquet, Claus Frederik Sørensen, and Fabrice Cognot, 'Historical European Martial Art: A Crossroad between Academic Research, Martial Heritage Re-creation and Martial Sport Practices', *Acta Periodica Duellatorum*, 3 (2015), pp. 5–35.

[70] Bukart, 'Limits of Understanding', p. 12.

[71] *Ibid*, p. 19.

challenges as HEMA practitioners in interpreting and recreating a physical activity (in this case the performing of music) from an imperfect collection of sources (musical notation and original instruments) in a search for a historical authenticity of style. Those working in the field have determined that, in the end, there is too much within performance that comes from modern sensibilities and beliefs about how the performance should sound. Even when a piece of music and the instruments on which it is played is understood in its broad historical and cultural context, the 'rightness' of the interpretation is, in the end, still contingent on the modern sensibilities of the performer and audience.[72]

Quite simply, there is too much missing for us to truly recreate medieval swordplay. Whether it be as straightforward as the fact that neither participant in the reconstruction is really seeking to put a sword through their opponent's head, or as complex as how one takes a step (which is different after a lifetime walking in modern shoes on modern pavements from how a medieval person may have done), in the end what we have is a modern interpretation of a medieval cultural experience, not an authentic recreation of that original practice. HEMA, for all its attention to the original source material, is in that respect no different to the demonstrations of the Victorian 'kernoozers', or the swashbuckling fights of stage and screen, or the combats of the re-enactor. They are all modern interpretations and adaptations. One might say that they are simply the latest of the cultures of the medieval sword.

[72] On this, see Lydia Goehr, *The Imaginary Museum of Musical Works: An Essay in the Philosophy of Music* (Oxford, 1994).

Conclusion

IN THIS BOOK I have sought to offer a broader understanding of the sword in the high Middle Ages, arguing for three interconnected, but distinctive 'cultures'. Whilst recognising the importance and complexity of the noble culture of the sword, I have sought to get away from the modern preconceptions of them as purely high-status rarities; magical symbols of royal or knightly power, instead offering an alternative culture that places the sword in the hands of the middle classes. They used the weapon as a symbol of their aspirations for noble status, and their desire to participate in the masculine world, but where swordsmanship was, perhaps, as much an intellectual as it was a martial pursuit. Finally, I have argued that our own attempts to represent, interpret and understand the place and use of the medieval sword have resulted in a third 'culture' of the medieval sword, one that is played out on the movie and television screens, or at Renaissance fairs and historical fencing *salles*, where the need to get it 'right' is tempered by the desire for it to look or feel right, and the underlying fear that, in recreating medieval combat, someone might actually get hurt.

The sword of the high and late Middle Ages was every bit as special, but also far more mundane than we have been led to believe. Whilst the sword of the Anglo-Scandinavian tradition of the early Middle Ages had been forged by smiths using knowledge that was arcane, verging on the supernatural, the sword of our period was a product of industrial processes: water-powered trip-hammers and blast furnaces.[1] No longer the rare and treasured heirlooms of an elite group within a martial elite, we find swords in the hands of magnates and merchants, students, and soldiers. Where once they had been imbued with magical force, cursed, or carrying the power to grant victory, even the swords of the great heroes of the mythical past had lost much of their magical aura. Christianity too had cost the sword something of its power and agency. The belief that an object might have a destiny of its own, that it had power to act for the good or ill of those who possessed it, was a pagan one, that denied the supreme power of the Almighty. Victory in battle came from God. The sword thus became a vehicle for God's grace and power. In the hands of the heroes of epic and romance relic-bedecked blades would slaughter the ungodly, but the strength to do so came direct from the Lord.

Ironically, perhaps, the decoration on the blade became more magical than it had been. In the early Middle Ages, it was the maker's name that was dominant on the blade, whilst runes and incantations are almost unheard of. In the high Middle Ages,

---

[1] Sixt Wetzler and Peter Johnsson, "I am the Sword", *Das Schwert: Gestalt und Gedanke*, p. 15.

we find many blades adorned with esoteric inscriptions that are best understood as pious and invocatory phrases.

Those inscriptions may not just have been requests for divine aid, however. The sword remained a symbol of power and status, an integral part of the creation of knights and kings. Here again the Church was a central player, co-opting the sword for its purposes. It retained the spiritual sword, long since adopted as a metaphor for the spiritual struggle, but granted its temporal counterpart to those in authority – kings and knights – so that they might wield it in defence of the Church. This transfer of power was physically enacted through the passing of a sword from the officiating prelate, via the altar, to the candidate. The inscriptions on so many blades that appear to be the same biblical passages and prayers used in such rituals suggest that some if not all of the swords so decorated may have served in these rites, as an aide-memoire to them during, or a memento of them thereafter.

A sword with a history continued to be a powerful symbol. Just as in the early medieval period, such a sword gave added legitimacy to its holder. Whether it be the weapon of an Arthurian hero, the ornate sword of an emperor, the ancient-looking sword of a dragon-slaying forebear, or a rusty old blade that had come over with the Conqueror, such swords leant their *gravitas* and historical weight to the holder's position, reinforcing his power.

The transference of power through the giving of a sword was not solely in the hands of the Church. Kings might present swords to counts, mayors, and royal officials as a mark of delegated authority. Rules for the bearing of such swords (and their sheaths and belts; the whole ensemble had significance) defined when and how such weapons were to be carried. Bearing swords became a potent symbol of authority and are one of the few examples where original medieval weapons retain their function to this day.

A sword might well denote noble status and authority, but its ownership was no longer confined to that elite. Amongst the gentry – the lesser landowners, merchants and guildsmen, apprentices and clerks – the sword was also a possession which, like other aspects of the chivalric culture which this group had adopted, was adapted to suit their needs and interests. They were not yet wearing swords as a matter of course. Their culture was not yet that of the Renaissance where every gentleman had a sword at his hip as a mark of his status and his readiness to defend that status immediately. Private quarrels that came to sword blows were rare and were often the result of premeditation. The dominant culture of the sword amongst this professional urban elite was of buckler-play and fencing. Swordsmanship for these men was primarily a sport to be played in the back alleys and mews, and amongst the taverns and brothels. Like the ludic pastimes of the nobility, such activities were viewed with distrust by the authorities. Just as the tournament could become a place of sedition and unrest, so too the schools of fence were often seen as places of iniquity and breeding grounds for disorder. Yet, by the fifteenth century the pursuit was becoming more acceptable, and some of those who taught and practiced the art of fencing were finding themselves being called upon by the authorities, even employed by them, rather than shut down and prosecuted.

The varied cultures of the sword make it difficult to draw conclusions as to how the sword was used. Too often our sources skip the gory detail, or add to it to make the combat seem more glorious and the protagonists more fearsome or valiant. The marks on weapons and remains offer tantalising hints as to the blows that caused them, but nothing more than that. The *fechtbücher* that seem to lay out the nature of sword combat so clearly provide a glimpse only into one form of combat, the single combat of the judicial combat or the duel of honour, a specialised form that had even professional warriors coming to their authors to learn.

The *fechtbücher* may not even really tell us how swordsmanship was taught and learnt in the period. The bulk of them were most certainly not intended as do-it-yourself manuals. They were the product of a particular type of swordsmanship. For all that the likes of Fiore and Talhoffer may have courted the nobility and sought their patronage, the methods and the style of fighting they taught were very much that of the fencing school, of the bucker-playing urban professional. Other texts, like HS3227a, were the jotted notes of men for whom fencing was just one of the many subjects that a gentleman of their status should be interested in. All of the authors of these texts were of this same stratum in society; non-noble but aspirational of noble status, educated in or at least *au fait* enough to use the same pedagogical language as the universities that so many of them seem to have lived near. Even if they were not actually teaching swordplay as if they were leading a class in rhetoric, when it came to setting their concepts down on paper, it was that style of classical and formal pedagogy that became the structure of their works.

For those seeking to recreate medieval swordsmanship in the modern world this poses huge problems. The core source materials from which we look to draw our lessons cannot serve as a manual for study. They are too often designed as much to obfuscate as to elucidate and leave too much unspoken or unexplained. They offer a type of swordsmanship that was artificial even for its original students, let alone for us today. Besides, it is not enough to simply recreate the techniques of medieval swordsmanship. If we truly want to understand the way in which the sword was used in the Middle Ages, then we must also recognise the complexity and breadth of the historical context in which the sword appeared, and that may prove a greater challenge than deciphering Lichtenawer's *zedel*.

Glossary

I HAVE TRIED NOT to use too many technical terms in this book; however the following appear relatively frequently, and these definitions (though not definitive) may prove useful.

Arming Sword

In modern terms, this is a catch-all for any medieval sword designed to be wielded in one hand, and so serves as a synonym for the classic 'knightly' sword. It was originally a fifteenth-century term denoting the sword that was worn on the belt, as a backup to the main weapon (whether a **longsword**, pollaxe, bow, or whatever).

Baselard

A form of dagger or short sword, with a distinctive I-shaped grip. The term may have been less specific in the medieval period, being used to refer to any large dagger or small sword.

Bearing Sword

A sword displayed as a symbol of power and authority, generally born by a 'sword-bearer' before or behind the individual whose rank or status is being represented. Some of these were purpose made as ceremonial symbols, and could reach massive proportions (like the **greatsword**) but they could equally well be 'real' swords.

Bind/Binding

The moment where two swords are in blade contact, 'bound' together.

Blossfechten

German term referring to combat out of armour. The opposite of **harnischfechten**.

Buckler

A small, normally round shield with a centre grip, used in conjunction with an **arming sword**. In the fourteenth century, the main combination of weapons used in non-noble ludic swordsmanship.

Centre of Balance

The physical, precise point on a sword where its weight is equally distributed to each side.

Centre of Percussion	The point of the blade which has the least vibration and thus delivers the best cut.
Counter	In the **fechtbücher**, and in **HEMA** practice, a **play** undertaken in opposition to an opponent's attack. See also **remedy**.
Cross	The part of the **hilt** running perpendicular to the blade which protects the hand, often mistakenly referred to as the 'Quillons', a post-medieval term.
Dusack	From the Czech *tesák* (lit. *fang*), a sixteenth- and seventeenth-century single-edged curved bladed sword, akin to a **falchion**. Also developed as a practice weapon or **foil**, with a short, thick, curved 'blade', made of wood or leather. It had no hilt, the handle being a hole cut within the width of the blade itself. These practice weapons continue to be used in the modern practice of **HEMA**.
Épée	Literally 'sword' in French, but in modern sports fencing it refers to the weapon and discipline, in which the whole body is a target and for which 'right of way' rules do not apply.
Estoc	A form of the **longsword** specifically designed for thrusting, with a long, narrow blade, sometimes without a cutting edge. A variant was also developed for boar hunts, with a spatulate tip and a bar partway down the blade to prevent the blade going to deep.
Falchion	A single-handed, broad-bladed, single-edged sword, often with a cusped or clipped tip.
False Edge	The edge of a sword blade that faces towards the wielder's body.
Fechtbuch / Fechtbücher	A German term used by modern HEMA practitioners and researchers to describe any medieval or early modern text connected with the teaching of fencing.
Feder / Federschwert	A nineteenth-century neologism to describe a sixteenth-century training sword, designed to have the heft of a **longsword** whilst reducing the impact of either cut or thrust. It is characterised by a flexible narrow and **rebated blade** with a wide section adjacent to the **cross** known as the *schilt*, which helps to provide a realistic **heft** to the blade. Now a common form of weapon used in the practice of **HEMA**.[1]

---

[1] For a discussion of the term, see D. Jaquet, '"…schirmen mit Federklingen": Towards a Terminology

Foil	A form of sports fencing in which only the trunk is a target and where 'right of way' rules are enforced. Also, the weapon used in that form of combat and, colloquially, any weapon used in sports fencing.
Fuller	A groove or grooves running down the centre of a blade. Often referred to as the 'blood groove' and popularly explained as a feature to prevent swords becoming stuck in wounds, the reality is that they are designed to reduce the weight of a blade whilst retaining its stiffness.
Greatsword	A sword larger than a **longsword**, often approaching six feet in length, designed to be used in two hands. Predominantly a weapon of the sixteenth century, they often have ornate hilts and are sometimes confused with **bearing swords**. Often referred to using the German term *zweihänder*, a nineteenth-century term. See also **Montante** and **Spadone**.
Guard	Either the section of the **hilt** protecting the hand (see also **cross**) or (in the **fechtbücher**, and in **HEMA** practice) the offensive or defensive posture taken by a fighter, from which all attacks and defences are taken.
Half-sword / Half-swording	A technique for using a longsword in armoured combat (**harnischfechten**), in which one hand is placed halfway down the blade, to facilitate the tip being worked into the gaps between elements of harness.
Harnischfechten	A German term referring to combat in armour. The opposite of **blossfechten**.
Heft	The way in which a sword feels and moves in the hand. A combination of its weight and balance.
HEMA	'Historical European Martial Arts'. The modern practice of recreating medieval swordsmanship through the study of **fechtbücher** or other fencing treatises, using analogues of period weapons.
Hilt	A term to describe the pommel, grip and **cross** of a sword.
Longsword	A sword designed to be used in either one or two hands. Longer than the **arming sword** but shorter than the later **greatsword**.

---

of Fencing Swords (1400–1600)', *The Sword: Form and Thought*, ed. Lisa Deutscher, Mirjam Kaiser and Sixt Wetzler (Woodbridge, 2019), pp. 24–40.

Malchus	A German synonym for **falchion**, from the name of the servant whose ear was severed by St Peter in the garden of Gethsemane.
Messer	Literally 'knife' but used to refer to a knife similar in form to a **falchion**, being single-edged and commonly (but not invariably) with a clipped tip. Sometimes conflated with the terms *haus-* or *bauernwehr* ('house- or farm-weapon'), *messer* refers to a fencing weapon whilst the latter are catch-all terms for a utility knife (akin to the modern machete).
Montante	Iberian name for a form of **greatsword**.
Plays	In the **fechtbücher**, and in **HEMA** practice, a term used to describe a particular technique of swordplay.
Pommel	The shaped weight at the end of the sword that helps to counterbalance the weight of the blade.
Rapier	A sword for the robe, that is to say a sword made to be worn with civilian clothing. A development of the late fifteenth and sixteenth centuries, it had an increasingly long and slender, blade, with an ornate guard.
Rebated blade	A blade either designed or altered to have no point or edge, to serve as a **foil**, **feder,** or **waster**.
Remedy	In the **fechtbücher**, and in **HEMA** practice, an action taken to counter an opponent's **play**. A **counter-remedy** is the action taken to oppose a **remedy**.
Ricasso	A section of a blade towards the **hilt** which is unsharpened.
Sabre	A single-handed sword, often single-edged and with a curve, designed for cutting. In sports fencing the discipline in which the whole body above the waist is a target.
Schilt	The wide section of a **feder** blade close to the cross that serves to give the weapon a more sword-like **heft**.
Seax	An early medieval knife with a broad, single-edge blade and a clipped tip.
Smallsword	A late seventeenth-century development of the **rapier**, designed to be easily worn with everyday clothing. Characterised by a needle-like blade and simple hilt. With a small, slim blade, it is the precursor to the modern sports fencing foil and épée.
Spadone	Italian term for a form of **greatsword**.
Tang	The portion of a blade around which the hilt is mounted.

The Strong	In the **fechtbücher**, and in **HEMA** practice, the section of the blade closer to the hilt, offering the most resistance to pressure from an opponent's sword in the **bind**.
The Weak	In the **fechtbücher**, and in **HEMA** practice, the top section of the blade, furthest from the hilt, and the least able to resist the pressure from an opponent's sword in the **bind**.
True Edge	The edge of a sword blade that faces towards the wielder's opponent.
Tuck	English word for an **estoc**.
Waster	Historically, a wooden cudgel or stave used in place of a sword for practice and play. In modern terms a practice weapon made of wood or nylon.
Zetteln/zedel	'notes' or 'epitomes', written in rhyming couplets attributed to the fourteenth-century fencing master Johannes Liechtenauer as cryptic summaries of his teachings. First appearing in the anonymous 'Pol Hausbuch' (GNM Ms 3227a), they come down to us through various manuscripts prepared by those purporting to be his students, who provide explanatory glosses of them.

Bibliography

Manuscript Sources

Bible of Roda, BnF Latin 6 (3)

Bodleian Library Ashmole Ms 1146

Bodleian Library Ashmole Ms 1147

Chief Justice's Roll, 29 Edw III, Hilary term, NA CP40/380

Codex Manesse, Große Heidelberger Liederhandschrift, Cod. Pal. germ. 848

Court of Common Pleas: Brevia Files, TNA C 47/2/64

Court of Kings Bench: Plea and Crown Sides: Coram Rege Rolls, TNA KB 27/220/105-7d

The Douce Apocalypse, Bodleian MS. Douce 180

Duarte I, *The Book of Horsemanship by Duarte I of Portugal*, trans. Jeffrey Forgeng (Woodbridge, 2016)

Froissart, Jean, *Chronicles*, Besançon, Bibliothèque municipale, ms. 864

———, *Chroniques sire Jehan Froissart*, Besançon, Bibliothèque municipale, ms.865

———, *Chroniques sire Jehan Froissart*, BnF MS Français 2644

Guiron le Courtois, BnF MS NAF 5243

The Harley Psalter, BL Harley MS 603

The Littlemore Anselm, Bodleian Library MS. Auct. D. 2. 6

Montauban, Regnault de, *Rédaction en prose*, 4 vols., BnF, MS Arsenal 5072-75

Talhoffer, Hans, *First Manuscript*, Copenhagen, Det Kongelige Bibliotek, MS Thott.290.2º

Ordo ad Coronandum regem et reginam Francorum, BnF Latin 1246

Phébus, Gaston, *Livre de la chasse*, BnF MS 616, fol. 94r-94v

Queen Mary Psalter, BL Ms Royal 19B xv

Smithfield Decretals, BL Royal 10 E IV

Statuts de l'Ordre du Saint-Esprit au droit désir ou du Noeud, étably par Louis d'Anjou, roy de Naples et de Sicile, en 1352, 1353 et 1354, BnF MS 4274

Wigmore Inventories, British Library Add.MS 60584

Wigmore Inventories, TNA E 163/4/48 (2e), E 101/333/4 and E 372/179 (22.d)

Published Primary Sources

Alfieri, Francesco Fernando, *L'arte di ben Maneggiare la Spada*, trans. James Clark. https://wiktenauer.com/wiki/Francesco_Fernando_Alfieri#Lo_Spadone_.28.22 The_Greatsword.22.29 (accessed 1 August 2021)

Bar-sur-Aube, Bertrand de, 'Girart of Vienne', *Heroes of the French Epic*, trans. M. Newth (Woodbridge, 2005), pp. 281–472.

Bayeux Tapestry Digital Edition (revised edition), edited by Martin K. Foys (Saskatoon, 2011), http://www.sd-editions.com/Bayeux/online (accessed 21 August 2022).

The Beauchamp Pageant, ed. Alexandra Sinclair (Donington, 2003)

Beowulf, trans. Howell D. Chickering, Jr (New York, 2006)

Brooks, Terry, *The Sword of Shannara Trilogy* (London, 2002)

Calendar of Close Rolls of the Reign of Henry III: AD 1237–1242, ed. H.C. Maxwell Lyte (London, 1911)

Calendar of Coroner's Rolls of the City of London, A.D. 1300–1378, ed. Reginald Sharpe (London, 1913)

The Calendar of Letter Books of the City of London, ed. Reginald R. Sharpe, 11 vols. (London, 1899–1912)

Calendar of the Plea and Memoranda Rolls of the City of London: Volume 1, 1323–1364, ed. A.H. Thomas (London, 1926)

'Capitulare Mantuanum', *Monumenta Germaniae Historica: Capitularia Regum Francorum, Nova Series 1*, ed. Gerhard Schmidt (Hanover, 1996)

Carmen de Triumpho Normannico, trans. Kathleen Tyson (Scotts Valley, CA, 2013)

Cartulaire des comtes de Hainaut, de l'avènement de Guillaume II à la mort de Jacqueline de Bavière [1337–1436], ed. L. Devillers (Brussels, 1881)

Castle, Egerton, *Schools and Masters of Fence from the Middle Ages through to the Eighteenth Century*, 2nd edn. (London, 1893)

La Chanson de Guillaume, ed. Duncan McMillan (Paris, 1949)

The Book of Chivalry of Geoffroi de Charny: Text, Context, and Translation, trans. and ed. Richard Kaeuper and Elspeth Kennedy (University Park, PA, 1996)

Chaucer, Geoffrey, *The Canterbury Tales*, trans. David Wright (Oxford, 2011)

The Chivalric Biography of Boucicaut, Jean II le Meingre, trans. Craig and Jane H.M. Taylor (Woodbridge, 2016)

The Chronicle of London, ed. H.N. Nicholas (London, 1827)

Chronicle of the religious of Saint-Denys: containing the reign of Charles VI, from 1380 to 1422, ed. and trans. M.L. Bellaguet, 6 vols. (Paris, 1839–44)

'Collectio Capitularium Ansegisi', *Monumenta Germaniae Historica: Capitularia Regum Francorum, Nova Series 1*, ed. Gerhard Schmidt (Hanover, 1996)

The Continuations of the Old French "Perceval" of Chretien de Troyes, Volume 1: The First Continuation, ed. William Roach (Philadelphia, PA, 1949)

Corthey, Adolphe, *Français et Prussiens: Armes Blanches et armes à feu* (Paris, 1887)
———, *Fencing Through the Ages*, trans. Chris Slee (Brisbane, 2015)

The Coventry Leet Book; or Mayor's Register, Containing the Records of the City Court

Leet or View of Frankpledge, A.D. 1420–1555, with Divers Other Matters, trans. and ed. Mary Dormer Harris (London, 1907)

Domesday Book: A Complete Translation, ed. A. Williams and G.H. Martin (London, 2002)

Figueyredo, Diego Gomes de, *Memorial of the Practice of the Montante*, trans. E. Myers and S. Hick (n.p., 2009)Forgeng, J., *The Art of Swordsmanship by Hans Lecküchner* (Woodbridge, 2015)

Froissart, Jean, *Chronicle of England, France, Spain, and the Adjoining Countries, from the Latter Part of the Reign of Edward II to the Coronation of Henri IV*, trans. T. Johnes (New York, 1857)

———, *Ouevres de Froissart*, trans. Baron Kervyn de Lettenhove, 25 vols. (Osnabruck, 1967)

———, *Chroniques*, ed. Siméon Luce et al, vol. 2 (Paris, 1869)

Furnivall, F.J. (ed.), *Hymns to the Virgin and Christ, the Parliament of devils, and other religious poems* (London, 1865)

De Gamez, Gutierre Diaz, *The Unconquered Knight: A Chronicle of the Deeds of Don Pero Niñó, Count of Bucha*, trans. Joan Evans (Woodbridge, 2004)

Sir Gawain and the Green Knight, ed. and trans. W.R.J. Barron (Manchester, 1998)

Gesta regis Henrici Secundi Benedicti abbatis / The Chronicle of the Reigns of Henry II and Richard I, A. D. 1169–92; Known Commonly under the Name of Benedict of Peterborough, ed. William Stubbs, 2 vols. (London, 1867)

Goudourville, Henri de, *Escrimeurs Contemporains* (Paris, 1899)

von Günterode, Heinrich, *De Veris Principiis Artis Dimicatorie* (Wittenberg, 1579)

History of William Marshal, ed. A.J. Holden, trans. S. Gregory, 3 vols. (London, 2002)

Hymns to the Virgin and Christ, the Parliament of devils, and other religious poems, ed. F.J. Furnvall (London, 1895)

Hoveden, Roger of, *Chronica*, ed. W. Stubbs, 4 vols. (Cambridge, 1868–71)

Hutton, Sir Alfred, *The Sword and the Centuries* (London, 1901, reprinted Barton under Needwood, 2003)

Joinville, Jean de, *Vie de Saint Louis*, ed, and trans. Jacques Monfrin (Paris, 1998)

Joinville and Villehardouin: Chronicles of the Crusades, trans. M.R.B. Shaw (London, 1961)

Great Britain, The Statutes of the Realm, 9 vols. (London, 1963)

Knyghthode and Bataile, eds. Roman Dyboski and Z.M. Arend (London, 1935)

Laxdœla Saga, trans. Magnus Magnusson (London, 1975)

Lewis, C.S. *The Lion, The Witch and the Wardrobe*, The Chronicles of Narnia (London, 2001)

Libere, Fiore De'i, *Fior Battaglia*, Getty MS Ludwig XV 13, trans. Colin Hatcher. https://wiktenauer.com/wiki/Fior_di_Battaglia_(MS_Ludwig_XV_13) (accessed 1 August 2021)

Il libro di Montaperti (An. 1260), ed. Cesare Paoli (Florence, 1889), pp. 373–4

The Life and Death of Cormac the Skald, trans. W.G. Collingwood (London, 1903)

Lull, Ramon, *The Book of the Order of Chivalry*, trans. Noel Fallows (Woodbridge, 2013)

Malmesbury, William of, *Gesta Regum Anglorum*, ed. and trans. R.M. Thomson and M. Winterbottom, 2 vols. (Oxford, 1998–9)

Meyer, Joachim, *Gründtliche Beschreibung der Kunst des Fechtens* (Strasbourg, 1570), vol I, 10v. Transcribed Michael Chidester, trans. Mike Rasmusson. https://wiktenauer.com/wiki/Joachim_Meyer#Sword (accessed 1 August 2021)

Mitty, Jean de, 'La Société d'Encouragement a L'Escrime', *La Grande Dame: revue de l'élégance et des arts / publiée sous la direction de F.G. Dumas*, ed. F.G. Dumas (Paris, 1894), pp. 97–100

Monmouth, Geoffrey of, *The History of the Kings of Britain*, trans. Lewis Thorpe (London, 1966)

La Chronique de Enguerran de Monstrelet: en deux livres, avec pieces justicatives 1400–1444, ed. L. Douët d'Arcq, 6 vols. (Paris, 1857–62)

Moorcock, Michael, *The Dreaming City* (New York, 1972)

Morte Arthure, ed. G.G. Perry (London, 1865)

Munimenta Gildhallae Londoniensis: Liber Albus, Liber Custumorum et Liber Horn, ed. H. Riley (London, 1859)

Musset, L., *The Bayeux Tapestry*, trans. R. Rex (Woodbridge, 2005)

Of Knyghthode and Bataile, ed. Trevor Russell Smith and Michael Livingston (Kalamazoo, MI, 2021)

Matthaei Parisiensis, monachi Sancti Albani, Chronica Majora, ed. H.R. Luard, 7 vols. (London 1872–80)

Matthew Paris's English History. From the year 1235 to 1273, trans. J.A. Giles, 3 vols. (London, 1852–4)

Parliament Rolls of Medieval England, ed. Chris Given-Wilson, Paul Brand, Seymour Phillips, Mark Ormrod, Geoffrey Martin, Anne Curry and Rosemary Horrox (Woodbridge, 2005)

Pisan, Christine de, *The Book of Deeds of Arms and of Chivalry*, trans. Sumner Willard, ed. C.C. Willard (University Park, PA, 1999)

The Poems of Laurence Minot, ed. John Hall (Oxford, 1914)

Political Poems and Songs Related to English History, vol. I, ed. Thomas Wright (London, 1859)

'The Post-Vulgate Merlin Continuation', trans. Martha Asher, *Lancelot-Grail: The Old French Arthurian Vulgate and Post-Vulgate in Translation*, gen. ed. Norris Lacy, vol. VIII (Cambridge, 2010)

Proceedings and Ordinances of the Privy Council of England, ed. Sir Harris Nicolas, vol. VI (London 1837)

Ravaton, Hugues, *Chirurgie d'armée, ou, Traité des plaies d'armes à feu, et d'armes blanches: avec des observations sur ces maladies.* (Paris, 1768)

Records of Medieval Oxford Coroners' Inquests, the Walls of Oxford etc., ed. H.E. Salter (Oxford, 1912)

Robert le Diable: Roman d'Aventures, ed. E. Löseth (Paris, 1903)

Rowling, J.K., 'The Sword of Gryffindor.' *Pottermore*, 10 August 2015, https://www.pottermore.com/writing-by-jk-rowling/the-sword-of-gryffindor (accessed 1 August 2021)

Select Cases from the Coroner's Rolls, AD 1265 – 1413, with a Brief Account of the History of the Office of the Coroner, ed. Charles Gross (London, 1896)

Select Documents of English Constitutional History, George Burton Adams and Henry Morse Stephens (London, 1906)

'Sir Gowther', *The Middle English Breton* Lays, ed. Anna Laskaya and Eve Salisbury (Kalamazoo, MI, 1995), pp. 263–307

'Starhemberg Fechtbuch', *Accademia Nazionale dei Lincei Cod.44.A.8* https://wiktenauer.com/wiki/Starhemberg_Fechtbuch_(Cod.44.A.8) (Accessed 1 August 2021)

Statuta Antiqua Universitatis Oxoniensis, ed. Strickland Gibson (Oxford, 1931)

Sturluson, Snorri, *The Prose Edda*, ed. and trans. J.L. Byock (London, 2005)

Speculum Regale: Ein altnorwegisher Dialog, nach Cod. Arnmagn. 243 Fol. B, ed. O. Brenner (Munich, 1881)

Sylvius, 'Lettre de Belgique', *Le Figaro* (16 May 1894)

'Talhoffer Fechtbuch', *Königsegg-Aulendorf Collection, MS XIX.17-3. https://wiktenauer.com/wiki/Talhoffer_Fechtbuch_(MS_XIX.17-3)* (accessed 1 August 2021)

'Talhoffer Fechtbuch', Det Kongelige Bibliotek MS Thott.290.2° https://wiktenauer.com/wiki/Talhoffer_Fechtbuch_(MS_Thott.290.2%C2%BA) (accessed 1 August 2021)

Talhoffer, Hans, *Medieval Combat: A Fifteenth-Century Illustrated Manual of Swordfighting and Close-Quarter Combat*, trans. and ed. Mark Rector (London, 2000)

Testamenta Eboracensia, Or Wills Registered at York, Illustrative of the History, Manners, Language, Statistics, &c., of the Province of York from the Year 1300 Downwards, vol. 3, ed. James Raine and John William Clay (London, 1865)

The Medieval Art of Swordsmanship: Royal Armouries I.33, ed. Jeffrey Forgeng (Leeds, 2018)

The Saga of King Hrolf Kraki, ed. J. Byock (London, 1998)

The Song of Roland, trans. G. Burgess (London, 1990)

The Song of the Cid, trans. Burton Raffel (London, 2009)

Tolkien, J.R.R., *The Hobbit* (New York, NY, 2012)

———, *The Fellowship of the Ring: Being the First Part of The Lord of the Rings* (New York, 2012)

———, *The Two Towers: Being the Second Part of The Lord of the Rings* (New York, 2012)

———, *The Return of the King: Being the Third Part of the Lord of the Rings* (New York, 2012)

The Tournaments at Le Hem and Chauvency, trans. Nigel Bryant (Woodbridge, 2020)

The Trial of Jeanne d'Arc, trans. W.P. Barrett (New York, 1932)

Troyes, Chrétien de, *Arthurian Romances*, trans. W.W. Kibler (London, 1991)

Vegetius: Epitome of Military Science, trans. N.P. Milner (Liverpool, 1996)

The Earliest English Translation of Vegetius De Re Militari, ed. G. Lester (Heidelberg, 1988)

The Ecclesiastical History of Orderic Vitalis, ed. and trans. M. Chibnall, 6 vols. (Oxford, 1969—1980)

Wace, *Roman de Rou*, trans. Glyn S. Burgess (St Helier, 2002)

Zimmer Bradley, Marion, *Mists of Avalon* (New York, 1983)

Secondary Sources

Aird, W., *St Cuthbert and the Normans: The Church of Durham 1071–1153* (Woodbridge, 1998)

Allmand, Christopher, *The De Re Militari of Vegetius: The Reception, Transmission and Legacy of a Roman Text in the Middle Ages* (Cambridge, 2011)

Ambühl, Rémy, *Prisoners of War in the Hundred Years War: Ransom Culture in the Late Middle Ages* (Cambridge, 2013)

Amburger, J. Christoph, *The Secret History of the Sword: Adventures in Ancient Martial Arts* (Burbank, CA, 1996)

Androshchuk, Fedir, *Viking Swords, Swords and Social aspects of Weaponry in Viking Age Societies*, Statens Historiska Museum, Studies 23 (Stockholm, 2014)

Anglo, S., 'Anglo-Burgundian Feats of Arms: Smithfield, June 1467', *Guildhall Miscellany*, 2 (1965), pp. 271–83

———, *The Martial Arts of Renaissance Europe* (New Haven, CT, 2000)

Appleby, Jo, Rutty, Guy N., Hainsworth, Sarah V., Woosnam-Savage, Robert C., Morgan, Bruno, Brough, Alison, Earp, Richard W., Robinson, Claire, King, Turi E., Morris, Mathew, and Buckley, Richard, 'Perimortem Trauma in King Richard III: a Skeletal Analysis', *The Lancet*, 385.9964 (17–23 January 2015), pp. 253–9

Armstrong, Jackson, 'The Development of the Office of Arms in England, c.1413–1485', *The Herald in Late Medieval Europe*, ed. Katie Stevenson (Woodbridge, 2009), pp. 9–28

Astrup, E.E., and Martens, I. 'Studies of Viking Age Swords: Archaeology and Metallurgy', *Gladius*, XXXI (2011), pp. 203–6

Aurell, Martin, *The Plantagenet Empire, 1154–1224*, trans. David Crouch (Harlow, 2007)

———, *The Lettered Knight: Knowledge and Aristocratic Behaviour in the Twelfth and Thirteenth Centuries*, trans. Jean-Charles Khalifa and Jeremy Price (Budapest, 2017)

———, *Excalibur, Durendal, Joyeuse: La Force de l'épée* (Paris, 2021)

Ayton, Andrew, *Knights and Warhorses: Military Service and the English Aristocracy Under Edward III* (Woodbridge, 1999)

Barber, Richard, *The Reign of Chivalry* (Woodbridge, 2005)

———, 'Arthurian Swords I: Gawain's Sword and the Legend of Weland the Smith', *Arthurian Literature*, XXXV (2020), pp. 1–20

———, *Magnificence: Princely Splendour in the Middle Ages* (Woodbridge, 2020)

Barber, Richard, and Barker, Juliet, *Tournaments: Jousts, Chivalry and Pageants in the Middle Ages* (Woodbridge, 2000)

Barker, Juliet, *The Tournament in England, 1000–1400* (Woodbridge, 2003)

Barnes, Mike, 'William Hobbs, Fight Director on Swashbuckling Classics "The

Duellists" and "Rob Roy", Dies at 79', *The Hollywood Reporter*, 20 July 2018, https://www.hollywoodreporter.com/news/william-hobbs-dead-fight-director-swashbuckling-classics-duellists-rob-roy-was-79-1128567 (accessed 1 August 2021)

Barrett, Edward, *Ceremonial Swords of Britain: State and Civic Swords* (Stroud, 2017)

'Battle of the Nations: Rules for Buhurt Categories', *Battle of the Nations*, n.d. http://www.new.botn.info/wp-content/uploads/2019/10/Rules-for-BUHURT-CATEGORIES_v1.0.2-1.pdf (accessed 1 August 2021)

Bauer, Matthias Johannes, 'Fechten Lehren, mitt verborgen vnd verdeckten worten', *Das Schwert – Symbol und Waffe*, eds. L. Deutscher, M. Kaiser, and S. Wetzler (Leidorf, 2014), pp. 163–70

———, 'Teaching How to Fight with Encrypted Words: Linguistic Aspects of German Fencing and Wrestling Treatises of the Middle Ages and Early Modern Times', *Late Medieval and Early Modern Fight Books Transmission and Tradition of Martial Arts in Europe (14th-17th Centuries)*, eds. Daniel Jaquet, Karin Verelst, and Timothy Dawson (Leiden, 2016), pp. 47–61

Beaumont, C.L. de, *Fencing: Ancient Art and Modern Sport* (Worthing, 1978)

Benati, C., 'À la guerre comme à guerre but with caution: Protection charms and blessings in the Germanic tradition', *Brathair*, 17.1 (2017), pp. 155–91

Berard, C.M., *Arthurianism in Early Plantagenet England, from Henry II to Edward I* (Woodbridge, 2019)

Biborski, Marcin, and Stępínski, Janusz, 'Szczerbiec (the Jagged Sword) – The Coronation Sword of the Kings of Poland', *Gladius,* XXXI (2011), pp. 93–148

Binard, Fanny, and Jaquet, Daniel, 'Investigation on the collation of the first fight book (Leeds, Royal Armouries, Ms I.33)', *Acta Periodica Duellatorum*, 4.1 (2015), pp. 3–21

Blackett, Sir Edward and Baron de Cosson, 'The Conyers Falchion', *Armes and Armures* (Royal Armouries Library 03984)

Blair, Claude, *European and American Arms* (London, 1962)

———, 'The Sword Catalogue', *The Crown Jewels: The History of the Coronation Regalia in the Jewel House of the Tower of London* (London, 1998)

Blair, Claude, and Delamer, I., 'The Dublin Civic Swords', *Proceedings of the Royal Irish Academy*, 88C (1988), pp. 87–142

Bodemer, Heidemarie, 'Das Fechtbuch: Untersuchungen zur Entwicklungsgeschichte der bildkünstlerischen Darstellung der Fechtkunst in den Fechtbüchern des mediterranen und westeuropäischen Raumes vom Mittelalter bis Ende des 18. Jahrhunderts', Unpublished PhD thesis (Stuttgart, 2008)

Bogaerts, Ilse, 'Representations of executioners in Northern France and the Low Countries', *ICOMAM Conference October 2009 Proceedings* (Leeds, 2012), pp. 149–65

Bonne, Jeanne-Claude, 'The Manuscript of the *Ordo* of 1250 and its Illuminations', *Coronations: Medieval and Early Modern Monarchic Ritual*, ed. János M. Bak (Berkeley, CA, 1990), pp. 58–70

Bork, Robert, *The Geometry of Creation: Architectural Drawing and the Dynamics of Gothic Design* (London, 2016)

Boulton, D'Arcy, 'Classic Knighthood as Nobility Dignity: The Knighting of Counts and Kings Sons in England, 1066–1272', *Medieval Knighthood V: Papers from the Sixth Strawberry Hill Conference 1994*, ed. Stephen Church and Ruth Harvey (Woodbridge, 1995), pp. 41–100

Bourke, Joanna, *An Intimate History of Killing* (London, 1999)

———, *Deep Violence: Military Violence, War Play, and the Social Life of Weapons* (Berkeley, CA, 2015)

Boutell, Charles, and Fox-Davies, Arthur Charles, *English Heraldry* (Whitefish, MT, 2003)

Bradak, B., and Heslop, Brandon, *Lessons on the English Longsword* (Boulder, CO, 2010)

Brault, Gerard J., *Early Blazon: Heraldic Terminology in the Twelfth and Thirteenth Centuries with Special Reference to Arthurian Heraldry* (Woodbridge, 1972)

Bretel, Jacques, 'The Tournament at Chauvency', *The Tournaments at Le Hem and Chauvency*, trans. Nigel Bryant (Woodbridge, 2020), pp. 61–122

Brooks, Robert, 'The truth, the half-truth & nothing like the truth', *Hotspur School of Defence*, 22 October 2019, https://www.hotspurschoolofdefence.com/blog/the-truth/ (accessed 1 August 2021)

Brundage, James A., *The Medieval Origins of the Legal Profession: Canonists, Civilians, and Courts* (Chicago, 2008)

Brunning, Sue, *The Sword in Early Medieval Northern Europe: Experience, Identity, Representation* (Woodbridge, 2019)

Bruso, Steven, 'Bodies Hardened for War: Knighthood in Fifteenth-Century England', *Journal of Medieval and Early Modern Studies*, 47.2 (2017), pp. 255–77

Bumke, Joachim, *Courtly Culture: Literature and Society in the High Middle Ages* (New York, 2000)

Burkart, Eric, 'Die Aufzeichnung des Nicht-Sagbaren. Annäherung an die kommunikative Funktion der Bilder in den Fechtbüchern des Hans Talhofer', *Das Mittlealter*, 19.2 (2014), pp. 253–301

———, 'The Autograph of an Erudite Martial Artist: A Close Reading of Nuremberg, Germanisches Nationalmuseum, Hs. 3227a', *Late Medieval and Early Modern Fight Books Transmission and Tradition of Martial Arts in Europe (14th-17th Centuries)*, eds. Daniel Jaquet, Karin Verelst, and Timothy Dawson (Leiden, 2016), pp. 451–80

———, 'Limits of Understanding in the Study of Lost Martial Arts: Epistemological Reflections on the Mediality of Historical Records of Technique and the Status of Modern (re-)Constructions', *Acta Periodica Duellatorum*, 4.2 (2016), pp. 5–30

———, 'Body Techniques of Combat: The Depiction of a Personal Fighting System in the Fight Books of Hans Talhoffer (1443–1467 CE)', *Killing and Being Killed. Perspectives on Bodies in Battle*, ed. Jörg Rogge (Bielefeld, 2017), pp. 105–25

Cadilhac-Rouchon, Muriel P., 'Revealing Otherness: A Comparative Examination of French and English Medieval Hagiographical Romance', Unpublished PhD (Cambridge, 2009)

Canby, Vincent, 'Spirites 'Three Musketeers' (no 6)', *The New York Times*, 4 April 1974, p. 32

Carpenter, D., 'King Henry III and Saint Edward the Confessor: The origins of the cult', *EHR*, CXXII (2007), pp. 865–91

Cartlidge, Neil, *Heroes and Anti-Heroes in Medieval Romance* (Cambridge, 2012)

Catholica Anglicanum: An English-Latin wordbook dated 1483, ed. S.J.H. Heritage (London, 1881)

Cerri, Guiseppe, *Trattato teorico pratico della scherma di bastone* (Milan, 1854)

Chandler, Jean, 'The guild and the Swordsman', *Acta Periodica Duellatorum*, 2.1 (2014), pp. 27–66

Cherry, J., 'Symbolism and Survival: Medieval Horns of Tenure', *The Antiquaries Journal*, 69 (1989) pp. 111–18

Chidester, Michael et al., *Wiktenauer*. https://wiktenauer.com (accessed 1 August 2021)

Chouinard, Maxime, 'Very Perilous: A sword wounds compendium by the surgeon Ravaton', *HEMA MISFITS (I don't do longsword)*, 2 April 2020, https://hemamisfits.com/2020/04/02/very-perilous-a-sword-wounds-compendium-by-the-surgeon-ravaton/#_ftn1 (accessed 1 August 2021)

Clanchy, Michael, *From Memory to Written Record* (Oxford, 1993)

Claussen, Samuel A., and Sposato, Peter, 'Chivalric Violence', *A Companion to Chivalry*, ed. Robert W. Jones and Peter Coss (Woodbridge, 2019), pp. 99–118

Clemens, J. 'On the Pell', *ARMA: The Association for Renaissance Martial Arts*, n.d. http://www.thearma.org/essays/pell/pellhistory.htm#.XpHlfchKjDY (accessed 1 August 2021)

———, 'What did Historical Swords Weigh?', *ARMA: The Association for Renaissance Martial Arts*, n.d. http://www.thearma.org/essays/weights.htm#.YHQBT-hKjDA (accessed 1 August 2021)

———, 'The Myth of Edge-On-Edge Parrying in Medieval Swordplay', https://www.thearma.org/essays/edgemyth.htm#.YyiOZXbMLD4 (accessed 19 September 2022)

'Code of Safety for Combat Activities', *Society for Creative Anachronism*, n.d. http://www.themcs.org/documents/MCS%202012%20Code%20of%20Safety%20for%20Combat%20Activities.pdf (accessed 1 August 2021)

Cognot, F., 'L'armement Médiéval: Les Armes Blanches dans les Collections Bourguignonnes. Xe – Xve Siècles', Unpublished PhD thesis (Paris, 2013)

Cohen, Richard, *By the Sword: Gladiators, Musketeers, Samurai Warriors, Swashbucklers, and Olympians* (London, 2002)

Contamine, Philippe, *Pages d'Histoire Militaire Medievale (Xive-Xve Siecle)* (Paris, 2005)

Coronations: Medieval and Early Modern Monarchic Ritual, ed. János M. Bak (Berkeley, CA, 1990)

Corrsin, Stephen D., 'The Historiography of European Linked Sword Dancing', *Dance Research Journal*, 25.1 (1993), pp.1–12

———, *Sword Dancing in Europe: A History* (Enfield Lock, 1997)

Coss, Peter, *The Knight in Medieval England, 1000–1400* (Stroud, 1993)

———, *The Origins of the English Gentry* (Cambridge, 2003)

———, 'The Origins and Diffusion of Chivalry', *A Companion to Chivalry*, eds. Robert W. Jones and Peter Coss (Woodbridge, 2019), pp. 7–38

The Engineering of Medieval Cathedrals, ed. Lynn T. Courtenay (London, 1997)

Cramer, Michael, *Medieval Fantasy as Performance: The Society for Creative Anachronism and the Current Middle Ages* (Lanham, MD, 2009)

Crombie, Laura, *Archery and Crossbow Guilds in Medieval Flanders, 1300–1500* (Woodbridge, 2016)

Crouch, David, *The Image of Aristocracy in Britain, 1000–1300* (London, 1992)

———, *Tournament* (London, 2005)

———, 'The Violence of the Preudomme', *Prowess, Piety and Public Order in medieval Society*, ed. C. Nakashian and D. Franke (Leiden, 2017), pp. 87–101

The Crown Jewels: The History of the Coronation Regalia in the Jewel House of the Tower of London (London, 1998)

Cunha, E., and Silva, A.-M., 'War Lesions from the Famous Portuguese Medieval Battle of Aljubarrota', *International Journal of Osteoarchaeology*, 7 (1997), 595–9

Curry, Anne, *Agincourt: A New History* (London, 2005)

Dale, Johanna, *Inauguration Rituals and Liturgical Kingship in the Long Twelfth Century* (York, 2019)

Das Schwert: Symbol und Waffe, eds. L. Deutscher, M. Kaiser, and S. Wetzler (Leidorf, 2014)

Davidson, H.R. Ellis, *The Sword in Anglo-Saxon England: Its Archaeology and Literature* (Woodbridge, 1994)

Deacon, Jacob Henry, 'Prologues, Poetry, Prose and Portrayals: The Purpose of Fifteenth century Fight Books According to the Diplomatic Evidence', *Acta Periodica Duellatorum*, 4.2 (2016), pp. 69–90

———, '"Falsely Accused by the Villain"? A Fishy Trial by Combat in Fifteenth-Century London', *Martial Culture in Medieval Town*, 20 November 2019, https://martcult.hypotheses.org/404 (accessed 1 August 2021)

Medieval Warfare: A Reader, ed. Kelly DeVries and Michael Livingstone (Toronto, 2019)

Depping, G.B., *Wayland Smith: A Dissertation on a Tradition of the Middle Ages* (London, 1847)

Dittmar, J.M., Mitchell, P.D., Cessford, C., Inskip, S.A., and Robb, J.E. 'Medieval injuries: Skeletal trauma as an indicator of past living conditions and hazard risk in Cambridge, England', *American Journal of Physical Anthropology* (2021), pp. 1–20

Dronke, Ursula, *The Poetic Edda 1: Heroic Poems* (London, 1969)

Duby, Georges, 'Les "jeunes" dans la société aristocratique dans la France du Nord-Ouest au XIIe siècle', *Annales: Économies, Sociétés, Civilisations*, 19.5 (1964), pp. 835–46

———, *The Chivalrous Society*, trans. C. Postan (London, 1977)

Ducklin, Keith & Waller, John, *Sword Fighting Techniques: A Manual for Actors and Directors* (London, 2001)

Dugdale, W., *Monasticon Anglicanum*, ed. J. Caley, H. Ellis, and B. Bandinel, Vol. VI (London, 1830)

Dunn-Pattison, R.P., *The Black Prince* (London, 1910)

Dupuis, O. 'Organization and Regulation of Fencing in the Realm of France in the Renaissance', *Acta Periodica Duellatorum*, 2 (2014), p. 233–54

———, 'The Roots of Fencing from the Twelfth to the Fourteenth Centuries in the French Language Area', *Acta Periodica Duellatorum*, 3.1 (2015), pp. 37–62

———, 'Timeo Clipeos et Plagas Ferentes, or the Accidental Death of a Fencing Master in 1331', *Martial Culture in Medieval Town*, 20 April 2020, https://martcult.hypotheses.org/926 (accessed 1 August 2021)

Dykstra, Robert R., 'Lies, Damned Lies, and Homicide Rates', *Historical Methods: A Journal of Quantitative and Interdisciplinary History*, 42.4 (2009), pp. 139–42

Eads, Valerie and Garber, Rebecca L.R., 'Amazon, allegory, swordswoman, saint? The Walpurgis images in Royal Armouries MS I.33', *"Can These Bones Come to Life?" Insights from Reconstruction, Reenactment and Re-creation*, ed. Ken Mondschein (Wheaton, IL, 2014), pp. 5–23

Easton, Matt, 'Sword Carrying Laws in Medieval England', *Schola Gladiatoria*, 11 November 2013, YouTube, https://www.youtube.com/watch?v=9rp3nve9CJk (accessed 1 August 2021)

———, 'Medieval Laws Concerning Weapons', *myArmoury.com Discussion Forums*, 27 March 2011, http://myarmoury.com/talk/viewtopic.22719.html (accessed 1 August 2021)

Elmslie, J., 'Single-Edged Blade Types', *Das Schwert: Gestalt und Gedanke*, eds. B. Grotkamp-Scepers, I. Immell, P. Johnsson, and S. Wetzler (Solingen, 2015), endpapers

Fabian-Wittenborn, M., 'Schwertfrauen' und 'Schwertadel' in der Urnenfelder- und Hallstattzeit?', *Das Schwert. Symbol und Waffe*, ed. Lisa Deutscher, Mirjam Kaiser, and Sixt Wetzler (Leidorf, 2014), pp. 51–64

Faltot, Fanny, 'Les Mémoires de Philippe de Vigneulles', Unpublished PhD thesis (Paris, 2015)

Farrell, Keith, 'Trying to Simulate a Real Fight', 24 April 2017, https://www.keithfarrell.net/blog/2017/04/trying-simulate-real-fight/ (accessed 1 August 2021)

———, 'Sparring and Fighting', 21 May 2018, https://www.keithfarrell.net/blog/2018/05/sparring-and-fighting/ (accessed 1 August 2021)

———, 'The development of historical technique in modern HEMA tournaments', 27 August 2018, https://www.keithfarrell.net/blog/2018/08/the-development-of-his-torical-technique-in-modern-hema-tournaments/ (accessed 1 August 2021)

———, 'Attacking the Hands in Sparring', 17 September 2018, https://www.keithfarrell.net/blog/2018/09/attacking-the-hands-in-sparring/ (accessed 1 August 2021)

Forrest Evangelista, Nick, and Granet, Elijah, 'Fencing', *Encyclopedia Britannica*, 30 April 2019, https://www.britannica.com/sports/fencing/ (accessed 1 August 2021)

ffoulkes, Charles, and Capt. Hopkinson, E.C., *Sword, Lance and Bayonet: A record of the arms of the British army and navy* (Cambridge, 1938)

Fiorato, V., Boylston, Anthea, and Knusel, Christopher, *Blood Red Roses: The Archaeology of a Mass Grave from the Battle of Towton, AD 1461* (Oxford, 2000)

Flori, Jean, 'Les Origines de l'Adoubement Chevaleresque: Étude des Remises d'Armes et du Vocabulaire qui les Exprime dans les Sources Historiques Latines jusqu'au Début du XIIIe Siècle', *Traditio*, 35 (1979), pp. 209–72

Forehand, Brookes, 'Old Age and Chaucer's Reeve', *PMLA*, 69.4 (1954), pp. 984–9

Forgeng, J., 'Owning the Art: The German Fechtbuch Tradition', *The Noble Art of the Sword: Fashion and Fencing in Renaissance Europe 1520–1630*, ed. Tobias Capwell (London, 2012), pp. 164–75

Gardela, Leszek, *Women and Weapons in the Viking World: Amazons of the North* (Philadelphia, PA, 2021)

Geibig, Alfred, *Beiträge zur morphologischen Entwickluisevodermrtes im Mittelalter: Eine Analyse des Fundmaterials vom ausgehenden 8. bis zum 12. Jahrhundert aus Sammlungen der Bundesrepublik Deutschland* (Neumünster, 1991)

Gevaert, Bert, and van Noort, Reinier, 'Evolution of Martial Tradition in the Low Countries: Fencing Guilds and Treatises', *Late Medieval and Early Modern Fight Books*, ed. Daniel Jaquet, Karin Verelst, and Timothy Dawson (Leiden, 2016), pp. 376–409

Geldof, M.R., '"And describe the shapes of the dead". Making sense of the archaeology of armed violence', *Wounds and Wound Repair in Medieval Culture*, eds. L. Tracy and K. DeVries (Leiden, 2015), pp. 57–80

Goehr, Lydia, *The Imaginary Museum of Musical Works: An Essay in the Philosophy of Music* (Oxford, 1994)

Goodall, John, *The English Castle* (London, 2011)

Gräf, Julia, 'Fighting in women's clothes. The pictorial evidence of Walpurgis in Ms. I.33', *Acta Periodica Duellatorum*, 5.2 (2015), pp. 47–71

———, 'Walpurgis: The first lady of traditional Fencing', *Cote du Golfe School of Fencing*, 10 October 2018, https://traditionalfencing.wordpress.com/2018/10/10/walpurgis-the-first-lady-of-traditional-fencing/ (accessed 1 August 2021)

Grossman, David, *On Killing: The Psychological Cost of Learning to Kill in War and Society* (New York, NY, 2009)

———, *On Combat* (Mascoutah, IL, 2012)

Grünzweig, Friedrich, *Das Schwert bei den "Germanen" Kulturgeschichtliche Studien zu seinem "Wesen" vom Altertum bis ins Hochmittelalte* (Vienna, 2009)

———, 'Siegschwert und álög: literarisevoderiv oder Reflex eines kulturellen Phänomens?', *Das Schwert: Symbol und Waffe*, eds. Lisa Deutscher, Mirjam Kaiser and Sixt Wetzler (Leidorf, 2014), pp. 187–96

Hager, Katherine Rose, 'Endowed with Manly Courage: Medieval Perceptions of Women in Combat', Unpublished MA dissertation (Clemson, SC, 2018)

Hambling, Craig, 'Posh Bucklers: The Noble Use of Ignoble Objects' paper presented to the International Medieval Congress 2021 (online), 5 July 2021

Hammer, Carl, 'Patterns of Homicide in a Medieval University Town: Fourteenth-Century Oxford', *Past and Present*, 78.1 (1978), pp. 3–23

Hanawalt, B.A., 'Violent Death in Fourteenth- and Early Fifteenth-Century England', *Comparative Studies in Society and History*, 18.3 (1976), pp. 297–320

Hanley, Catherine, *War and Combat 1150–1270: The Evidence from Old French Literature* (Cambridge, 2003)

Hanner, Brent, 'The King's Mirror as a Medieval Military Manual', *De Re Militari*, n.d. https://web.archive.org/web/20110805101755/http://www.deremilitari.org/resources/articles/hanner.htm (accessed 1 August 2021)

Harrington, Joel F., *The Faithful Executioner: Life and Death in the Sixteenth Century* (London, 2013)

———, *The Executioner's Journal: Meister Frantz Schmidt of the Imperial City of Nuremberg* (Charlottesville, 2016)

Harvey, J.H., 'The Tracing Floor of York Minster', *The Engineering of Medieval Cathedrals*, ed. Lynn T. Courtenay (London, 1997), pp. 81–7

Havens, Earle, *Commonplace Books: A History of Manuscripts and Printed Books from Antiquity to the Twentieth Century* (New Haven, CT, 2001)

Hawkins, Quentin, 'The Meat Cleaver', *Military illustrated*, 112 (September 1997)

Hayes, Sean, 'Memory and Performance: Visual and Rhetorical Strategies of Medieval Martial Arts Texts', *"Can These Bones Come to Life?" Insights from Reconstruction, Reenactment and Re-creation*, ed. Ken Mondschein (Wheaton, IL, 2014), pp. 62–9

Hegg, Victor, 'English and Norwegian Military Legislation in the Thirteenth Century. The Assize of Arms of Norwegian Military Law', Unpublished MA Dissertation (Bergen, 2021)

'Help Us Decipher This Inscription - Medieval manuscripts blog', blogs.bl.uk, 3 August 2015, British Library. https://blogs.bl.uk/digitisedmanuscripts/2015/08/help-us-decipher-this-inscription.html (accessed 1 August 2021)

Hergsell, Gustave, *Talhoffers Fechtbuch aus dem Jahre 1467; gerichtliche und andere Zweikämpfe darstellend* (Prague, 1887)

Hermann, Raphael, Dolfini, Andrea, Crellin, Rachel J., Quanyu Wang, and Uckelmann, Marion, 'Bronze Age Swordsmanship: New Insights from Experiments and Wear Analysis', *Journal of Archaeological Method and Theory*, 27 (2020), pp. 1040–83

Hester, James, 'A few leaves short of a quire: Is the "Tower Fechtbuch" incomplete?', *Arms and Armour*, 9 (2012), pp. 20–24

———, '"To Adorn the Great at light of Mars": Armed Fighting Techniques of the Late Middle Ages', Unpublished PhD Thesis (Southampton, 2018)

———, 'Battle Damage on Arms and Armour', *School of Mars*, 15 April 2020, YouTube. https://www.youtube.com/watch?v=HSDS-p88Fyk (accessed 1 August 2021)

———, 'Battle Damage on Ceremonial Swords', *School of Mars*, 25 August 2020, YouTube https://www.youtube.com/watch?v=hn4qLxTUSFE (accessed 1 August 2021)

Hewitt, J. *Ancient Armour and Weapons in Europe from the Iron Period of the Northern Nations to the End of the Thirteenth Century* (Oxford and London, 1855)

Hils, Hans-Peter, *Meister Johann Liechtenauers Kunst des langen Schwertes* (Frankfurt-am-Main, 1985)

Hobbs, William, *Techniques of the Stage Fight: Swords, Firearms, Fisticuffs and Slapstick* (London, 1967)

———, *Fight Direction for Stage and Screen* (London, 1995)

Hodges, C.C. 'The Conyers Falchion', *Archaeologia Aeliana*, Series 2, 15 (1892), pp. 214–17

Hosler, John D., *Henry II: A Medieval Soldier at War, 1147–1189* (Leiden, 2007)

Hoss, Stefanie, 'A Theoretical Approach to Military Belts', *Rimska Vojna Oprema U Pogrebnom Kontekstu* (Zagreb, 2010), pp. 317–26

———, 'Cingulum Militare: Studien zum römischen Soldatengürtel Des 1. bis 3. Jh. n. Chr.', Unpublished PhD thesis (Leiden, 2011)

Hudson, William, 'Norwich Militia in the Fourteenth Century', *Norfolk Archaeology*, 14 (1901), pp. 295–301

Huther, Heinz, *Die Passauer Wolfsklingen: Legende und Wirklichkeit* (Passau, 2007)

Israel, Uwe, 'Die Fechtbücher Hans Talhoffers und die Praxis des gerichtlichen Zweikampfs', *Die Kunst des Fechtens*, ed. Matthias Johannes Bauer and Elisabeth Vavra (Heidleberg, 2017), pp. 93–132

Jackson, R.A. 'The *Traité du Sacre* of Jean Golein', *Proceedings of the American Philosophical Society*, 113–14 (1969), pp. 305–24

Jaquet, D., 'Fighting in the Fightschools, late XVth, early XVIth century', *Acta Periodica Duellatorum*, 1.1 (2013), pp. 56–9

———, 'Six weeks to prepare for combat: Instructions and practices from the fight books at the end of the middle ages, a note on ritualised single combats', *Killing and being Killed: Bodies in Battle*, ed. Jörg Rogge (Mainz, 2018), pp. 131–64

———, '"…schirmen mit Federklingen": Towards a Terminology of Fencing Swords (1400–1600)', *The Sword: Form and Thought*, ed. Lisa Deutscher, Mirjam Kaiser, and Sixt Wetzler (Woodbridge, 2019), pp. 24–40

———, 'Dancing on the rope, swallowing knives, juggling with daggers. Sword players in the 15th century', *Martial Culture in Medieval Town*, 15 April 2021, https://martcult.hypotheses.org/1240 (accessed 24 February 2022)

Jaquet, Daniel, Sørensen, Claus Frederik, and Cognot, Fabrice, 'Historical European Martial Art: A Crossroad between Academic Research, Martial Heritage Re-creation and Martial Sport Practices', *Acta Periodica Duellatorum*, 3 (2015), pp. 5–35

Jaquet, Daniel, Demésy, Tuaillon, Audrey, and Tzouriadis, Iason-Eleftherios, *Historical European Martial Arts: An International Overview* (Chungcheongbuk-do, 2020)

James, Simon, 'The point of the sword: what Roman-era weapons could do to bodies – and why they often didn't', *Waffen in Aktion. Akten der 16. Internationalen Roman Military Equipment Conference (ROMEC), Xantener Berichte 16*, ed. A.W. Busch and H.J. Schalles (Xanten, 2010), pp. 41–54

Jesch, Judith, 'Let's debate female viking warriors yet again', *Norse and Viking Ramblings*, http://norseandviking.blogspot.com/2017/09/lets-debate-female-viking-warriors-yet/ (accessed 1 August 2021)

Johns, Susan, *Noblewomen, Aristocracy and Power in the Twelfth-Century Anglo-Norman Realm* (Manchester, 2013)

Johnsson, Peter, 'Geometry and the Medieval Sword', *Das Schwert: Gestalt und Gedanke,* eds. B. Grotkamp-Scepers, I. Immell, P. Johnsson, and S. Wetzler (Solingen, 2015), pp. 16–27

———, 'Higher Understanding and Deeper Reckoning', *Peter Johnsson – Sword Smith,* n.d. https: http://www.peterjohnsson.com/higher-understanding-and-deeper-reckoning/ (accessed 1 August 2021)

———, 'The Søborg Sword: A Study of a 12th Century Weapon', *Peter Johnsson – Sword Smith,* n.d. http://www.peterjohnsson.com/the-soborg-sword/ (accessed 1 August 2021)

Johnston, M., *Romance and the Gentry in Late Medieval England* (Oxford, 2014)

Jones, P.E., 'The Surrender of the Sword', *Transactions of the Guildhall Association,* III (London, 1968), pp. 8–13

Jones, Randolph, 'How Waterford won its civic sword: the battle of Ballymacaw', *The fifth annual Dr. Niall Byrne memorial lecture,* The Medieval Museum, Waterford (4 November 2016), https://www.academia.edu/35007211/2016_How_Waterford_won_its_civic_sword_the_battle_of_Ballymacaw (accessed 12 January 2022)

Jones, Robert W., *Bloodied Banners: Martial Display on the Medieval Battlefield* (Woodbridge, 2010)

———, *A Companion to Chivalry,* ed. Robert W. Jones and Peter Coss (Woodbridge, 2019)

———, 'þen hentes he þe healme, and hastily hit kisses: The symbolic significance of donning armour in medieval romance', *Battles and Bloodshed: The Medieval World at War,* ed. Lorna Bleach and Keira Borrill (Newcastle upon Tyne, 2013), pp. 25–38

———, 'Heraldry and Heralds', *A Companion to Chivalry,* ed. Robert W. Jones and Peter Coss (Woodbridge, 2019), pp. 139–58

Kaeuper, Richard, *Chivalry and Violence in Medieval Europe* (Oxford, 2001)

———, *Holy Warriors: The Religious Ideology of Chivalry* (Philadelphia, PA, 2009)

Karras, Ruth, *Boys to Men: Formations of Masculinity in Late Medieval Europe* (Philadelphia, PA, 2002)

Keen, Maurice, *Chivalry* (New Haven, 1984)

———, *The Origins of the English Gentleman* (Stroud, 2002)

Kellett, Rachel, *Single Combat and Warfare in German Literature of the High Middle Ages: Stricker's Karl der Grosse and Daniel von dem Blühenden Tal* (London, 2008)

———, 'Royal Armouries MS I.33: The judicial combat and the art of fencing in thirteenth- and fourteenth-century German literature', *Oxford German Studies,* 41.1 (2012), pp. 32–56

———, 'Guts, Gore and Glory: Representations of Wounds Inflicted in War in Medieval German Literature', *Battles and Bloodshed: The Medieval World at War,* ed. Lorna Bleach and Keira Borrill (Newcastle upon Tyne, 2013), pp. 161–76

Kleinau, Jens P., '1440 – 1459 Luithold III of Königsegg', *Hans Talhoffer,* 11 July 2011, https://talhoffer.wordpress.com/2011/07/11/who-was-luithold-of-konigsegg/ (accessed 1 August 2021)

Knoll, Vilém, 'Executioners' Swords – Their Form and Development: A Brief Summary', *Journal on European History of Law*, 3.1 (2012), pp. 158–61

Krüger, Günter, '"daz Swert ze tragen, ze furen und ze halden". Eine kleine Kulturgeschichte des zeremoniellen Schwerttragens', *Das Schwert: Symbol und Waffe*, eds. L. Deutscher, M. Kaiser, and S. Wetzler (Leidorf, 2014), pp. 197–205

de Labroderie, O., Maddicott, J.R., Carpenter, D.A., 'The Last hours of Simon de Montfort: A New Account', *English Historical Review*, 115.461 (2000), pp. 378–412

Latham, John, 'The Shape of Sword Blades', *Journal of the Royal United Service Institution*, vol. VI (London, 1863), pp. 410–22

Legg, L.G.W., *Coronation Records* (London, 1901)

Le Goff, J., 'A Coronation Program for the Age of Saint Louis: The *Ordo* of 1256', *Coronations: Medieval and Early Modern Monarchic Ritual*, ed. János M. Bak (Berkeley, CA, 1990), pp. 46–56

Leland, John, 'Pardons for Self-Defence in the Reign of Richard II: The Use and Abuse of Legal Formulas', *Creativity, Contradictions and Commemoration in the Reign of Richard II: Essays in Honour of Nigel Saul* ed. Jessica Lutkin and J.S. Hamilton (Woodbridge, 2022), pp. 121–34

Leng, Rainer, *Katalog der deutschsprachigen illustrierten Handschriften des Mittelalters. Band 4/2½fg. 1/2, 38. Fecht- und Ringbücher* (Munich, 2009)

Lewis, Jason, 'Identifying sword marks on bone: Criteria for distinguishing between cut marks made by different classes of bladed weapons', *Journal of Archaeological Science*, 35 (2008), pp. 2001–8

Lewis, M. '"Names of great virtue and power": the sword Szczerbiec and the Christian magical tradition', *Waffen- und Kostümkunde*, Heft 2 (2021), pp. 1–28

Liddy, C.D., 'Land, legend and gentility in the Palatinate of Durham: The Pollards of Pollard Hall', *North-East England in the Later Middle Ages*, ed. C.D. Liddy (Woodbridge, 2005), pp. 75–95

Lieberman, M., 'A New Approach to the Knighting Ritual', *Speculum*, 90.2 (2015), pp. 391–423

Loades, Mike, *Swords and Swordsmen* (Barnsley, 2010)

———, *The Blow-by-Blow Guide to Swordfighting in the Renaissance Style*, dir. Mike Loades (Running Wolf Productions, 1991)

Maddicott, J.R., *Simon de Montfort* (Cambridge, 1995)

Marek, L., 'The Blessing of Swords. A new look into inscriptions of the *Benedictus* – type', *Acta Militaria Mediaevalia*, X (2014) pp. 9–20

Martindale, Jane, 'The Sword on the Stone: Some Resonances of a Medieval Symbol of Power (The Tomb of King John in Worcester Cathedral)', *Anglo-Norman Studies*, XV (1993), pp. 199–241

Mason, Emma, 'The Hero's Invincible Weapon: An Aspect of Angevin Propaganda', *The Ideals and Practices of Knighthood: Proceedings of the Fourth Strawberry Hill Conference*, ed. C. Harper-Bill and R. Harvey (Woodbridge, 1990), pp. 121–38

McInnes, Ian, 'Heads, shoulders, knees and toes: Injury and Death in Anglo-Scottish Combat, c. 1296–1403', *Wounds and Wound Repair in Medieval Culture*, ed. L. Tracy and K. DeVries (Leiden, 2015), pp. 102–27

———, '"One man slashes, one slays, one warns, one wounds". Injury and Death in Anglo-Scottish Combat, c. 1296–c. 1403', *Killing and Being Killed: Bodies in Battle: Perspectives on Fighters in the Middle Ages*, ed. Jörg Rogge (Mainz, 2021), pp. 61–78

McLaughlin, Megan, 'The Woman Warrior: Gender, Warfare and Society in Medieval Europe', *Women's Studies*, 17 (1990), pp. 193–209

Mclean, Will, 'Outrance and Plaisance', *Journal of Medieval Military History*, 8 (2010), pp. 155–70

McPeak, William J., 'The Falchion – Short Sword that Made Good', *Command*, 41 (January 1997), pp. 62–4

Melville, N., *The Two-Handed Sword: History, Design and Use* (Barnsley, 2018)

Memorials of London and London Life in the 13th, 14th and 15th Centuries, ed. H.T. Riley (London, 1868)

Miller, Rory, *Meditations on Violence* (Wolfeboro, NH, 2009)

Mitchell, Piers D., *Medicine in the Crusades: Warfare, Wounds and the Medieval Surgeon* (Cambridge, 2004)

Moffat, Ralph, 'The Medieval Tournament: Chivalry, Heraldry and Reality. An Edition and Analysis of Three Fifteenth-Century Tournament Manuscripts', Unpublished PhD thesis (Leeds, 2010)

———, *Medieval Arms & Armour: A Sourcebook. Volume I: The Fourteenth Century* (Woodbridge, 2022)

Moffet, Randall, 'The Military Organisation of Southampton in the Late Medieval Period, 1300–1500', Unpublished PhD thesis (Southampton, 2009)

Moilanen, Mikko, *Marks of Fire, Value and Faith. Swords with Ferrous Inlays in Finland during the Late Iron Age (ca. 700–1200 AD)* (Turku, 2015)

Molloy, Barry, 'Martial Arts and Materiality: A Combat Archaeology Perspective on Aegean Swords of the fifteenth and Fourteenth Centuries BC', *World Archaeology*, 40.1 (2008), pp. 116–34

Mondschein, Ken, 'Daggers of the Mind: Towards a Historiography of Fencing' (https://www.whitman.edu/fencing/Articles/daggersofthemind.htm, accessed 28 March 2022)

Morillo, Stephen, 'Milites, Knights and Samurai: Military terminology, comparative history, and the problem of translation', *The Normans and their Adversaries at War*, ed. R. Abels and B. Bachrach (Woodbridge, 2001), pp. 167–84

Muhlberger, Steven, *Jousts and Tournaments: Charny and the Rules for Chivalric Sport in Fourteenth-Century France* (Union City, CA, 2002)

———, *Deeds of Arms: Formal Combats in the Late Fourteenth Century* (Union City, CA, 2005)

Müller, Jan-Dirk, 'Bild—Vers—Prosakommentar am Beispiel von Fechtbüchern. Probleme der Verschriftlichung einer schriftlosen Praxis', *Pragmatische Schriftlichkeit im Mittelalter. Erscheinungsformen und Entwicklungsstufen*, ed. H. Keller et al. (Munich, 1992), pp. 251–82

———, *Deeds of Arms: Formal Combats in the Late Fourteenth Century* (Union City, California, 2005)

Müntz, Eugène, 'Les épées d'honneur distribuées par les papes pendant les xIVe, XVe, XVIe siecles', *Revue de l'art chrétien*, 32 (1889), pp. 400–11

Murray, Alan V., 'Introduction: From Mass Combat to Field of Cloth of Gold', *The Medieval Tournament as Spectacle: Tourneys, Jousts and Pas d'Armes, 1100–1600*, ed. Alan V. Murray and Karen Watts (Woodbridge, 2020), pp. 1–6

Nall, Catherine, *Reading and War in Fifteenth-Century England: From Lydgate to Malory* (Cambridge, 2012)

Neat, Helen, 'Depictions of violence in *Floriant et Florete*: Inter- and intertextual patterns', *Battles and Bloodshed: The Medieval World at War*, ed. Lorna Bleach (Newcastle upon Tyne, 2014), pp. 177–98

Neuschel, Kristen B., *Living by the Sword: Weapons and Material Culture in France and Britain, 600–1600* (Ithaca, NY, 2020)

Nickel, Helmut, 'A Knightly Sword with Presentation Inscription', *Metropolitan Museum Journal*, 2 (1969), pp. 209–10

Nicolle, D., *Arms and Armour of the Crusading Era, 1050–1350: Islam, Eastern Europe and Asia* (Cambridge, 1999)

Norling, Roger, 'A Call to Arms!' *HROARR*, 4 July 2012, https://hroarr.com/community-news/a-call-to-arms/ (accessed 1 August 2021)

Norman, A.V.B., *The Rapier and the Smallsword, 1460–1820* (London, 1979)

Novati, Francesco, *Flos Duellatorum, Il Fior di Battaglia di Maestro Fiore dei Liberi da Premariacco* (Bergamo,1902)

Oakeshott, Ewart, *The Archaeology of Weapons* (London, 1960)

———, *Records of the Medieval Sword* (Woodbridge, 1991)

———, *The Sword in the Age of Chivalry* (Woodbridge, 1994)

Palmer, Jeff, 'The Golden Years of Hollywood', *The Fight Master*, 1.1 (April 1978), pp. 22–4

Panhuysen, Raphaël, and Dijkstra, Menno, 'By Wounds Made Worthy? Interpreting Sharp Bladed Trauma in the Early Medieval Cemeteries of Maastricht and Rijnsburg (the Netherlands)', *Rural Riches and Royal Rags? Studies on Medieval and Modern Archaeology Presented to Frans Theuws*, ed. Mirjam Kars, Roos van Oosten, Marcus Roxburgh, and Arno Verhoeven (Leiden, 2018), pp. 43–55

Papal Encyclicals Online, https://www.papalencyclicals.net/councils/ecum10.htm (accessed 30 August 2022)

Parker, David, 'The Importance of the Commonplace Book: London 1450–1550', *Manuscripta*, 40 (1996), pp. 29–48

Patton, Sir J. Noel, 'Notes on the sword of Battle Abbey, formerly in the Meyrick Collection', *Proceedings of the Society of Antiquaries of Scotland*, 10 (1874) pp. 462–75

Peirce, Ian, *Swords of the Viking Age* (Woodbridge, 2002)

Peterson, Jan, *De Norske Vikingesverd* (Kristiania, 1919)

Petri, Ingo, 'Material and properties of VLFBERHT swords', *Sword: Form and Thought*, ed. L. Deutscher, M. Kaiser, and S. Wetzler (Woodbridge, 2019), pp. 61–88

Phillips, Matthew, 'Urban conflict and legal strategy in medieval England: The case of Bishop's Lynn, 1346–1350', *Urban History*, 42.3 (August 2015), pp. 365–80

Price, Brian R. 'The Martial Arts of Medieval Europe', Unpublished PhD thesis (Denton, TX, 2011)

Price, Neil, Hedenstierna-Jonson, Charlotte, Zachrisson, Torun, Kjellström, Anna, Storå, Jan, Krzewińska, Maja, Günther, Torsten, Sobrado, Verónica, Jakobsson, Mattias, and Götherström, Anders, 'A Female Viking Warrior Confirmed by Genomics', *American Journal of Physical Anthropology* (2017), pp. 1–8

———, 'Viking Warrior Women? Reassessing Birka Chamber Grave Bj.581', *Antiquity*, 93.367 (February 2019), pp. 181–98

'Priority (Right of Way) in Foil Fencing', *London Fencing Club*, n.d. https://www.londonfencingclub.co.uk/news/106-priority-right-of-way-in-foil-fencing (accessed 1 August 2021)

Provinciaal Overijssels Museum, *Thuis in de late middeleeuwen: het Nederlands burger-interieur 1400–1535* (Waanders, 1980)

Radulescu, R., *The Gentry Context for Malory's* Morte Darthur (Cambridge, 2003)

Gentry Culture in Late Medieval England, ed. R. Radulescu and A. Truelove (Manchester, 2006)

Wigmore Castle, North Herefordshire: Excavations 1996 and 1998, ed. S. Rátkai (Abingdon, 2017)

Rawlings, Dave, 'No fencing Schools in London Allowed, c. 1300', *Schola Gladiatoria Forum*, 4 April 2006, http://www.fioredeiliberi.org/phpBB3/viewtopic.php?f=4&t=231& (accessed 1 August 2021)

———, 'No Swords and bucklers in London Please', *Schola Gladiatoria Forum*, 25 April 2006, http://www.fioredeiliberi.org/phpBB3/viewtopic.php?f=4&t=447&start=0& (accessed 1 August 2021)

Regalia: Les instruments du sacre des rois de France, les honneurs de Charlemagne (Paris, 1991)

Reynolds, Susan, 'Eadric Silvaticus and the English Resistance', *BIHR*, 54 (1981), pp. 102–5

Richards, Jeffrey, *Swordsmen of the Screen: From Douglas Fairbanks to Michael York* (London, 1977)

Richards, William, *The History of* Lynn, 2 vols. (London, 1812)

Richardson, H.G., 'The Coronation in Medieval England: The Evolution of the Office and the oath', *Traditio*, 16 (1960), pp. 111–202

Richardson, Malcolm, *Middle Class Writing in Late Medieval London* (London, 2016)

Richardson, Thom, 'The Bridport Muster Roll of 1457', *The Royal Armouries Yearbook*, 2 (Leeds, 1997), pp. 46–52

———, *The Tower Armoury in the Fourteenth Century* (Leeds, 2014)

Robertson, Isobel Rennie, 'Wayland Smith: A Cultural Historical Biography', Unpublished PhD Thesis (Leeds, 2020)

Roman Imperialism and Provincial Art, ed. Sarah Scott and Jane Webster (Cambridge, 2003)

Rossi, Carla, 'A proposal for the interpretation of the inscription on the British Museum sword', *academia.edu*, n.d. https://www.academia.edu/14828685/A_

proposal_for_the_interpretation_of_the_inscription_on_the_British_Museum_
sword (accessed 1 August 2021)

Russell, M.J. 'Hired Champions', *The American Journal of Legal History*, 3.3 (1958),
pp. 242–59

———, 'Accoutrements of Battle', *Law Quarterly Review*, 99.3 (1983), pp. 432–6

Saul, Nigel, 'The Commons and the Abolition of Badges', *Parliamentary History*, 9
(1990), pp. 302–15

———, *For Honour and Fame: Chivalry in England, 1066–1500* (New York, 2011)

Schmid, W.M., 'Passauer Waffenwesen', *Zeitschrift für Historische Waffenkunde*, 8
(1918–20), pp. 317–42

Schmidt, Herbert, *The Book of the Buckler* (Berlin, 2015)

Schmitt, Georg, 'Die Alamannen im Zollernalbkreis', Unpublished PhD thesis
(Stuttgart, 2005)

Schulze-Dörrlamm, Mechthild, *Die Salier Das Reichsschwert: Ein Herrschaftszeichen
des slaiers Heinrich IV und des Welfen Otto IV* (Sigmaringen, 1995)

Roman Imperialism and Provincial Art, ed. Sarah Scott and Jane Webster (Cambridge,
2003)

Scalini, Mario, *The Armoury of the Castle of Churburg* (Udine, 1996)

Seitz, Heribert, *Blankwaffen*, 2 vols. (Braunschweig, 1965)

Siraisi, Nancy G., *Medieval and Early Renaissance Medicine: An Introduction to
Knowledge and Practice* (Chicago, 1990)

Sjursen, Katrin, *Peaceweavers' Sisters: Medieval Noblewomen as Military Leaders in
Northern France* (Ann Arbor, MI, 2011)

———, 'The War of the Two Jeannes: Rulership in the Fourteenth Century',
Medieval Feminist Forum, 51.1 (2015), pp. 4–40

Skemer, D.C., *Binding Words: Textual Amulets in the Middle Ages* (Philadelphia, PA,
2006)

Skoda, Hannah, *Medieval Violence: Physical Brutality in Northern France, 1270–1330*
(Oxford, 2013)

Slocum, Kay Brainerd, '"Confrérie, Bruderschaft" and Guild: The Formation of
Musicians' Fraternal Organisations in Thirteenth- and Fourteenth-Century
Europe', *Early Music History*, 14 (1995), pp. 257–74

The Society for Creative Anachronism Inc. Fencing Masters' Handbook (Milpitas, CA,
2020)

'Society for Creative Anachronism Newcomer's Portal: Armored Combat', *Society for
Creative Anachronism*, n.d. http://welcome.sca.org/armored-combat/ (accessed 1
August 2021).

Spierenburg, P., *A History of Murder: Personal Violence in Europe from the Middle Ages
to the Present* (Cambridge, 2008)

Sposato, Peter, 'A Local Feud in the midst of National Conflict: The Swynnerton--
Staffords of Sandon Feud, Staffordshire 1304–34', *Staffordshire Studies*, 19 (Spring
2010), pp. 15–42

Stalsberg, Anne, 'Herstellung und Verbreitung der Vlfberht-Schwertklingen. Eine
Neubewertung', *Zeitschrift für Archäologie des Mittelalters*, 36 (2008), pp. 89–118

Stępínski, Janusz, Zabniski, Grzegorz, and Nosek, Elzbieta Maria, 'Metallographic examinations of St Peter's Sword from the Archdiocesan Museum in Poznan', *Waffen-und Kostumkunde*, 57.1 (January 2015), pp. 19–62

Stevenson, Katie, 'Introduction', *The Herald in Late Medieval Europe*, ed. Katie Stevenson (Woodbridge, 2009), pp. 1–8

Stewart, Mary, *The Hollow Hills* (London, 1973)

Stuart, K., *Defiled Trades and Social Outcasts: Honor and Ritual Pollution in Early Modern Germany* (Cambridge, 2006)

Sword: Form and Thought, eds. Lisa Deutscher, Miriam Kaiser, and Sixt Wetzler (Solingen, 2019)

Taylor, Craig, *A Virtuous Knight: Defending Marshal Boucicaut (Jean II Le Meingre, 1366–1421)* (Woodbridge, 2019)

The Age of Chivalry: Art in Plantagenet England, 1200–1400, ed. J. Alexander and P. Binski (London, 1987)

The History of Parliament: the House of Commons 1386–1421, ed. J.S. Roskell, L. Clark, and C. Rawcliffe (London, 1993)

'The History of the Modern HEMA Movement', *Historical European Martial Arts Resources*, n.d. https://historicaleuropeanmartialarts.com/2020/05/30/the-history-of-the-modern-hema-movement/ (accessed 1 August 2021)

'The Realities of Combat', *netvike.com*, n.d. https://www.netvike.com/wounds-from-combat.html (accessed 1 August 2021)

Thompson, Kenneth J., 'Chaucer's Warrior Bowman: The Roles and Equipment of the Knight's Yeoman', *The Chaucer Review*, 40.4 (2006), pp. 386–415

Thordeman, Bengt, *Armour from the Battle of Wisby, 1361* (Highland Village, TX, 2010)

Thorndike, Lynn, *University records and Life in the Middle Ages* (New York, NY, 1975)

Thuis in de late middeleeuwen: het Nederlands burgerinterieur 1400–1535 (Waanders, 1980)

Tlusty, B. Ann, *The Martial Ethic in Early Modern Germany* (Basingstoke, 2011)

———, 'Invincible Blades and invulnerable Bodies: Weapons Magic in Early Modern Germany', *European Review of History*, 22.4 (2015), pp. 658–79

Tobler, Christian Henry, *In St George's Name: An Anthology of Medieval German Fighting Arts* (Wheaton, IL, 2010)

Toohey, Kathy, 'The Swords of King Arthur', *The Grail Quest Papers* (Sydney, 2000), pp. 26–38

Tracy, Larissa, and DeVries, Kelly (eds.), *Wounds and Wound Repair in Medieval Culture* (Leiden, 2015)

Graf Trapp, Oswald, *The Armoury of the Castle of Churburg* (London, 1929)

Tzouriades, Iason-Eleftherios, '"What is the Riddle of Steel?": Problems of Classification and Terminology in the Study of Late Medieval Swords', *The Sword: Form and Thought*, ed. Lisa Deutscher, Mirjam Kaiser and Sixt Wetzler (Woodbridge, 2019), pp. 3–11

Uebel, M., 'The Foreigner Within: The Subject of Abjection in *Sir Gowther*', *Meeting the Foreign in the Middle Ages*, ed. A. Classen (London, 2002), pp. 96–117

Van Emden, Richard and Piuk, Vic, *Famous 1914–1918* (Barnsley, 2009)

Verbruggen, J.F., *The Art of Warfare in Western Europe During the Middle Ages*, trans. Sumner Willard and R.W. Southern (Woodbridge, 1997)

Vilart, Franck, and Simonneau, Henri, 'City Heralds in the Burgundian Low Countries', *The Herald in Late Medieval Europe*, ed. Katie Stevenson (Woodbridge, 2009), pp. 93–110

Wagner, E., *Cut and Thrust Weapons*, trans. John Layton (London, 1967)

Wagner, T., Worley, J., Blennow, Holst, A., and Beckholmen, G. 'Medieval Christian invocation inscriptions on sword blades', *Waffen- und Kostümkunde*, 51.1 (2009), pp. 11–52

Wagner, T. and Worley, J. 'How to make swords talk: an interdisciplinary approach to understanding medieval swords and their inscriptions', *Waffen-und Kostumkunde*, 55.2 (2013), pp. 113–32

Wall, J., 'The Conyers Falchion', *Durham Archaeological Journal*, 2 (1986) pp. 77–83

Waller, John, 'Thoughts & Ideas: John Waller, Head of Fight-Interpretation, Royal Armouries, Leeds, UK', *ARMA: the Association for Renaissance Martial Arts*, n.d, http://www.thearma.org/spotlight/JohnWaller.htm#.YHRs3uhKjD4 (accessed 1 August 2021)

———, 'Chapter 13: Combat techniques', Fiorato, V., Boylston, Anthea and Knusel, Christopher, *Blood Red Roses: The Archaeology of a Mass Grave from the Battle of Towton, AD 1461* (Oxford, 2000), pp. 148–54

Warren, Michelle R., *History on the Edge* (Minneapolis, MN, 2000)

Wassmansdorff, Karl, *Sechs Fechtschulen (d.i. Schau- und Preisfechten) der Marxbrüder und Federfechter aus den Jahren 1573 bis 1614; Nürnberger Fechtschulreime v.J. 1579 und Rösener's Gedicht: Ehrentitel und Lobspruch der Fechtkunst v.J. 1589: eine Vorarbeit zu einer Geschichte der Marxbrüder und Federfechter* (Heidelburg, 1870)

Welle, Rainer, *" und wisse das alle höbischeit kompt von deme ringen": Der Ringkampf als adelige Kunst im 15. und 16. Jahrhundert* (Pfaffenweller, 1993)

Wenham, S.J. 'Anatomical interpretations of Anglo-Saxon weapon injuries', *Weapons and Warfare in Anglo-Saxon England*, ed. S.C. Hawkes (Oxford, 1989) pp. 123–39

Wetzler, Sixt, 'Überlegungen Zur Europäischen Fechtkunst', *Das Duell : Ehrenkämpfe vom Mittelalter bis zur Moderne*, ed. Ulrike Ludwig, Gerd Schwerhoff, Barbara Krug-Richter (Konstanz, 2012), pp. 61–76

———, 'Combat in Saga Literature: Traces of martial arts in medieval Iceland', Unpublished PhD (Tübingen, 2017)

Wetzler, Sixt and Johnsson, Peter, "I am the Sword", *Das Schwert: Gestalt und Gedanke*, eds. B. Grotkamp-Scepers, I. Immell, P. Johnsson and S. Wetzler (Solingen, 2015), p. 15

Wheeler, R.E.M., *London and the Vikings* (London, 1927)

Wierschin, Martin, *Meister Johann Liechtenauers Kunst des Fechtens* (Munich, 1965)

Wilkinson, Frederick, *Those Entrusted with Arms: A History of the Police, Post, Customs and Provate Use of Weapons in Britain* (London, 2002)

Wilkinson, Louise J., 'Gendered Chivalry', *A Companion to Chivalry*, ed. Robert W. Jones and Peter Coss (Woodbridge, 2019), pp. 219–40

Wilks, Michael, *The Problem with Sovereignty in the Later Middle Ages* (Cambridge, 1963)

Williams, Alan, 'A metallurgical study of some Viking swords', *Gladius*, XXIX (December 2009), pp. 121–84

———, 'Crucible steel in medieval swords', *Metals and Mines. Studies in Archaeometallurgy*, ed. S. La Niece, D. Hook and P. Craddock (London, 2007), pp. 233–42

———, *The Sword and the Crucible: A History of the Metallurgy of European Swords up to the 16th Century* (Leiden, 2012)

Williams, Howard, 'Viking Warrior Women: An Archeodeath Response – Part 1', *Archeodeath*, https://www.howardwilliamsblog.wordpress.com/2017/09/14/viking-warrior-women-an-archeodeath-response-part-1/ (accessed 1 August 2021)

Wilson, Guy, 'John Waller – A Life Remembered', *Arms and Armour*, 15.2 (2018), pp. 113–21

Windsor, Guy, 'How to spot the bullshit in any martial arts drill, and what to do about it', 8 October 2013, https://guywindsor.net/2013/10/how-to-spot-the-bullshit-in-any-martial-arts-drill-and-what-to-do-about-it/ (accessed 1 August 2021)

———, 'Why you should train with sharp swords, and how to go about it without killing anyone', *Chivalric Fighting Arts Association*, 18 February 2014, http://www.chivalricfighting.wordpress.com/2014/02/18/why-you-should-train-with-sharp-swords-and-how-to-go-about-it-without-killing-anyone/ (accessed 1 August 2021)

Winkler, Adam, *Gunfight: The Battle over the Right to Bear Arms in America* (New York, 2011)

Wolf, Tony, *Ancient Swordplay: The Revival of Elizabethan Fencing in Victorian London* (Wheaton, IL, 2012)

Woosnam-Savage, Robert, '"He's Armed Without that's Innocent Within". A Short Note on a newly Acquired Medieval Sword for a Child', *Arms & Armour: Journal of the Royal Armouries*, 5.1 (2008), pp. 84–95

———,- 'The Material of Middle-Earth', *Picturing Tolkien: Essays on Peter Jackson's* The Lord of the Ring *Film Trilogy*, ed. Janice Bogstad and Philip Kaveny (Jefferson, NC, 2011), pp. 139–68

———, 'Weapons', *1066 in Perspective*, ed. David Bates (Leeds, 2018), pp. 57–78

Woosnam-Savage, Robert C., and DeVries, Kelly, 'Battle Trauma in Medieval Warfare: Wounds, Weapons and Armour', *Wounds and Wound Repair in Medieval Culture*, eds. L. Tracy and K. DeVries (Leiden, 2015), pp. 27–56

Wright, Barbara, Unpublished transcriptions of the Wigmore castle inventories, from National Archives, E 163/4/48 (2e), E 101/333/4 and e 372/179 (22.d), and at the British Library Add.MS 60584

Yates, Frances, *The Art of Memory* (London, 1966)

Films

Cyrano de Bergerac, dir. Jean-Paul Rappeneau (UGC, 1990)

Don Q: The Son of Zorro, dir. Donald Crisp (Elton Corporation, 1926)

Excalibur, dir. John Boorman (Orion Pictures, 1981)

Game of Thrones, created by David Benioff and D.B. Weiss (HBO, 2011–-2019)

Kingdom of Heaven, dir. Ridley Scott (Scott Free Productions, 2005)

Ladyhawke, dir. Richard Donner (Twentieth-Century Fox, 1998)

Pirates of the Caribbean, dir. Gore Verbinski (Walt Disney Pictures, 2003)

Prince Valiant, dir. Henry Hathaway (Twentieth-Century Fox, 1954)

Raiders of the Lost Ark, dir. Stephen Spielberg (Paramount Pictures, 1981)

Robin and Marian, dir. Richard Lester (Columbia Pictures, 1976)

Rob Roy, dir. Michael Caton-Jones (United Artists, 1995)

The Black Pirate, dir. Albert Parker (Elton Corporation, 1926)

The Black Shield of Falworth, dir. Rudolph Maté (Universal Studios, 1954)

The Chronicles of Narnia: The Voyage of the Dawn Treader, dir. Michael Apted (Twentieth-Century Fox, 2010)

The Duellists, dir. Ridley Scott (Paramount Pictures, 1977)

The Iron Mask, dir. Allan Dwan (Elton Corporation, 1929)

The Lord of the Rings, dir. Peter Jackson (New Line Cinemas, 2001–-2003)

The Man in the Iron Mask, dir. Randall Wallace (United Artists, 1998)

The Mark of Zorro, dir. Fred Niblo (Douglas Fairbanks Pictures, 1920)

The Northman, dir. Robert Eggers (Regency Enterprises, 2022)

The Three Must-Get-Theres, dir. Max Linder (Max Linder Productions, 1922)

The Three Musketeers, dir. Richard Lester (Momentum Pictures, 1973)

Viking Warrior Women, dir. Stuart Strickson (National Geographic, 2019)

Vikings, created Michael Hirst (MGM Television, 2013–-2020)

Index

Armour and Weapons